THE PRODUCT MARKETING HANDBOOK

FOR Software

THIRD EDITION

by Merrill R. Chapman

edited by Gail Ostrow

Dedicated to Ruth, Lili, and of course, Charlie.

The Product Marketing Handbook for Software, Third Edition

Copyright ©1999 by Aegis Resources, Inc.

Printed in the United States of America

http://www.Aegis-Resources.com

ISBN: 0-9672008-0-6

Creative Director: Jo-Ann Campbell

Production & Design: *mle design* • 213 Cider Mill Road, Glastonbury, CT 06033

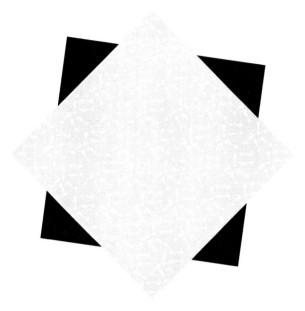

Foreword

Simply put, this is the definitive guide for sales and marketing professionals who need to successfully navigate the tricky and tumultuous waters of the computer and software industry. In the 18 years I've worked in sales and marketing for billion dollar companies such as IBM and Hewlett-Packard, major software firms such as Ashton-Tate and Lotus Development, and in the two companies I've started from the ground floor (Lyriq International and now Miacomet, Inc.), the one thing you quickly learn is that our business changes every three years. You must constantly challenge yourself and your assumptions or face failure. If you don't start with an approach and methodology that promotes excellence, you will not get a second chance. The **Handbook** provides that start.

It does so by discussing and illuminating proven marketing principles and methods that lead to sales success and by providing the tools you need to succeed. Its combination of checklists, templates, case studies, and methodologies are invaluable to understanding not just how companies succeed (and fail), but why. Many successful companies, including my own, use **The Product Marketing Handbook for Software** to consistently get results.

Whether you are just starting out in this industry, or a scarred marketing veteran, you will gain insight and invaluable knowledge from the ***Handbook***. I have not seen anything that is better written or more thorough in presenting all aspects of the industry's sales and marketing process. Good luck and good selling!

Randy Hujar

CEO–Miacomet, Inc.

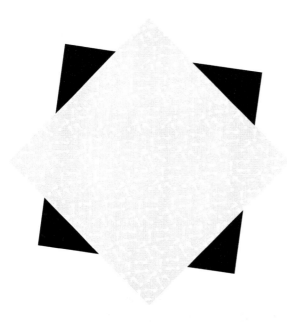

Table of Contents

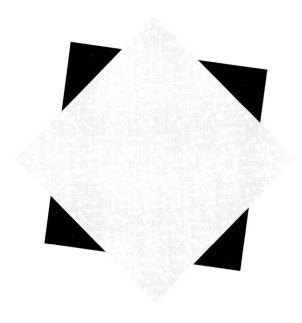

Preface

Welcome to the 3rd Edition of *The Product Marketing Handbook for Software*. Since the publication of the earlier editions, the **Handbook** has become the standard text for software companies seeking to learn and teach their staffs successful software marketing. Many companies use the **Handbook**'s checklists and procedures to structure and plan their marketing efforts and activities. To facilitate these efforts, all the checklists, templates, and forms used in the **Handbook** are on the accompanying disk so you can use and modify them as you see fit. (If you misplaced your disk, or received the **Handbook**, without it, go to www.Aegis-Resources.com to obtain the latest versions of these files.)

WHAT'S NEW IN THE THIRD EDITION

In the last five years, the software industry has continued to undergo unceasing change. And the **Handbook** has kept pace with these changes; this third edition reflects the software world as it exists today. Industry experts have reviewed every section, and every topic speaks to today's software business realities. We know you will find the **Handbook** an invaluable resource as you plan and execute your company's mission-critical marketing plans and strategies.

- All appropriate sections have been updated.
- All checklists have been updated and expanded.

- The Electronic Marketing section has been rewritten to include the World Wide Web, electronic direct marketing, and other forms of E-marketing.

- The Product Positioning section has been updated to incorporate a simple yet powerful methodology for successfully executing this critical marketing task.

- The Channel Distribution section examines marketing development funds (MDF) programs in ever-greater detail, ranks many of the most common programs, and describes some of the channel's most dangerous financial practices.

- The Direct Marketing section now includes information on selling to the high-end customer, telemarketing, and infomercials. (Don't laugh. Intuit used them to take control of the small business accounting market.)

- New and contemporary focus stories have been added to most sections. (We've also kept the classics.)

- The Advertising section now incorporates a new methodology for creating, classifying, and targeting your ads.

- The PR and Product Review section includes new information on avoiding the marketing dangers of the World Wide Web.

- Direct sales- and VAR-class software have been given increased focus and attention.

- The glossary has been updated to reflect new industry terms and developments.

- The Software Marketing Pipeline has been updated.

- The Marketing Resources Appendix has been updated

We are confident that the 3rd edition of *The Product Marketing Handbook for Software* will help you shorten your marketing cycle, avoid costly mistakes, and, most importantly, sell more product. Best of luck!

Merrill R. Chapman

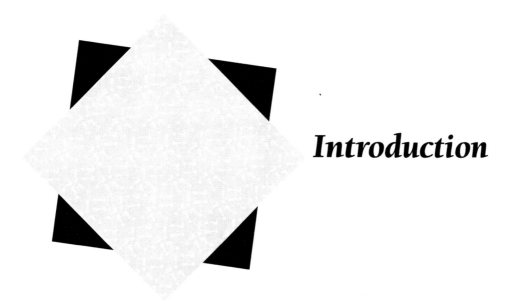

Introduction

Thank you for purchasing *The Product Marketing Handbook for Software,* 3rd edition. The **Handbook** is the most comprehensive guide to successful software marketing available and should be read and used by anyone who needs to manage or understand the software marketing process. Its descriptions of every aspect of software marketing will help you make better business decisions and boost your bottom line.

WHO SHOULD USE THIS HANDBOOK?

The **Handbook** can be used by any size organization. Larger software publishers can use it as a workbook for their product managers and as a tool to manage the marketing cycle and boost sales. Several major software publishers, such as IBM and Lotus, use the **Handbook** in just this way.

Start-up companies will find the **Handbook** is an invaluable educational tool and a blueprint for marketing success. Too many new publishers make basic mistakes—improperly positioning their product, creating category conflicts, or printing poorly-designed collaterals—that cost them thousands of dollars and precious time. Using the **Handbook** as your guide, you will shorten your marketing cycle, sell more product, and avoid making these mistakes.

THE SOFTWARE INDUSTRY TODAY

Since the publication of the first two editions, the U.S. software industry has continued its dynamic growth. The entire market now comprises over $94 billion, including retail, direct, and embedded applications. Growth in all these markets has been steady, in spite of recessions and problems in any one segment or company.

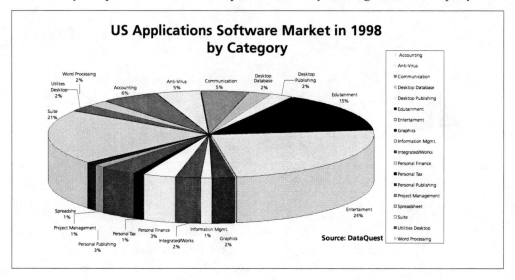

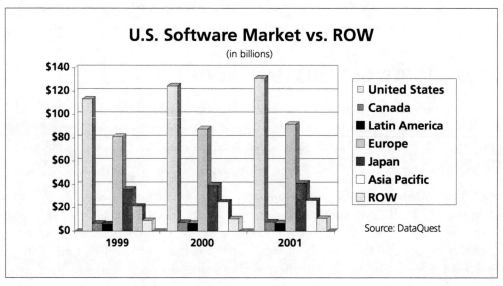

Figure 1 US Software Applications Market

As the software market has grown, so have competitive pressures and public awareness of the industry and its impact on their lives. Microsoft, for example, has gone from being an obscure software power to an international colossus, respected by many and feared by some. Its founder and leader, Bill Gates, has undergone the transformation from rich but unknown nerd to international celebrity and seminal figure in American business history, a man worthy of the fame and notoriety accorded earlier giants like Carnegie, Rockefeller, and Ford.

In an industry already driven by the relentless prod of technological innovation, the rapid growth of the Internet has acted on the market like a shot of steroids in a weightlifter's biceps. The promise of the information age delivered by the World Wide Web (hereafter referred to simply as "the Web") to every home has caused the home market to grow faster than the business market. This, in turn, has sparked ruthless competition among manufacturers, resulting in steeply decreasing prices at the same time that speed, storage, and memory is increasing and graphic displays grow ever larger.

This relentless growth has caused a flood of new categories and titles to come market. But the gods of success have not smiled equally on everybody. Apple has stumbled to the brink of oblivion (again). Former hardware and software giants like Commodore, Ashton-Tate, and WordPerfect have disappeared. The Internet superstar Netscape was purchased by AOL. Even mighty IBM has been humbled by changing times.

The reasons for failure have not changed since the first two editions of the **Handbook**. In many cases, companies have stumbled or failed not because of poor technology, but because they didn't understand the marketing process. The U.S. software market is a demanding one—its consumers are prosperous, knowledgeable, and fickle. They have little interest in dealing with wrongly-positioned products, confusing pricing, and badly-conceived collaterals. The need to understand and properly execute marketing basics has never been more important

The **Handbook** is designed to help you understand that process and assist you in the critical tasks of positioning, launching, and sustaining products in today's ultra competitive software arena. It describes, in detail, the different tasks marketing managers in the software industry must accomplish. In turn, each task is broken down into a series of goals and steps that must be completed for your product to be successful.

There are usually two things that stand between a software product and the market. The first is the product itself. If the publisher has misread the market's desire to purchase the product, if the product cannot perform up to market expectations, or if the product is fatally flawed technically, then no expert or theory can help. Only you, or your company, know the truth about your product.

The second is the execution of a successful marketing plan, which incorporates these fundamental tasks:

Positioning: The clear description to the market of a product's functionality and purpose, both in relation to itself and its competition. Your product positioning drives every aspect of your marketing.

Launching: Releasing the product to the marketplace.

Distributing: Making the product available to buyers.

Sustaining: Maintaining sales and market share through marketing, advertising, and sales promotions.

The principles of successful marketing are well known. There are no secrets, no "magic marketing bullets," that guarantee success. While there are many books that describe various marketing theories and concepts, what has been missing is a book that assists marketers in executing programs and evaluating results.

The 3rd edition of *The Product Marketing Handbook for Software* fills that gap. Written and researched by software industry experts, its focus is on the bottom line and the successful strategies that will enable you to manage effective marketing campaigns. The *Handbook*'s checklists help you plan the nuts and bolts of a product launch, and evaluate and deploy the different marketing, advertising, and promotional programs used by successful software marketers.

ORGANIZATION

The *Handbook* is divided into the following sections:

- Positioning, Pricing, and Naming.
- Channel Distribution.
- Collaterals.

- Public Relations and Product Review Programs.
- Advertising.
- Sales Promotions.
- Direct Marketing.
- Bundling.
- Internet and Electronic Marketing.
- Trade Shows.

Each section contains detailed descriptions of the specific marketing tasks, focus stories, and checklists. The focus stories recount actual marketing situations, including major and minor mistakes and disasters. Read them carefully. By learning from these stories, you can start earning your advanced degree from the "See What They Did? Now Don't Do That" school of marketing!

THE CHECKLISTS

We have chosen to use checklists to categorize marketing tasks because they are easily and quickly adapted to different needs. Many different programs exist that fit marketing activities into some form of predefined process. If you are currently using such a program, the checklists can provide added benefit and value to your system. If you are not, then the checklists can serve as the foundation for creating your own system.

The *Handbook* uses two types of checklist: the Objectives/Evaluation Checklist and the Success Checklist. In the preparation/planning phase of your marketing activities, review the Objectives portion of the specific checklist(s) and decide which objectives best fit your marketing plan. For each objective chosen, enter a specific target goal—generally a number or a percentage. This is the "what you will do" part of your plan, and should include measurable and quantifiable objectives.

After you determine your objectives, you then use the Success Checklist to implement your plan, stepping through all the activities that promote a successful effort in the particular marketing area. This is the "how you do it" part of your plan. After implementation, revisit the Objectives/Evaluation Checklist(s) and use the Evaluation column to record what was actually accomplished, evaluating how well you did with respect to your initial objectives.

Tracking the success (or failure) of your marketing activities will help you build a marketing "bible" of what does and doesn't work for your product and company. Over time, you will possess an "at-a-glance" record of your marketing performance and be able to quickly identify areas of critical weakness and repair them.

The checklists are very comprehensive. How you use them depends on the structure of your company and its individual resources. Regardless, each relevant task on a checklist must be completed. Your goal is to complete them as efficiently and cost-effectively as possible. The **Handbook** will help you do just that.

THE DISK

To further assist you, all of the **Handbook's** checklists are contained on the accompanying disk in 7-bit ASCII format. Any text editor, word processing application, or business-presentation package can read them. The checklists can be quickly printed out as is, or edited and converted into overheads, handouts, etc. Feel free to alter them to meet your particular needs and strategies.

Use the disk to complete the checklists while referring to the ones in the book for insight and planning purposes (e.g., assigning particular sections to the appropriate individuals in your organization).

The files are arranged on the disk in two directories: Objective and Success. In addition, there are two additional files:

adreview.asc	The advertising evaluation form.
read.me	A description of what's on the disk and information about the author of the 3rd edition of *The Product Marketing Handbook for Software*

THE APPENDICES

The appendices provide additional information relevant to a successful software product marketing strategy.

Appendix A: Basic Marketing Concepts and Organization describes the basic marketing organization functions by title and responsibilities.

Appendix B: Product Marketing Cost Matrix outlines in broad terms the costs for basic marketing tasks.

Appendix C: Marketing Resource Directory provides a starting point for locating marketing consulting, products and services.

Appendix D: Software Marketing Pipeline provides a detailed description of when each marketing task occurs in the overall plan and in relation to all the other marketing tasks.

THE GLOSSARY

Every industry develops its own internal vocabulary or "jargon" to help facilitate quick communication. The software industry is no exception. The Glossary helps demystify "software speak" and close the communication gap.

CONTACTING US

In an industry as dynamic and changeable as software, new trends, ideas, and challenges are constantly appearing. As in the past, we are always delighted to hear from you and rely on communications with our readers to help keep us up to speed. To reach us, you can send E-mail to RickChapman@compuserve.com or visit our web site at www.aegis-resources.com.

And best of luck with your software marketing!

ACKNOWLEDGEMENTS

I need to particularly thank my editor, Gail Ostrow, for the long hours and insight she brought to the *Handbook*, even if she did make me take out my favorite story about Microsoft and online manners! I'd also like to thank Ray and Jo-Ann Campbell of *mle design* for the long hours they spent on layout and design. I also owe Randy Hujar, Gary Skiba, Tom Anderson, Jan Matthews, Jerry Duro and everyone who assisted in providing me with the information and stories that make up the heart of the 3rd Edition a huge debt of gratitude.

My special thanks to Dataquest for the market information and data they supplied for the 3rd Edition of *The Product Marketing Handbook for Software*.

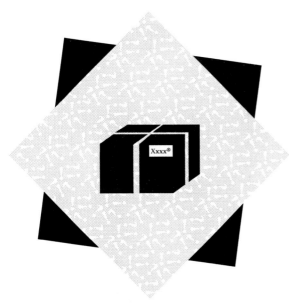

Positioning, Pricing, and Naming

Can you market a product without knowing who would want to buy it? Of course not. Yet you'd be surprised how many software publishers develop and market products without a clear understanding of their product's position in the market place.

Positioning is the foundation of all marketing activities. Until you define your product, its target market, and the reasons why the market would want to buy it, you cannot begin to market it. This is why every marketing group's first critical responsibility is to position the product. And this positioning must be clear and logical, both to your company and the market place. A company that does not understand or believe in its own product positioning cannot successfully sell its products to the market place.

Product positioning requires that you answer these fundamental questions:

- What category or type of product am I selling?
- What class of product am I selling? (In the retail market, usually low-end or high-end. In VAR markets, a middle ground **may** exist.)
- What are the significant features and benefits of the product with respect to the target audience's expectations? Other products in this category?

1

After answering these positioning questions, you can successfully:

- Build a product that meets the competitive specifications of the market in which it is competing.
- Target the audience which wants to buy and use your product.
- Price the product realistically and competitively.
- Focus on the channel partners who can provide you with maximum product push through the distribution system.

KEY ELEMENTS OF POSITIONING
Product Category

To categorize a product is to clearly define what type of product it is and who is likely to use it. This is the most crucial task in the product positioning process. Software, by nature, is always an abstraction and can be difficult for a buyer to visualize and understand.

ENCAPSULATION

The ultimate goal of the categorization process is **encapsulation**. Conceptually, a properly encapsulated product consists of a series of carefully structured ideas and concepts that are self-supporting, internally logical, and capable of being communicated to potential buyers with a minimum of confusion. The ultimate goal of the encapsulation process is to create a marketing identity for the product that automatically triggers these concepts, ideas, and associations in the buyers' minds without having them to "think" about it.

CONCEPTUALIZATION

The cornerstone of successful encapsulation is **conceptualization**. In the case of software, which is an abstract product to begin with, the best way to achieve conceptualization is to connect the product to the real and the physical.

Sometimes, this process presents little challenge. For example, few people have trouble envisioning a word processor as a typewriter in a computer (though one day, few people will know what a typewriter is) or a software database as the equivalent of an electronic file cabinet.

Other products, however, are more challenging. A classic example is Lotus Notes. If you're in the industry, you've certainly heard about it. Take a minute and think about what you know about this product. What, exactly, does it do? Does any particular image or symbol spring to mind when you think about it? Unless you use it, probably not. If you're like most people, several phrases may spring to mind like **Groupware**, **Replication**, **Documents**, and **Workflow Management**. But you are probably unable to connect the product to any coherent image or concept. The Lotus Notes documentation, rather pathetically, highlights this problem best:

> ***What Is Notes Anyway?***
>
> People have been asking that question since the beginning of time (or at least since Notes first came onto the market). It has been hard for people to define Notes because you can use it to do so many things.
>
> *(from the Notes 4.0 Beginner's Guide)*

As you can imagine, the Lotus sales force had a great deal of trouble explaining why someone should buy Notes when the company that publishes it can't explain what it is.

Many marketing newcomers make the mistake of claiming that their product is new and revolutionary. This is not the benefit you may assume it to be. A new and unique product has no existing "marketing frame of reference," and requires the publisher to educate the market by:

- Describing the product features that make it unique.
- Deciding where to advertise the product.
- Educating the reviewing and reporting press about the product.
- Deciding what type of distribution system, if any, is appropriate for the product
- Convincing the appropriate elements of the distribution system to take a chance on a new product.

SHELTERS AND UMBRELLAS

There are several things a company can do to build a clear visual image around a hard-to-conceptualize product. The first is to consider initially positioning the product around a **"shelter"** or an **"umbrella."**

A "shelter" is a product or concept that is already clearly established in the mind of the buyer. This positioning tactic works best when the product is clearly related to the shelter. For example, as Web technology is integrated into existing applications, products are increasingly described as "Web-enabled" word processors, spreadsheets, databases, etc. It is not necessary to spend much time conceptualizing these products —time and the market have already done it. To return to Notes for a minute, the growth of the Web finally allowed Lotus to position Notes as a Web-server application. But, even with this leg up, Notes still has a nebulous identity in the market.

An "umbrella" is a related concept that provides an initial mental reference point. An example of this idea in action is when Xerox introduced a new product for managing faxes. Instead of proclaiming it as a new product in a new category, Xerox positioned it as an extension of existing fax technology.

It may not always be feasible, or desirable, to use a shelter or an umbrella to help position a product. In some cases, a product may simply not fit an existing category, or there may be marketing baggage associated with that category you don't wish to carry.

VISUALIZATION

The key to successful conceptualization is visualization, accomplished by creating a **visual identity** for the product, combining the visual identity with favorable images and ideas, and then extending the result to appropriate surroundings and circumstances.

Visual Identity

Developing a strong visual identity for a product requires finding a clear and widely understood object or process that can be equated with the product. Sometimes, this is easy—there is a natural mental connection between a typewriter and a word processor, and it is easy to explain the benefits of the latter as opposed to the former. One simply has to hold up a bottle of Wite•Out to make the point.

At other times the job is harder. Again, consider Notes. There are many concepts and images that might match the product's capabilities. Notes could be thought of as "staffware," a group of people in a box who pop out and start to manage a business. You might reach for a sports metaphor and picture Notes as a referee managing the rough and tumble of your office. You might try a science fiction theme, and present Notes as an efficient android or robot that manages data. Or you could think of Notes as an electronic post office, the choice Microsoft made when it initially positioned Exchange, its competitor to Notes.

Image Creation and Attachment

The next step is **image creation and attachment**, combining the basic visual identity or concept with favorable images and ideas. Let's step outside the computer industry for a minute to get a different perspective. Let's look at dough. Yes, dough. Now, in and of itself, just about everyone knows what dough is, what it looks like, and what you do with it. And visually, dough is not much to look at.

Now, just how does one make dough desirable? Fun? Enticing? You build a man made out of dough. He's rather sexless and childlike in appearance, with a round little tummy, a high squeaky voice, and a high-pitched giggle (a series of characteristics common to babies, creatures with strong appeal to women, the principal purchasers of dough). We're talking about the Pillsbury Doughboy, of course, and he imparts to dough about as an attractive an image as you could expect it to possess.

Layering

Finally, after combining visual identity and basic images, the layering process can begin—extending the visual identity and its image to appropriate circumstances and surroundings. For instance, our Doughboy becomes ubiquitous on morning breakfast shows and around major holidays, both times when people are more likely to be thinking about and using baked products. The concept Pillsbury wishes to build in your mind is that dough is the Pillsbury Doughboy who appears at Christmas, who makes you think of delicious things and makes you want to buy dough. Pillsbury dough, to be precise.

The company faced with a difficult conceptualization challenge often has to commit to a two-track marketing process. The first track focuses on building the marketing relationship between the product and concept. This is usually done through ads, collaterals, presentations, media, etc. At the same time, the concept must be incorporated and integrated directly into the final product description. If this doesn't sound easy, it's not. It can be particularly difficult for a new or small company without deep pockets, which is why sheltering or finding an umbrella can be a more attractive option.

MARKETING VOCABULARY

The next step after conceptualization is to build a supporting "marketing vocabulary" around the concept. In high-tech marketing, the foundations of this vocabulary are **jargon** and **buzzwords**. Jargon consists of industry-specific slang and acronyms. Buzzwords are words and phrases that describe desirable features and characteristics.

There is a natural tendency for jargon to evolve into buzzwords. A classic example is the term WYSIWYG (what you see is what you get), which was coined by MicroPro founder Seymour Rubinstein, publisher of one-time, market-leading, word processor WordStar, to describe the product's text-formatting abilities. When first coined, it had a specific technical meaning; it described a text editor that formatted words in a fashion similar to that of a typewriter. Now, WYSIWYG functions as a buzzword. A product that has "WYSIWYG" is good, and one that lacks WYSIWYG is not as good.

DESCRIPTORS

Once the appropriate jargon and buzzwords have been identified or created, we turn our attention to "descriptors," short, pithy, catch phrases and sentences built from your marketing vocabulary that perform several functions simultaneously in the mind of the buyer. For one thing, they reassure the buyer about the nature of the purchase. For example, you don't care if a toothpaste is "easy to use," but you'd like your spreadsheet to be. For another, they serve as category cues, often letting the buyer know more about the nature of the product being discussed. "Powerful and full-featured" means "high-end." "Powerful multimedia technology" often means no more than the program is on a CD-ROM.

Descriptors can also incorporate **"validators**;" that is, words and phrases that "prove" the truth of the assertions being made. "Market leading," "Endorsed by," and "*PC Magazine* Editor's Choice," are all good examples of common validators.

DESCRIPTIONS

Concepts, basic vocabulary, and descriptors are combined to create a product description. Ideally, the description is internally logical and consistent, and cues the mind of the buyer almost immediately, describing precisely what the product is, its key characteristics, and the compelling reason(s) to buy it.

REPETITION AND INTEGRATION

The final keys to successful encapsulation are **repetition** and **integration**. Repetition is always critical, but even more so when dealing with the product that is difficult to conceptualize. In this case, the marketing campaign must relentlessly and continuously repeat, almost to the point of physical pain, the company's visual concept of the product and its encapsulated description. The ultimate goal is to establish a mental link between product and concept that is as clear as the link between a word processor and a typewriter.

Integration consists of incorporating the concept, images, and vocabulary you've built to describe and support the product into all aspects of your marketing activities.

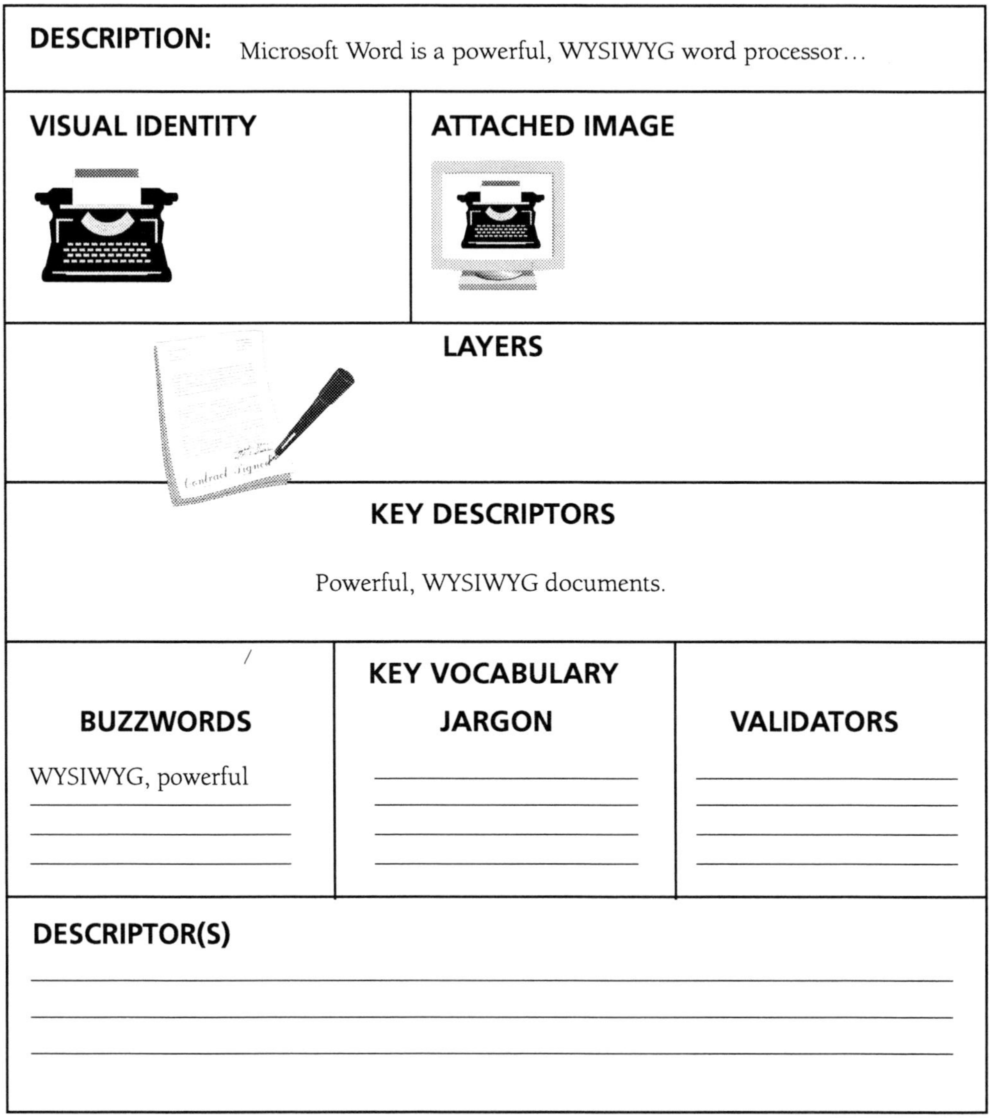

DESCRIPTION: Microsoft Word is a powerful, WYSIWYG word processor...

VISUAL IDENTITY	ATTACHED IMAGE

LAYERS

KEY DESCRIPTORS
Powerful, WYSIWYG documents.

BUZZWORDS	KEY VOCABULARY JARGON	VALIDATORS
WYSIWYG, powerful		

DESCRIPTOR(S)

Figure 1-1. The Conceptualization Process

Product Class

It is a natural tendency to divide a market into low, middle, and high segments. This is dangerous in the retail software market. Because of the historical ranges in price for low- ($99) and high-end ($995) software, there is little pricing "room" in the middle. This is especially true after standard discounting is factored into the pricing equation.

Throw in the current heavy discounting taking place in many application markets, and mid-level pricing often either leaves money on the table or makes the product too expensive to compete at the low end. The numbers in Figure 1-2 help illustrate this point; the upper reaches of mid-level pricing bump into the discount ranges for high-end products. Most buyers·will opt for the extra "chrome" if they're not paying too much for it.

Retail Pricing Chart				
Class	**Low SRP Price**	**High SRP Price**	**Low Street Price***	**High Street Price***
Low end	$80	$250	$48	$150
Mid level	$250	$450	$150	$270
High end	$500	$600	$300	$359
*Discount prices assume 40% discount off SRP.				

Figure 1-2. Retail Price Points

As a result, the trend in the retail markets is for a product to either occupy the low or high end of the spectrum, especially for applications in the major and secondary categories. For example, there are no "mid-level" spread-sheets. There is the high end (Lotus, Quattro, Excel) and the low end (the various "Works-type," products like Microsoft Works, Cassady and Green's KISS, and some shareware products). Many niche markets are not able to support even two pricing tiers, and prices tend to cluster around the benchmark established for a particular category.

A mid-level price range can exist in VAR, mini and mainframe markets; however, there is a constant trend for mid-level products to migrate to the high end. A good rule of thumb is to avoid mid-level pricing and positioning in a market that is undergoing price constriction.

Features and Benefits

When discussing features and benefits in relation to positioning, the key point to remember is that a product's capabilities must logically fit into market expectations for that product category and class. For example, no word processor can be considered a "high end" product if it lacks a spell checker. On the other hand, the presence of real-time network simulation capabilities in a network design tool identifies this product category as high end. Too often, software publishers rely on abstract technical nitpicking to justify a class claim. The fact that your word processor is written with a leading-edge development tool and its code is a marvel of software engineering doesn't make it a high-end product if the spell checker isn't there. While many PC users do care about technology (in accordance with the "more chrome than you" school of consumer desires), the message must show something getting done more quickly and efficiently because of the technology—not in spite of it.

POSITIONING MISTAKES

A positioning mistake is the most costly of all marketing errors because your positioning strategy drives every aspect of your marketing. Unclear, contradictory, or conflicting product positioning will immediately begin to sabotage these efforts. If not corrected, it can destroy your product marketing, and even your company.

The most common positioning mistakes are:

- Pricing mistakes. For instance, assigning a product a suggested retail price that places it in the "middle" of a category. We'll cover pricing mistakes in greater detail in the *Pricing* section of this chapter.
- Releasing a product whose feature set does not justify the product's class claim.
- Failing to properly conceptualize and encapsulate a product. People rarely buy something when they don't know what it is (as Lotus found out with Notes).
- Creating a category conflict by trying to sell two products that occupy the same position in a particular product category. This is the most difficult positioning mistake to rectify, and often has long-term strategic consequences, as the focus story illustrates.

FOCUS STORY: WHAT'S IN A NAME?
Companies

MicroPro International

Microsoft

Products

MicroPro: WordStar and WordStar 2000

Microsoft: Windows 95 and Windows NT

Marketing Overview

A positioning mistake can create massive disruption in a company's marketing plans. Perhaps the most classic example is MicroPro International's fatal marketing disaster with WordStar and WordStar 2000. Once a titan in the industry, few people remember how dominant MicroPro once was.

Many of the events leading to MicroPro permanently losing its market-leading position in the word processing market can be traced to its release of WordStar 2000 in 1985. At the time, MicroPro was not ready to release an upgrade to WordStar. Miscommunication and a breakdown in the company's product development cycle led to their developing a new word processing product (despite the company's original intention to create no such thing). Desperate, MicroPro decided to make this product the focus of its future sales and marketing efforts in word processing. They called it WordStar 2000. The original product, WordStar, remained on the dealers' shelves. Both products were priced at $495.

RESULTS

The decision proved disastrous. The WordStar user base rejected WordStar 2000, requiring MicroPro to invest more in enhancing and marketing WordStar. The similarity in product names had MicroPro endlessly attempting to explain the difference between the two products instead of selling them. The distribution system, faced with trying to remember which product was which, frequently ended up selling MS-Word or WordPerfect. There was only one of each of those.

Ultimately, the company began to split internally along WordStar/WordStar 2000 fault lines. At one point, the head of the WordStar product development team forbade team members from talking with WordStar 2000 programmers. (A neat trick, since both programming teams worked in the same building.) After several years of this, MicroPro permanently ceded its leadership in the word processing market to MS-Word and WordPerfect.

A more recent example of a naming and positioning problem is Microsoft's ongoing positioning conflict between Windows 95/98 and Windows NT—now Windows 2000 (the more things change…). Industry insiders have always known that Windows 95 was never supposed to exist in its current form. Originally designed to be a 16-bit upgrade to Windows 3.X, 95 abruptly got a new makeover and direction when it looked like OS/2 was gaining ground in the market place. The overly bulky and resource-hungry Windows NT, originally promised as the upgrade to 16-bit Windows, was quickly hustled off stage and repositioned as a LAN alternative to

Novell's Netware, where it had tremendous success. Windows 95 was then introduced as the "real" desktop environment Microsoft had been promising. Its huge marketing campaign achieved tremendous sales success.

Microsoft's execution of its "have NT go somewhere else" strategy was masterly, but its success lulled the company into complacency. Both Windows products have sold well, especially given IBM's and Novell's past marketing ineptitude. But over time, the positioning problem grew in the critical desktop arena. Windows NT has always been available in a "workstation" (PC) version, and is now directly competing with Windows 95. After all, they're both called Windows. They're both 32-bit operating systems. The desktop versions are comparably priced. They even look alike. So, which to buy?

Microsoft tried to help customers make the decision via its inept "Two Nags Racing" ad, which ran in 1996 (if you dig up the June *Infoworld*, it's a two-page spread.) It featured a picture of two horses running neck and neck with the caption "You see a horse race. We see two thoroughbreds." Well, yes, but the horses **are** racing. And as we all know, only one horse can win. So, which customer is going to ride the losing steed? Faced with such a choice, corporate America paused. Two years after the release of Windows 95, over 60% of the U.S. corporate market was still using Windows 3.X. This didn't seem to particularly bother Microsoft; after all, business would have to upgrade sooner or later and they only had one choice. A Microsoft choice. Right? Right.

And then Java appeared. With its siren call of "write once, run anywhere," corporate America, frozen in place by indecision, decided to give the newcomer a close look. Perhaps this was a safer choice than attempting to pick the right pony in the OS sweepstakes. Microsoft, taken by surprise, was forced to "embrace" Java through a humiliating agreement to license it from rival Sun. That done, Microsoft has spent enormous amounts of time, effort, and money trying convert the supposedly platform-independent Java into a proprietary extension of Windows (whichever Windows).

To complicate matters further, Linux, a freeware OS bundled with source code, began making considerable gains in the market. Bundled with the freeware Apache web-server application by such firms as Red Hat Software, Linux has begun to nibble away at both NT's and Netware's market share, and catch the imagination of the market place. The basic Linux business model is simple (and Microsoft, of all companies, should understand and appreciate it.) Drain money out of the operating systems market and make money selling applications. This concept has particular appeal to companies like Corel and Lotus, who would dearly like to reset the competitive terrain and fight over ground where their chief competitor does not possess an overwhelming strategic position by dint of ownership of the operating environment.

As of this writing, Java's future and the Linux's ultimate success are unclear. What is clear is that Microsoft's situation would have been very different if the market were focused on how to upgrade from Windows 3.X and not what to upgrade to. If you give your customers reasons to shop, be assured they will.

LESSONS

The failure to position products clearly led to the loss of dominance for one company (MicroPro) and a threat to market dominance for the other (Microsoft). The lesson should be clear. It is not possible, over time, to sell two products occupying the same category into the same market segment. If you try, you will either A) break your company into warring camps, or B) freeze your customer base with indecision, encouraging them to look elsewhere for a simple answer to their shopping problem or, C) both.

Recovering From Positioning Mistakes

There are several corrective actions a company can take to repair a positioning mistake. First, the problem must be diagnosed. Is the product's feature set at odds with market expectations for this product? If so, development must respond as quickly as possible to remedy this deficiency, while marketing executes a series of promotions, PR releases, and interim price changes to offset the problem.

If a product is poorly conceptualized, then your marketing is failing in its primary responsibility and needs to be revamped. Most problems in this regard stem from failing to undertake this critical task in the first place.

Most difficult to remedy is a category conflict. If two of your products occupy the same market niche, you must reposition one or both of the products. This is never an easy or enjoyable exercise. One reason is that you may have executed an effective marketing strategy for **both** products. Unfortunately, it is in the inherent nature of a category conflict to negate all your good works and turn them to dust.

Repositioning Strategies

There are three repositioning strategies to choose from when you need to remedy a category conflict: re-price, resign (kill), or re-categorize the product.

Re-price

This is the easiest strategy and often the least effective; it often becomes necessary if you've failed to properly connect features and benefits to a product's category and class. An interesting example of this recently took place in the CAD marketplace. CADKey, a major high-end competitor, re-priced its flagship product from $4000, the benchmark for this category and class of product, to $495 SRP (even less in some cases), expecting the market to stampede toward them in a mad rush to take advantage of the offer.

They were bitterly disappointed. In fact, the market ran away from them in fear instead. The problem was one of credibility. In the high-end CAD market, extensive product support and after-sales resources are considered key features/benefits. At the new price, CADKey's users were convinced they would lose these key benefits.

Resign

Let's look at the most logical approach. If you have two products occupying the same market position, discontinuing one of them is, in theory, a clean way to handle the problem. Of course, financial issues may prevent this. In MicroPro's case, by the time the company awoke to what it had done, WordStar 2000 accounted for about 30% of company revenues. MicroPro could not afford to give up that cash.

In some cases, the product is very good, fills a real need, and your business needs it—in which case it may be best to **re-categorize** the product by rethinking your category, class, and features/benefits claims.

Re-categorize

Re-categorizing, the last of your options, is usually a messy, expensive, and time-consuming activity. You have to completely revisit your basic positioning and recast it. Hopefully, when you are done, your product occupies a different market and faces different competitive and product realities.

There are three strategies to choose from when you need to re-categorize a product: **Go Somewhere Else**, **Facade**, and **Sweep the Board**.

Go Somewhere Else

Microsoft's repositioning strategy when it initially released Windows NT was a **Go Somewhere Else** strategy. As it became apparent that the product was going to miss the existing desktop hardware profile by a wide margin, Microsoft repackaged NT as a network operating system only. But this "Go To the Network" approach only worked because NT had that inherent capability. You can't always count on your product being able to do double duty for you in this fashion. Also, since NT is **still** also a desktop OS, it continues to be drawn, inexorably, into conflict with Windows 9X.

Facade

Facade is a more difficult strategy to execute. The author implemented a facade strategy at MicroPro after becoming WordStar 2000's product manager. After evaluating the situation and various options, WordStar 2000 was re-christened a word publisher.

And what, you ask, was a word publisher? Well, a word publisher was a word processor with exceptional laser printing capabilities, a particular strength of the product at that time. However, this claim could not withstand market scrutiny; in reality, there was no such thing as a "word publisher." The claim to differentiation was sustainable only as long as WordStar 2000 was superior to the competition in this area—a short lived and ultimately hollow claim. But, in the short term, the campaign worked. Sales and market share increased. The strategy bought MicroPro some time and maneuvering room.

A more contemporary, albeit unintended, example of a facade strategy was Word Perfects' ill-fated attempt in 1994 to re-position its fading word processor as a "document processor" And what was a document processor? Oh, a word processor with more fonts, graphics, web support, and a whole slew of new features. An upgrade, not a new category. Like WordStar 2000, nothing about the feature set or target audience justified this grandiose claim of a new category, and the campaign quickly ground to a halt.

When to Use Facade

If circumstances dictate a Facade strategy, there are several tactical moves that can help its execution, including:

- Selling similar products into different distribution channels. For example, selling one version of a code base into a vertical mark and the other into a horizontal, can, for the short term, (typically one release cycle), help keep similar products out of each other's way.

- Adding at least one key feature to one of the products. Again, even if the code bases are similar, a single major feature targeted to a segment within a market can offer temporary cover.

- Using service, support, and add-ons as to differentiate the products. Again, this offers some temporary cover.

It's important to remember that even if these tactical advantages are used, their effectiveness is short term. The goal of using Facade is to buy time—to maneuver yourself out of having to explain the differences between the two products so that you can talk about what the products are and why the buyer wants them. (Do not make the mistake of believing your own propaganda.) When done correctly and with finesse, a Facade strategy provides the opportunity to decide if it is possible to resign a product, either via a migration strategy or "merger," Go Somewhere Else, etc. By its nature, Facade is a transitional strategy.

Sweep the Board

Finally, we come to **Sweep the Board**, the most grandiose of all re-categorization strategies. This strategy is an attempt to proclaim that the current rules are now obsolete, and that everything, including market share, is now up for grabs. Current examples of Sweep the Board are Sun's Java initiative and the market's enthusiasm for Linux, both of which are designed to break Microsoft's stranglehold on the crucial OS market, and replace it with a "new" (in the case of Java, if you don't remember the p-System) technology. Will it work? Who knows? For Sweep the Board to be effective, everything must break just right. It is a high-risk strategy with a potential high reward. And note the players involved. Sun, Oracle, IBM, all big companies with deep pockets. Sweep the Board is a strategy best employed by such companies.

BRANDS AND BRAND BUILDING
What Is a Brand?

First, it is important to understand what a brand is. It is not, nor can it ever be, a product. This is a hard concept for many marketers to grasp. Yes, you can buy a company. And you can buy its brands. However, you can never sell these brands to the customer. All you can ever sell is products or services.

That's because a brand is a symbol, an intangible entity created and charged by dint of product excellence, unceasing PR, advertising, and good collaterals, with **positive** equity. The ultimate goal of investing in a brand is the ability to charge a premium for a product (typically, between 5% and 15%), or to increase market share, or both. Figure 1-3 helps illustrate this principal.

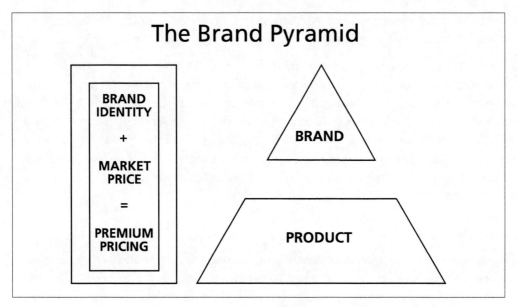

Figure 1-3. Brand Equity

Please note the emphasis on positive equity. It is quite possible for a brand's equity to change from positive to negative, and when this occurs, you no longer have a brand. Instead, you have a liability or an "anti-brand," if you will. WordStar is a classic example of a brand's equity changing from a positive to negative. At the beginning of the 1980s WordStar represented power and market dominance; by the 1990s, WordStar stood for hard-to-use and out-of-date.

Brand Components

While intangible in and of itself, a brand, paradoxically, consists of tangible components. These can, but do not have to, include:

- **A spokesman or spokeswoman**. Like the brand, these individuals possess certain qualities intended to support and build brand equity. And like a brand, a spokesman's equity can change from positive to negative. For example, we can assume the product manager for the word processor O.J. Simpson used to write his book was praying that the former Hertz spokesman would never mention their product by name.

- **Music**. Jingles and tunes have always supported products. Famous examples include the "I'd like to teach the world to sing" campaign used by Coke (people are still suffering from that one) and "Thus Spake Zarathrustra" (from the movie "2001, A Space Odyssey"). Few computer products have ever been identified with a memorable melody or song, except perhaps Microsoft's appropriation of the Rolling Stone's "Start Me Up" to support the rollout of Windows 95.

- **A cartoon or mythical creature**. Remember Speedy Alka Seltzer? Joe Isuzu? IBM's Little Tramp? And of course, the Duracell Bunny. (You caught that, correct?) Yes, one of the problems with these characters is that they can subsume the product they're supposed to support. While the ubiquitous Bunny has worked magnificently as a branding symbol for batteries, it is not clear whether Duracell or Eveready benefits more.

- **Distinctive design, colors, and pictures**. Of all brand components, these are often hard to remember or tie to any product. One example everyone remembers is the Yellow Pages, which, of course, are very yellow. A more subtle example is the "bite" in the Microsoft logo, which represents a "byte." The function of design and color is to "invade" the mind quietly, remaining present as a constant whisper to the subconscious.

Where Do Brands Come From?

Brands arise from one of two sources. The first is as a result of product success, which is the key to understanding their importance. Most brand identities spring from this source. For example, Proctor and Gamble was able to persuade the American Dental Association that Crest toothpaste really did help prevent cavities. For a time, Crest was the only toothpaste able to make this claim, and the moms and dads of America flocked to buy a product that could objectively back up its claim to be "better."

Building upon this success, Proctor and Gamble was able to build a brand around Crest. Over time, a whole family of related Crest-brand products were introduced, such as mouthwash, dental accessories, variants of the toothpaste, etc. In the software industry, companies such as Lotus, WordPerfect, Borland, and most notably Microsoft, have built brand strategies focused on superior products, then extended their success to other products.

This is not to say that the process is always successful. For instance, do you think that because you've (Lotus) created the world's best selling spreadsheet (1-2-3), you can sell a new word processor (Manuscript)? Or that because you're the largest computer company in the world (IBM), you can dictate a new microcomputer bus (MCA) and new operating system (OS/2) to the industry? All on the strength of previous product success and brand identity?

Branding

Branding is a deliberate attempt to create a brand using PR and marketing campaigns. Intel's "Bunny People" campaign is a classic example of this process. (I know, they look like little spacemen to me too.) Beginning with its "Intel Inside" campaign, the company embarked on a program to make its company a consumer brand. Prior to these efforts, the only people in the world who were aware of Intel were industry insiders and analysts concerned with technology stocks. But for the last several years, dancing technicians in fluorescent clean suits have been selling the idea that Intel makes computers sing and boogie. Probably not one in 20 people understands that the basis for all this disco'ing and singing is an extension to the chip's instruction set, nor does Intel want to tell them about that. What it **does** want is for you to believe that if your computer doesn't have Intel in it, your system will be as exciting as Alan Greenspan testifying before Congress on the prime rate. Intel is hoping that this campaign will help it sell its chips at a premium and maintain its market dominance.

As you can imagine, Intel's branding campaign has cost millions. Few companies can afford this type of expenditure. Nor can most companies afford the cost to defend a brand name when things go wrong, like they did with the infamous 1995 "The Pentium Can't Count" fiasco. Shortly after the chip's release, a bug was found in its internal software that caused it to improperly round off numbers in certain complex calculations. Now, a bug in a chip's embedded code is not a new phenomenon. Practically every major CPU released by Intel, Motorola, AMD, etc., is accompanied by an "errata" sheet listing known problems. Engineers are used to dealing with these problems, and devising workarounds.

However, as Intel quickly found out, the general consumer who bought a computer with "Intel Inside" because it makes it exciting, is **not** used to dealing with these problems. Intel failed to understand this marketing reality, and after a futile attempt to avoid the inevitable, issued a recall to replace millions of perfectly good chips with better ones. The whole mess ended up costing Intel about $500 million, and left the company with a greatly enhanced appreciation of the "power of brands," both for good and bad.

Brand Integration and Persistence

The final elements in the brand-creation process are integration and persistence; that is, ensuring that brand components and messages are incorporated into every aspect of the company's marketing. For example, when a company creates its collaterals, a common "look and feel" of design should be woven through all pieces. The text of each piece should repeat key marketing messages and vocabulary. Key brand components, such as a musical set piece, should be repeated anytime the product or company logo is shown (the Intel "ta dah ta dah" jingle you constantly hear in their ads is a good example of this). The goal is to create an immediate recognition in the mind that buying a particular product also brings the buyer the intangibles represented by the brand.

Brand Attachment

Once a brand has been created, a choice must be made as to where it will be "attached."

- A related product.
- A group of products not related to the initial product.
- A division or component of a company.
- A company.

An example of attaching brand identity to a company and not a product is Microsoft's recent "Where do you want to go today?" advertising campaign. Microsoft hopes to convince potential buyers that their products have unique qualities of "futureness" and "modernity;" that they have the ability to take you anywhere in the world you want to go. It doesn't matter which Microsoft product you buy; if it's a Microsoft product, it must, by definition, have these qualities.

Brand Limitations

On the face of it, who can argue with the concept of brands? They sound wonderful. Create an enticing image or belief, attach it to your products and *voila!* Watch the profits roll in! But there are pitfalls.

- **Brands are expensive to create.** Remember, you can't sell them. That means every dollar spent on their creation comes out of your marketing budget. And it's always difficult to calculate just how many incremental copies of a particular product a branding program is selling.

- **Brands must be defended.** This sounds logical and easy. As Intel discovered, it's not. There are practical problems. It can be difficult to justify investing substantial sums into an abstraction that has no direct impact on sales. When things go wrong, a high degree of coordination between product marketing, upper management, and PR is needed to set things right. And many technology companies do not understand the damage that an anti-brand can wreak on a successful product.

- **Brands cannot be infinitely extended.** Coca Cola found this out in the 1980s with the great Coke clothing disaster. You may remember this. For a short time, you could buy jeans, shirts, T-shirts, sweats, etc. with the Coke logo. It **sounded** like a good idea, until they discovered that people had no great desire to turn themselves into walking billboards for a soft drink, and they were left with mountains of unsold clothing

- **Brands do not allow you to simply raise prices at will.** Many companies have found this out the hard way. Through the '80s, Porsche and Mercedes raised the prices of their products seemingly in defiance of the laws of economics. When they were done, a fun little two-seater you could have bought for $14K in 1982 cost almost $50K, and a small family sedan (the 190) that sold for $15K cost $45K. Then Mazda introduced the Miata for about $15K and Porsche's sales disappeared. Toyota and Nissan introduced full-sized luxury sedans for $30K and Mercedes gave up U.S. market share and profits by the bucketful.

Should Your Company Invest in Branding?

For small companies, this is usually an easy question to answer. Don't bother. Save your money and time and focus on establishing your product as a winner in its respective market arena. The issue of whether you can extend the product's identity to other products only becomes relevant once you have established product visibility and superiority,

For larger companies, the question is more complex. While Intel's consumer brand program stumbled into a major marketing *faux pas*, Intel will tell you in that in the end, the program is worth it. They believe that consumers prefer to buy computers with "Intelness" inside and are willing to pay a premium for the privilege. If you believe you have the opportunity, resources, and ability to create this kind of brand loyalty and identity, then branding can make sense.

Before making any decisions however, ask yourself one final question. Try to name one software product that has achieved success due to a "great" branding program. It's a difficult task. Practically every product you can name has achieved success by creating excellent products, and surrounding them with successful marketing programs.

PRICING

The key to successful pricing is proper positioning. Remember, your product's positioning drives all aspects of your product marketing. Many publishers make the mistake of pricing a product before establishing its positioning. When you do this, you are making your decisions in a vacuum. You may get lucky and get it right the first time, but don't count on it. Proper positioning and good marketing intelligence provide the reality check you need to price your product correctly.

Setting prices is often the most contentious and difficult issue facing a company. It is particularly difficult in the software industry because of its periodic price wars. While most publishers have not "officially" changed their retail prices, competitive upgrades, special offers, and plain old-fashioned discounting have effectively cut the street prices of many popular products by 70% or more. While hardware prices decline more predictably due to fixed costs, the inevitability of price erosion over time is a given in the software industry.

The result is that publishers have discovered that they must be flexible in pricing. In the U.S. market, cutting prices to achieve a sales goal will not always succeed, and conversely, refusing to cut prices based on previous notions of "brand equity" will sometimes fail. This does not mean it is always necessary to resort to blind discounting.

Pricing Goals

Software companies have two primary objectives when pricing a product. They are:

- Maximize profits
- Maximize market share

Which objective a company decides to make a priority depends on its marketing strategy. The ongoing price wars in the software industry are driven by a desire to maximize market share at any cost.

SRP vs. ESP Pricing Models

The PC retail price market was almost exclusively driven by the suggested retail price (SRP) structure until 1995, when several publishers, foremost among them Microsoft, announced they were dropping SRPs in favor of allowing the "market" to decide prices. (Microsoft promptly instituted a manufacturer's advertised price (MAP) program to fix prices of Windows 95 and 98.) Industry watchers proclaimed the end of SRPs and the beginning of ESP (estimated street price, also sometimes referred to as "cost plus"). Many benefits were claimed for the change: customers wouldn't have to pay "inflated" SRPs, street pricing would be more honest, and software pricing would have more integrity. Figure 1-4 illustrates the differences between the two pricing models.

SRP	$500	ESP	No SRP
Distributor Discount	-50%	Sell to Distributor	$250
Distributor Markup	+10%	Distributor Markup	+10%
Price to Reseller	$275	Price to Reseller	$275
Reseller Markup	+20%	Reseller Markup	+20%
Street Price	$330	Street Price	$330

Figure 1-4. SRP vs. ESP Model

Of course, this is all nonsense. Few buyers ever purchase products at SRP. The SRP model functions as a useful yardstick for calculating discounts and establishing product positioning; all channel discounts, end-user discounts, upgrade prices, etc., can be quickly derived from it. Both end users and resellers find the SRP a useful device for "keeping score" of a product's price structure. Resellers in particular like SRPs as they allow them to run promotions offering "steep" discounts.

On the other hand, ESP pricing makes comparison shopping more difficult (at least when we're talking about the real world. Neither system prevents a savvy Internet-shopper from searching for the best price). Unless special advertised promotions are being run simultaneously in different chains by the same company, the consumer must comparison shop store-by-store to find the best price. This benefits larger publishers who can afford to dominate precious shelf space with promotional and MDF (marketing development funds) dollars.

The upshot of all this maneuvering is that most companies have retained SRPs, though they sometimes cloud the issue with nomenclature like "recommended street price" (RSP), estimated retail price (ERP), etc. Only a company that refuses to assign any suggested price of any sort can claim to have a true ESP.

MAP Pricing

As proof that the more things change, the more they stay the same, look at the growth of MAP programs. This is an SRP with teeth. MAP programs allocate marketing funds to the distribution system in return for not discounting a product under an SRP or ESP. Microsoft and other large publishers are fond of them, using them to "defend" their price and the product's perceived value.

Which Pricing Model Should You Use?

No hard and fast rules exist in the industry. Most customers still find it useful to know a product's SRP and, in a sense, demand the publisher assign one to each product. In addition, if your product will be sold through the software distribution system (the channel), you will probably find an SRP useful. Standard discounting practices will lower the SRP to ESP levels anyway. SRP pricing can also be useful in establishing a higher perceived value for a product, particularly applications aimed at smaller, more focused market like CAD or high-end DTP. An ESP structure may be suitable for lower-end products, or for applications you can support with extensive store-based promotions and advertising. MAP pricing should only be implemented by publishers with deep marketing pockets.

VAR Pricing

Publishers of VAR-class products usually do not have to worry about either SRPs or ESPs. Prices are determined by the competitive parameters of the market in which you compete. Your discount structure reflects the usual 30 to 40 percentage "points" off the SRP the distribution system requires in order to sell your product profitably. Figure 1-5 illustrates price points for a representative sample of VAR markets.

Accounting (niche or vertical markets)	$1K to $5K (dependent on market and features wanted)
CAD	$2.5K to $15K
Distributed Budgeting	$1K to $10K
E-commerce	$5K to $100K
Enterprise Resource Planning (ERP)	$50K to $50M (dependent on number of business functions integrated within ERP framework)
Network Design Tools	$2.5K to $20K
Time and Attendance	$5K to $50K

Figure 1-5. Typical VAR market price points

Positioning and Pricing

A fundamental mistake many marketing managers make is resetting a product's price independently of its position. In almost all cases, the product's position will and should drive its pricing. And once the price point for a particular product category has been established, the two factors develop a symbiotic relationship. A product's category dictates it be priced within a particular range. If the product's price does not match the levels expected for that category, consumers will often not take the product seriously, as Borland found out with Quattro Pro.

FOCUS STORY: DEATH BY HYUNDAI

Company

Borland (Inprise)

Marketing Overview

Once seemingly poised for industry greatness, Borland is today a shell of itself. Borland was a $500 million dollar firm in the early 1990s. Today, it staggers from quarter to quarter with announcements of layoffs, losses, and executive reorganizations. The company even decided it would be prudent to change its name (to Inprise. It's supposed to remind you of the enterprise.) Once a power in desktop applications, Borland was forced out of these markets, and today is refocused on its roots as a publisher of development tools for programmers.

Several factors contributed to Borland's fall, including a botched acquisition of Ashton-Tate that sparked an internal positioning war (Paradox vs. dBase), missed product deadlines, and inept marketing programs, exemplified by its infamous slash-and-burn pricing war in support of Quattro Pro.

Quattro Pro was Borland's entry in the high-end spreadsheet sweepstakes. Originally introduced as a value-priced alternative to Lotus 123, Borland had over time repositioned the product as a high-end competitor to both 123 and Excel. Determined to gain market share at any cost, Borland began a series of price promotions and reductions designed to achieve this goal. From an SRP of $495 (at that time the benchmark for high-end spreadsheets) Borland steadily reduced Quattro's price until the product hit the $29.95 price point.

As pricing dropped, sales increased as the first wave of buyers rushed in to take advantage of the bargain. However, as the price continued to drop, sales began to level off, then decrease. The reason was simple. Borland's pricing was destroying the product's credibility. No one could figure out how Borland could make money at these prices, and many suspected they were losing their shirt on Quattro Pro (and they were.) Companies that lose money tend to go out of business, and who wants to own an orphaned product?

The credibility issue proved fatal. Borland ran ads proclaiming that buying Quattro Pro was like "Being Offered a Lexus for the Price of a Hyundai." To understand the problem with this, imagine yourself in a Hyundai dealership and being approached by a salesman. Imagine the salesman telling you about a new car that is equal in every way to a Mercedes Benz 300E. The same quality steel. The same powerful engine. The same impeccable fit and finish. And it's true! Objectively, the two cars are the same. An independent government agency published a report attesting that the two cars are the same. Would you believe the salesman? Would you buy the Hyundai?

LESSON
Positioning drives pricing. At a certain point, price cutting no longer attracts bargain hunters, but instead destroys product credibility. If the only way you can sell a product is by cutting the price past the point of credibility, then perhaps you shouldn't be selling this product.

Pricing Points and Tiers

Each segment of the software market has, over time, developed recognized price points and tiers for the different types and classes of software in the retail and VAR markets. These pricing structures have proven surprisingly durable over the past 20 years, changing little. Figure 1-6 outlines some basic price points for particular major retail markets and sub-markets. Note that different sub-markets can have different price tiers. For example, it is rare to find word processing add-ons with SRPs much higher than $149.95. Development environments, such as compilers, on the other hand, often have SRPs or ESPs that equal or exceed that of the flagship DBMS or language product. A publisher must always research both market and sub-market pricing to price a product competitively.

RETAIL MARKET PRICE POINTS	LOW-END SRP	HIGH-END SRP
Business Applications	$99.95	$999.95
Education & Entertainment	$19.95	$59.95
Add-ons (Products that add functionality to the main product)	$89.95	$149.95
Word Processing	$89.95	$299.95
Office Suite	$89.95	$499.95
DBMS	$69.95	$695.95
Web and Internet Products	$29.95	$699.95
Niche Products (includes utilities, small business, home management, etc.)	$69.95	$149.95

Figure 1-6. Common retail market price points

Price Point Persistence

Another important factor to note in the pricing decision is the "persistence" of price points. The current office-suite market provides a good example of this principal in action. Up until the early 1990s, standalone word processor and spreadsheet applications cost $495 SRP, with discounting dropping the price to between $279 and $349 on average.

The office suite has subsumed the main part of these markets, but the $495 price remains, occupied by this relatively new product category. Price wars suppressed SRPs for a time in this market, but as Microsoft achieved 90% plus market share, prices have returned to historical retail and discount levels.

The Creation of Price Structures

Once established, an SRP or widely publicized ESP forms a pricing structure the publisher must "live in," especially when dealing with the distribution system. No company, especially a market's number two, can expect to unilaterally overturn them by fiat. Instead, they must be respected and if changed, changed in an evolutionary manner. There are many factors that contribute to a market's price points. One is the price relationship between hardware and software. Companies that compete in the $1000 and under hardware markets traditionally have low software prices. It is difficult to sell an office suite for $495 to someone who has purchased a $995 computer.

In other cases, price points are set by competitive pressures, audience and volume expectations, and the need to compete. Sometimes, a price point can be established because of a key player's past actions.

A good example is the low price of PC desktop operating systems. The key products, DOS (still), Windows 95/98 and Windows NT, OS/2 (a bit), and the various commercial versions of Linux are all available for between $49.95 and $89.95 (street price, not SRP). These low prices were established by IBM in 1981 with the introduction of the original IBM PC. Originally, three operating systems were offered: DOS, CPM/86, and the UCSD P-System. DOS cost $40, CPM/86 $295, and the P-System, $695. DOS quickly crushed its competition, and from that point on, PC users have been accustomed to paying very little for their PC desktop OS.

IBM learned how difficult it was to "reset" a price point when they introduced OS/2 1.0 in 1987. Despite its greatly increased capabilities, one of the key reasons for its initial rejection was its high price of $295. It took years, but IBM finally learned its lesson. When OS/2 3.0 Warp was released, it had an SRP of $129.95. Adjusting for inflation, that's the same price as PC DOS 1.0. Windows 95 and 98 sell for approximately $90, lower than the 1981 inflation-adjusted benchmark. Windows NT upgrade version, by the far the most popular version of the product, sells for approximately $130. Commercial versions of Linux range between $49.95 and $99.95. It will be difficult, if not impossible, to ever persuade consumers they should pay much for a desktop OS.

Price Wars

Vicious price wars periodically rock the software industry, with the inevitable casualties. We've seen what happened to Borland. Word-processing giant WordPerfect was purchased by Canadian upstart Corel at fire sale prices, who went on to lose millions selling Corel Office against Microsoft Office. Lotus gave up its independence to IBM. In all cases, these price wars have been driven either by the desire to expand market share or the need to protect an installed base. In many cases, they have damaged all the participants, but this doesn't stop companies from employing the "price bomb" when their competitive blood is up.

Competitive Upgrades and Upgrades

Competitive and regular upgrades remain popular alternatives to simply cutting prices. Competitive upgrades offer special pricing for purchasers of competing products; regular upgrades ostensibly require a user own a previous version of the same product. Both upgrades are widely available through the reseller channel.

The competitive upgrade, pioneered by Borland, functions as an attack on a competitor's installed base as well as a means to generate volume sales. Both types offer a discount off SRP ranging between 50% and 80%. They remain a common method of discounting for several reasons:

- Maintaining a traditional retail SRP or ESP helps the publisher maintain pricing credibility.
- SRP pricing allows resellers to build attractive discount offers around a product.
- In the event a company succeeds in driving its competition from the market, publishers want the ability to quickly "climb back up" the pricing ladder to more profitable price points.
- The SRP is a useful pricing benchmark.
- A certain percentage of users continue to purchase at "standard" prices, despite the widespread availability of competitive upgrades and introductory offers. These users represent incremental profits for publishers.

PRICING DEFINITIONS

Pricing definitions cover a wide array of products and programs. Among the most common are:

1. **List prices**. These, in turn, include:
   - The unit price. The single-unit retail price.
   - Multiple-quantity price. The retail price for multiple purchases, such as packs of 10, 20, 50, etc.
     - Server price. The retail price for a unit of software that runs on a server and supports multiple workstations.
     - Workstation price or "requester" price. Workstation prices are either concurrent or individual. In concurrent pricing, the user buys a license for a given number of accesses to a product; e.g., 25 users can log in and use the server-based product. In individual pricing, the buyer purchases a license for each "seat" or user who will be accessing the program.
   - Upgrade price. This is the single-unit retail price for a qualified upgrade to a licensed product.
   - Site license. The price for a product that can be distributed by the purchaser throughout a specified site. Site licenses can include the right to duplicate disks and documentation.

- Volume purchase agreement price. A purchase contract for a volume quantity of a product. It differs from a site licenses in that the buyer obtains full product.
- OEM price. The price set for selling your software to a hardware manufacturer or another publisher.

2. **Channel prices**. These are the prices charged distributors and resellers who buy directly. The standard pricing model covers the most common scenarios, but all kinds of special deals, volume discounts, and promotional arrangements exist, and are in a constant state of flux.

3. **Promotional Prices**. These can include:
   - Competitive upgrade price. The price offered the owner of a competing product as an inducement to switch.
   - Corporate evaluation price. The price for product provided for corporate evaluation. (No publisher provides evaluation software for individuals). This pricing can include fully functional as well as limited-function product.
   - Industry courtesy price. Usually a limited-time offer to promote a product in a particular industry, such as selling a product at a special price to software developers.
   - Value Added Reseller (VAR) price. This is the price for selling products to a VAR to package with their product(s).
   - Dealer evaluation copy price. This is similar to the evaluation copy price, but is designed to allow dealers and their sales personnel to buy software for in-store education and demonstration purposes.
   - Employee purchase price. The price for an employee to purchase the product.
   - Internal use price. The price for products used internally. This pricing is usually used only by large companies.

4. **Government Price**. These are prices charged to federal, state, and local agencies. Often they are driven by government purchasing requirements. For example, U.S. law has recently changed to allow agencies to buy items under $2.5K without going out to bid via a request for proposal (RFP).

Pricing Guidelines

Despite the fluid pricing environment vendors find themselves in, there are some basic rules that should be considered (thought not slavishly followed).

- Do not calculate discount by only considering retail prices; factor in discounted prices as well. Once discounts prices are factored into a pricing equation, it may become apparent that there is not much room to maneuver in the "middle" of a market's price structure. This is particularly true for software.

- Do not establish a price differential less than 20% of equivalent products. Doing so raises the "it's too good to be true" question in buyers' minds.

- Remember that while buyers are excited by price cuts, the distribution system is often indifferent. In fact, a steep reduction in price lowers the volume of dollars flowing through the channel and can make other, higher-priced products more attractive.

- Using price to differentiate your product is most effective when the product is offered for a special price on a limited-time basis or, in the case of software, as a competitive upgrade.

- Unless you are the undisputed market leader in your product category, do not try to change the existing SRP structure. Only a market leader can do that, and even they are very reluctant to do so. If you need or want to compete on price, use promotional pricing.

- Deep discounting against an established category leader with deep pockets is usually not an effective promotional tactic. In fact, history shows it is counterproductive in the long run.

NAMING PRODUCTS

The primary function of naming is to support the product's positioning of the product. There are three classes of names: descriptive, suggestive, and arbitrary. Below are some familiar examples:

> **Descriptive**: Microsoft Word
> **Suggestive**: Documagix's PaperMaster
> **Arbitrary**: Corel's Paradox

Picking names is something of a black art. Companies choose names for a wide variety of reasons, not all of them rational. For example, Mitsubishi Corporation gave its first series of American cars Italianate names (i.e., Tredia, Cordia, etc.). It seems a puzzling choice. Italian cars have never had a particularly good reputation in the U.S. The trend caught on in high tech, and it now seems that every computer ends with a vowel: Aptiva. Infinia. Achieva. Figaro (just kidding). Whimsy is apparently a staple of Japanese car naming: one successful car is called the Fair Lady in Japan because a top executive liked the Broadway musical "My Fair Lady."

Whimsy is the not the exclusive property of the Japanese. Apple's Lisa computer, the forerunner to the Macintosh, was named after Apple founder Steven Jobs' daughter. Of course, Macintosh and Newton seem logical plays on the corporate name, but think what the future of the company might have been had they used "Granny Smith."

It is rare to find instances where a product's name, by itself, leads to marketing success. It is much easier to find examples where a naming mistake has led to major product and corporate headaches. For example, consider "Windows NT." Now, as you probably know, "NT" stands for "New Technology." This is rather nifty, and if you were a Microsoft systems programmer coding away on NT it must have felt good to be working on the latest and greatest. Of course, if Windows NT was new technology, it logically follows that anything else, including Windows 98, is, well, "Old Technology." And who wants to work on or buy old technology? The key to naming success is to focus less on the creative aspects of the process and more on the trademark, translation, and positioning issues, as our focus story further illustrates.

WARP SPEED! ENGA...ERR, LET'S TOKE ON THIS
Companies

> IBM
>
> Novell

Marketing Overview

A recent example of naming agony was the release in 1995 of version OS/2 3.0, now known, unfortunately, as "Warp." The genesis of this truly unfortunate moniker began with IBM's habit of using code names lifted from the popular and seemingly eternal TV and movie series, "Star Trek." Previous beta versions of OS/2 were named "Ferengi" and "Klingon," (alien races on the show), and the 3.0 beta version was called Warp (as in "warp speed," as in really really fast). It seemed an excellent idea! OS/2 had been criticized as being slow, though this was more a function of memory requirements and set-up than a technical deficiency. "Star Trek" was cool, futuristic, and familiar, a seemingly perfect match of product image to functionality. But as Warp neared its release date, IBM puzzled over what to call the released product, until Chairman Lou Gerstner decreed that the product should be known as…"Warp."

Which seemed a good idea at the time. IBM moved ahead, and designed a marketing campaign built around a Star Trek theme. They even rented a hall in New York City and invited hundreds to see Patrick Stewart, current captain of the starship Enterprise to help roll out the product in a gala event. (Stewart was a no-show.)

The only problem is that no one at IBM had bothered to check with Paramount, owner and guardian of the Star Trek franchise and all related trademarks and marketing rights, what they thought of this idea. Now, Paramount had no right to trademark the name "warp; SciFi writers had been using the phrase since the 1930s. But IBM's public use of "Klingon" and "Ferengi" had annoyed them, and Paramount wasn't about to let IBM appropriate Star Trek for their own marketing purposes. Sharp letters were sent to IBM and threats voiced. As a result, IBM decided to drop any Star Trek marketing concepts for Warp.

This was a problem. Without a cool futuristic concept tied to the word and the product, IBM had to rely on the traditional meanings of the word. Like "bent." "Twisted." "Warped" out of shape. And other, less conventional meanings. For instance, if you were alive during the 1960s (if you **remember** the 60s), "warped" was something you became after ingesting certain substances that time and experience have shown to be bad for memory recall and possibly your genetic heritage.

The result was that IBM ending up creating a very odd advertising and marketing campaign redolent of hash brownies and magic mushrooms. Twisty "Age of Aquarius" type was splashed across ad posters all over the land proclaiming that people were "warping" their computers. One ad had Phil Jackson, coach of the mighty Chicago Bulls and the flower child of NBA basketball with the New York Knicks in the 1970s, smiling through his bushy mustache at the prospect of "warping" his computer. Everyone, of course, was thrilled at running a psychedelic, warping operating system that smoked dope and went "groovy" when you asked it to retrieve a file. OS/2's current 1% market share attests to this.

Novell's naming problems, on the other hand, were a bit less colorful, but no less self-inflicted and painful. As Netware began to lose its grip on the NOS market, the company, as is often the case, began to thrash about for quick fixes. The growth of Intranets, internet systems set up internally to facilitate corporate communications and information exchange, seemed to fit naturally with Novell's LAN strategy. In a burst of inspiration, Novell decided to drop the Netware name, and call its new versions "Intranetware."

The results were not good. Everyone immediately assumed that Novell had discontinued Netware and began to ask what had happened to the product? After all, there was still a huge market for conventional LANs, and it seemed Novell no longer stocked such an item. After a year or so of trying to explain to the market that, "no, Novell still sold LANs and that Intranetware was also a LAN product, but with Intranet capability as well as all those terrific LAN abilities traditionally associated with Netware," Novell gave up and returned to the tried, true, trusted, and blessedly familiar "Netware" (now with Intranet capabilities) name.

LESSONS

It's a very good idea to check for all trademark rights and issues, as well as checking the dictionary before you name a product. Think about all the possible alternative meanings of the name you've chosen. Also, check with the existing user base and prospective new purchasers before giving up a highly recognized product or brand name. You can learn a lot quickly and save a great deal of money.

Trademarks

One common reason for renaming a product is the desire to register it as a trademark. A famous example is Intel's introduction of the Pentium microprocessor, previously known as the 586. Intel decided to change the name after it became clear that it wasn't going to be allowed to trademark a series of numbers. Also, despite the recent craze to trademark every conceivable combination of syllables and vowels known to mankind, it is important to remember that trademarking a name is not always a desirable thing. In some cases, you may wish to use a simple, familiar concept, such as "Windows," to describe your product.

Key Naming Issues

When assigning a new name, or considering changing an existing name, consider the following questions:

- Does the name support or undermine the product's positioning?
- Can the name be confused with another of your products, or a competitive product?
- Can the name be trademarked?
- Have you referred to the product as 1.0? If so, don't. Call the product 1.1, or 1.5. First versions scare people.

- Do you want the name to relate to other company products?

- Can you picture the product name on resellers' shelves?

- Can the name be shrunk down to an inappropriate acronym? Does it lend itself to an undesirable pun? ? (For instance, one company once introduced a VAR program that shrank to "CPR.")

- Does the name translate into an inappropriate or scatological term in a foreign language?

- Will the name infringe on a protected trademark? (Protected is the key word. Microsoft, for example, claims "Windows" as a trademark, but has never been granted a trademark on the name. It can trademark the name "Microsoft Windows.")

- Do you want the name to support a "family" or brand name identity? For example, Microsoft's Word, Software Publishing Corporation's "Harvard" family of products (Harvard Graphics, Harvard Draw, Harvard Mapping, etc.).

- Have you avoided, if possible, "extenders" that are overworked, such as "Extra," "Plus," "Enhanced," "Improved," etc.?

THE NAMING PROCESS

There are two basic methods companies can use when naming products. One is to brainstorm internally and develop a list of possible names. This method has the advantage of being comparatively quick and inexpensive. It is used by both large and small companies: Pentium and Unisys are just two examples of names that were generated internally by major computer companies.

The other method is to use a naming consultant or specialist. The individual or firm will research names for audience reaction, associations, nuances of meaning, dissonance, etc. Costs can range from $5K to over $150K.

Regardless of which method you use, prospective names must always be checked for trademark violations. Never depend on an outside ad or PR agency to handle this process. Your attorney can and should handle the trademark search for you. Costs range between $1 to 5K, with additional international filings averaging about $1K per country.

TESTING NAMES

The final point to remember about naming is the need to test, check, and call. Large companies can afford to call in professionals and let them uncover any potential problems. Small publishers often can't, but even informal testing can tell you a lot. IBM could have saved itself a lot of money if they had made some phone calls to Paramount. All MicroPro and Novell needed to do was discuss their respective naming concepts with some users. In all cases, a great deal of grief and money would have been saved by the exercise of common sense.

POSITIONING, PRICING, & NAMING OBJECTIVES/EVALUATION CHECKLIST

OBJECTIVES	EVALUATION

Positioning Goals

1. Clearly establish product category, class, and pricing
Measured by:

> Feedback from press _____ _____ _____
>
> Feedback from sales force _____ _____ _____
>
> Customer data from
> direct sales _____ _____ _____
>
> Vertical market(s) activity _____ _____ _____
>
> User registration information _____ _____ _____

Pricing Goals

1. Determine the price where you can sell the most product and achieve maximum profits
Measured by:

> Different price points _____ _____ _____
>
> Market research _____ _____ _____
>
> Competitive analysis _____ _____ _____

2. Maximize market share
Measured by:

> Competitive analysis _____ _____ _____
>
> Channel reports _____ _____ _____
>
> Formal market research _____ _____ _____

Naming Goals

1. Choose effective name
Measured by:

> Positive feedback from market
> research (target audience,
> influencers, consultants, etc.) _____ _____ _____
>
> No mocking references or
> inappropriate puns in press _____ _____ _____
>
> No trademark or copyright
> problems _____ _____ _____
>
> No translation problems _____ _____ _____

POSITIONING, PRICING, & NAMING SUCCESS CHECKLIST

POSITIONING

1. **Determine product's position with respect to the following:**

    ### A. Category
    ☐ What is it? _____
    ☐ What does it do? _____
    ☐ Encapsulation strategy _____
    ▪ Conceptualization (physical connection) _____
    ▪ Use Shelters/Umbrellas? _____
    ▪ Visualization? _____
    ▪ Image creation _____
    ▪ Attachment _____
    ▪ Layers _____
    ☐ Marketing vocabulary _____
    ▪ Buzzwords _____
    ▪ Jargon _____
    ▪ Validators_____
    ▪ Descriptors_____
    ▪ Repetition and integration _____
    ☐ Repositioning Strategy _____
    ▪ Re-price _____
    ▪ Resign_____
    ▪ Re-categorize_____
    ○ Go Somewhere Else _____
    ○ Facade _____
    ◈ Different distribution channel?_____
    ◈ Feature differentiation?_____
    ◈ Service and support differentiation? _____
    ○ Sweep the board _____

    ### B. Class
    ☐ High-end _____
    ☐ Mid-range _____
    ☐ Low-end _____

C. Features and benefits _____
- ☐ What's new, different, better, etc.? _____
- ☐ Who will buy this product? _____

D. Price
- ☐ What's the right price for this product? _____

2. **Research target audience**
   - ☐ Strongly recommended, especially for new products _____

3. **Present product position internally**
   - ☐ Is position understood and believed? _____
   - ☐ Does sales force agree with it? _____

4. **Incorporate position into marketing plan** _____

5. **Brand strategy**
   - ☐ Brand from products? _____
   - ☐ Brand building? _____
   - ☐ Brand Components _____
     - ▪ Spokesman/woman _____
     - ▪ Music _____
     - ▪ Cartoon/mythical creature _____
     - ▪ Distinctive color/design/pictures _____
   - ☐ Brand Integration and Persistence? _____
   - ☐ Brand attachment _____
     - ▪ Related product _____
     - ▪ A group of products _____
     - ▪ A division or component of your company _____
     - ▪ Your company _____

PRICING

1. **Determine price model you will use**
   - ☐ SRP _____
   - ☐ ESP _____
   - ☐ MAP _____

2. **Develop a pricing model to establish price points for every price category. Compare your price for each category with your competitions' prices. Avoid pricing too high or leaving money at the table.**

A. List price

- ☐ Unit _____
- ☐ Multiple quantity _____
- ☐ Server _____
- ☐ Upgrade _____
- ☐ Site license _____
- ☐ Volume purchase _____
- ☐ OEM _____
  - ▨ Retail SKU _____
  - ▨ Special build _____
  - ▨ Special packaging _____
  - ▨ Limited function version _____

B. Channel price

- ☐ Distributor _____
- ☐ Reseller _____

C. Promotional price

- ☐ Competitive upgrade _____
- ☐ Corporate evaluation copy _____
- ☐ Industry courtesy _____
- ☐ VAR _____
- ☐ Dealer evaluation copy _____
- ☐ Employee purchase _____
- ☐ Internal use _____
- ☐ Government _____

NAMING

1. **Determine whether or not you need a new or different name**

   A. New product or product line _____

   B. New module/edition _____

   C. Existing name isn't working _____

   - ☐ Name does not support product's position _____
   - ☐ Product has changed significantly _____
   - ☐ Name connotes antiquated or negative images _____
   - ☐ Product breadth changes—becomes a family or series _____

2. **Evaluate whether or not you are in a position to change name**

   A. Do you have enough money to:

   ☐ Conduct adequate research _____

   ☐ Change target audience awareness (advertising, direct mail, etc.) _____

   B. Do you have enough time to:

   ☐ Conduct formal market research _____

   ☐ Conduct formal naming sessions _____

   ☐ Obtain legal approval(s) _____

   ☐ Explain change to sales force _____

   C. Does name have too much "in market" equity?

   ☐ Decide to keep third-party product name _____

3. **NAMING PROCESS**

   A. Decide you need a new name _____

   B. Determine if you will hire outside naming consultant

   ☐ How much will it cost? _____

   ☐ Do you have the time (4-8 week process)? _____

   ☐ Requires contract and nondisclosure agreement in place _____

   C. Determine type of name you want

   ☐ Descriptive (JetPrinter) _____

   ☐ Suggestive (Documagix) _____

   ☐ Arbitrary (Acrobat) _____

   D. Conduct target audience research

   ☐ Formal—through consultant _____

   ☐ Informal—in-house _____

   E. Run naming session

   ☐ Brainstorm _____

   ☐ Vote on names _____

   ☐ Select up to 15 _____

   F. Select final name _____

   G. Conduct legal research _____

   H. Reserve name with U.S. Patent and Trademark Office _____

   I. Reserve name with international agencies _____

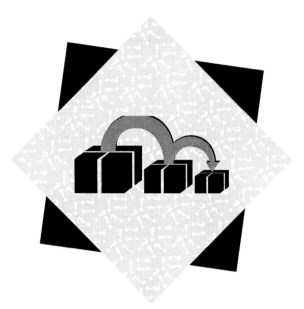

2

Channel Distribution

The U.S. market for software has grown from approximately $100 million in 1981 to an estimated $124 billion by the end of the millennium. Of that figure, approximately 70% flows through the U.S. distribution system for software, often referred to as "the channel." A software vendor desiring to achieve maximum growth must learn to enter, understand, negotiate with, and employ this system to its best advantage.

NEW TRENDS IN DISTRIBUTION

The last several years have seen the development of several new trends in distribution, each of which has the potential to permanently change the marketing environment publishers inhabit, and needs to be carefully tracked and analyzed as events unfold. The most important are:

- **Apple Computer's near-death and rebirth**. Apple's market share and revenue collapse transformed the Macintosh from the leading alternative to the Windows/Intel duopoly into a niche player. Under Steve Jobs' leadership, Apple has made something of a financial recovery, but the platform is no longer a viable mainstream competitor. And while Apple retains its grip on the printing and 2-D graphics market, it has not carved out a dominant position for itself in 3-D graphics and as a web development and server tool.

Apple's travails have also led to a shrinkage in its retail presence, forcing developers of retail-class software to focus more closely on niche, electronic, and direct marketing (DM) strategies to sell their products.

- **The Microsoft intimidation factor**. During Microsoft's long campaign to win market acceptance for Windows, it usually presented an open and smiling face to smaller publishers and even major competitors. After achieving complete operating system dominance however, Microsoft turned far less friendly. Smaller publishers often found themselves crushed as Microsoft used its OS leverage to swell profits while buying or burying competitors.

As a result, a subtle backlash against developing new products for the Window/Intel platform has begun, expressing itself in interest in Java and Linux development, and a reluctance to commit to building new Windows-based products. Not surprisingly, Microsoft has begun to display a bit less of a heavy hand, and has announced it will actively encourage and fund new development for its platform via an ISV startup program administered by its Developer Relations Group. Astute publishers may be able to use this situation to their advantage when developing applications for new markets and audiences.

- **The rise of open-source computing**. Interest in both is driven by the anarchic nature of software developers, distaste for Microsoft, and Microsoft's violation of the fundamental laws of marketing in its positioning of Windows 9X and NT. Prodded by Linux, Sun's Java is now also distributed via a more limited version of the open source model, though it does require developers who use its source code in commercial applications to pay Sun royalties.

The Linux open source model was actually pioneered by Richard Stallman of The Free Software Foundation and GNU (Gnu's Not Unix) fame, and requires that the operating system be distributed with source code at no charge. Furthermore, any modifications to the source must, in turn, be redistributed for free with the source code. This does not prevent a company from packaging up a version of the product and offering it for sale, much as companies package collections of freeware and shareware and sell them. What the user purchases is a CD, convenience, and in some cases, support. Your local CompUSA does a brisk business in sales of boxed versions of Red Hat and Caldera Linux for about $40 to $50 each (about the price of the original PC DOS) as well as in sales of the handful of commercial applications.

Strategically, the distribution of Linux and Java under open-source agreements threatens to drain profitability away from the commercial sale of operating systems. This, of course, represents a direct threat to Microsoft's bottom line and its absolute domination of the software industry via its control of the operating environment. One hopes that Microsoft appreciates this ironic turn of events, since the company has specialized in draining profits away from competitors by converting commercial categories into freeware zones, as recently demonstrated in the struggle for the web browser market between Microsoft's Internet Explorer and Netscape's Navigator.

But despite the utopian claims of open-source and freeware proponents, the laws of economics cannot be repealed. Few people are interested in consigning themselves to poverty so that others can buy cheaper software, and new commercial applications for Linux are appearing with price tags firmly attached. While Linux may remain free, its success depends on a commercial market surrounding it.

What Linux does offer for the software publisher is a level playing field, and a chance to enter new markets free of Microsoft's dominance and predatory behavior. As of this writing, only a few publishers have fully committed to the development of commercial applications for open-source products. But every publisher needs to consider whether or not to make this commitment.

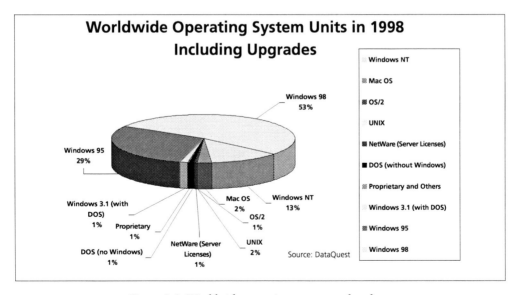

Figure 2-1. Worldwide operating system market shares

THE INTERNET AND THE CHANNEL

Finally, of all the forces bearing down on today's software channel, it is the Internet that has the potential to affect the most profound and lasting changes. Several years ago the author wrote an article about the current state of "bricks-and-mortar" retailing in which he decried the lack of choice in the current system, and asked how someone with special needs could easily and quickly locate and buy the right software solutions?

The Internet's explosive growth has answered that question. It allows limitless segmentation and distribution of any type of software. And nothing is more suited to electronic distribution than software, which is simply an abstraction riding a stream of electrons onto your hard disk. Of course, the current Internet backbone, your phone system, is not very good at delivering a 100-megabyte office suite application to your PC. But the rapid spread of cable modems and DSL technology has the potential to change this.

Also underway is the development of what some call "weblications" or more prosaically, web software hosting. Under this model, a publisher or channel partner runs and maintains applications for web-based servers. The concept is being explored and supported by giants like Microsoft and IBM, and is already in use in the U.S. hospitality and sales force automation (SFA) markets.

The U.S. distribution system is well aware of the Internet's potential power. In a world of true electronic distribution, what need for warehouses, pallets, and expensive channel marketing programs? Talk privately with channel executives about the future of software and distribution, and their uncertainty becomes evident. (They feel a bit better about hardware, since no one has figured out yet how to deliver a PC over the phone.)

Despite this, conventional distribution remains a powerful force in software marketing. If you are selling a retail-class product with broad market appeal, the Internet is just a one stop on the path to general acceptance. Despite the growth of Internet access, people have had a lifetime of reading about products and buying them in stores, and this won't change in the short-term. In the long run however, the Internet will permanently alter software distribution. And it is only right that this is so. After all, it is the software industry that is inventing the Internet. In the meantime, many software publishers must still understand and operate in a conventional distribution environment.

PUSH VS. PULL

When discussing the channel, the terms "push" and "pull" are frequently used.

Push refers to the channel pushing products through the distribution system up to the point of sale. Pull refers to the creation of demand that pulls product out of stores and into buyers' hands.

A successful marketing plan combines these two forces into a coherent whole.

ONE VS. TWO-TIER DISTRIBUTION

Distribution strategies are either one- or two-tier. In a one-tier system, you sell product directly to resellers, bypassing distributors. In a two-tier approach, you sell product to a distributor, who, in turn, sells product to resellers. Most publishers use a combination of the two.

Both approaches have advantages and disadvantages. A one-tier system gives the publisher more control over pricing, product margins, and sales forecasting and is the system most favored by companies selling VAR-class products. The downside is that the publisher must warehouse, ship, track, and manage inventory for all their resellers. And, as a company becomes larger, managing inventory becomes more difficult; the larger and more successful a company becomes, the more difficult these tasks become.

From a practical standpoint, most publishers discover that 100 to 150 resellers is the maximum number they can effectively manage. Beyond this, the drain on internal resources becomes untenable. In such cases, publishers find it necessary to segment their reseller base into different tiers, and "off load" low activity resellers into two-tier distribution.

A two-tier strategy gives a publisher fast access to a large reseller base and eliminates the need for a professional warehousing operation. The major disadvantage is cost: the major distributors make their profits by extracting what are called marketing development funds (MDF) to support a wide variety of marketing and promotional programs. Regardless of whether these programs benefit the publisher, the distributor intends to profit handsomely.

It is important to remember that in the U.S., the channel does not create markets for products. That responsibility is left to the publisher. The natural response from publishers is always "then why should I give away money to a group of middlemen? Why not keep the extra margin for myself, or use it to fund end-user promotions?"

This observation has natural appeal, but ignores logistical realities. Few publishers can match the major distributors' skills in warehousing, stocking, and shipping product. Their access to the reseller base is an invaluable strategic asset to any publisher. Just as important is the fact that many major resellers are not interested in tracking, receiving, and returning goods from dozens of suppliers and insist on purchasing most of their product from distributors.

Distribution also plays a role in establishing your company's credibility. One of the key questions corporate buyers ask when purchasing product is "is this product widely available, widely supported, professionally packaged, and professionally marketed?" A product cannot gain access to distribution unless it meets these criteria. Channel availability is a key factor in many buying decisions.

DISTRIBUTORS

A distributor purchases product from publishers for resale to resellers. The major distributors do not distribute products directly to end users, although they do ship product to "corporate resellers" who then "resell" product to their "customers." Their primary role is to provide:

- Quick access to a large base of qualified resellers.
- Credit terms to resellers.
- Limited technical support.
- Promotional opportunities to resellers.

Distributor Categories

Software distributors can be divided into several broad categories, including:

- International distributors such as Ingram, Tech Data, and Merisel.
- National distributors such as American Software and Hardware, Micro Central, and D&H Distributing.
- Specialty distributors such as Electronic Arts, which distributes products through its affiliate label program.

RESELLERS

Resellers purchase product from publishers and distributors for resale to the public and can be categorized into a number of different categories.

Bookstores

Bookstores usually carry a limited selection of edutainment titles, though some do carry a few entertainment and business products. Some bookstores such as Borders purchase directly from a publisher while others rely on rackjobbers.

Catalogers: PC Connection, MicroWarehouse, PC Zone

Catalog resellers rely on-mail programs and magazine advertising to sell software; they vary considerably in the strategies and tactics they employ, as well as in the markets they address. The number of software titles carried by catalogers can range from the handful carried by Damark to the roughly 4,500 listed in PC Connection.

Many catalog resellers list only a percentage of the titles they sell in their catalogs. PC Connection, for example, includes approximately 60% of the products stocked in their warehouse. Publishers should note that being listed in a catalog does not mean the cataloger is carrying the product in their inventory; in such cases, they order product from the publisher on an "as-sold" basis.

Approximately 70% to 75% of the products inventoried by a catalog reseller are software related, though up to 80% of their revenue is generated from hardware sales, due to hardware's higher price points.

A key component of a cataloger's business model is selling ad space. For the major catalogs, prices range between $17K for a full page and $1.5K for a spot placement (box thumbnail, short product blurb). Discounts are offered for multiple placements, and catalogers are aggressive in pursuing promotional and bundling opportunities.

- Quick access to huge audiences. Even smaller books claim drops of over 500K per catalog, with two to three issues per year. Large companies, such as Mac and PC Warehouse, may drop over one or two million issues per catalog per month.

- Faster initial access to a "known" channel entity. Whereas only 1% to 2% of new products are accepted by the large distributors, catalogers are far more open to new offerings. Typically, 10% to 15% of new products reviewed will be accepted for placement. If you have an SRP, catalog margins will range between 40% to 50% or a 20% to 40% markup under cost plus.

- The opportunity to barter for space. Most catalogers accept product in lieu of cash up front.

Catalogers avoid stocking inventory, especially of new products. Until you've demonstrated that your product has consistent sell through, the cataloger may stock as few as a dozen copies, or attempt to purchase product via a distributor "pass through" arrangement (the distributor tracks sales to the reseller and passes through the results to the publisher).

In evaluating whether to work with a cataloger, consider the negative factors:

- Circulation claims can be highly exaggerated and many catalogers are less than religious about eliminating duplicates from their mailing lists. Since catalogers charge for ads based on their claimed circulation, they have little incentive to worry about multiple drops to an individual or location. As a rule of thumb, discount all circulation claims by at least 30%. In some cases, a 40% to 50% figure may make even more sense.

- For disk-based programs, and some games, 30-day, no-questions-asked guarantees can be a problem. Returns on these products tend to be high, either due to copying, price shopping, or simple buyer's regret. Depending on your product, you may not want to offer such a guarantee,

- Catalogers can unexpectedly change price points. In theory, the publisher and reseller negotiate the product's price before the catalog mails. However, catalogers can and do change their prices unilaterally, which has a heavy impact on sales and promotions. If a cataloger changes prices without your agreement, you can refuse to pay, or negotiate for an additional placement at no cost or a reduced price. Also, be careful of price changes after the first placement in a multiple-appearance deal. Some publishers have had the nasty experience of seeing a successful placement's sales abruptly dry up when the next catalog dropped with a new non-competitive price.

- Many of the general catalogs are ineffective in selling games and low-end lifestyle software. This is a change from a few years ago, when they were fairly effective vehicles for these products. Specialty catalogs focusing on these markets may be a better choice.

- Drop timing is critical for certain products. For products with seasonal appeal, for example, a missed drop date can seriously hurt sales or a promotion. It's not uncommon for catalogs to miss dates by several weeks. If this happens to you, be prepared to negotiate for additional appearances in future issues for free or at a reduced price.

- Restrictions on appearances can add to costs. Some of the major catalogs do not allow publishers to buy a limited or focused number of appearances—October, November, December for entertainment products, for example. You need to decide whether you want to appear in extra, unprofitable drops as the price for appearing in a peak sales period.

Internet-Only Resellers: Egghead.Com, Cyberian Outpost

A new category of reseller, these Internet stores offer E-commerce sites, large selections of software in every category, and competitive pricing. In some cases, the reseller simply ships retail boxes; in others, the buyer can choose to download the product directly. This ability allows new publishers to build a marketplace position and start making sales before making the expensive commitment to build conventional packaging. Many of the points made about catalogers apply to Internet-only resellers when negotiating stocking and advertising.

While these sites are currently market and media darlings, customers sometimes have a different viewpoint after they deal with their tough return policies, which come as something of a shock to consumers used to kid glove treatment from conventional resellers. For instance, Egghead.com requires the customer to obtain an RMA, and charges a 15% restocking fee unless the software is defective. (On the other hand, CompUSA's recent introduction of a 15% restocking fee on returned opened hardware merchandise may make this less of an issue.) The customer is also responsible for packing and shipping returns.

Mass Merchants: Costco, Wal-Mart, Best Buy, FYE

Mass merchants comprise several sub-categories, such as catalog showrooms, consumer electronics stores, retail and wholesale department stores, office superstores, and warehouse clubs. In theory, mass merchants have the potential to reach huge buying audiences.

You should consider the following factors when planning your participation with a mass merchant.

- The importance of packaging and pricing as mass merchants have little interest in features and technical issues.

- Quick inventory turnover. Poorly selling product will be terminated after 90 days.

- The complete lack of support. If a product requires extensive hand holding, the mass merchant will simply ask the buyer to return it for credit rather than provide support.

- The importance and expense of in-store merchandising, including replacing damaged product, setting up in-store demo systems, providing in-store collaterals, and so on. Costs for these merchandising efforts can be considerable; Wal-Mart, for example, has over 2800 locations nationwide.

It is important to note that it is still an open question as to how profitable it is to sell software, particularly high-end retail business applications, through mass merchants. Rack jobbers currently manage software distribution in several major retailers and some discounters. In such an environment, software is truly looked upon as a commodity and high SRPs are a problem due to shrinkage. Support is critical; software returns can range as high as 30% because of support issues and customer fickleness. Rack jobbers like companies that offer 800 number support, but few software companies like the expense of 800 numbers. Finally, mass merchants prefer to deal with major customers directly, and usually demand best price though they can rarely deliver the type of highly qualified audience found in a CompUSA or Fryes.

Rack Jobbers: Good Times, Handleman

Rack jobbers manage shelf space in a store, turn over a percentage of the revenue generated by the section to the store, take a percentage for payment, and give what's left to the publisher. The economic justification for the rack jobber, over and above the simple fact that the publisher has no choice, is that the jobber has "special knowledge" and skills for dealing with the particular store or chain.

To a limited extent, there is some truth in this claim. For instance, mass merchandisers and national wholesalers do have their own peculiarities. Wal-Mart, for example, tried to dictate to the software industry a packaging size that maximized the Wal-Mart shelving system. Led by Microsoft, the industry refused, but Wal-Mart still pressures smaller publishers to build stocking units (SKUs) to their format.

However, the real reason for using rack jobber is that by aggregating clients, the wholesaler can lower administrative overhead and obtain the best price. Rack jobbers justify their existence by promising their clients best price, and the competition to service a Wal-Mart or K-Mart is fierce. For software publishers, the battle is fought over your bottom line.

The Rack Jobber Financial Model

A quick look at the rack jobber financial model is instructive. Once the reseller's discount and the rack jobber's management fee are factored in, the publisher's portion usually averages out to about 15% of SRP, leading to some interesting marketing economics.

Take, for example, a product with a$34.95 SRP, a popular price point for "edutainment" titles (the word is an amalgam of education and entertainment). A 15% share of SRP works out to $5.25 per sale. Now, subtract your COG, between $1.50 and $2.00, on average. You now have about $3.00 per unit. Now, remember to subtract advertising, development, support, and returns processing costs, etc., which comes to another $2.00. You are now making about $1.00 per unit. Your net revenue for the same unit using conventional distribution and its standard discount is between $12 and $14.

The upside of rack jobbing is reach. For example, Wal-Mart has over 2800 stores nationwide visited annually by over 200 million shoppers. A big audience. Assume you sell five products per store per month, a not uncommon run rate for a Wal-Mart. For 14,000 units a month, or 168,00 per year, you realize $168K in revenue. An incremental opportunity certainly, but no financial windfall.

Software-Only Chains: Electronic Boutique

A category once dominated by Egghead, these reseller strongholds are the country's in-door malls. The term ""software-only" is somewhat misleading because most of these resellers also carry a limited selection of small popular peripherals and accessories; however the bulk of their revenue is from software sales. Most software-only resellers highlight entertainment programs, with limited opportunities to sell any other class of software. A typical software-only profile includes:

- A product selection of 500 to 1,200 titles.
- Discounts ranging from 10% to 40%.
- Floor space averaging between 1,000 and 1,500 square feet.
- A professionally merchandised location, with high-quality, point-of-purchase displays.

Specialty Resellers: ComputerWare (Apple specialist)

Specialty resellers focus on developing expertise in an application category or for a particular platform. For example, a reseller specializing in graphics may feature:

- A service bureau offering slide, typesetting, scanning and multimedia fulfillment.

- Rental stations.
- Seminar and training services.
- System integration sales and services.
- A specific hardware platform.

Opportunities for selling software are completely dependent on the business model and markets addressed.

Storefront Resellers: Computerland, PCW

Storefront resellers are the oldest, most established element of the reseller channel. They traditionally sell a mix of hardware and software to walk-in customers from a storefront location. Their focus is on hardware so they limit their software inventory to the market leaders in the major categories. Most will, however, special order any title requested by a customer.

Superstores: CompUSA, Fryes

Superstores are the dominant reseller category in the retail software market. Floor space averages around 25,000 feet per location, with upward of 1,500 Windows, Linux, Mac, and OS/2 software titles carried in stock. In addition, most will special order any product, though this means little in terms of sales and market awareness. In addition to software, superstores stock a wide range of peripherals, networking hardware, fax machines, and other accessories at very competitive prices (end-user discounts average between 30% and 40%), and usually offer house brands in some of the major hardware categories.

Publishers who want their products on superstore shelves need to run a product approval and MDF gauntlet designed to discourage all but the most determined and well-funded. A new publisher must usually establish strong demand via direct marketing, catalog appearances, Internet marketing and good product reviews before a superstore will consider stocking their product.

Value Added Resellers (VARs): DataMedic Corporation (Medical Billing)

VARs sell customized solutions for a variety of systems, and base the resources and services they offer on their market and specialty. VAR solutions usually consist of a range of hardware and software components integrated to solve a business problem or enhance the capabilities of a given system. VARs cover a wide range of application needs, from the more familiar realms of database management and desktop publishing to medical imaging and bank restructuring.

Small players dominate the VAR market. Although 10% of VARs generate revenues of $20 million or more per year, the annual revenue of about 70% of VARs is $5 million or less, with 50% under $2 million.

It is up to the publisher to find the right VAR for their products. VARs consider themselves consultants in many respects and, as such, can be the source of a strong third-party sell for a new product. However, since the publisher's software is often used to create proprietary VAR solutions, your product is not likely to acquire strong brand awareness no matter how much product the VAR sells.

Customer pull for a product exists in the VAR market, but it is less important since the customer typically relies on the VAR's expertise. These resellers will recommend less well-known products if they feel they best fit the customer's needs.

VARs do sell popular retail products if they are easily integrated into their solutions. A VAR specializing in selling and installing medical billing systems may, for example, bundle an office suite with their main product so they can claim to offer a total office-automation solution.

VAR PRODUCT PURCHASING

While VAR discount margins generally match those offered to other resellers, the solution-selling nature of VAR business necessitates different requirements for product purchasing and authorization. Publishers may charge an initial authorization fee that includes the right to sell and market the product in a given area. This fee can range from as little as $200 to over $10K for high-end products, and cover product revisions and technical support. Publishers may waive the initial fee for unique reasons or if the VAR achieves a minimum sales goal. The VAR/Publisher contract is usually for one year and is subject to reauthorization fees varying from zero to 20% or more over the previous year's cost when a new contract is negotiated.

VARs with a direct publisher relationship purchase product as needed and are usually billed net 30 to 45 days. Many contracts include a prepayment bonus ranging between 1.5% and 3%. Different types of contractual arrangements can include:

- Direct delivery and billing of the product to customers by the publisher combined with a pass along on money earned to the VAR. This arrangement is most often used with high-cost items or special-license agreements.
- Monthly or quarterly payments to the publisher by the VAR based on the total number of units sold over a given period. This arrangement is most often used

when proprietary software is sold for modification and a runtime version is not necessary.

White Box Resellers: Computer Renaissance, PC Club

These resellers are a fairly new addition to the channel, and focus primarily on selling generic hardware systems and peripherals to local governments, system integrators, and hobbyists. These resellers also accept trade-ins, and frequently sell used software on consignment. They sell a limited amount of software, with the selection confined to a handful of mainstream business applications and utilities.

KEY CHANNEL RELATIONSHIPS

Once a publisher has made the decision to work with a distributor or reseller, it is important to develop a basic understanding of the company's organizational structure and responsibilities. There is a strong degree of overlap in titles and responsibilities between these two channel components, and we have indicated which positions are found in each.

Inbound Sales Manager (Reseller)

The individual responsible for managing the activities of floor sales representatives.

Outbound Sales Manager (Reseller)

The individual responsible for managing field sales personnel and activities.

Product Manager (Distributor, Reseller)

The individual responsible for managing the reseller's marketing of a product or product market category. A major product is sometimes assigned a separate marketing manager, but the trend is to assign products by category.

Promotions Manager (Distributor, Reseller)

The individual responsible for administering, tracking, and measuring the reseller's different promotions.

Purchaser/Buyer (Distributor, Reseller)

The individual responsible for administering the purchasing of product from publishers and distributors. In consumer electronics, a buyer is very influential in the purchasing decision-process; however, in the retail software market, this influence varies widely from reseller to reseller. Often the buyer's function is mainly administrative, with little influence on buying decisions.

A favorite trick of reseller product managers under pressure from publishers to purchase product is to claim that the "purchasing manager" makes this decision. This is almost never the case, and the claim is usually the opening to a negotiation for the publisher's participation in a promotion or MDF program. Once the publisher has agreed to participate, discussions about the incremental amount of product the reseller will buy usually proceeds with no mention of the purchasing manager.

Sales Personnel (Reseller)

Inside and outside sales people have an average longevity of six to 18 months. A person who exceeds this average is often a premier salesperson, one whose success and knowledge gives them influence with the reseller's sales staff. It is important to identify these sales "stars" and provide them with special attention and support; the rest of the reseller's sales staff will often turn to them for advice on which publisher's products they should sell.

The chance of a publisher's product succeeding with a reseller improves markedly if supported by in-house reseller "evangelists." Identifying these people requires detective work and effort on the publisher's part. Once identified, supporting them with training and support tools should be a high priority of your sales force.

Because of high turnover, you must constantly communicate your sales and marketing message to the reseller's sales staff. Failing to do so will lead to rapidly losing reseller mindshare. And even though turnover is high, many of the sales managers and sales people will move to other companies where they will recommend and sell your products.

Store Manager (Reseller)

The individual responsible for the managing the store. Although it is important to develop good relations with store managers, they are usually unconcerned about an individual product unless it accounts for a disproportionately large percentage of sales. Direct your energies to the store personnel who specialize in selling your product category.

Telemarketing Manager (Distributor, Reseller)

The individual responsible for managing the reseller's or distributor's telemarketing operations and staff.

RESELLER AUTHORIZATION PROGRAMS
Basic Types

There are two types of authorized reseller programs: "substantial" and "instructional." A substantial authorized reseller program is a serious attempt to work with and build business for a select group of resellers, and is often the cornerstone of building a VAR reseller base. These programs also offer the strategic benefit of "locking" in a VAR base since resellers have limited bandwidth and must carefully evaluate how many authorized reseller programs to participate in. An instructional program is primarily an effort by the publisher to build a mailing list of resellers who stock or sell a product and build retail channel recognition.

Both types of programs have their place in channel marketing efforts, depending on the nature of your product and its target market. However, implementing and managing a substantial authorized reseller program takes a significant amount of expense and effort. Consider carefully whether you are willing to make such a commitment. Of course, there is a third alternative—no authorized reseller program at all. Often, however, the benefits of implementing at least an instructional program are well worth the comparatively modest costs and effort.

INSTRUCTIONAL AUTHORIZED RESELLER PROGRAMS

In an instructional program, resellers interested in selling a product apply for authorization. After their acceptance in the program, they usually receive store copies of the product at reduced prices or at no charge, merchandising materials, and are placed on the publisher's mailing list. In some cases, the publisher lists authorized resellers on its web site and allows customers to search for a reseller by regions. The publisher periodically mails materials to the reseller, stays in touch via telemarketing, and possibly refers low-level leads to the reseller base. These programs do not commit the reseller or publisher to anything specific.

From the publishers' standpoint, the value of instructional programs lies in the development of high-quality mailing lists. These are valuable marketing assets, providing publishers with the ability to reach resellers selling or interested in selling a publisher's products—invaluable aid in conducting a wide variety of sales and marketing activities

The instructional approach is appropriate for products that are easy for customers to buy and install, do not require system integration, are widely distributed, "pulled" rather than "pushed" through the channel, and have an initial SRP of less than $1,000.

IMPLEMENTING AN INSTRUCTIONAL AUTHORIZED RESELLER PROGRAM

The process of implementing an instructional program contains the following:

- Distributing authorized reseller application kits containing an information form at trade shows, and in response to all reseller inquiries(via mail or E-mail).
- A compelling reason to fill out and return the form. The best inducement is a great deal on a store copy of your product—but only if they return the form.
- Consistent follow-through with your authorized reseller base. Authorized resellers should be targeted for sales field activities, periodic electronic and conventional mailings, new product information, demos, etc. If your product is retail oriented, you may want to direct customers via collaterals provided to authorized resellers. (This should be implemented only if your company is constantly checking its resellers to make sure they actually stock your product.) Remember that all lists become quickly dated. An effective way of keeping them current is by periodic telephone campaigns to your authorized base.

ELEMENTS OF AN INSTRUCTIONAL AUTHORIZED RESELLER PROGRAM

There are five basic elements to an instructional program:

- **The registration form**. It should be simple, capturing only the most basic information for future marketing purposes.
- **Free or very low-cost store copy purchase program**. If you are going to charge, keep the cost to $15 or $20, covering only your mailing and handling costs. We recommend no charge.
- **A low-cost employee purchase program**. Again, the cost should be low enough to persuade the reseller to take advantage of the offer. Unless a sales representative wants product for their own use, they are not likely to pay $50 for a product so that they can learn to sell it for you. A reasonable price is $15.
- **An authorized reseller's kit**, including product information, article reprints, and distributor availability information.

- **A reseller order form for a no-charge promotional literature pack**, including five to 10 product fact sheets and a demo disk.

SUBSTANTIAL AUTHORIZED RESELLER PROGRAMS

Substantial authorized reseller programs are best put in place for products that require extensive support or installation, have high SRPs (often $1,000+), and are VAR oriented. A substantial program provides an incentive to a reseller to make a strong commitment to recommend and sell your product as part of a solution. This means the publisher must strongly support their authorized resellers, protect their product margins, and restrict product distribution. Key issues to be considered are:

- **Stocking requirements**. A publisher undertakes a substantial authorized program because it believes the reseller will sell significant quantities of product. The program must therefore require that the reseller buy and inventory reasonable quantities of product to demonstrate their commitment.

- **Ongoing training and re-certification of authorized resellers**. If you don't have marketing bandwidth to dedicate to these activities, you should not implement this type of program.

- **Communications and support**. In addition to mailings, telephone contact, and field sales support, a publisher needs to plan for reseller councils, close contact by senior management with select resellers, sell-through programs, special access to technical support, Intranet support, and more.

- **Protected margins**. If a publisher sells product through substantial authorized resellers while also selling it through other channels, it must provide special pricing to its authorized resellers to help them compete with corporate resellers. This is legal, as long as you clearly identify and enforce authorization requirements. This also means selling direct to your authorized resellers.

- **Lead referrals**. Since publishers must refer closeable leads to its authorized resellers, it must have a system for capturing, qualifying, and distributing leads. At the same time, it must provide prospective end users with the names of authorized resellers. And it must never, never undercut the reseller's price in order to take an account direct. Taking accounts direct should be reserved for situations where a customer insists on dealing directly with the publisher, or in cases where a regional reseller must provide support for a customer with national or international requirements. In such cases, the reseller can remain part of the deal as a subcontractor, work under a predetermined formula with other resellers, or receive a substantial "account management fee" to ensure they are repaid for their efforts.

DECIDING TO IMPLEMENT A SUBSTANTIAL AUTHORIZATION RESELLER PROGRAM

Consider carefully why resellers would commit their time, money, and resources to your product, especially if you are a new or emerging company. Market players like Microsoft and Novell can establish exhaustive authorization requirements because they have the financial strength to support their programs, the sophistication to supply resellers with real value-added selling advantages, and have managed their channel so that their authorized resellers have a marketing advantage against the competition.

ELEMENTS OF AN INSTRUCTIONAL AUTHORIZED RESELLER PROGRAM

For participating resellers, the benefits of an authorization program should include:

- **Increased reseller visibility and enhanced marketing image**. A publisher must build a perceived value—support, service, quality—to encourage the reseller to be authorized.

- **Authorized reseller kits that provide comprehensive information about the product, company, services, and programs**. These kits jump start reseller sales efforts by anticipating customer questions and providing answers.

- **Demonstration product at very attractive prices or at no cost**, depending on whether or not the reseller is paying an authorization fee. At most, the cost to resellers for demonstration product should equal the product's BOM plus administrative costs: approximately $25 to $50. Providing low-cost software or free software also helps to ensure that resellers sell the most up-to-date version of the product.

- **Seminars and training**. These are vital elements in any substantial authorization program. They assist resellers in learning the products, as well as how to market and sell them.

- **Assistance with reseller direct marketing programs**. Publishers often provide resellers with materials for their mailings or with a turnkey mailing service.

- **Special technical services**. Some VAR resellers may need a way to integrate their proprietary products with yours. To support this, you must have an established system that includes designated publisher contacts and engineers to provide assistance.

- **Access to communications vehicles**, including newsletters, integration into the publisher's Intranet, and regular mailings and electronic notifications to authorized resellers with relevant information about upcoming events, product updates, success stories, promotions, and services.

- **Cooperative advertising**. Co-op funds are accrued against purchases and reimburse the reseller for a percentage of advertising, direct mail, trade shows, collaterals, training, and demonstration product purchases.

- **Lead referral programs that provide qualified leads to authorized resellers**. A good program builds reseller loyalty and commitment to your products.

- **Regional trade show support** that helps resellers present your product in the best light.

- **Membership in a reseller advisory council**, which enable you to incorporate reseller ideas and suggestions into your marketing programs and build an open dialogue with your channel. Discussions typically cover product development and feature issues, support, services, and all aspects of marketing and selling the product. You will be expected to actively respond to suggestions and follow-up on council commitments.

GAINING ACCESS TO THE CHANNEL

Making the decision to use the channel is only half of the equation. Persuading the channel to carry your product is the other. Every major distributor and reseller is constantly bombarded with submissions from new vendors. Initially, few of these products are selected. If yours is one of the lucky few, you should understand that despite talks of "contracts" and "commitments," you are there on a consignment basis. Do not expect to be paid unless or until all of your product in the distributor's warehouse has been moved out into the reseller channel. Then be prepared to wait to be paid.

Products that make the cut usually fit the following criteria:

- **The new product is published by an established company with products already carried by the distributor or reseller** (i.e., Lotus, Netscape, Microsoft, etc.).

- **The new product fits in a category that the distributor or reseller has identified as an important niche or opportunity**. For instance, after Windows 3.0 first shipped, it was comparatively easy for a Windows-specific product to gain distribution. Internet utilities now enjoy greater channel acceptance than other product categories.

- **The distributor or reseller has a close personal relationship with all or some of the principals in the company.**

If you don't meet these criteria, be prepared to work your way through the distributor or reseller's selection process and demonstrate user demand for your product.

THE DISTRIBUTOR AND RESELLER SELECTION PROCESS

While the actual bureaucratic process differs from company to company, the following steps are common to all distributor and reseller evaluation programs:

- In almost all cases, the publisher should first contact the individual or department at the distributor or reseller responsible for new product evaluation and provide a brief description of the product and company. Then request a vendor profile form.

- Fill out the vendor profile form and return it, along with a copy of the product, to the distributor or reseller. Many companies also include a full or abbreviated copy of their business plan, describing the market opportunity their product addresses.

The distributor or reseller then either rejects or accepts the product for evaluation. Most products are rejected because:

- The distributor or reseller perceives no demand for the product.

- The publisher has failed to clearly explain the product's target audience.

- The publisher only sells one product. A one-product company is perceived as less stable and more likely to fail than one with multiple offerings. Also, the channel likes to be able to swap slower selling titles with more popular ones.

- The product, including packaging and contents, is unprofessionally or unacceptably packaged by channel standards. The standards are different for VAR- and retail-class software. However, VAR-class software is expected to be professional in appearance even if not engineered for retail shelving.

- The company is new or unknown to the distributor or reseller.

- The product is unavailable through distributors. Major resellers prefer to buy new or niche products through distributors.

Don't be unduly discouraged by an initial rejection. Most new products from small companies are rejected an average of three times before finally being accepted for distribution by a major distributor or reseller. The average time between submission and acceptance ranges between 12 and 18 months.

DEMONSTRATING PRODUCT DEMAND

While your product is undergoing channel evaluation, there are several steps you should be taking to demonstrate and build demand for the product, including:

- Persuading independent resellers to carry the product. Approximately 25% of the reseller base consists of independents or regional chains. These companies are more open to carrying new products, often on a consignment basis. If the product sells, such resellers will start calling their distributor and asking for the product to be stocked.

- Persuading direct-response catalogers such as PC Mall, MacWarehouse, Tiger Software, Multiple Zones, etc. to carry the product. These companies are open to new opportunities because their inventory is minimal and they charge a fee for inclusion in their catalogs. There is little or no risk involved for them. Be forewarned—if the product sells, you must be ready to supply inventory quickly. These catalogers do massive mailings and can quickly provide visibility for your product.

- Implementing direct-mail programs. However, these programs are no panacea for small or new publishers offering retail-class products. While they can help a company build market presence, many buyers will not purchase products from new or unknown companies. Even if they prefer to buy by mail, they'll wait to see if the product is available through retail where they can look at the product and know that the company is legitimate and stable.

- Implementing electronic direct marketing (EDM) programs. You can quickly generate initial sales using E-commerce.

- Investigating bundling opportunities: offer your product as a premium with another established product, approach a hardware firm looking to add value to their product, or similar strategies.

- Working with manufacturers' representatives, especially representatives with distributor and reseller experience. A manufacturer's representative is an individual or company whose business is to represent a series of different products. Such representatives function as "salesmen" for hire, and allow you to put a sales force into the market without incurring the expense of building an internal one. Some representatives have excellent contacts with major distributors and resellers, who rely on their judgment and industry expertise when evaluating products.

- Considering international distribution, particularly through Canada, Western Europe, and Mexico. Most of the major distributors and resellers have subsidiaries in these countries. If a product is distributed through them, the parent company will be more inclined to evaluate that product favorably.

- Approaching a smaller or regional distributor. Most publishers automatically approach a major distributor with their product. However, smaller or specialist distributors are often more receptive to new products, especially well-focused, niche opportunities. Acceptance by a smaller distributor helps build interest on the part of larger players.

- Obtaining favorable product reviews. A "*PC Magazine* Editor's Choice" award, for example, can go a long way in persuading a distributor or reseller to give your product a favorable evaluation.

DISTRIBUTOR MARKETING DEVELOPMENT FUNDS PROGRAMS

Distributor marketing development funds (MDF) programs vary from distributor to distributor and only the largest publishers are offered the opportunity to participate in them. Smaller publishers are offered the chance to participate in a subset of the distributor's sales and promotional programs. This is not always the disadvantage it would seem to be. It is important to remember that a distributor's business model calls for their marketing programs to be paid for by the vendors and publishers, and that MDF programs represent a vital part of a distributor's revenue stream.

MDF programs represent a source of tremendous danger for unwary and unprepared publishers. Regardless of the type or scope of the MDF program, a reliable rule of thumb is that it will cost at least 100% more than similar programs developed in-house or by independent marketing contractors. Note, however, that vigorous negotiations can sometimes transform an MDF swine into a gleaming marketing pearl.

The state of MDF is in constant churn, with new programs constantly being introduced, poor performers retired, and old favorites resurrected. Despite all this activity, the basic MDF elements remain constant.

Ad Placements

Distributors can provide publishers premium placement (middle, front, back) in major trade journals and publications. However, the most common placement is a thumbnail picture of the product accompanied by a dozen other thumbnails of other products. The primary purpose of these ads is to demonstrate the distributor's inventory strength, not push a particular publisher's product. Nevertheless, the added exposure can be beneficial to small publishers. Costs range between $4K and $20K.

Basic Participation Fees

These are up-front payments publishers make to distributors in exchange for their agreeing to stock your product. These fees are hallmarks of large distributors, and rarely charged by smaller firms or regionals. Supposedly this money pays to cover the distributor's costs for adding your product to its inventory system. For instance, before distribution giant Ingram will even consider stocking your product in its warehouses, you must pay over $10K in MDF. After that, you have about six months to boost sales volume to $40K per month, or Ingram will drop you from its vendor list unless you agree to pay an extra $3K per quarter.

Buying Incentive Programs

These incentive programs are exemplified by Merisel's "Frequent Buyer" and Ingram's "Go with Ingram" programs. They reward resellers points for volume purchases which can be traded for purchases or prizes, typically trips, merchandise, or cash. They are funded by participating publishers who contribute an additional 1% to 2% in margin to the distributor. Small- to medium-sized publishers should expect to have no control over how these funds are used by the distributor. Larger publishers are sometimes able to direct the disbursement of their contribution. Most publishers are unable to discern any benefit from these programs.

Catalogs

A mailing to resellers listing different products at special promotional prices. Costs range from $1.5K to $8K per placement. Effectiveness varies widely based on your product and the publication's target audience.

Detailing Programs

These programs ensure that your product is correctly priced and positioned in a retail sales environment. Typical costs range between $40 and $60 per store. An independent detailing service can offer similar services for between $25 and $45 per store.

Direct Marketing Programs

Distributors offer a wide range of DM and EDM programs aimed at resellers. Costs are usually double those of similar in-house programs. Judge your participation carefully, based on the target audience and type of mailing.

Drop Shipping

Distributors can provide drop shipping to end users on behalf of resellers. Distributors tend to tread very lightly in this area, as they are sensitive to charges of channel conflict. Drop shipping is of increasing value to hardware vendors, but the Internet makes the issue less important to software publishers.

Public Relations

The distributor sends out press releases about your product or company. Costs range between $1.5K and $5K per year. Not usually an effective use of PR resources.

Publications

Distributors publish a wide variety of magazines, newsletters, videos, etc., and all of them are tied into various MDF and co-op programs. Resellers read these publications to help them determine which products are "hot" and to discern marketing trends. However, they rely on the end-user press for serious qualitative information.

Distributors also offer programs in which ad space is shared with different publishers. Many of these placements involve thumbnail pictures of the product accompanied by a brief description and price. Effectiveness varies widely based on the publication and target audience. Costs range between $1K and $10K.

Product Management Services

An employee of the distributor or reseller ostensibly acts a "product manager" for your product category. In reality, they act as a distributor promotions manager. Costs range between $5K and $10K per year. Paying for these programs is usually a complete waste of money.

Reviews and Evaluations

Distributors do provide product reviews and evaluation advice; however, this is heavily influenced by the promotional dollars you spend with them. Resellers are aware of this, and rely on the end-user press for reviews and product evaluation information. Costs for reviews are usually buried in your advertising fees; a good review costs about $500 to $1.5K.

Reseller Presentations

The best example of this program is Merisel's "Softeach" program, which offers publishers the opportunity to demonstrate their products, position them to resellers, and discuss the best way to sell them. Most publishers regard the program as an effective way to reach resellers, but it is costly. A typical six-city tour cost between $30K and $100K. Depending on the cities visited, a publisher can present products to approximately 1000 to 3500 resellers over a two-month period.

Tech Data's and Ingram's programs are smaller in scope, and usually involve one- or two-night mini shows held in local hotels. Costs range between $1.5 and $7K per event. The publisher provides all personnel, software, and hardware. These programs do offer some potential value to publishers who want to meet local independent resellers and consultants. However, they are not useful in building business with superstore or software chains, since their upper management does not attend these functions.

Special Promotional Pricing

Promotional pricing can mean two- or three-for-one pricing, discounts, bundles, rebates, etc. These programs have the advantage of giving the distributor more incentive to move product, and are fairly effective in building extra push **if** combined with strong pull marketing. If allowed to spawn out of control, special pricing programs damage a publisher's pricing structure as the distributor's warehouse fills up with unsold merchandise (often referred to as "stuffing" the channel).

SPIFs

Special performance incentive funds. A SPIF is a gratuity paid to a sales representative in return for selling a particular item. SPIFs straddle the line between MDF and true promotional programs. (See the *Sales Promotions* chapter for more information.) Large distributors currently discourage direct SPIFs, preferring to encourage their sales forces with contests tied to reaching sales goals. Smaller distributors still prefer SPIFs.

Technical Training

The publisher pays to provide technical training to a distributor. Costs range between $1K and $2K per hour. A complete waste of money.

Telemarketing Programs

The best example is Ingram's **Sales Wizard** telemarketing program, which is a two-week program during which Ingram calls about 2500 resellers touting product promos and introductions. The cost is $10K. This is one of Ingram's most esteemed programs, requiring "committee" approval before you are permitted to participate.

It should be noted that Ingram **must** do this type of calling regularly, whether or not a publisher pays for it. Their relationships with resellers are perhaps their most important asset. Distributor telemarketers call resellers regularly and develop a personal rapport with many of them.

However, don't overestimate the value of this. While the reseller may take the telemarketer's call, their ability to influence sales is limited. The resellers assume their distributor reps are being spiffed, and take all recommendations with a big grain of salt. Furthermore, this type of program is effective only with independents and small chains. Large resellers have centralized ordering systems and often restock inventory via electronic purchasing so their individual stores cannot be influenced by these calls. Also, when the distributor rep calls, your product is not the only one mentioned. A Sales Wizard call can cover up to half-a-dozen special offers and promotions.

By contrast, you can run a similar in-house program that focuses exclusively on your product for about half of what Ingram charges. In all fairness, you can anticipate that a distributor will close more sales than you will due to their reseller relationships. You must decide whether the distributor's credibility and close rate justify the premium they charge for this service. In some cases, the answer is yes.

Trade Show Participation

Distributors can make trade floor space available by assigning vendors a demo station or pedestal in their booth. It is customary for the publisher to run a promotional program in conjunction with their appearance at the show. This can be a valuable opportunity to gain exposure for smaller or new publishers who cannot afford the expense of attending a major show such as COMDEX. Costs range between $2K to $10K for booth space only.

Vendor Nights

This is a key activity for creating push and consists of visiting, alone or with other vendors, the distributor's sales and telemarketing people either during or after business hours to demonstrate and discuss your product. The telemarketing group is at the heart of any distributor organization. These individuals are in constant contact with resellers and can provide significant push into the stores.

The presentation usually consists of a quick product demo, a positioning statement, a quick overview of the product's features and benefits, and usually an incentive or SPIF for the telemarketers. Sell scripts and specification sheets are commonly used to support these efforts. Depending on the terms negotiated or the publisher's influence with the distributor, publisher sales personnel may be on the selling floor during a product rollout to reward the telemarketers immediately after each sale.

These presentations are usually very effective in generating incremental sales; the more time you can spend with the telemarketers, the better. Costs range between $1.5K and $2.5K at larger distributors, and are often free at smaller ones.

Web Site Listings

These are of some value if you don't overpay for the privilege. Costs range between $500 and $10K per month. Good value for your money can be found at the lower end of the spectrum. Anyone who pays $10K to appear on any channel web site is wasting money. Remember that your banner will be rotating through the page with other banners.

RESELLER MARKETING DEVELOPMENT FUNDS PROGRAMS

Like distributors, resellers offer a wide variety of MDF programs. The crucial difference between them is that reseller programs are aimed at buyers, not at another layer of distribution. Like distributor programs, all program costs are paid by the publisher.

Ad Placements

Same as for distributors.

Bundling

Several major resellers sell private label hardware (CompUSA sells the CompUSA PC-line, for example). As part of adding value to their offerings, these resellers may offer bundling opportunities. Most resellers will try to purchase product at prices ranging from 80% to 90% off SRP.

Demonstration Days

Demo days are special events held in reseller locations or sometimes at a local hotel or similar facility. Their objective is to boost floor traffic through a reseller's facility and gain incremental sales for a vendor. Usually, though not always, demo days are held during a major product's update or launch. These programs are very effective in creating sales, but expensive to implement. Average cost is $35 to $50 per store per day. Please note that the store only provides electricity—computers, personnel, collaterals, tables or demonstration facilities, and all other related costs are the publisher's responsibility.

Detailing Programs

Same as for distributors.

Direct Marketing Programs

Costs for these DM programs are similar, but they may offer greater benefit because they target potential customers. Typically, the program integrates the publisher's participation in a catalog with a DM piece to the reseller's customer base. The publisher pays for inclusion in the offer, special positioning (if a catalog mailing), and usually offers the product at a special promotional price, while the pays for production and fulfillment. Carefully evaluate the different programs offered; you may find a bargain.

In-store Audio

In-store audio programs play promotional blurbs over poor-quality systems that few people listen to. Generally a waste of money.

In-store Kiosks

Currently implemented by CompUSA, this program lists your product in an in-store Kiosk along with several hundred other products. The kiosk does **not** periodically cycle your product through its display screens. The cost is $3K, and you must participate if you appear on this reseller's shelves. Several publishers interviewed called this program "the biggest waste of money in the industry."

In-store Merchandising

In-store merchandising programs have grown in importance over the last three years as superstores and mass merchants become important factors in software retailing. The objective is to grab the store's strategic "sight lines" and shopping areas for your product. The ultimate goal is to secure the lion's share of either impulse buyers or those thinking about a particular type of product but undecided about which one to buy. The most popular form of in-store merchandising is the end-cap (described in the *Collaterals* chapter). End-caps are usually effective in increasing sales, and resellers know it. Costs range from $7K to over $60K, depending on the promotional period and duration and the particular reseller.

Product Management Services

Same as for distributors.

Planograms

A planogram is a standardized display of items established on a chain-wide basis. Good examples can be seen in your local Office Max, Staples, or mass merchant. At your local Wal-Mart, the planogram is assembled and maintained by a rack jobber, while office product stores maintain theirs internally. The product mix is constantly reviewed by the reseller for sales performance, and slow sellers are quickly yanked. Criteria for acceptance are profitability, minimal support requirements, and quick turnover. Stores are given updated planograms on a 30-, 45-, or 60-day basis, and store managers usually have little to say about it.

Product placement in the planogram is critical. The most valuable locations are the left top and center of the display. The least desirable are the right side and bottom rows, particularly the right bottom. Products are usually grouped by category, with impulse-buy titles scattered strategically throughout the display. Product mix within most planograms is heavily slanted toward edutainment, SOHO, and commodity titles ($24.95 and under). Within the major business categories, only the top three sellers by category have a chance of being included.

Point-of-Purchase Buyout Programs

Point-of-purchase buyout programs allow publishers to "buy" desirable merchandising locations in one or more of the reseller's stores. Desirable locations include near the register, windows, walls, and ceilings. These programs are usually, but not always, integrated into a more comprehensive in-store merchandising program.

Sales and Product Training

This can be hands-on product training or marketing presentations given by publisher personnel to store sales representatives either at the store or an off-site location, such as a hotel conference room. Most resellers do not charge publishers for the privilege of training their sales representatives. Always participate if possible.

SPIFs

Same as for distributors.

Special Promotional Pricing

Similar to distributor programs.

Reseller Ad Placement

Most opportunities for ad placement are usually found with catalog resellers such as PC Connection, Mac or MicroWarehouse, Multiple Zones, etc.

Reseller Publications Placement

Opportunities in this area are currently limited as reseller publications about product trends and capabilities are not taken seriously by buyers. Most placements are part of direct-marketing programs.

Trade Show Participation

Similar to distributor programs.

Vendor Nights

Similar structure and costs as distributor programs. Of course, the telemarketers and sales representatives will be talking to potential customers, not another distribution tier, making these programs an even more useful investment.

Web Site Listings

Reseller web site listings are of slightly greater value if the reseller has a vigorous E-commerce component to their business. As with distributors, a $10K charge for a listing is ludicrous.

EVALUATING YOUR MDF PARTICIPATION

When evaluating MDF programs, a marketing manager should first ask one simple question: can this program generate incremental sales for my product? The answer, as you might expect, is not easily determined. While you should always ask the distributor or reseller to provide proof of effectiveness, do not expect them to provide that proof. Even if the program is of marginal or no value, your MDF expenditures are happily carried to their bottom line.

Publishers should take the following steps to determine the effectiveness of such programs:

- **Create a matrix of all available MDF programs**.

- **Establish the timeline over which you will track results**. A suggested starting point is three months before the beginning of a promotion. The end date should be two to three months after the promotion ends.

- **Create your marketing baseline**, including all base channel-marketing expenditures.

- **Analyze which MDF programs best address the market segments that best fit your product's positioning**. For example, a catalog reseller's direct marketing program is probably not a good fit for a product with an SRP of $199 or above. Then, analyze costs.

- Finally, **measure return on investment (ROI) against expenditures**. If you don't see significant incremental sales from participating in an MDF program, then it's time to reassess your participation.

There are several techniques available for judging the effectiveness of different programs. But, remember that many distributor and reseller MDF programs (Frequent Buyer, direct marketing, lead generation, etc.) address overlapping audiences. With this in mind, test different programs with different distributors and resellers. This will allow you to develop a profile of a channel partner's strengths and weaknesses.

It is also a good idea to participate in programs incrementally; over the course of a year, participate in different programs at different times. In the case of multiple products, test different programs with different products. Again, the goal is to build a profile of channel capability. You will find that different distributors and resellers have different strengths and weaknesses, even when comparable programs have almost identical functions and costs.

Negotiations

Distributor and reseller representatives will always tell a publisher that the terms of their MDF and co-op programs are set—no negotiations allowed. This is nonsense. Everything is negotiable. Terms, money, prices, returns. Too many marketing managers make the mistake of not tracking what other companies and competitors are up to. If you do, you'll quickly discover that there is very little that is "standard" in the world of MDF. Gathering the right type of intelligence can greatly increase your leverage in MDF negotiations.

THE CHANNEL DANGER ZONE

Special perils await the unwary in the world of distribution and MDF, financial traps that have killed small publishers and even wounded bigger game. To help you survive, we now examine some of the snares and pitfalls thrown in the path of the unprepared publisher. Forewarned is forearmed.

Contract Conundrums

A publisher must always read distributor and reseller contracts very carefully. For example, distributor Micro Central sent out contracts charging publishers a 5% "penalty" if they signed an agreement with another distributor! This 5% "gotcha" was equal to the amount of inventory held by Micro Central, and was assigned to **standard** contracts. Such penalties **might** be part of a distributor exclusive, an agreement where the channel partner provides extensive marketing support and commits to large buy-ins of product in return for sole stocking rights.

Resellers have their own set of contractual tricks. CompUSA is infamous for its "slippage penalties," fees it charges publishers if their product is not available for sale when advertising breaks. These fees can include one-half the advertising costs or a substantial up-front penalty as high as $10K, whichever is **higher**! CompUSA will attempt to collect this fee if even one store has not received inventory "by the Tuesday prior to the ad break date..." Now, if you're a publisher who's just noticed this charming deduction attached to your receivable's inventory statement, just try and prove your product arrived on a timely basis at CompUSA locations. Good luck.

Detailing Woes

A frequent problem is the lack of follow-through on agreed upon in-store detailing despite the fact that the publisher may have paid for service. It is not uncommon for a publisher to walk into a store location and find product stacked up in back rooms instead of being positioned neatly and attractively on shelves. The problem is compounded when the reseller does not allow the publisher to hire its own detailing company to correct the situation.

Grand Opening Day Appearances

These are one of the channel's biggest boondoggles, and almost always a waste of time. Resellers often double standard MDF costs for participation in opening-day appearances, but few publishers have ever been able to associate increased sales with opening-day MDF expenditures.

Double Charge Backs and Switch-Offs

These are perhaps the most insidious practices and can quickly turn black ink very red indeed. A double charge back occurs when a reseller charges a product return back to the publisher's receivables, then turns around and charges their distributor for the same batch of returned goods. The distributor then applies the charge against the unfortunate publisher, who must then figure out why their payables are growing at an alarming rate.

When confronted with the facts, everyone shrugs and blames the problem on "poor record keeping." It now becomes the problem of the publisher, who is bounced back and forth between the reseller and distributor in an attempt to be reimbursed. In many cases, the reseller or distributor will offer the publisher participation in some MDF program in lieu of the cash owed. To protect yourself against these practices, make sure you carefully track returns from all channel partners, prohibit transshipping arrangements (you agree to allow a distributor to take back product from a reseller to whom you ship product directly) in your contract, and manage your receivables carefully.

A switch-off is a variant of the double charge back. In this case, marketing funds you've allocated to a reseller to be spent with one distributor are applied to a different distributor. Often you'll find out about a switch-off only after you've approached the distributor to call in a favor you haven't "earned." The best way to protect yourself from switch-offs is to insist on a contractual agreement that gives you sign-off rights on special expenditures for all channel-to-channel marketing programs.

Slow Payment

The channel is notorious for slow payment. Waiting periods of 45, 60, 90, 120 days and even longer are not uncommon. In effect, publishers often find themselves acting as the channel's "bank," but without benefit of earning interest on your loans. These problems are by no means confined to slow- moving products; indeed, if your product is not moving it will be promptly shipped back to you minus your MDF expenditures. Rather, it is successful publishers with products that have demonstrated demand who suffer from "The Curse of the Ancient Receivables."

The answer to the problem is careful monitoring of your channel receivables and a willingness to get tough. If a channel partner won't pay, cut them off and send them to collections. Of course, use common sense when making this decision. You're going to have to sometimes bend a bit, and a laggard but consistent payer can be managed. But don't be afraid to lower the boom on someone who abuses your cash flow. If your product has proven demand, you can always find another distributor or reseller to carry it. Despite their power, even a major distributor cannot afford to lose the goodwill and business of successful publishers.

FOCUS STORY: THE ART OF THE DEAL

Companies

Egghead, CompUSA, Microsoft, IBM

Product(s)

Windows 3.1, IBM DOS 6.1

Market Overview

In 1991, Microsoft released Windows 3.1 to universal fanfare. The product received kudos from the press and the public rushed to buy. Shortly after the release, it appeared to channel watchers that Egghead Software, then a leading bricks-and-mortar reseller with over 180 stores, had scored a major coup. It was offering Windows 3.1 to buyers for $49.95, at least $10 lower than any competitor. Observers proclaimed that Egghead was going to sell "a million of em."

Well, not quite. Egghead sold a large number of Windows 3.1, but not near the amount projected. Some observers attributed the shortfall to bundling, some to direct sales, some to increased competition from superstores. Whatever the reason, Egghead had pallets full of unsold Windows 3.1.

The normal reaction of a reseller in this position is to ship the product back to the publisher. However, Egghead was unable to do this. The *quid pro quo* of Egghead's deal with Microsoft was "you get the crazy low price, and you have to sell it."

And that's what Egghead did. It took time, and it ruined two financial quarters, but Egghead finally sold it all. It bundled, cut prices, used the product as a loss leader, and finally cleared its inventory.

Contrast Egghead's agreement with the one between CompUSA and IBM, which in 1993 was ready to launch a major campaign for IBM DOS 6.1. CompUSA asked IBM for an exclusive promotional program and IBM agreed. The total budget for the promotion was approximately $250K and stipulated that:

- IBM provide the product to CompUSA for sale one week before its official release.
- IBM provide special promotional pricing.
- IBM provide personnel for in-store product demos.
- IBM provide T-shirts, banners, balloons and other in-store collaterals to support the promotion.
- IBM place radio and print ads for the product.
- IBM provide PCs to the CompUSA stores for the product demos.

Marketing Goals

IBM projected it would sell one-third of the year's forecasted sales for this product in one week. This was an unrealistic goal and CompUSA probably knew it. However, they were quite happy to take IBM's money.

OUTCOME

The release of IBM's product through CompUSA did well, but did not come close to the projected sales goals. After the 30-day promotional period was up, CompUSA shipped the unsold product back to IBM, who paid the shipping costs. Since all existing stock had been shipped to CompUSA, IBM was not able to fill orders coming in from other sources, and sales were lost.

LESSONS

The primary lesson to learn here is that you must negotiate. Every year new publishers repeat IBM's mistakes in almost every aspect. All that changes is the product and the details of the fiasco.

In the case of CompUSA and IBM, the negotiations were completely one-sided. IBM could have and should have attached several conditions to its MDF spending, such as:

- Insisted on a no-returns policy. This might have given CompUSA more incentive to help IBM develop a more realistic sales projection.
- Asked CompUSA for matching funds. Again, this would have given CompUSA some incentive to help plan and successfully execute the promotion.

  Not "front-loaded" the promotion so heavily. IBM could have spaced out their promotional efforts over time, perhaps three months. This would have allowed them to compare MDF expenditures with ROI and judge whether some of their money was better spent elsewhere.

Another important lesson is that the channel's appetite for MDF is insatiable. Do not expect a "channel partner" to tell you that you are spending money foolishly. It is up to you to make this determination, based upon measurements of effectiveness and after tough negotiations.

Co-op Programs

Traditionally, a co-op program is based on the accrual of matching funds, typically between 1% to 2% of the product's channel price, between the publisher and the distributor or reseller. The publisher "banks" these funds for the distributor or reseller, and matches them when the channel partner carries out marketing activities (ads, demo days, special presentations, etc.) that benefit the publisher.

Over the years, this concept of co-op has changed. Most distributors and resellers now expect the publisher to fund all "co-op" programs, transforming them into simply another MDF program.

Co-op programs should be just that, cooperative in nature. If the distributor or reseller is unwilling to provide funds or significant resources that translate directly into publisher savings, the program is not a co-op program. Evaluate it as just another MDF program and subject it to the same scrutiny.

Establishing Effective Co-op Programs

To establish an effective co-op program, several steps should be implemented:

- **Insist all participants tell you in advance of their co-op-based marketing plans** so you can plan and track your co-op expenditures.
- **Develop a tracking and evaluation system that tells you specifically what co-op activities are planned**. For example, ask to see copies of co-op ads being placed that focus on your product. Then, ask for a copy of the actual ad when it runs. Do not make this system overly complex or no one will use it.
- **Track results from co-op programs through resellers' sell-through figures**.

Without these controls, co-op programs quickly degenerate into MDF expenditures.

Deciding How To Spend Money

Once you have gained access to the channel, decide on your participation strategy. As the focus story illustrates, you cannot depend on the channel to help you decide how to spend your money. Some resellers and distributors will, on occasion, steer a publisher clear of programs that are not appropriate for them. If that is the type of relationship you have developed with your channel partners, great. Nevertheless, a publisher must always track and take responsibility for its channel expenditures.

There are two strategies you can consider. One is a "lighthouse" strategy, which focuses on a particular channel partner or partners and seeks to do a first-class job with them in the hopes of attracting other channel participants. The second is a general-channel strategy, which is only feasible if you are a large publisher with deep pockets. However, even with large publishers, a lighthouse strategy can be the best one as the channel has a limitless capacity to soak up marketing funds. Even the largest publishers have difficulty tracking and making sense of the results of the many different programs that can be running at any one time.

ALTERNATE CHANNELS
Shareware

Shareware is software distributed by developers and publishers for free trial use. Buyers can try the product, test it, and decide if it satisfies their needs. If so, they are required to purchase the product. In return, they receive product documentation, their product is registered, and they are eligible for updates and product fixes and enhancements. Shareware is **not public domain** software, which is released for unlimited use without any obligation or expectation of payment.

Shareware products are widely available for the PC, Macintosh, Linux and Unix platforms in every product category, from CAD to word processing. Utilities and telecommunications programs are the most popular shareware programs, followed by Internet tools, editors, and games. Most users obtain shareware by copying the program from a friend, buying a disk or CD from a shareware distributor, or downloading the product from a web or FTP site.

The benefits of the shareware model are:

- Start-up costs are very low.
- A product can obtain widespread distribution quickly.
- The user base that develops around shareware products is very loyal as users can usually reach the developer quickly and discuss problems with "the source."
- Products that succeed in the shareware market can be enhanced and introduced into the traditional retail software market.

Shareware distribution to sales conversion rates range between 1% and 10% depending on the product category, reviews, and price.

Try Before You Buy (TBYB)

Try Before You Buy (TBYB) is a variant of the shareware concept, with the important exception that the product is either crippled or limited in some critical aspect or shuts down after X amount of time or X number of uses. Many retail products are now being offered on a TBYB basis, with distribution to sales conversion rates ranging between 5% and 40%, again depending on the product category, reviews, and price. High-end TBYB programs are most effective when integrated with direct and electronic direct marketing programs and direct selling efforts.

OEM Distribution

OEM distribution occurs when an independent software vendor's (ISV) product is integrated into another software publisher's product, such as Microsoft's use of Inso Corporation's spelling and hyphenation products in MS-Word. An OEM product differs from an add-on or bundled product in that the OEM code is "baked into" the core product and, from the users' viewpoint, has no separate identity. It is not uncommon for an add-on to be so successful that a publisher decides to incorporate it on an OEM basis.

THE OEM CHANNEL ENVIRONMENT

The OEM selling environment is technical and characterized by word-of-mouth advertising among industry insiders. Few formal programs or publications currently exist that cover the specific needs and challenges of OEM selling. Success is predicated on an intimate understanding of the technology, its benefits to customers, and personal relations.

OEM CHANNEL MARKETING PROGRAMS

Few formal mechanisms exist for OEM marketing. Most selling opportunities arise when a publisher becomes dissatisfied with a current supplier, or when competitive pressure makes it necessary to quickly add certain features to a product. Within the industry, a small network of consultants specialize in knowledge of the various available technologies.

OEM RELATIONSHIPS

Key to a successful ISV/OEM relationship is establishing regular communications between the two partners. ISV publishers often make the mistake of failing to notify the OEM of product upgrades and refinements to their product This can lead to the ISV missing opportunities to quickly and easily add enhancements to their product.

Another important factor is product reviews. OEM publishers expect ISVs to defend or at the least assist in the defense of their product's reputation in the reviewing press. If, for example, a major consumer publication reviews E-commerce shopping cart technology, the OEM publisher will expect marketing and technical help in correcting mistakes or bringing some of the product's subtleties to the reviewer's attention.

THE OEM REVIEW PROCESS

When evaluating a product for OEM inclusion, the OEM's marketing group will ask the following questions:

- What does this product do that the core product doesn't?
- If the company already uses such a technology, why should they use this new technology instead?
- Can this technology be adapted to my product to offer a unique competitive advantage?
- What new markets or niches does this product address?
- What proof exists to substantiate the ISV's product claims?

The ISV should be ready to provide competitive matrices, marketing material, and other corroborating evidence to document their marketing and technical claims.

The OEM's development/integration group will have different concerns.

- What is the type and quality of support provided by the ISV? If the development work involves hardware support, a sample unit will need to be provided.
- What is the quality of the documentation provided by the ISV? Are any test suites included with the code? Intranet support?
- How stable and reliable is the code? How much time will they have to spend debugging the product?
- How modular is the product? The more modular and "black box," the better. Such products are easier to port to new platforms or adapt to different languages.

OEM FINANCIAL ISSUES
Royalty Rates

Royalty rates typically range between $.50 and $1.50 per unit with a negotiated cap. This rate **can** reach as high as 30% of the product's wholesale price if it is unique and addresses a narrow niche; however, these cases are comparatively rare. Factors that impact royalty negotiations include:

- The amount of OEM technology already incorporated in the product. While a royalty rate of $1.00 seems inconsequential, several OEM inclusions can raise the bill of materials of a typical high-end software product considerably ($15 to $25 on average).

- The potential sales volume. The higher the volume, the lower the royalty offered.

- Competitive pressures. If the publisher is under intense pressure from the market to add a particular feature, they'll be willing to offer a higher royalty.

- The length of the contract. Typical contracts are for three to five years.

Outright Purchase

In many cases, the OEM publisher will offer to buy the ISV's product outright and incorporate it into their own core technology. This is often the case when the ISV has a low-volume sales rate and a royalty agreement would be of little benefit. Such purchase agreements usually include:

- A maintenance contract to handle minor upgrades and bug fixes.

- An agreement to provide major upgrades on a contractual basis.

AFFILIATE LABEL DISTRIBUTION

Affiliate label distribution (ALD) is a re-marketing agreement between a smaller publisher and a larger one (the affiliate), typically one with high-level visibility and an established distribution channel. Unlike an OEM relationship, the small publisher retains its separate identity, may take a role in developing the product's pull marketing, and finances their push programs through the affiliate publisher. ALD agreements generally run for two to three years and are exclusive, although the exclusivity may be tied to a specific selling territory, such as North America. These relationships are sought by small publishers desiring to build a corporate and product identity but who cannot afford the cost of channel marketing.

Affiliate Label Distribution Costs

Generally, the affiliate publisher receives between 58% and 72% of the SRP. They in turn resell to the channel with a 10 to 12 point markup, or 52% to 55% of SRP. Some affiliates split the receipts 75% (affiliate) and 25% (publisher) and pay the publisher 30 days after shipment. This arrangement allows the affiliate publisher the flexibility to manage a wide variety of channel MDF programs.

Affiliate Label Distribution Concerns

While the goal of ALD is to build and maintain a corporate identity, the power of the affiliate's brand identity may subsume the smaller publisher. To prevent this, the smaller publisher may have to devote more marketing resources than originally budgeted to educate and inform the market of their existence. There can also be differences of opinion between the publishers about the type of marketing messages to be communicated, packaging requirements, copy, and the product's presentation to the channel.

A final point of concern is that creating awareness of the smaller publisher's product within the affiliate's sales force can be difficult. In many cases, the affiliate publisher is selling many different titles from a variety of smaller publishers. The smaller publisher has no control over the affiliate's sales compensation structure, and must communicate sales goals and promotions through the affiliate's management, which makes it difficult to track performance, respond to problems, and encourage the affiliate's sales force to focus on their product.

CHANNEL DISTRIBUTION OBJECTIVES/EVALUATION CHECKLIST

OBJECTIVES   **EVALUATION**

1.   Establish a retail market for the product
%sales from retail   _____ _____ _____

2.   Establish a VAR channel for the product
% sales from retail   _____ _____ _____

3.   Quickly move product to market
Monthly run rates   _____ _____ _____

4.   Build a large reseller base
 # resellers carry product _____ _____ _____
*# SKUs shipped
(for direct resellers)*   _____ _____ _____
*# SKUs in monthly reports
(indirect)*   _____ _____ _____

5.   Build a strategic position in the market
*% increased reseller
recommendation rate*   _____ _____ _____
% increased reseller mindshare _____ _____ _____
% increased buyer mindshare _____ _____ _____
*# orders from channel for
other product(s)*   _____ _____ _____
*# orders from channel for
new product(s)*   _____ _____ _____
*# new channel promotion
proposals*   _____ _____ _____

6.   Quickly establish market visibility
 # calls to company   _____ _____ _____
*# channel press articles,
reviews, etc.*   _____ _____ _____
*# calls from other resellers
and distributors*   _____ _____ _____
*# product reviews, first-looks,
and articles in press*   _____ _____ _____

OBJECTIVES   **EVALUATION**

7. **Penetrate specific market segments**
    % increased market share
    in each segment   _____   _____   _____
    % increased run rates
    v.a.v. competition   _____   _____   _____

8. **Decrease in-house warehousing, shipping, and inventory management activities**
    % sales handled by distributors   _____   _____   _____

CHANNEL DISTRIBUTION SUCCESS CHECKLIST

1. **Select distribution model**_____
   - ☐ One-tier _____
   - ☐ Two-tier _____
   - ☐ Combination _____
   - ☐ Affiliate Label_____
   - ☐ Shareware _____
   - ☐ OEM _____
   - ☐ TBYB _____

2. **Select distributor (s)**
   - ☐ International_____
   - ☐ National _____
   - ☐ Specialty _____
   - ☐ Other _____

3. **Select reseller(s)**
   - ☐ Bookstores _____
   - ☐ Catalogers _____
   - ☐ Internet-only _____
   - ☐ Mass merchants_____
   - ☐ Rack jobbers_____
   - ☐ Software-only chains_____
   - ☐ Specialty _____
   - ☐ Storefront_____
   - ☐ Superstores _____
   - ☐ VARs _____
   - ☐ Whitebox _____

4. **Identify key distributor personnel**
   - ☐ Product marketing manager _____
   - ☐ Promotions manager_____
   - ☐ Purchaser/buyer _____
   - ☐ Telemarketing manager_____

5. Identify key reseller personnel

☐ Inbound sales manager _____

☐ Outbound sales manager _____

☐ Product marketing manager _____

☐ Promotions manager _____

☐ Purchaser/buyer _____

☐ Sales personnel _____

☐ Store manager(s) _____

☐ Telemarketing manager _____

6. Establish authorized reseller programs

INSTRUCTIONAL _____

☐ Authorization form _____

▨ How distribute and obtain _____

▨ Compelling reason to fill out and return _____

▨ Easy to fill out _____

☐ Program elements

▨ Employee product purchase _____

▨ NFS product _____

▨ Promotional literature pack _____

▨ Consistent follow through _____

SUBSTANTIAL

☐ Authorization form _____

▨ Compelling reason to fill out and return _____

▨ Consistent follow through _____

☐ Program elements _____

▨ Cooperative advertising _____

▨ Direct marketing assistance _____

▨ Distribution and marketing _____

▨ Employee product purchase _____

▨ Lead referral programs _____

▨ NFS product _____

▨ Promotional literature pack _____

▨ Regional trade show support _____

▓ Reseller councils _____

▓ Seminars and training_____

▓ Special technical services _____

7. **Complete Distributor/reseller Identify selection process**

☐ Contact new product evaluation _____

☐ Demonstrate demand _____

☐ Direct marketing results _____

☐ E-commerce sales _____

☐ Product reviews _____

☐ Fill out and return form _____

☐ Send copy of business plan _____

☐ Send sample of product _____

8. **Identify which MDF programs you will participate in**

    A. Distributor

☐ Ad placement _____

☐ Basic participation fees _____

☐ Bundling _____

☐ Buying incentive program_____

☐ Catalog _____

☐ Contract field services_____

☐ Co-op _____

☐ Detailing _____

☐ Direct marketing _____

☐ Drop shipping _____

☐ Product management _____

☐ Public relations_____

☐ Publication placement_____

☐ Reseller presentations _____

☐ Reviews and evaluations_____

☐ Special promotional pricing _____

☐ SPIFs _____

☐ Technical training _____

☐ Telemarketer presentation _____

☐ Trade show participation _____

☐ Vendor nights _____

☐ Web site _____

☐ Other _____

B. Reseller

☐ Ad placement _____

☐ Basic participation fees _____

☐ Bundling _____

☐ Buying incentive program_____

☐ Catalog _____

☐ Contract field services_____

☐ Co-op _____

☐ Direct marketing _____

☐ Drop shipping _____

☐ In-store merchandising _____

    ▨ Audio announcements_____

    ▨ Banners _____

    ▨ Brochures _____

    ▨ Demonstration days _____

    ▨ Detailing _____

    ▨ End caps _____

    ▨ Kiosks _____

    ▨ Point of purchase (window front, cashier counter)_____

    ▨ Posters_____

    ▨ Shelf talkers _____

☐ Special promotional pricing _____

☐ Product management _____

☐ Public relations_____

☐ Publication placement_____

☐ Reseller presentations _____

☐ Reviews and evaluations_____

☐ Special promotional pricing _____

☐ SPIFs_____

☐ Technical training _____

☐ Telemarketer presentation _____

☐ Trade show participation _____

☐ Vendor nights _____

☐ Web site _____

☐ Other _____

9. **Coordinate channel activities**

☐ Account sales representatives _____

☐ Channel sales representatives _____

☐ Inbound manager _____

☐ Outbound manager _____

☐ Product Marketing _____

☐ Promotions manager_____

☐ Purchaser _____

☐ Store manager _____

☐ Telemarketer manager _____

10. **Develop launch plan**

A. Focused _____

☐ Which distributors? _____

☐ Which resellers?_____

B. General _____

11. **Implement launch plan**_____

12. **Track and evaluate results**_____

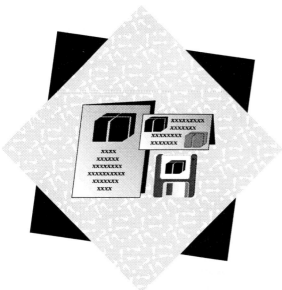

3

Collaterals

The variety of marketing tools that support your marketing and sales efforts are collectively referred to as collaterals. Effective, well-designed collaterals can:

- Generate sales leads.
- Support direct sales efforts.
- Support direct marketing efforts.
- Support sales promotions.
- Create and maintain a product image.
- Create and maintain a company image.

Collaterals comprise a wide range of materials but are divided into three basic categories:

- Those intended for end-users.
- Those aimed at the distribution system or "channel."
- Those designed to support either an end-user or channel promotion.

THE CORPORATE IDENTITY PROGRAM

A corporate identity program drives the creation and development of your collaterals. If you are a start-up publisher, the program establishes a baseline "look and feel" for all your company's materials. If you are an established publisher, the program must also incorporate the positioning factors discussed in the *Positioning* chapter of the *Handbook*. When completed, your corporate identity program should provide the following deliverables:

- A company logo.
- A company tag line, if you have decided to create one.
- A series of graphics templates and guidelines designing your collaterals.

Optional deliverables can include:

- Custom art or images designed exclusively for your company.
- A corporate piece.
- A high-level piece for a flagship product.

After you finalize your corporate identity, you can incorporate its basic elements into your end-user, channel, and merchandising collaterals.

END-USER COLLATERALS

Designed for distribution to potential purchasers and users of your product(s), end-user collaterals are more widely disseminated and more expensive to produce than "channel" collaterals. Print or production runs of 10,000 pieces or more are not uncommon, depending on the product and scope of your marketing efforts. Below we list the most common end-user collaterals.

Brochures

A brochures is typically a four-color piece that highlights your products, though it is sometimes also used as a company piece. It discusses key product benefits and solutions and should be professionally designed and well written.

Case Studies

Case studies, or success stories, describe how a customer uses your product to successfully overcome an operating roadblock or to solve a particular business problem. They are almost always commissioned by the publisher and developed by its Marcom group. Case studies are highly factual, and should not contain overt marketing hyperbole. They usually focus on the actions of an individual or group within a particular industry and the issues and solutions specific to that industry.

The goal of a case study is to build credibility within an industry by providing proof, with references, that your software is appropriate to its needs. The design of these pieces should be simple but professional, and they can be printed in two or four colors. Well-written case studies can do double duty as both conventional handouts and as articles for placement in specific magazines and periodicals.

Elements of a Successful Case Study

Case studies should be researched and developed with great care. After all, in most cases these are **your** customer(s) you are writing about, and you want them to be happy with the story you tell. To help ensure this, pay attention to the following:

- **Use a professional writer to write the story**. If you don't have a writer on staff, use a contractor. Bad grammar, awkward phrasing, and ill-considered word choices will make you and your customer look foolish.

- **Send final copy to the person or people being profiled and obtain written approval for the story**. In the case of larger companies, be prepared to obtain approval from their legal department as well.

- **Plan well ahead**. If you're profiling a larger company, expect the case study to take between 60 and 180 days to be written, checked, and approved before it can be put into production. Keep in mind that answering your questions will not be your customer's highest priority. Be patient, diplomatically persistent, and prepared to go away if asked.

- **Do NOT change approved quotes unless you obtain specific permission to do so**. If you decide that existing quotes need to be changed, resubmit the case for approval. This second approval cycle may take longer, as people often have better things to do than tell the same tale twice.

- **Use industry-specific terms and phrases**. This will help make the piece more "immediate," believable, and compelling to the target audience.

- **Offer the company some inducement or "thank you" for their cooperation**: a reduced price on an upgrade, extra support, or perhaps special pricing on an ancillary product or product module. This will help keep the door open for future studies and references. And it's always a good idea to frame the study and personally present it to the person(s) you profiled. You can be sure that the next time you visit that customer, the piece will be hanging on the wall of their lobby, office, or cubicle.

Common Vertical Markets for Case Studies

- Agriculture
- Construction
- Defense
- Education
- Employee leasing
- Finance (banking, brokerages)
- Government
- Healthcare (hospitals, nursing homes, hospices, assisted living)
- High-tech (hardware, software)
- Hospitality (hotels, restaurants, amusement and theme parks)
- Insurance
- Legal
- Manufacturing
- Mining
- Retail
- Transportation (air, rail, trucking)
- Unions

Comparison Sheets

Comparison sheets are the most notorious of all collateral pieces. They typically contain a matrix comparing competitive products on features, price, and support. Surprisingly enough, the company sponsoring the comparison always wins. While many end-users profess to put little faith in such comparisons, comparison sheets are generally regarded as highly effective collaterals. However, companies must be careful. If your statements about competing products vary too widely from the truth, you may receive a call from the other firm's attorney wishing to discuss the matter. Also, note that comparison sheets are illegal in some countries (e.g., Germany).

Corporate Piece

A corporate piece is usually an elaborate, four-color, multi-page brochure that provides a high-level overview of a company and its products. The design is elaborate, featuring glossy paper, high-quality graphics and art, and elegant text. Larger companies eschew a small form factor in favor of an 8.5" x 11" layout.

Corporate Backgrounder

This is a simple collateral designed for/by a publisher's PR department briefly describing the company's mission, products, key officers, and key corporate contacts. It can be produced internally, usually on corporate letterhead. Backgrounders are often the core component of a press kit.

Demo Disk

A demo disk is a collateral fairly unique to the computer hardware and software markets, though other industries have begun using them as well. They contain a self-running or interactive series of animated screens and displays highlighting a product's capabilities. While expensive to create and produce, demo disks can be one of the most effective tools to persuade someone to buy a product. Demo disks can be made available through a variety of electronic media, including floppy disks, CD-ROMs, and the Internet.

Demo disks function both as end-user and channel collaterals. At the reseller level, they are a staple and a successful publisher of any size is expected both to produce them and update them on a regular basis. Resellers often use a demo disk as a stand-in "sales rep" because a good demo allows a potential buyer to inspect the product while the sales representative handles other floor traffic.

As end-user collateral, demo disks are used in a variety of ways. They are popular as giveaways at trade shows and are often used as "bounce-back" pieces in advertising and direct-mail campaigns. They have been bound into magazines and can be posted on web sites and FTP sites for downloading and viewing.

ELEMENTS OF A SUCCESSFUL DEMO DISK

A successful demo disk incorporates the following elements:

- A clear presentation using color and sound.
- A fairly brief and straightforward presentation. About five minutes is the maximum anyone will watch a demo disk.
- Viewing options that allow the potential customer to terminate the demo or select specific segments of particular interest.
- Encourages the potential customer to buy the product **now**. Options include printing out an order form or offering to fax an order to an 800 number, or a direct link to a web site where the product can be purchased.

To encourage reseller and channel use, demos are often integrated into promotions. For instance, to receive a free T-shirt, a sales rep may be required to sit through the demo and fill out a simple questionnaire when the demo ends. One publisher built a disk that "knew" when a complete demo had been given and automatically entered the viewer into a contest for a free computer.

In today's demanding multimedia environment, many demo disks are now distributed on CDs. This is entirely appropriate. However, smaller companies can consider using floppy disks. Data compression and installation to hard disk allow succinct and effective demos, and floppy disks are still more universally supported and available than any other storage device.

DEMO DISK COSTS

Production costs for a good demo disk range from $7.5K to $60K. Therefore, you would be wise to consider additional ways to use the demo, such as part of a buyer promotion (i.e., call and get a free demo disk) or as an advertising bounce-back piece.

Demo Templates

Demo templates are pre-configured data for use with application demos or presentations. In many cases, the templates are industry-specific and designed to support sales efforts by a VAR channel or direct sales force into a specific vertical market. More sophisticated templates sometimes incorporate screen- and keystroke-capture programs, such as Lotus ScreenCam, to automate all or portions of the presentation.

Electronic Presentations

Inexpensive laptops and color projectors have made transparency and slide presentations almost extinct. Today, an electronic presentation is an electronic slide show created with either Lotus' Freelance, Microsoft's PowerPoint, Astound, or a similar package. You should avoid using manual presentation material unless absolutely necessary as customers will expect your presentation technology to reflect the times.

Electronic presentations are one of the most "fluid" types of collateral, since they can be easily altered as needed. To ensure consistency of appearance and message, have your in-house staff or a professional graphics service develop a set of templates and distribute them to all your marketing and sales personnel.

Folders

Folders are usually high-quality stock pieces (80lbs and over) designed to hold other collaterals and a business card. They are often used for press kits and direct-selling or solution-selling environments.

Newsletters

Newsletters are one of the most widely discussed and rarely implemented of all collaterals. They always **sound** like a great idea, but the reality is another matter as they are labor intensive, require professional writing, and to be effective must be published and distributed on a regular basis. Smaller publishers often find the work associated with creating and maintaining a newsletter too great a drain on their scarce marketing resources.

On a more optimistic note, the growth of the web has made publishing electronic newsletters easier, though nothing about the web has changed the need for the newsletter to be cleanly and professionally written. However, like conventional newsletters, electronic newsletters must be published on a regular basis to be effective, and the marketing overhead associated with them remains high.

Not for Sale (NFS) Software

NFS software is usually fully functional product given away to induce the buyer to purchase the product; as such, it is the most expensive collateral of all to produce. This is in large part because of the normal COG of the package—between $20 and $30 dollars for a major business application—and because it can be difficult to persuade someone to buy something when they have received it for free.

Publishers use a variety of tactics to deal with the cost issue. In some cases, NFS software for resellers contains only a limited version of the documentation, which is the most expensive component in the package. In other cases, publishers distribute NFS product with a number of limitations including:

- Scaled back documentation.
- Pre-registered product.
- Requiring product registration before the product can be used.
- Requiring the product be delivered in person by a sales representative.
- Marking the product prominently "Not for Sale" to discourage resellers from selling it.

- Refusing to allow NFS product to be registered.

In all cases, the goal is to discourage losing actual sales to NFS software.

Presentation Binders

Outbound sales teams or marketers use this collateral to hold slides, overheads, pitch books, and so on. The presentation book can be thought of as the print equivalent of a collateral CD.

Reprints

Reprints are reproductions of product reviews and stories by the press. They are very effective collaterals as the reader is inclined to believe the material, particularly if the reprint is from a respected publication like *PC Magazine* or *InfoWorld*. Reprints cost money, but if the review or story is highly favorable, it is well worth the expense to obtain copies to distribute to customers and key accounts.

Specification Sheets

Specification sheets are usually inexpensive 8-1/2" x 11" two-color handouts, designed for sales personnel and prospects that need a quick product overview. The copy should be crisp and succinct.

System Overview

This type of collateral is usually used late in a solution-selling cycle. The system overview functions like a mini-product manual, detailing key product capabilities and functions.

Try Before You Buy Software (TBYB)

An increasingly popular alternative to NFS software and demo disks is try before you buy (TBYB) software. Often downloaded from web or FTP sites, it is a full version of the product that can be used either for a set period of time or a set number of uses. The potential buyer can try the program and even enter data (hopefully offering an incentive to purchase the product). If users like the product they can call a fulfillment number (almost always a toll-free call) or access a web site to purchase the product and obtain an unlocking code.

There are several advantages to account for the increasing interest in TBYB software, including:

- It offers even a small publisher an immediate means of widespread distribution.

- It provides a distribution channel for niche and non-retail oriented software.

- It provides 100% buyer registration.

- It has a lower COG since it doesn't require packaging or printed documentation.

Videos

Videos (perhaps one day to be called DVDs) are used in both VAR and retail markets. They are relatively expensive and time consuming to produce, and a smaller publisher should carefully consider whether they are worth the time and expense. In a VAR market, videos are most commonly used as an alternative to a conventional case study. When used in this venue, remember the following:

- **Use professional talent to create your videos**. "Homegrown" efforts can be spotted immediately, and can leave a bad impression.

- **Focus on customers who use your product to solve real problems**. Let them tell their stories, and avoid distracting voice-overs and special effects.

- **Restrict video to 15 minutes**. This is the maximum time anyone will watch a video, even when the audience directly identifies with the people and problems presented.

- **Avoid a hard sell**. If the video begins to sound and look like an infomercial, you may alienate your audience.

- **Plan on running the video in person**. Most videos left for later viewing are tucked away and never loaded into a VCR.

As a retail tool, videos are most useful in establishing an ongoing point-of-sale (POS) presence in a reseller's location. In most cases, setup and use of the video will be part of an MDF program. When planning the video's production, remember that:

- **Professional talent is even more critical in POS presentations**. Mix compelling graphics with visuals of customers using the product in real surroundings and situations.

- **Use close-ups of the package on the shelf** to help visually cue the potential buyer to find and pick up the product.

- **Use a minimum of screen shots**; they are dull and can make your video look like an expensive keystroke demo. It is a good idea, however, to quickly demo how easy the product is to install and use out of the box.

- **Avoid the use of talking heads; voiceovers are more effective in a POS environment**.
- **Use music as a background element**. An overly catchy or obtrusive melody may focus the buyer's attention on the tune, not the product.
- **Retail videos should not exceed 4-1/2 to 5 minutes**. POS tapes should repeat continuously, with a two-second blank space between loops.

Web Sites

A web site, in addition to functioning as a distribution mechanism, is also collateral and, as such, its design should consider the following:

- **Do not scatter collateral items throughout the site**. People are used to picking literature from convenient racks. Your site should function as an analog equivalent.
- **Design your conventional collateral for web posting**. And remember that most printers are filled with 8.5" x 11" paper.
- **White papers, datasheets, specification sheets, case studies and reviews are the best collaterals for web posting**.

The Impact of the Web on Collaterals

In spite of predictions to the contrary, the Web has not sparked new types of collaterals, except for the ubiquitous banner, which we discuss in detail in the *Advertising* and *Electronic Marketing* chapters of the **Handbook**. With the exception of newsletters, whose format fits the web milieu quite well, few people actually read on the Web, choosing instead to print out material for later comparison shopping.

The Web **has** had a major impact however on your ability to provide almost immediate access to your marketing materials. Your web site functions very well as an information kiosk, providing quick and easy distribution of specification sheets, white papers, reviews, etc. Previously, publishers relied on direct sales forces, direct marketing, and the Channel system to distribute collaterals to potential customers. These conventional efforts are very expensive and distributors and resellers have little interest in stocking and providing collaterals unless paid handsomely for the privilege via an MDF program.

Publishers have also begun to experiment with providing product documentation on their web sites. While some publishers worry that this will make it easier for the competition to steal their ideas, other publishers point out that competitors can easily gain access to your documentation if they want to, so it's not worth worrying about. What is worth considering are the benefits you can achieve:

- You can update and disseminate new documentation to your users almost immediately.
- You can lower your printing and fulfillment costs by publishing updates on the web.
- You can lower (though not eliminate) competitive snooping by placing or using a password-protected area on your web site or requiring a log-in to view product documentation.
- You can learn more about your customers and their needs by requiring them to identify themselves when accessing the documentation,

It is important to note that nothing about publishing your documentation on a web site relieves you of the need to create properly edited, well-structured, easy-to-read manuals with useful tables of contents and indices. Also, you should anticipate paying a premium in time and money for creating manuals that are formatted for both printing and web publishing.

White Papers

White papers are a special type of collateral aimed at reviewers, power users, influencers, key corporate purchasers, and developers. They are usually between five and 25 pages long, and discuss key product technology, market trends, and high-level development and use issues. The tone is serious, often technically oriented, and designed to "talk up" to the audience. Designs are usually very simple and heavy on text, and the piece may be printed in one, two, or four colors. White papers are most often used in a solution-selling environment, though they occasionally support retail-class products.

Well-designed and content-rich white papers are perceived to have greater intrinsic value than other types of collaterals. If not overly biased toward your company or product, a white paper can often be circulated within a company or group for educational purposes or as part of an internal evaluation process. For this reason, white papers have found increasing utility as direct-marketing response or "bounce-back" pieces, both via conventional mail and web sites.

CHANNEL COLLATERAL

A common mistake made by many software newcomers is confusing channel and end-user collaterals. They are different, and should be created to achieve different goals. Channel collaterals should:

- **Be inexpensive to produce**. In many cases, four-color art and fancy graphics are wasted on distributors and resellers. Pieces should at most be two- or three-spot color.
- **Highlight the key benefits to the channel of selling a product**.
  - *Ease of selling*. This product won't sit on store shelves.
  - *Profitability*. You make money selling this product.
  - *Tie-in to other sales*. Selling this product makes it easier to sell another product, or adds margin to an existing sale (e.g., selling a clip art collection along with a draw package).
  - *Quality technical support*. The channel won't have to support this product.
  - *Customer pull*. Selling this product will increase store, catalog, or telesales activity.
- **Highlight the top three reasons to sell the product**. Most sales representatives will not learn more than three facts about any product.
- **Not be overproduced**. Channel collaterals are read by the channel, not end-users, and quantities should reflect this.
- **Be customizable**. Many VARs and solution-oriented resellers prefer to have their address and local contact information, not yours, printed on your collaterals. Your datasheets, specification sheets, and similar collaterals should provide space for the reseller to easily add this information.

An important point to remember is that pouring large amounts of end-user collaterals directly into the channel is generally a waste of money. Few retail-oriented resellers bother to keep catalog and brochure racks stocked with material unless the publisher provides them an incentive to do so through an MDF program. Much of the end-user collaterals given to these resellers ends up collecting dust in their storerooms. The only way to ensure that end-user collaterals in retail stores are reaching potential buyers is to use a field sales force or detailing firm to monitor and manage these collaterals. And this can be an expensive proposition.

Channel collaterals are less varied than end-user collaterals and print runs range from 500 to 2.5K pieces. The most popular channel collaterals are:

Collateral CDs

A collateral CD is a relatively new development in software marketing; it can be conceptualized as a "collateral" store on a CD. Designed primarily for use by a direct sales force or a reseller channel, the CD contains most of a company's secondary collaterals, including demos, specification sheets, white papers, etc. High-level collateral such as the corporate piece may be excluded to preserve quality and presentation values. This approach allows the sales representative or reseller the ability to provide a customer with needed collaterals even when stocks of company-provided materials are low or not available. The files are usually formatted in HTML or Adobe PDF for quality printing by a print shop or high-resolution color printer.

Comparison Sheets

Channel comparison sheets include merchandising comparisons and information as well as feature breakdowns. They are printed in black-and-white or two-color.

Corporate Identity Manual

A corporate identity manual describes where and how a company's corporate and product logos can be used as part of a reseller's marketing programs. It will also describe clearly what is not permitted, and provide samples and templates for the reseller.

Logos

As part of a personalization program, some publishers make their corporate and product logos available for use by resellers. A corporate identity program governs how these can be used.

Sell Scripts

Sell scripts are often provided to a reseller or distributor's telemarketing sales force to help them quickly sell a product. If intended for a distributor group, the sell script should focus on:

- Ease-of-sales.

- Margin.

- The product's dollar volume.

- Ease of support.

- The product's leadership position in the market (resellers like to sell winning products).

If intended for end-users, the script should focus on:

- The positioning and target audience for the product.

- Three key features and benefits of the product. Do not overload the script with technical details. Telemarketers do not spend much time on any one call and are not expected to be technical mavens.

- The price of the product, and any incentive to purchase. If there is such an incentive or special offer, the offer's end date should be clearly called out.

Specification Sheets

Channel specification sheets are simpler than end-user specification sheets and are usually black and white. They are often handed out to a reseller's telemarketing and direct sales group, and highlight price, support, and ease-of-sale issues.

Ordering Channel Collateral

Many publishers print channel and end-user collaterals without giving any thought to how their distribution system will order them. Order forms can easily be created in-house, and printed or posted to a web site. You want to make it easy for the reseller channel to order and restock your collaterals.

MERCHANDISING COLLATERAL

Merchandising collateral is a special class of channel collateral designed for placement in retail locations and to support VAR-oriented promotional programs. It is expensive to produce and should be built on an "as-needed" basis with a close eye kept on quantities and costs. However, do not expect to build this type of collateral, walk into a reseller's location, and freely merchandise their store. Some independents and resellers may allow a publisher's sales representative with whom they have a personal relationship to do this, but it isn't something you can count on.

In addition to banners, posters and signs, the most common types of merchandising collateral are:

- **End-cap Displays**. End-caps are a type of shelf talker placed at the end of a shopping aisle, designed to attract buyers down an aisle to your product.
- **Floor Stacks**. A floor stack is a collection of product boxes stacked in a strategic location on a selling floor. For maximum impact, the product's package should be designed with this use in mind.
- **Kiosks**. Kiosks are self-standing displays usually containing product and collateral, which function as extra shelf space dedicated to your product.
- **Mobiles**. Mobiles are hanging displays consisting of various graphic elements. They are often placed near cash registers and other strategic locations in the store.
- **Monitor Wraps**. This type of collateral fits around the outside of a monitor.
- **Sell Sheets**. A sell sheet, also called a datasheet, describes a product's key features and benefits and is a two- or four-color 8.5" x 11" handout.
- **Shelf Talkers**. A shelf talker is a card or flap attached to a retailer's shelf to draw attention to a product as the customer walks down the aisle.
- **Tent Cards**. A tent card, usually a piece of cardboard stock assembled into a tent, box, or pyramid shape, is an inexpensive collateral best suited to small display areas where store personnel closely control the selling-floor environment.

PROMOTIONAL COLLATERALS

Promotional collaterals are handouts and giveaways that support direct, channel, and direct-market promotions, and run the gamut from Beanie Babies to T-shirts. A list of the more popular types includes:

- Coffee mugs.
- Carryalls.
- Diskette holders.
- Hats.
- Mouse pads.
- Mouse holders.
- Pens.

- Shopping bags.
- T-shirts.
- 3M Post-it note dispenser.
- Watches.

How to use promotional collaterals effectively is discussed in detail in the *Promotions* chapter of the *Handbook*.

Producing Collaterals

Contrary to popular opinion, there is nothing glamorous or exciting about producing the different brochures, specification sheets, white papers, shelf talkers and other collaterals required to support your software product(s). Coordinating text creation and approval, checking designs, copy editing text, doing press checks, etc., are tedious and time consuming. To create successful collaterals, a company must implement a formal process of creation and review controlled by the marketing group. Once established, it is the responsibility of the marketing group to request inputs and suggestions from the company's other functional groups. For instance, when the sales force requests a case study to assist their sales efforts in a specific market segment, they must be prepared to provide the marketing group with the following essential information:

- **Key marketing vocabulary and concepts in the industry or market segment.**
- **Qualified contacts and experts willing to be quoted.**
- **Important issues and challenges unique to the industry or market segment.**

Armed with this information, the marketing group can incorporate these points into your collaterals and manage their production.

A corporate piece or brochure for a flagship product should be reviewed by the heads of the functional groups before production. This is usually not necessary for less critical collaterals. In all cases, it is a mistake to involve any other functional group in the production details.

Design and Production Tips

While it is beyond the scope of the *Handbook* to instruct you on graphics design, we can provide some practical tips and advice, including:

- **Be aware that design choices have a serious impact on price and production**. For instance, a "full bleed" design (printing right up to the edge of the paper) requires using oversized paper stock and larger printing plates. Set-up costs will also be higher. Complex designs requiring different elements to overlap can cause registration problems (control of printing one element over another). Consider using white space to separate text and graphics. As a rule, the more intricate and complex the design, the more costly it will be to produce.

- **Involve your printer in the design process when possible**. Many graphics designers and illustrators have little experience with the actual printing process. A good printer can work with your graphics group to minimize unnecessary additional costs. (However, be aware of hidden charges from your printer. They may charge for production consulting.)

- **Don't forget black-and-white**. A well-designed-and-white piece, especially one that uses spot varnish for dramatic effect (the varnish is regarded as a second color), can be very effective.

- **Instead of commissioning custom photos, use stock photos from a stock photography house, or from a local commercial photographer**. Also, consider purchasing royalty-free clip art and image collections; they are a worthwhile investment.

- **Don't overpay for paper**. Contrary to what many expect, 80 to 100lb domestic coated paper, the type used for most higher-quality collaterals, is the **least expensive** stock you can buy (due to the high volumes produced of this paper). Matte-type paper (no gloss) usually costs more.

- **Know which printer to use for which job**. There are three types of printers: quick, sheet set, and web-press.
  - *Quick printers rely primarily on copy machines and inexpensive offset presses that print on standard pre-cut stock.* Use a quick printer for very small runs and on an "as-needed" basis.
  - *Sheet set printers employ four- and six-color presses that are capable of printing on large sheets of paper, which are cut to size after printing.* A sheet set printer is often the most cost-effective for print runs up to 100K.

- *Web-press printers use large, high-capacity presses that can print on even larger sheets of paper and are the most cost effective for print runs of 500K and up. They have high set-up and operational costs.*

- **You have three options when purchasing printing**: 1) *dealing directly with the printer,* 2) *using a print broker, or* 3) *having the design agency hire the printer.* Option 1 or 2 is usually your best choice, depending on the amount of time you can afford to spend on shopping for printers. With option 3, you will almost certainly pay more.

- **Submit major print jobs to multiple printers for competitive quotes**.

- **Don't overpay for four-color printing**. While set-up and press time do cost more, premiums of 100% or more are not reasonable. Four-color work should never cost more than 50% to 70% more than black-and-white, and comparison shopping can find even better prices.

- **Most internal or corporate letterhead is printed on 24 lb paper for appearance**. However, an automatic folding and stuffing machine for internal direct mail efforts may not work well with this heavier stock. Plan on using 20lb paper if the corporate letterhead doesn't work.

- **Review all bluelines, color keys or electronic proof versions**—sometimes called Irises. These are proofs made from the plates or directly from the printer's high tech proofing system used to approve work before going on press. Changes made at this point are still affordable.

- **If you are shipping printed collaterals to other locations, drop test your boxes from a height of at least six feet before sending them out**. A box of 1,000-80lb specification sheets weighs between 50 and 60lbs, and can easily overwhelm a standard cardboard shipping box when dropped or mishandled. Using special tapes and reinforced boxes may be wise. And always assign a value to your boxes when shipping so you can recover damages ($100 is a good starting point; it will motivate shippers to be a bit more careful with your materials).

Cost of single offset plate	$100
Cost of film (one color)	$50 to $80
Time-on-press charge per hour	$200
Cost of setup (four-color)	$100 to $250
Cost of stock photo	$100 to $2,000 (can depend on size of print run)
Cost-per-thousand of 80lb. glossy stock (8 1/2 x 11)	$12

Figure 3-1. Breakdown of typical printing costs

Agency/designer concepts to publisher	4 to 7 days
Publisher concept approval cycle	2 to 3 days
Design layout and copy to publisher	4 to 5 days
Layout and copy approval cycle	2 to 3 days
Revise and prepare final materials	5 to 7 days
Materials approval cycle	1 to 3 days
Final changes made to materials; sent to printer	1 to 2 days
Printer makes plates, film separations, bluelines	4 to 7 days
Final review cycle by publisher	1 to 4 days
Printing/folding/binding	5 to 10 days

Figure 3-2. Sample production schedule for four-color brochure

FOCUS STORY: TOO MANY COOKS SPOIL THE COLLATERAL

Company

Stromberg, LLC
59 Elm St
New Haven, CT 06497

Market Overview

Stromberg, LLC is a start-up company resulting from the merger of Jason Data Systems, a secondary competitor in the computer-based time and attendance market, and the remains of Stromberg, once a leader in providing electromechanical time clocks and stamps. The computer-based time and attendance market primarily targets companies where punching a time clock is part of normal business operations. A complete computer-based time and attendance solution usually consists of a database designed to total employee clock punches, an interface to a payroll package or program, and a computer time clock connected to a server or workstation via a LAN or serial cabling. Most time and attendance publishers focus on selling their products into specific vertical niches, though the leading publisher in the industry, Kronos, with estimated 1998 revenues of approximately $230M, sells into all major verticals. Most publishers sell to this market directly or through a one-tier reseller channel, though a few have tried to sell at retail via two-tier distribution.

In terms of collateral, Stromberg was starting at ground zero, with not even an acceptable company logo available for use. Much of the existing Jason collaterals were simply not suited for widespread distribution. For example, the demo disk they had been distributing since 1996 contained numerous typos and misspellings, which is typical of a small company that doesn't have a professional collaterals production and review program or the internal resources and talent to manage its marketing.

After completing the required corporate identity program, over thirty new pieces were commissioned and the collateral creation cycle began. It immediately bogged down, as numerous sales people involved themselves in the production process, with the inevitable poor results. For instance, a series of vertical case studies was commissioned by the marketing group and written by a professional writer. After first drafts had been received, revised, and laid out, some of these pieces were submitted to the sales force for (ostensibly) high-end review. Despite repeated warnings to avoid copy editing and proofing, the pieces were returned with literally dozens of pointless, and in many cases, incorrect changes. (Internally, the sales group circulated the pieces among themselves with no system to control revisions, leading to the spectacle of mistakes being introduced while other mistakes were being corrected or missed.) Worse, user quotes were significantly changed (a giant no-no), and industry-specific language was stripped out due to the sales reviewers' ignorance of the particular vertical markets being profiled.

In the meantime, in something of a rogue operation, the sales group continued to insist on blundering ahead in parallel with its previous "system" of creating collateral. This resulted in printing business cards that had obsolete addresses and incorrect titles, and the printing of thousands of soon-to-be-obsolete product brochures with an incorrect business address.

RESULTS

The breakdown in the collateral production process delayed the printing of desperately needed pieces by 60 to 90 days. In addition, thousands of dollars were wasted in making and correcting unnecessary revisions, and marketing programs dependent on receiving collaterals on a timely basis were either cancelled or delayed.

A more insidious cost was the time wasted by the sales force trying to do other peoples' jobs. Properly copy editing and revising over 30 pieces takes two marketing people approximately ten days to complete (and this does not include initial design and writing, revisions, and layout). There are few organizations that can afford to have its sales force take a hiatus from selling while they moonlight as copy editors and proofreaders.

LESSONS

Stromberg's marketing efforts would have been more effective if upper management had allowed marketing to manage the collateral process, limited the input of the sales group to high-level comments and suggestions, and insisted that the sales group focus on the job of selling product. It is important for a publisher to remember that collateral is not "literature." Most pieces will not remain in stock for more than a year, if that long, and obsessing over every word and phrase is a self-defeating exercise. The best collaterals, assuming they are cleanly designed and well written, are ones that are available to support the company's marketing efforts.

CONCLUSION

To succeed in building and using collaterals effectively, keep in mind these key factors:

- **Collaterals can close a sale**. Your collaterals should always contain an offer to buy and instructions on how to do it.
- **Build collaterals to need**. Keep initial print runs conservative. Basic end-user and channel collaterals can usually be built quickly.
- **Don't pour end-user collateral down the channel**. If a channel partner requests large amounts, find out where it is going. When a reseller requests collaterals, make sure they are properly distributed and end up in the hands of end-users.
- **Merchandising collaterals must be managed once placed in the field**. This may require cleaning, updating, or refurbishing. And make sure you have permission to put them in the store.
- **Keep track of NFS software programs**. These can quickly grow out of control and start costing you sales.

- **Consider placing collaterals on the product CD**; there is usually plenty of space left over to include upgrade, promotional, and other product materials.

PACKAGING

While it is often not considered collateral, your product's package is a very important piece of collateral—it is often your first direct marketing contact with a buyer. In a retail environment, your packaging functions as a company sales person talking directly to the buyer and should present your company at its best and most persuasive. In many cases, your product's packaging is your first and last chance to make a good impression. If you make a bad one, you may never have another chance to persuade a ready buyer to purchase your product.

Packaging Objectives

Well-designed packaging can:

- Act as a powerful sales presentation tool.
- Encourage buyers to pick up the package.
- Function as a sales center for the life of the product.
- Protect the product, both in the retail and user environment.
- Help establish a company image.
- Differentiate your product from the competition.

Packaging Basics—The Design

The package lives in many different places: a reseller shelf, photographed in an ad, on a purchaser's shelf or desk, perhaps even on television and its design should take these possibilities into account. Design factors to consider include:

- **The package's photographic appearance**. How will the package look when shrunk to appear in a trade publication or ad?
- **Its size and shape**. Consider the different types of shelving on which the package will reside. If a product will not fit a reseller's shelves, you have a fundamental problem.
- **Survivability**. The retail environment is harsh and packages are frequently stacked in different ways. Key survivability features include:

- *An internal cardboard package or stiffener to help protect the package against crushing and ending up in "rough goods" pile.*

- *Shrink wrapping.* This protects against fingerprints, moisture, everyday handling, and bundle breaking.

- *A shellac finish to protect against finger prints if your package is not shrink-wrapped.* Shellacking also allows you to build a "flap front" box and bundle a brochure directly into the product's packaging. The downside is that flap boxes are more prone to shelf damage from fraying and toppling, and to avoid the problem some store personnel tape the box shut—defeating the purpose of the design.

- *Printing the product name **on all six sides** of the package.* This will help prevent the package from "drowning" in a sea of competitive packages. You cannot control how your package will be stacked or presented in different resellers.

• **Package colors**. If your package is done in white and beige, will it stand out in a retail environment of bright fluorescent lighting and white shelves? Yellow and red traditionally gain the greatest retail "eyeshare," but if everyone's package is yellow or red, you may not want to create a "me-too" appearance.

• **Printing the company name and logo on the cardboard box or manila envelope** in which you ship upgrades or product sold via direct marketing.

• **Placing endorsements from key influencers on your packaging**. This tactic is useful both for retail- and VAR-class products.

• **Using five-color printing for special impact**. A clear shellac (the fifth color) over a logo or picture can impart a remarkable 3-D effect to your packaging.

• **Leaving some open space on the front of the package for placing promotional stickers, awards, and announcements in the future**, if needed.

• **Buyer interaction with the package**. This is frequently overlooked in many packaging designs. Points to consider include:

- *Make your package easy to open.* A difficult-to-open package is frustrating and the buyer may scatter and lose the contents, including the all-important registration card and any in-the-box catalogs or promotions.

- *Pre-engineer the sequence and presentation of key material in the packaging.* For instance, a "lift off" design forces the buyer to sort through any papers, cards, and catalogs before reaching the product, and it's easier to control the order in which the buyer sees the registration card, a catalog, or promotional offering. With an open-from the-top design, placing all materials in an envelope offers similar benefits.

- *Registration card placement.* To help increase registration card returns, some publishers use Velcro to attach the registration card directly to the disk or CD case.

Packaging Basics—The Outside of the Box

Items that should appear on the outside of the box include:

- **A bar (UPC) code**. This must be included as most distributors and resellers no longer accept products that are not bar coded. Refer to *Appendix C: The Marketing Resource Directory* for bar code vendors.

- **Well-written copy about your product** that emphasizes and reinforces the product's position and includes:
  - *A clear statement about the benefits of the product on the front of the box.* If the buyer has to wait until the back of the box to find out what the product does, odds are high that the package that says it first will be picked up first.
  - *Highlights of key product benefits and the problems this product solves.*
  - *Answers to buyer objections to this class or type of product.*
  - *Emphasis on the product's unique features.*
  - *Comparisons against other products*, if necessary or appropriate.

- **Company name and address**. A phone number is optional (depending on how you wish to handle support and registration issues).

- **Basic hardware and software requirements**, including:
  - *The minimum hardware and random access memory (RAM).*
  - *Any system software requirements (Windows 9X, Windows NT, Linux, or UNIX).*

- **Copyright and trademark acknowledgments**.

- **Award medallions**. *PC Magazine, PC Week, InfoWorld, Windows Magazine,* and *MacWorld* are among the most recognizable names to buyers. (Obtain permission from these publications before printing their endorsement.)

- **Endorsements from experts or recognized specialists in your market** (this approach is almost completely overlooked by most publishers).

Packaging Basics—The Inside of the Box

A package must contain the following:

- The registration card.
- The product on CD-ROM or disks.
- The documentation.

Optional items can include:

- A keyboard template.
- A coupon or catalog book.
- An index card containing support and customer service numbers
- A tip sheet with common questions, problems, and solutions. This is an underutilized technique for decreasing support calls.
- Collaterals for different products
- Addenda or supplemental documentation. These are often used to document aspects of a product that constantly change, such as driver support.

The Registration Card

If you're not using an electronic registration system, the registration card is the most important piece of collateral in the box, and should be the first thing the buyer sees when opening the package. Returned registration cards represent an opportunity to tell users about new product developments, offer them new or ancillary products, and sell them upgrades. Unreturned registration cards represent lost opportunity and dollars. A publisher should always spend the time and effort to create a compelling reason for users to read and return their registration. An active, up-to-date registered user list is a valuable commodity and a potential source of incremental revenue.

Designing an Effective Registration Card

An effective registration card is self mailing, postage paid, and asks only for key information, such as the buyer's name, address, E-mail address, the date of purchase, etc. Many registration cards ask a seemingly endless list of questions about the buyer's hardware, software, company size, number of computers at a site, etc., and so on. Most buyers don't bother to answer these questions, and the appearance of a long list makes may even cause them to throw the card away. If you really want a buyer to fill out a long questionnaire, make sure it is understood that this part of the registration process is optional. Thank them for their cooperation, and don't make their registration incentive depend on filling out the entire form.

If you allow other companies access to your list, the card should also offer the option to not be included on such lists. If you are offering an incentive to register the product, display the incentive prominently on the card.

Effective Incentives

The best way to ensure a high registration card return rate is to provide an incentive. Without one, even an effective registration card will probably generate only a 15 to 20% average return. An enticing incentive can double that. The most effective incentives offer a tangible reward for returning the card. Among the most popular are:

- T-shirts. This ranks at the top. Everyone loves them. Of course, at between four and seven dollars per shirt, this can be expensive.
- Coffee mugs.
- Mouse pads.
- Complimentary magazine subscriptions.
- Supplementary or add-on products. These rank very close to T-shirts.
- Entrance in a contest. This is usually not very effective, because most people believe they won't win. (Have **you** ever won a contest?)

Make sure the incentive offer is clearly visible and attractively presented. Do not bury it in the package or make it hard for the user to find. Even the least effective incentives should increase the product's registration return percentage by 25% or better.

Electronic vs. Conventional Registration

The past few years have seen the introduction of various commercial electronic registration systems and companies. In some cases, publishers have made the decision to develop their own internal systems. However, the hidden overhead associated with supporting the fulfillment half of electronic registration makes this option less desirable than it initially appears.

Electronic registration's ultimate goal is to achieve software marketing nirvana, 100% capture of the installed user base; the most effective conventional systems typically achieve no more than 30% to 40% registration (and this is very rare). Depending on the registration and fulfillment options chosen, electronic registration systems can achieve registration rates of between 40% and 99%.

ELEMENTS OF AN ELECTRONIC REGISTRATION PROGRAM

While individual features and costs vary, all electronic registration products incorporate the following elements:

- **The use of a software development kit** (SDK) used by the publisher to "bake" the electronic registration code into their product and display registration messages to the user.

- **Various options and software switches used to implement different registration options**, including the ability to prohibit use until registration, shut down the program after X number of days of use, shut down after X number of program accesses, display "nag" screens urging the customer to register, slow product loading, etc.

- **Various fulfillment options**, including the ability to provide unlock codes electronically via a direct modem connection (almost always an 800 class connection), web site registration, 24 x 7 800-number fulfillment, etc.

While electronic systems perform as advertised, their use has been limited by several factors. The most important is the royalty overhead added to the product's COG when using electronic registration, typically between $.75 and $3.00 per transaction, depending on the cost of the product, projected number of registrants, and which fulfillment options are included.

Users often react negatively to "forced" or required registration, and some publishers have been forced to disable such options. Retail markets typically display the highest resistance to required registration, though certain markets, such as small business accounting, have been able to implement this requirement.

SHOULD YOU USE ELECTRONIC REGISTRATION?

In most cases, the answer is yes. Incredible as it seems, many publishers still fail to understand the value of identifying and marketing to their installed base. Electronic registration is the most effective means of capturing this base for future marketing efforts. In many cases, even product sold for bundling, as a loss leader, or as shareware, should incorporate an electronic registration capability so as to build a base on which to market future products and upgrades.

However, there are reasons **not** to use electronic registration, including:

- The product is a "one shot wonder," and no sequel or add-on is ever planned, and no similar products will ever be marketed to the customer base. This is rare.
- Your product is sold almost exclusively via a direct sales force, and all customers are pre-registered.
- The cost structure of your product cannot support the royalty overhead of a commercial solution. In such cases, consider whether a home-grown solution integrated with web site registration can function as a possible alternative.

Packaging Basics—Retail Shelf Exercises

Perhaps the most useful thing a marketing manager can do when planning retail product packaging is walk through the aisles of a retail outlet and inspect what the competition is doing. Pick up some packages. Are product hardware and software needs clearly listed? How "self selling" are the packages you see? Do they contain a clear statement of what the product does on the front of the box?

Stores are also a good place to see new packaging designs in action and to pick up current trends on color, styles, and copy. And always make a quick stop to the remainders section of the store. You're sure to pick up some good "bad" examples there.

Packaging Costs

It is possible to spend a great deal of money on elaborate and intricate packaging. Some of the most *avant garde* examples are found in entertainment software. For business software however, overly elaborate packaging is probably ineffective in generating extra sales and therefore a waste of money. Also remember that all packaging costs are negotiable based on the volume and market conditions.

The following table details typical packaging costs for a range of products; it should be used as reference only. Quantity assumed is 10K.

Using Your Registered Users List

Many publishers make the mistake of not marketing to their registered users list until it is time to release an upgrade. Over the course of a year (the usual period between major releases), as much as 50% of the list can become obsolete. There are several things you can do to keep your list current:

- Offer it for sale to publishers in complementary but not competitive markets.
- Offer users a chance to buy incremental upgrades, add-ons, or complementary products.
- Survey users on how they're using your product, what they would like to see in the next release, what they don't like, etc. Remember to offer them an incentive to participate in the survey as well as an opportunity to buy something.

Let creativity be your guide. But above all, do not allow the list to become stale. Even if a survey or incentive program only breaks even, it is worth doing in order to keep the list current and up-to-date. It will pay for itself many times over when upgrade time approaches.

FOCUS STORY: THE BAD, THE REALLY BAD, AND THE EXTREMELY UGLY

Companies

Computer Associates

IBM

M-USA

Novell

Street Technologies

From the "Its not what you say, its how you say it" school of packaging:

CA-Simply Accounting on support:

> "All registered users are allowed two free telephone support calls. Additional coverage is available through the SupportPlus Program."

(I'm allowed, eh? Is that after I eat my spinach, or before?)

M-USA's Pacioli 2000 on support:

> "If you have any questions when using Pacioli 2000, the answers are as close as your telephone. When you call us for technical support, we'll be there to help you free of charge for 30 days."

Both support offers are, in practical terms, comparable, but whom would you rather buy from?

And now for "This Is the Worst Piece of Collateral Ever Developed" school of marketing (no, this is *not* a joke):

The front of Street Technologies brochure for its Street Trainer multimedia product says:

"How to eliminate half your work force."

The inside says:

"Get the other half to use your software!"

The front panel has a red background with white lettering, which seems appropriate for a marketing message apparently designed to provide an excuse for the resuscitation of communism.

And this example from the "You'd Better Know Your Market or Else!" university of collateral design:

IBM produced an OS/2 brochure whose front piece showed a yuppie type flinging open a window to explore the wonderful new world of OS/2. Behind the window was a viscous green mass in which the yuppie had immersed his face. It looked a lot like what happens when the Blob ingests its teenage victims.

Worse for IBM was that the design appeared to customs officials in several Arab (Egypt and Saudi Arabia, among others) countries as vaguely blasphemous. The yuppie with his hands up in the air in a square window reminded the authorities there of someone praying to Mecca. All brochures sent to these countries were either returned or confiscated and destroyed.

From the "Where Did You Get Those Pecs?" school of promotional design:

Novell's disastrous Novell Market Messenger promotional CD-mailer. Designed to distribute a CD hawking Novell reseller services, the mailer was cleverly designed to resist opening by anyone lacking the strength to rip phone books apart with their bare hands. (Actually, it's easy to open the package if you mark the sequence for the user.) After mailing 50K, Novell reengineered the package to make it obvious how to open it. In the meantime, the vigorous workout offered by the package was, we're sure, enjoyed by all.

LESSONS

Always talk nicely to your customers. Think about what you're saying in your collaterals. For instance, threatening people with unemployment if they use your software is probably not a powerful marketing message. If your collaterals are going to be used internationally, send samples to the country where they will be used and ask your employees or the appropriate authorities to review them. Test all mailers and special items for design and implementation. Obtain test samples and tear them apart, making notes as you do. Any potential problems should become quickly apparent.

Documentation Trends

The trend over the past years has been to cut back on product documentation. Thick books have been replaced by skinny manuals and on-line help systems. This has been driven by pricing pressures, the widespread acceptance of Windows, the subsequent standardization of basic program usage, and the growth of third-party publishers who sell books focused on getting the most out of various software products.

Your market and users determine the extent of your product's documentation. If you are selling a $3K CAD package, your customers will probably insist on complete and comprehensive documentation. If you are selling a basic disk utility or a simple application, less documentation may be acceptable.

Many publishers choose to provide basic printed documentation with the product and the rest on a CD or electronic manual, which are often created using electronic book (E-book) software. The user can view and move around in the formatted documentation and print out relevant pages. There are several advantages to this approach. One is that the product COG can be substantially lowered. Another is that updated documentation can be developed and quickly distributed over a web or FTP site with far less expense to the publisher than with conventional documentation.

COLLATERALS OBJECTIVES/EVALUATION CHECKLIST

OBJECTIVES	EVALUATION

Marketing Goals

1. Increase sales

*% increased SKUs shipped
to channel* _____ _____ _____

% increased direct sales _____ _____ _____

*% increased direct marketing
response rates* _____ _____ _____

2. Increase registration card returns or electronic registration:

*% increased registration
cards returned or registration* _____ _____ _____

3. Establish/enhance product visibility

*% increased calls to
company* _____ _____ _____

*% increased product
inquiries* _____ _____ _____

*% increased SKUs shipped
to channel* _____ _____ _____

% increased web site visits _____ _____ _____

% increased direct sales _____ _____ _____

*% increased mentions,
articles, reviews, etc.,
in press* _____ _____ _____

4. Act as successful presentation tool(s)

*% increased sales leads
generated* _____ _____ _____

*% increased calls to
company* _____ _____ _____

*% increased product
inquiries* _____ _____ _____

*% increased web visits and
collateral downloads* _____ _____ _____

OBJECTIVES   EVALUATION

Marketing Goals

5. **Survive in the retail environment**

    *# damaged packages
    returned*   _____ _____ _____

    *% merchandising
    collateral damaged*   _____ _____ _____

6. **Look good in advertising, promotional photographs, and via web downloads**_____

    *$ required for design/
    photographic rework*   _____ _____ _____

7. **Support sales promotions**

    *# pieces used in sales
    promotions*   _____ _____ _____

    *$ saved due to multiple
    use*   _____ _____ _____

Audience

1. **Do end-user collaterals focus on product features
    and benefits?**   _____ _____ _____

2. **Do channel collaterals focus on the advantages of selling
    the product?**   _____ _____ _____

COLLATERALS SUCCESS CHECKLIST

1. **Develop collaterals strategy, including objectives, budget, distribution scheme, and schedule** _____

2. **Obtain all necessary approvals**
   ☐ Product Marketing _____
   ☐ Finance _____
   ☐ Senior Management _____

3. **Assign collaterals coordinator** _____

4. **Select vendor(s)**

   A. Brief vendor(s) on product, audience, objectives, etc. _____

   B. Obtain quotes from printers, designers _____

   C. Set production schedule from development to distribution _____

   D. Define tasks, deliverables, responsibilities, etc. _____

   E. Generate "get started" purchase order(s) _____

5. **Information required for collaterals development**

   A. Product
   ☐ Advantages of selling product _____
   ☐ Description _____
   ☐ Hardware requirements _____
   ☐ Key differentiators _____
   ☐ Key exclusives _____
   ☐ Key features/benefits _____
   ☐ Key product messages _____
   ☐ Name _____
   ☐ Platforms supported
   ☐ Position _____
   ☐ Price _____

   B. Target audience
   ☐ End-user _____
   ▓ Demographics (age, title, sources, etc.) _____
   ▓ What is their perception of the product? _____

       ▨ What do they know about the product? _____

       ▨ What excites them? _____

☐ Channel _____

       ▨ What is their perception of the product?_____

       ▨ What do they know about the product? _____

       ▨ What excites them? _____

C. Competitive information

☐ Who, market share, strengths, weaknesses?_____

☐ Intelligence from their product launches, promotions, direct mail, etc. _____

D. Product(s) perception in market _____

E. Collateral(s) life cycle (end-user vs. channel) _____

F. Forecast quantities (end-user vs. channel) _____

G. Determine whether or not detailing company will be used _____

6.   Collaterals development process

A. Develop designs for testing _____

B. Develop designs for web viewing and downloading _____

C. Obtain high-level input from functional groups _____

☐ Important issues and problems _____

☐ Key marketing vocabulary _____

☐ Useful contacts and experts_____

D. Coordinate high-level review for appropriate collaterals_____

E. Test against sample target audience (in-store and channel) _____

F. Choose best concepts based on test results _____

G. Product Marketing provides:

☐ Packaging for photo shoot _____

☐ Screen shots _____

☐ Output samples_____

H. Vendor submits production and distribution cost estimates _____

I.   Budget approved (allow for overruns) _____

J.   Produce collaterals _____

K. Collateral proofing cycle (at least 3 edits)

☐ Product Marketing _____

☐ Development (for technical accuracy only)_____

L. Print collaterals

☐ Check design_____

☐ Involve printer in design process _____

☐ Use broker to select printer _____

☐ Contact printer directly _____

☐ Test for mail machine use _____

☐ Press check at start of each job _____

☐ Test/disassemble special collaterals _____

M. Distribute collaterals_____

☐ Drop-test shipping boxes _____

N. Track and evaluate results_____

O. Build/enhance and use registered users list _____

7. **Select collateral type(s)**

A. End-user

☐ Brochure _____

☐ Case Study_____

☐ Agriculture_____

☐ Construction _____

☐ Defense _____

☐ Education_____

☐ Employee leasing _____

☐ Finance (banking, brokerages)_____

☐ Government _____

☐ Healthcare (hospitals, nursing homes, hospices, assisted living) ____

☐ High tech (hardware) _____

☐ High tech (software)_____

☐ Hospitality (hotels, restaurants, amusement and theme parks) _____

☐ Insurance _____

☐ Legal _____

☐ Manufacturing _____

- ☐ Mining _____
- ☐ Retail _____
- ☐ Transportation (air, rail, trucking) _____
- ☐ Unions _____
- ☐ Other _____
- ☐ Comparison sheets _____
- ☐ Corporate backgrounder _____
- ☐ Corporate piece _____
- ☐ Demo disks _____
    - ▓ Color and sound? _____
    - ▓ Length approximately five minutes? _____
    - ▓ Viewing options? _____
- ☐ Immediate call to action? _____
- ☐ Demo Templates _____
- ☐ Industry specific _____
- ☐ Electronic presentation _____
- ☐ Folders _____
- ☐ Newsletters _____
    - ▓ Conventional _____
    - ▓ Electronic _____
- ☐ NFS software _____
- ☐ Presentation materials _____
    - ▓ Reprints _____
    - ▓ Specification sheets _____
    - ▓ System overview _____
    - ▓ TBYB software _____
    - ▓ Time limit _____
    - ▓ Usage limit _____
- ☐ Presentation binders _____
- ☐ Videos _____
    - ▓ Case study _____
    - ▓ Professionally produced _____
    - ▓ Focus on users _____
    - ▓ Running length approximately 15 minutes _____

- ▓ Avoids hard sell _____
- ▓ POS _____
- ▓ Continuous loops _____
- ▓ Length around five minutes _____
- ▓ Package close ups _____
- ▓ Professionally produced _____
- ▓ Minimum of screen shots _____
- ▓ Music as background element _____
- ▓ Strong use of graphics and user visuals _____
- ▓ Use of voiceovers _____
- ☐ Web Sites _____
- ☐ White paper _____

B. Channel

- ☐ Collateral CD _____
- ☐ Comparison sheets _____
- ☐ Corporate identity manual _____
- ☐ In-store (merchandising) _____
  - ▓ Banners _____
  - ▓ End-cap displays _____
  - ▓ Floor stacks _____
  - ▓ Kiosks _____
  - ▓ Mobiles _____
  - ▓ Monitor wraps _____
  - ▓ Posters _____
  - ▓ Sell sheets _____
  - ▓ Shelf talkers _____
  - ▓ Tent cards _____
  - ▓ Videos (POS) _____
  - ▓ Others _____
- ☐ Logos _____
- ☐ NFS software _____
- ☐ Order forms _____
- ☐ Sell scripts _____
- ☐ Specification sheets _____

C. Promotional

☐ Coffee mugs _____

☐ Carryalls _____

☐ Diskette holder _____

☐ Hats _____

☐ Mouse pads _____

☐ Mouse holders _____

☐ Shopping bags _____

☐ Pens _____

☐ T-shirts _____

☐ 3M Post-it note dispenser _____

☐ Watches _____

☐ Others _____

8. Packaging Design and Development

A. Exterior design/copy requirements

☐ What product is and what it does _____

☐ Key product features/benefits _____

☐ Answers to buyer questions _____

☐ Unique features highlighted _____

☐ Competitive comparisons _____

☐ Company name, address, and phone number _____

☐ Hardware/software requirements _____

☐ Media type inside box (disks or CD-ROM) _____

☐ Platform, version, module designations _____

☐ Copyright and trademark information _____

☐ Endorsements, award medallions, reviewer quotes _____

☐ UPC Code _____

B. Interior design, copy, and elements

☐ Mandatory inclusions _____

    ▨ Documentation _____

      ○ Web publish _____

      ○ Password protect _____

      ○ User log-on _____

- ☐ Product (disks or CD-ROM) _____
- ☐ Registration card _____
  - ▨ Asks only vital information_____
  - ▨ Call to action _____
  - ▨ Contains additional offer (optional) _____
  - ▨ Offers incentive_____
  - ▨ Postage paid _____
- ☐ Optional inclusions: _____
- ☐ Electronic registration_____
  - ▨ Required information option _____
  - ▨ Reminder option (nagware)_____
  - ▨ Time out/shut down option _____
  - ▨ Fulfillment in house _____
  - ▨ Fulfillment handled externally _____
- ☐ Keyboard template _____
- ☐ Coupon(s) and/or catalog(s)_____
- ☐ Additional add-on/promotional products (on CD)_____
- ☐ Index card containing support and customer service phone numbers _____
- ☐ Tip sheet outlining common questions, problems, and solutions _____
- ☐ Collateral for other product(s)_____
- ☐ Buyer survey (questionnaire) _____
- ☐ Supplemental documentation (errata, etc.) _____

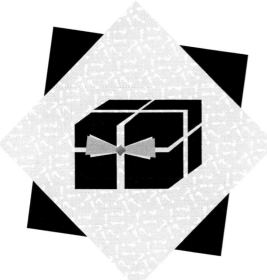

Public Relations and Product Review Programs

The essence of running successful a public relations (PR) campaign in the software industry is building and maintaining a favorable company image and obtaining good product reviews. The industry's most successful software company, Microsoft, was masterly in achieving these goals (though recently the company has had problems holding on to its sterling public perception). Spearheading the effort was the time and energy devoted to crafting Microsoft founder Bill Gates' image and reputation. Throughout the 1980s and 1990s, it has been difficult not to see pictures of Bill Gates holding a floppy disk, Bill Gates standing under a grove of redwoods, Bill Gates gazing into a monitor, Bill Gates talking about the information age (hastily revised to be the Internet as events overtook the old buzzword) etc., etc., etc., all the while expounding about the future of the PC marketplace.

The image created was of a friendly, non-threatening technical wizard—a kind of high-tech elf—an image completely at variance with Gates' PC-insider reputation as a tough-as-nails negotiator and ultra-shrewd businessman. The effort's zenith was reached when a writer for a major PC trade publication wrote that "Microsoft doesn't understand marketing, they just want to create great products." A PR department that obtains that kind of press has mastered the Zen of marketing!

Many authors make the mistake of thinking that PR campaigns begin with a product announcement and end with a product release. Nothing could be farther from the truth. The PR process is an ongoing one, and must be constantly managed. Microsoft and other successful companies have achieved their success by understanding this and making image building and review management integral parts of their marketing efforts.

IN-HOUSE VS. OUTSIDE PR SERVICES

Among larger publishers, PR is often handled by both external agencies and internal departments. The external agency may focus on coordinating large events, such as press conferences and major product events, while the internal department may focus on day-to-day activities and managing the ongoing product review process.

Many smaller firms hire external agencies to handle their PR. This may be a wise choice for a firm that needs to focus on product development. However, this does not mean that a small company can expect its PR agency to run on auto pilot. All publishers need to:

- Provide the agency with key positioning information about the product.
- Instruct the agency about the product's key features and benefits.
- Provide the agency with the names of key users of the product, if any.

Many PR firms advertise themselves as "full-service" agencies; they can provide, in addition to PR services, ad development, ad placement, collaterals development, event management, and so forth. Carefully evaluate all such claims. Many agencies excel in some areas, but are weaker in others. Select an agency based on its strengths and your needs and then hire additional specialists to work in the areas in which the agency may be weak.

Another factor to keep in mind is that bigger is not necessarily better in the world of PR. A smaller PR firm with good press contacts and specific knowledge of your market will do a better job for a smaller publisher than a large-name firm that covers dozens of markets.

PR SPECIALTIES

Like other marketing groups and functions, PR personnel tend to specialize in different areas.

- Corporate specialist. This individual focuses on building an overall corporate image. This type of PR is more suited to larger publishers; smaller ones should focus on obtaining good product PR.

- Product specialist. This individual focuses on developing a product's image and clarifying its market positioning.

- Investor relations specialist. This individual specializes in establishing and maintaining relationships with venture capitalists, private investors, and financial analysts.

- Writing specialist. This individual writes feature stories about products.

- Media specialist. This individual builds and maintains relationships with the editors and reviewers of the different publications that cover different market segments.

PR BASICS

Press Kits

A press kit is a collection of marketing collaterals designed to position your product to the press and assist them in writing about it. A basic press kit should contain the following:

- A company backgrounder.

- A product release statement. This is a one- to three-page document that provides a product overview emphasizing features, benefits, etc.

- Positive testimonials from beta and current users. This is an overlooked item that publishers need to pay more attention to. The press is always looking for independent sources to verify a company's PR statements. By providing them, you can help influence your company's image and reviews on an ongoing basis.

- The company's web site address (URL) and E-mail contacts.

- Optional items can include product photographs, comparison sheets, spec sheets, a 35mm color slide, and a white paper. White papers are usually reserved for business applications; in some cases however, entertainment and educational publishers use them if they think their technology is interesting enough to catch the press' interest.

- In some cases, a free copy of the product.

Press Conferences

A press conference is a formal meeting paid for and hosted by the publisher for members of the press. During the conference, the publisher makes a formal presentation, answers questions from the press, and provides some refreshment.

These meetings are usually held at a hotel or similar site.

Press conferences should be used sparingly as a PR tool. They are expensive, require extensive management, and are often unproductive. Unless your company has something truly earth shattering to announce, attendance tends to be sparse. This is because:

- Too many publishers have held conferences to announce products and alliances that proved to be without substance (vaporware, vaportalk).

- Editors and reviewers are usually too busy to attend more than a handful of these events.

- Members of the press are also reluctant to ask too many questions at press conferences for fear of being scooped by their colleagues.

Press Releases

The press release is the bedrock of PR activities; it is a simple document, usually no more than one or two pages long, released to relevant news and press organizations. Most are prepared by a member of the PR group, and focus on a single key announcement or event. A standard release includes the following:

- Contact information at the company and/or the PR firm. This should include an executive's name, direct phone line at work, home phone number (in case someone is working on a tight deadline and needs to contact the company after hours), E-mail address, fax number, and web site address.

- A heading announcing the new and significant event. The text should be succinct and to the point, highlighting only key changes and features. This is not the place for technical expositions.

- Standard positioning information on the company's products and services. This information will often be repeated, verbatim, from release to release. The point is to hammer home this vital information into the press' collective consciousness

- A quote from a senior manager.

- A quote from a research firm, if you have one. While companies like The Gartner Group do not review products, the press does look to these companies to validate technology and product categories.

- Key points about the product in the main body of the release.

- Standard style markers to signify the end of each page and the end of the final page. To indicate that another page follows, the center bottom of each page should have the word "more" printed inside dashes (i.e., –more–). To indicate the final page, print three pound signs at the bottom (###).

Once prepared, the releases are usually sent directly to targeted publications or released on services such as Business Wire or PR News Wire, which can send your release to the world or to selected industry segments.

Press releases should be prepared any time a significant event occurs at your company, such as:

- A new product release
- A new partnership or alliance
- A new distribution arrangement
- A significant personnel addition or change
- An important awards and reviews (a *PC Magazine* Editors Choice award, for instance).

The point of all this activity is to keep the press' awareness of your company alive and fresh. While no particular release is likely to have a tremendous effect on your company's visibility (unless you are dealing with a major crisis), the cumulative effect is to keep the press aware of your existence and interested enough to report on your activities.

Press Tours

The press tour is an effective, but relatively expensive and time-consuming method of building press relations. It consists of arranging for the key editorial personnel and analysts who cover your product category to meet with members of your senior management team. Press tour arrangements are usually made by the PR group, and are booked one to two months in advance. Their key objective is to build personal, face-to-face relationships. Once established, these are the most powerful and useful press contacts a company can possess.

The best time for a press tour is usually just before the release of a new product, service, or significant upgrade. Remember that the press' key objective is to gather items of interest that will generate new stories and exclusives for their readers. Try to avoid scheduling tours midway through a product's life cycle. While such tours can be useful in building personal relations, they will usually not generate increased editorial coverage.

The ideal press tour team consists of at least one member of upper management, one member of middle management capable of giving a comprehensive product demonstration (often the product manager), and a PR person.

Most press tour meetings last about an hour. The usual format is to give a quick, concise, informative overview of the company, the product, and the product marketing strategy. The nature of these meetings lends itself to small talk and speculations about industry directions, distribution trends, and other issues. It's fine to chat and establish personal relationships, but don't lose sight of the need to explain your product and your marketing mission.

After the tour, follow-up is vital to ensure the tour's ultimate objectives.

- Send the people you met with a thank you letter or E-mail repeating (subtly) your basic product and marketing message.

- Ship evaluation copies of the product to anyone in the meeting who requested them.

- Enter key points and notes about the people you met into your reviewer database.

- Send E-mail and press releases to the people you met on a regular basis to continue building the relationship.

Contacting the Press

Many publishers continue to rely on mailings and phone calls to talk to editors and reviewers, but e-mail has become a much more effective way to reach the press. Most editors and reviewers are advanced computer users, rely on E-mail, and tend to respond to it before turning to other notifications and contacts. You will do well to use electronic communications to manage your day-to-day PR.

User Groups

User group presentations, while often overlooked, are an effective way to develop favorable word of mouth for your product, test and refine product demonstrations, and even generate sales. All of the major metropolitan and most suburban areas host user groups. In many cases, the group will be glad to hear from you, and very happy to schedule you for a presentation to the membership. Larger groups may be divided into special interest groups (SIGs); you may be asked to present your product to a more tightly focused audience.

User groups vary widely in size and composition. Smaller groups tend to be a mixed bag, so your presentation should focus on the general benefits of your product and its most appealing features. However, remember that even at a smaller group, in addition to people learning how to run Windows or format floppies, you are also likely meet MIS employees from local businesses, resellers, VARs, and technology consultants.

At larger groups, your presentation can be higher level and focus more on an in-depth examination of your product's capabilities. Your audience may be a mixture of MIS specialists, consultants, and even senior managers such as CIOs and the occasional CEO. Major user groups typically hold their meetings in local hospitals or businesses with facilities large enough to handle their membership. In some cases, publishers have been lucky enough to meet managers from the firms hosting the group—with these contacts eventually leading to sales.

If you are going to appear before a user group, the following tips will help you prepare your presentation:

- Be prepared to bring all the necessary equipment needed to display your product. The type and quality of projectors and computers user groups can provide vary widely.

- Know your product thoroughly, and be prepared to vary from a standard demonstration. Members of the audience will pepper you with questions about what you're showing them, and may ask you to show them any feature at any time.

- Always offer the group a free copy of your product. Most groups will use it to publicize your appearance and hold a drawing for it at the end of the evening. Try to be the one who actually hands the product to the lucky winner (a picture of this wouldn't hurt).

- Always offer some form of discount on your product. Some publishers take orders on the spot, or give the group X amount of time to take advantage of the special discount or incentive.

- Do not pack up and leave after your presentation. Stay until the end of the session and allow members of the group who have questions to approach you and talk further about your product.

- Don't assume everyone in attendance will have his or her business card. Be prepared to capture the names, addresses, and phone numbers of any future prospects.

ESTABLISHING THE PR PROCESS

After a decision has been made to launch a product, the first PR activity is to designate an individual to act as the PR coordinator for the product. This person will manage the entire process of launching and maintaining PR relations for the product or product family. If your company has formally implemented a product team approach, the coordinator should develop a close working relationship with the team leader or product manager four to six months before any major announcement or PR campaign. Key dates should be set and regular meetings scheduled and held between PR and product marketing.

THE PR CYCLE

Every PR cycle has three phases.

- **Pre-announcement**. During this phase, press releases, market and product backgrounders, press kits, and all deliverables are created. As announcement date approaches, press kits are assembled.
- **Announcement day**. During this phase, activities from the pre-announcement phase are executed.
  - Press releases are sent over the wire to your press contact list.
  - In-person and to be conducted in person or over the phone interviews are scheduled.
  - Major press/consultant conferences or events are staffed and ready.
  - Press kits have been mailed so that publishers, editors, reviewers, and key influencers have them on announcement day. Kits should be in the hands of weekly publications at least a week before they go to press.
- **Post-announcement**. During this phase, trade shows, meetings, interviews, announcements of product promotions, development of success stories, and other follow-up activities are conducted.

PRE-ANNOUNCE PHASE

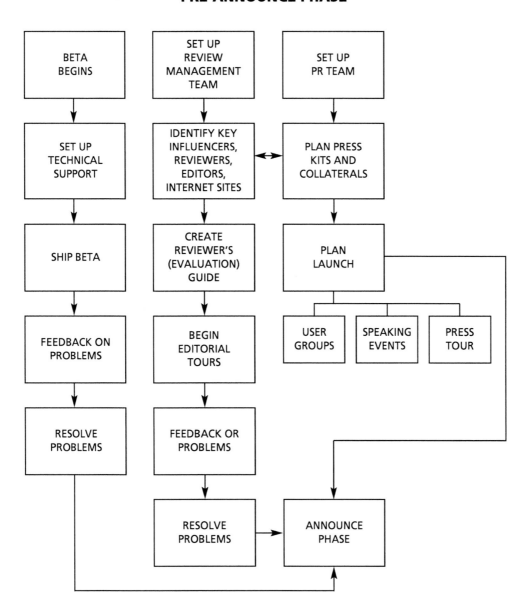

ANNOUNCE DAY PHASE

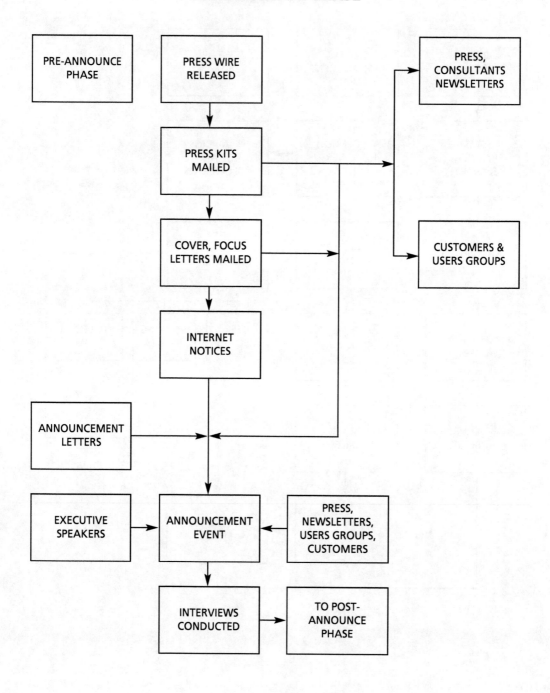

POST-ANNOUNCE PHASE

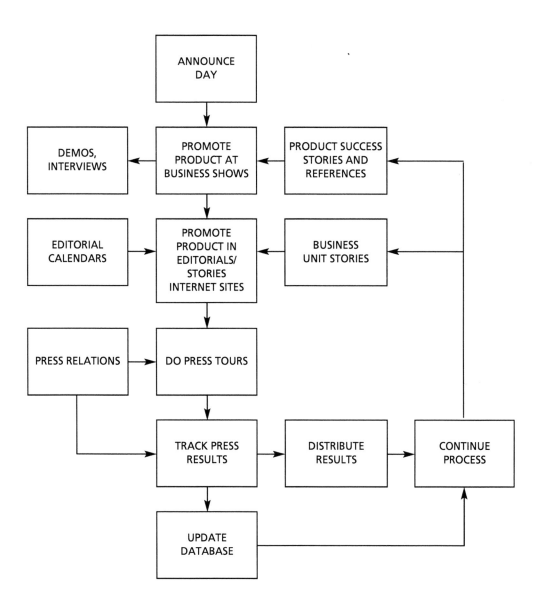

PRODUCT REVIEWS
Editorial vs. Publishing

Most large publications and media vehicles are divided into two areas, editorial and publishing. The editorial side is supposed to focus strictly on writing, reviewing, and reporting on the events and applications that the publication includes under its mission. The publishing side is the magazine's business operation, concerned with selling ad space, boosting circulation, and setting prices for the different types of ads and services offered.

In theory, a "Chinese wall" separates the editorial from the publishing side, and ne'er the twain shall meet. Supposedly, the two sides do not coordinate reporting with advertising: the amount of advertising you purchase has no effect on their reviews, and your position in the market will have no effect on the quality of the coverage you receive.

The reality, of course, differs from magazine to magazine and publisher to publisher. Some strictly enforce the publishing/editorial separation, others less strictly, some not at all. You will need to research each publication to find out the actual state of its Chinese wall.

Regardless of what you discover, it will be a rare occurrence (though not unheard of) when ad placement guarantees a favorable review. Nonetheless, a substantial advertiser does have the right to insist on at least the following from any publication in which it advertises:

- Your product is included in all roundups, first looks, and review specials that focus on your product category.

- You have the opportunity to discuss any misunderstandings about your product's category, design philosophy, or target audience with the reviewer or appropriate editorial personnel while the review cycle is underway. This does not mean that you will have the right to argue about bugs the reviewer finds, or insist the review be changed because you are not judged to be the best of class. You do, however, have the right to see that your product is compared against products of similar category, price, and target audience.

- Any mistakes or significant omissions by the reviewer are acknowledged by the magazine and corrections quickly published.

Beyond this, it is best to tread very lightly in your dealings with the editorial side, and apply a very deft touch indeed to managing your editorial/publisher relations.

Rely on personal relationships and good judgement to help you maximize your opportunities in this aspect of review management.

Product Reviews

Product reviews are absolutely critical to marketing success. It is true that a great review will not, in and of itself, ensure a product's success. It is almost impossible, however, to sell a product that has received poor reviews. And not only reviews affect product sales—bad press can go a long way toward killing a product, as the following focus story illustrates.

FOCUS STORY: IBM'S OS/2 PRESS MESS

Company

IBM

Product

OS/2

Market Overview

IBM's recent press relations history is a mixed one. In the pre-PC era, their strategy was a conventional but effective "big company" approach and garnered IBM a great deal of public respect. IBM invested in public charities, sponsorships of select TV and theater programs, advertising, and the usual editorial placements in a wide variety of different publications to build and maintain its public image.

IBM's successful strategy was regarded as a model of effective PR. However, as was true of most IBM marketing programs, its PR program was highly centralized, not designed to communicate with its product marketing groups, and technically ignorant. This did not work well in the new era of press reviews and analysis that sprang up in the 1980s and continues to this day. Powerful columnists and influencers such as John Dvorak and Jerry Pournelle had little interest in IBM's sponsorship of Hallmark's annual showing of a "Christmas Carol" or its contributions to the United Way. But they were very interested in discussing the newest and hottest technology, playing with the latest technical toys, and having their egos stroked by people who are knowledgeable about the industry.

Over time, IBM developed an involuntary two-track approach to PC press relations. The first track consisted of IBM's conventional PR program, which clanked along, oblivious to its increasing irrelevance in the new world.

The second track was an unruly back channel of former and current IBM employees who talked to the press on an *ad hoc* basis, churning out gossip and fueling speculation. A mini-industry of "IBM-watchers" sprang up, dedicated to deciphering the various statements and pronouncements of the different officers, divisions, and spokespeople.

Even worse was the fact that IBM had no formalized approach to managing its products' review cycles, a problem that has plagued IBM since the release of the IBM PC and one that continues to this day. Once an IBM software product is released, the product is on its own. Not surprisingly, very few IBM software products ever receive stellar reviews.

IBM's PR chickens came home to roost in 1995 when an amazing series of missteps helped to mortally wound OS/2. The timing could not have been worse. Contrary to skeptics' opinions, OS/2 was approaching general acceptance in late 1994. The continued delay in the release of Chicago (later Windows 95) had begun to erode sales of Windows 3.1 and the market was showing signs of restlessness.

Another factor in OS/2's favor was that the product was technically superior to Windows. Throw in Microsoft's increasingly public woes with the U.S. Department of Justice, and it seemed the "window" of opportunity for OS/2 was widening. The slow trickle of OS/2-specific applications coming to market began to swell. Sales of OS/2 through the retail channel became brisk. While OS/2 was far from achieving parity with Windows, it was close to achieving the status of a strong, permanent, second-place contender with significant market share. But at the height of this renaissance, a series of devastating press stories stopped OS/2's momentum in its tracks.

The first blow occurred when, in a major speech to business analysts, IBM CEO Lou Gerstner was quoted as saying that worrying about operating systems was fighting the "last war." Later in the speech, he added that it was too late for IBM to "go after the desktop." Several newspapers immediately reported this speech as an admission by IBM that OS/2 was a failure. *The New York Times* article was headlined "IBM Chief Concedes OS/2 Has Lost Desktop War."

The fallout was immediate and wide-ranging. OS/2 software vendors began to publicly question whether it made any sense to further invest in OS/2. Many large corporate accounts committed to installing OS/2 on an enterprise level announced they were reconsidering their positions. Key OS/2 advocates and columnists such as Will Zachman began to publicly question their support of OS/2.

The next, and even more devastating blow, came from a completely unexpected source. In his August 6th *New York Times* "Technology Column," Peter Lewis ran a story called "OS/2 No Longer at Home at Home." It was full of juicy quotes from an IBM spokesman. Among them: "OS/2 is a great operating system" but that "Sony's Betamax was a better system than VHS..." and "I'm going to put Windows 95 on the machines in my house."

What made the these quotes truly memorable was that they were made by David Barnes, IBM's Mr. OS/2 himself! Highly photogenic and comfortable in front of a crowd, Barnes had traveled thousands of miles over the previous three years conducting competitive demonstrations of OS/2 and Windows, been a keynote speaker at trade shows, and had appeared on radio and TV extolling OS/2's virtues. It was as if Bill Gates had been quoted saying that Windows was really an inferior product to OS/2 and he wouldn't be caught dead using the thing himself.

Reaction in the OS/2 community made the Gerstner *faux pas* seem insignificant. OS/2-friendly forums exploded. Tens of thousands of messages were posted electronically over the next several weeks, most asking for an explanation of Barnes' remarks. Famous long-time OS/2 aficionado James Fallows, author, columnist for *The Atlantic Monthly*, former editor of *US News and World Reports*, and now a Microsoft employee, posted several messages asking what on earth IBM was doing.

For several weeks, IBM did nothing: corrections weren't published, Barnes didn't write a letter of clarification to the editor of *The New York Times*, and an IBM spokesperson didn't appear on any online services, Usenet forums, or SIGs to correct or explain Barnes' statements.

Finally, after more OS/2 customers announced their defection from the product, IBM reacted. Barnes published a statement claiming that Lewis had taken his statements out of context. IBM assured everyone it was still committed to OS/2. Various IBM spokespeople made comforting noises. No one read any of these statements, and before Microsoft had even released Windows 95, OS/2 was truly dead.

IBM's response, or lack thereof, is a text book case of how not to manage the press. Cynics have pointed out that perhaps IBM was attempting to signal to the marketplace that it was discontinuing its support for OS/2. If true, it's hard to imagine a more self-defeating strategy. At the very least, IBM could have waited until after

Windows 95 had shipped to judge market response. But after the Gerstner/Barnes remarks, Microsoft could have waited another year to release Windows 95. It wouldn't have mattered.

LESSONS

There are several lessons to be learned from IBM's OS/2 experience, including:

- Perhaps most important, is the need to provide formal training for all product managers and marketing representatives on communicating with the press. This training should include profiles of the most prominent columnists and influencers, analysis of all relevant books and online sites, lessons on how to handle an obstreperous reviewer, uncovering and assuaging press and reviewer hostility, and so on.

- It is a mistake to cut off the product marketing staff from the press. Do not attempt to funnel all press relations through a Marcom department or a PR specialist. In the long run, this is a highly counterproductive strategy. PC reviewers and reporters do not enjoy talking exclusively to PR "flacks" (the mildest term they reserve for these people).

- The importance of developing a preplanned, detailed, rapid-response plan for major PR disasters, which should incorporate the following key points:

  - An initial response to a major print story should occur within 24 hours of the story. This helps ensure your response appears the next day in the major dailies.

  - A response to a major media story should take place within one hour (yes, an hour) to ensure that your response is run on **that** evening's radio and TV programs.

  - Upper management needs to know how to talk to the press. Brief and prepare them.

  - A curtailment of press contacts by middle management. During a major disaster, it is important that a unified and coherent message be transmitted to the press. After a reasonable period of time, middle management should resume contacts with the press, reinforcing the original message and maintaining good relations.

MANAGING A PRODUCT REVIEW PROGRAM
Goals

The minimum goal of a successful product review program is to obtain two highly favorable reviews from two of the major end-user publications (called "books" by industry insiders) and favorable reviews from the rest of the major books. A highly favorable review from one major book and an unfavorable review from another effectively cancel each other out. Remember that a well-run product review program cannot guarantee you will receive the top honors for your product; however, it can and will help your product earn the best reviews possible.

The goal of a successful editorial placement program will vary depending on your market and the type of press and editorial coverage your segment receives. A major segment, such as the CAD marketplace, supports between four and five publications. A secondary segment, such as time and attendance, often receives only partial coverage from related magazines.

First Looks and Features

In addition to reviews, there are also "first looks" and "feature" or "solution" stories. A first-look story is a brief overview of the product and description of the intended audience. It may be strictly informational, or the reviewer may include initial impressions of the product. A feature story usually focuses on a business problem or challenge solved by an individual or company using a product. Both types of stories, if favorable, are useful adjuncts to good reviews. Bad reviews, however, will negate their value.

Many mainstream publications do not review VAR-class products. Instead, industry-specific publications may review them, and the quality and influence of these reviews can and does vary widely. In these markets, well-written feature stories may be as valuable in building sales as positive reviews. The relative effectiveness of the two types of coverage must be decided market segment by segment.

The Internet explosion has also opened up more television opportunities for publishers. Programs like C-Net and Cool Tech cover new software products and technologies. But these appearances are still fairly hard to obtain, since the shows tend to focus on products that are of interest to a general audience. Entertainment, Internet-specific, and lifestyle products have the best chance of being selected for coverage.

Another area of opportunity often overlooked by publishers is local news outlets. Newspapers, regional magazines, and local business magazines in every major metropolitan center in the country publish columns on technology developments and new products. These local outlets represent an excellent opportunity to develop favorable coverage and press contacts.

Lead Times

You should plan on at least a five-month waiting period between product submission and publication. This is the minimum—some publications may require more time. In the case of smaller publications, these lead times can shrink to as little as two months. However, never expect that you can submit a product two weeks in advance of release and garner good reviews. In fact, don't expect the product to be reviewed at all.

Editorial Calendars, Personnel, and Services

Most PC publications plan their editorial coverage months, even a year, in advance. To ensure that your product is available for review or first looks, you should either call the publication and request a copy of their editorial calendar, or subscribe to a service like MediaMap or Press Access, which provide this data. Both services also offer software applications that assist you in managing the PR process if you are using their data. Another advantage is that they list key editorial personnel and the areas they cover.

The Internet Factor

To make things more interesting, software product marketers can no longer focus only on the traditional publications that cover their market(s). Increasingly, user groups and SIGs, both on the Internet and on the major services like CompuServe and AOL, play an important role in shaping and driving public opinion. Various web sites are dedicated to examining and covering particular products and markets. For example, the Happy Puppy, one of the pre-eminent entertainment sites, publishes reviews of new products, and a thumbs up or down from their reviewers can seriously impact sales of new games.

The Internet also makes reviews more persistent. Most of the major PC publications make back issues of their magazines available online. A potential customer need merely search the Internet for mentions of your product and quickly retrieve that less-than-favorable review from a key publication.

FLAMING

Finally, remember that companies, both formally and informally, use the Internet to hype their products and sometimes "flame" the competition. While you cannot be held responsible for what your employees do on their own time, you can set policy about what they do on your time. To avoid legal and marketing problems, consider the following guidelines when preparing your online marketing strategy:

- Establish a policy of no insults (flaming) on company time, no use of company equipment for flaming, and no use of a company's name while flaming, thus providing your company with some legal protection against slander and libel suits.

- Never attack a respondent personally, no matter what you think you know about them. Even if your information is correct, you'll usually be seen as a bully and a snoop. And your employees should also avoid giving out personal information about themselves to others online.

- Develop a policy of discouraging anyone but authorized employees to frequent forums/SIGs where your product or company is likely to be discussed. If they are absolutely determined to visit these places, encourage them to not discuss your company or products, and certainly not to identify themselves as employees of your company.

- Pick people with even tempers to monitor and participate in selected forums where your products and company are likely to be discussed. Warn them that once their position with the company is known, they must be prepared to deal with individuals who are unable to distinguish between people and products. Personal insults, nasty comments, and unpleasant invective must be deflected with a friendly cyber-shrug and a soothing word.

LAYING THE GROUNDWORK

The first step in preparing for the product review cycle is deciding who will oversee the review program. Within a PR group, the marketing communications manager often takes responsibility for this activity. The product manager should also play a major role in coordinating and participating in PR and review activities.

The Reviewer Database

The next step is to build a database of reviews and reviewers, containing names, magazine affiliations, copies of previous reviews, and an assessment of the reviewer's prejudices and attitudes toward your products and others in your category. The database should be available to and consulted by everyone involved in the product rollout and PR activities.

The Reviewer's Guide

The third step is to create a product review guide that *always* accompanies the product when it is sent to a reviewer. The guide must include the following:

- The product's positioning (category, class, and key features and benefits).
- The target audience.
- A profile of intended users and how they will use your product in their business.
- Supporting materials and testimonials.
- Names of key marketing and support contacts in the company.
- Names of beta users and key developers and/or influencers closely involved with your product. Of course, this only works if you have maintained good relations with these people.

Reviewer Handlers

The final task is to assign each reviewer an individual contact within the company. This contact should be matched to the reviewer's profile (a marketing-oriented reviewer should be matched to a marketing person, etc.). During the review preparation, the reviewer contact should remain in touch with the reviewer, offer help and clarification about the product's capabilities, and report back to the Marcom group. This process allows you to judge reaction to the product and address problems before the product's release and an unfavorable review.

IMPORTANT REVIEWS

Not all reviews are created equal. In different markets, different publication's reviews carry more weight and influence than others. Figure 4-1 lists some of the major computer publications in order of their estimated importance within categories.

PC Publications	Mac Publications
PC Magazine	Mac Week
Infoworld	MacWorld
PC World	
PC Computing	
PC Week	
Windows Publications	**Internet Publications**
Windows Magazine	InternetWeek
WindowsNT Magazine	Internet World
	EmediaWeekly
	Inter@active
	The Industry Standard
	NewMedia
Network Publications	**Channel Publications**
Network Computing	VAR Business Magazine
Network Magazine	Smart Reseller
Network World	Computer Reseller News
	Solutions Integrator
	Computer Retail Weekly

Figure 4-1. Major computer publications

MANAGING BAD REVIEWS

If your product receives bad reviews, there are several corrective steps you can take, including:

- Fix any technical flaws discovered in the product and update the user base and distribution system as soon as possible.
- Read the reviews and note any significant errors, then send a letter to the review editor pointing them out and asking for a printed correction. A quick response puts the reviewers on notice that you read your reviews, and that they need to be accurate and thorough. Editors react negatively to having to print frequent corrections.

- Read the reviews of other competitive products. If there are features or capabilities the reviewer liked in those products, you should consider whether to incorporate them in your product's next release.

- Prepare a white paper that points out any reviewer errors, misunderstandings, and technical corrective measures taken by the author or vendor. Ensure this piece receives widespread internet distribution to appropriate sites.

MEASURING YOUR REVIEWS

Other than reading your reviews and exercising common sense, a popular means of judging the amount (and to some extent "quality") of the press your product is receiving is to use a clipping service. These companies read the major daily and weekly newspapers, magazines, and trade publications; monitor the wire services, radio, network and cable television news broadcasts; and scan the various Internet forums and SIGs that discuss your product. They clip all articles, tape every broadcast that mentions any subject important to their clients, and even transcribe Internet gripe sessions. Most of these companies offer a range of services, including tallying the number of inches devoted to a company and its products, day-of-publication delivery, historical research, news clip analysis of public relations performance, advertising analysis of competitors, Internet activity analysis, and foreign press monitoring. New services specialize in total Internet scans, and look for every mention of your product in every Usenet group, SIG, forum, and web site.

Whichever route you take, the important thing to remember is that the product review cycle is unending; therefore, results and feedback should be factored in on an ongoing basis to continually improve the process, as well as your relationship with the reviewers.

PUBLIC RELATIONS AND PRODUCT REVIEW PROGRAMS
OBJECTIVES/EVALUATION CHECKLIST

OBJECTIVES	EVALUATION

1. Generate positive company image

positive articles, mentions,
   etc., in press   _____ _____ _____

press interviews with key
   development and
   marketing personnel   _____ _____ _____

2. Generate positive product launch coverage

publications carrying
launch announcement   _____ _____ _____

first-look stories   _____ _____ _____

feature stories   _____ _____ _____

user groups addressed   _____ _____ _____

attendees at special
launch events   _____ _____ _____

evaluation products
distributed   _____ _____ _____

Favorable mentions on
the Internet   _____ _____ _____

    World Wide Web   _____ _____ _____

    Usenet   _____ _____ _____

    SIGs/Forums on services   _____ _____ _____

    AOL   _____ _____ _____

    Compuserve   _____ _____ _____

    Prodigy   _____ _____ _____

    Other   _____ _____ _____

    _____ _____ _____

3. Generate favorable product reviews

highly favorable
   product reviews   _____ _____ _____

favorable product
   reviews   _____ _____ _____

unfavorable reviews   _____ _____ _____

OBJECTIVES	EVALUATION		

3. Generate favorable product reviews (continued)

Key favorable product feature(s) in reviews _____ _____ _____

Key unfavorable product feature(s) in reviews _____ _____ _____

4. Manage, mitigate, and eliminate poor product reviews

 # highly unfavorable reviews _____ _____ _____

% bugs/problems fixed in product _____ _____ _____

% review errors corrected _____ _____ _____

PUBLIC RELATIONS AND PRODUCT REVIEW PROGRAMS SUCCESS CHECKLIST

PRE-ANNOUNCEMENT PHASE

1. Determine who will provide PR services

- ☐ External vendor _____ . _____
- ☐ In-house department or staff _____

2. Assign PR coordinator

- ☐ PR Specialist _____
- ☐ Product Marketing _____

3. Develop and implement Internet and World Wide Web PR strategy

A. Develop "flaming" procedures and policies

- ☐ Response to "difficult" respondents _____
- ☐ No flaming on company time or equipment _____
- ☐ Sites to be avoided by non-authorized company personnel _____

B. Develop monitoring policy for

- ☐ SIGs/Forums _____
- ☐ Web Sites _____
- ☐ Usenet groups _____

C. Assign individuals to appropriate sites

3. Develop and implement review management process

A. Assign individual to manage review process and create team from:

- ☐ PR _____
- ☐ Product Marketing _____
- ☐ Support _____
- ☐ Development _____
- ☐ Senior Management _____

B. Establish meeting schedule _____

C. Create/update product reviewer database _____

D. Create/update product review guide and conduct internal product briefing

- ☐ Position product _____
- ☐ Profile intended user _____
- ☐ Include supporting materials and testimony _____

☐ Include company contact names and phone numbers_____

☐ Include names of beta users, key developers, influencers, etc. _____

E. Establish contingency program for bad reviews_____

F. Identify and assign product review company contacts_____

G. Establish feedback reporting procedure _____

H. Establish problem management procedure _____

I. Establish Internet PR and review search procedures _____

J. Subscribe to media services

☐ Clipping service_____

☐ Editorial Service _____ _____

K. Prepare evaluation product for distribution to reviewers _____

4. Identify key influencers and arrange interview schedule(s)

☐ Press_____

☐ Consultants_____

☐ User groups_____

☐ Newsletters _____

☐ Vertical market specialists _____

☐ Internal organizations (e.g., SIGs, user groups)_____

☐ Beta users _____

5. Establish beta test plan

☐ Select beta sites (key influencers, developers, corporate users)_____

☐ Complete nondisclosure agreements _____

☐ Ship beta product_____

☐ Collect and analyze beta feedback _____

6. Obtain key editorial calendars/schedules from authors and/or media services

☐ Reviews _____

☐ Reference stories _____

☐ Buyers' guides_____

7. Prepare press releases

8. Prepare Q&As _____

9. Prepare press kits

   A. **Determine quantity** _____

   B. **Plan distribution to coincide with announce day**

    ☐ Press kits must arrive one week in advance for weekly publications _____

    ☐ Other press kits can arrive on announce day_____

   C. **Develop contents**

    ☐ Backgrounder _____

    ☐ White paper _____

    ☐ Product release statement _____

    ☐ 35mm slide(s) _____

    ☐ Electronic images _____

    ☐ Testimonials _____

    ☐ Output samples _____

    ☐ Demo disk _____

    ☐ B&W glossies_____

    ☐ Color glossies _____

    ☐ Other _____

10. **Design and plan announce-day activities**

   A. **Arrange for press interviews with key development and marketing personnel**

   B. **Plan press conference**

    ☐ Prepare speech _____

    ☐ Select and train speakers _____

    ☐ Select/acquire conference facility _____

    ☐ Prepare demo _____

    ☐ Select and invite attendees _____

ANNOUNCEMENT-DAY PHASE

1. **Distribute press releases (1000+ over wire)** _____

2. **Hold press conference**

    ☐ Distribute press kits to attendees _____

    ☐ Mail press kits to non-attendees_____

3. **Conduct interviews with press (in person or on phone)**

    ☐ Key development personnel _____

    ☐ Key marketing personnel_____

POST-ANNOUNCEMENT PHASE (1-6 months)

1. **Conduct Press Tours**
    - ☐ Arrange for tour schedule _____
    - ☐ Pick tour participants _____

2. **Conduct more press interviews with key development and marketing personnel** _____
    _____

3. **Move product review management process into high gear**
    - ☐ Read all reviews and correct mistakes _____
    - ☐ Correct review errors and send letters to the editors _____
    - ☐ Read reviews of other products in your category/class _____
    - ☐ Prepare review corrective white paper _____
    - ☐ Set up and implement calling schedule for editors, reviewers, etc. _____

4. **Produce/place reference success stories** _____

5. **Implement tracking system for follow-up**
    - ☐ Develop quick-response mechanism for press and influencer inquiries _____
    - ☐ Track all inquiries and responses _____
    - ☐ Deliver and track evaluation product _____

6. **Ongoing activities**
    - ☐ Update reviewer database _____
    - ☐ Update product review guide _____

5

Advertising

Designing, buying, and placing conventional advertising is a frustrating experience for many software publishers. Advertising is expensive and takes a big bite out of tight marketing budgets. No one agrees on what makes a good ad. Magazines and web sites can measure circulation but must be blackmailed into providing response data. Many publishers secretly suspect that a full-page ad, run in black-and-white with block letters proclaiming "The product is good—buy it and stop wasting our time!" would probably work as well as a fancy agency-generated ad based on solid demographic research and loaded with the latest psychological cues. And in some cases, they're right.

DOES ADVERTISING WORK?

This may seem an odd question when you look at the major computer publications; their pages are overflowing with ads from a variety of software firms, both large and small. Clearly, these publishers believe their expenditures are generating a return on their investment.

However, what ads often generate is product awareness, not product sales. The constraints of space, money, and competitive pressure make conventional advertising a rather ineffective direct-response mechanism. After all, you're not the only company advertising. You're probably not the only one advertising in your product category.

Many small publishers make the mistake of placing an ad with the expectation that orders will start pouring in when the piece breaks. Instead, they are inundated with inquiries about the product, the company, where the product can be seen, requests for more information, etc. Other marketing elements, such as retail availability, product review programs, quality collaterals, direct and electronic mail programs, direct selling programs, etc., must already be in place for your advertising to work.

Measuring Advertising's Effectiveness

Standards for measuring advertising cost and ROI exist, and can serve as useful guidelines when planning an ad campaign. Some companies use a cost efficiency (CE) model, which defines the relative balance of effectively meeting reach and frequency goals at the best price. More common is the cost per rating point (CPP) system: the cost per one percent of buying advertising space in a given publication or venue. Most widely used is the cost per thousand (CPM) yardstick: the cost per 1000 people of buying advertising space in a given publication or media vehicle, derived by dividing the number of subscribers by the placement cost.

Where advertising does function as a direct-response vehicle, acceptable response rates normally range between .025% and 1%; the 2% to 3% figures seen in conventional direct mail are a rarity. Frequency of placement, type of publication, competitive factors, and editorial reviews all impact response rates.

In theory, therefore, your advertising ROI should be easy to calculate; simply track the number of sales or inquiries generated by your ad, divide by the number of subscribers, and you have your response rate. Total up your sales from the ad, subtract your ad costs and *voila*! You have your ROI.

Alas, reality is more complicated as there are many factors that make calculating advertising ROI very difficult indeed.

- Tracking sales through your channel. If a substantial amount of your product is sold via the channel, it is difficult to measure direct sales responses to advertising.
- The frequency of your advertising. On average, you must place an ad a minimum of three times to reach between 10% and 20% of the publication's readership. Size and number of ads in each issue, as well as how many competitors also advertise in its pages, affect this reach. It takes six to nine months of repeated placements to ensure that at least 60% to 70% of the

readership sees and reads your ad at least once. This means it can take months of repeat placements before you see sales increase as a result of your advertising.

- The publication's pass-along-rate. Some publications are handed off to other readers after the subscriber is finished, substantially altering your CPM calculations.

- The audience delivered. You may find that despite charts, surveys, and demographics demonstrating that a particular publication or media vehicle seems to be a perfect fit for your product, reality will prove otherwise. And in many cases, the only way to find this out is to experiment over time with different times and types of placement.

- The number of publications and media vehicles in which you are advertising. If you're running the same ad in three publications simultaneously, how do you determine performance by publication?

- The editorial terrain of the publication. For instance, the author once consulted with a company that was considering advertising in a major computer publication. Shortly before the ads were placed, the publication ran a review of the vendor's product category, and recommended that customers not purchase this type of product. Needless to say, the ads were placed in other publications.

Often, the most effective means of measuring response to an ad is by post-sales surveys. These surveys are useful for measuring ad awareness, the impact of your marketing message, and your position in the marketplace *v.a.v.* your competition. However, even surveys are not always able to precisely measure your advertising ROI. Of course, you should always code each and every ad you place. Without a code, tracking performance becomes a far more difficult task.

However, measuring advertising ROI is much easier in some markets and situations; for example, those distinguished by:

- A direct selling model with no channel.
- A highly focused niche or market audience.
- A limited number of appropriate publications or other vehicles in which to advertise.
- A limited amount of competition in your market.

However, these exceptions are usually short-lived. As your company and your market grow, you will inevitably need to employ other marketing mechanisms and perhaps develop a distribution channel; as you do, measuring advertising ROI will become more difficult.

THE IMPACT OF THE INTERNET ON ADVERTISING

The Internet has had far less impact on conventional advertising than first predicted. Its most famous contribution to advertising, the banner, has been over-hyped while under-performing for many publishers. It's also been an expensive addition to the marketing mix, with average banner CPM costs between $35 and $40 per thousand, while conventional print ads range between $5 and $20. In addition, the early promises that Internet ads would allow advertisers to immediately capture customer demographics while providing precise information on ROI have not yet been realized. Still, used properly, banners can generate incremental sales and increased market awareness, and they will play an increasingly greater role in the marketing equation. Please refer to the *Electronic Marketing* chapter of the *Handbook* for a more detailed discussion.

THE ADVERTISING FRAMEWORK

Advertising high-tech products requires a solid conceptual framework of how, where and why advertising works. The high-tech industry is littered with unsuccessful and ineffectual ads that were developed by professionals and placed at reasonable prices. To create successful ads, you must understand both the psychological and the physical mechanics of advertising. Only then can you begin to fashion advertising that effectively manages and shapes a buyer's perception of your company and products.

To that end, we have developed a new paradigm for understanding, creating, and evaluating your advertising. Using this structured approach, you will be able to classify ads, understand their basic emotional appeal, analyze their fundamental components, and examine the psychological world in which buying decisions take place. Armed with this new "ad space" model, you will create ads that attract and persuade customers to buy your products.

AD TYPES

There are only two kinds of ads: those that sell a company, and those that sell a product. The purpose of selling a company is to enhance the company's image and ultimately build brand equity, making it more likely that a prospective customer will buy the company's products and/or be willing to pay more for them. These ads usually focus on one of three themes:

- We're big.
- We're better.
- We're going to be around.

Do they work? Unless you can bring overwhelming force to the marketplace, as in the case of large companies such as Microsoft, Intel, or IBM, they are probably not worth the expense. Buyers tend to focus more on functionality and price issues and less on who the company is. In addition, the computer market has proven to be a bad place to brag about your longevity and invincibility. Remember Wang, Atari, Commodore, VisiCorp, MicroPro, or Ashton-Tate? High flyers like Borland and Corel have had their wings clipped, mega star Netscape was forced into AOL's embrace, mighty IBM has been humbled, and even Microsoft is concerned about Linux. Unless you have the deepest of pockets, you don't have the money to run these ads.

To understand why ads attract and persuade people to buy certain products, let's examine the four basic ad types: **transformational**, **transferal**, **protective**, and **assuagement**.

Transformational

A transformational ad is the most powerful of the four types as it literally promises to change you from one thing to another. Some of the most compelling examples of transformational ads are found in religious advertising. The power TV evangelists have over their followers and the seeming ease with which they coax dollars from their mainly blue-collar audiences is quite astounding. At their core, religious ads promise to hurl the devil from your body, scrub your soul clean enough to allow you to enter heaven, and, in some cases, cure you of physical sickness. A very powerful claim, and one with universal and eternal appeal.

Children are always receptive to transformational ads. Many successful children's toys and publications focus on transformation; indeed, a popular line of toys is called "Transformers." Most successful comic books portray an ordinary individual transformed into a superhero or heroine via bites from radioactive spiders, exposure to chemicals, visitations from aliens, or something equally fantastical.

And secular adults are hardly immune to the power of transformational advertising. A quick look at the plethora of ads for cosmetic potions that promise to turn the middle aged into fresh-faced youngsters, and exercise devices that will transform couch potatoes into muscular athletes confirms this. The eternal appeal of these ads can be judged by shopping at any outlet or garage sale, where last year's ab smasher, herbal panacea, and miracle cream can be picked up at a fraction of their original price, replaced by this year's biceps pounder and miracle vitamin.

Despite its undoubted power, transformational advertising has been infrequently used in business software marketing, though some Internet advertising has edged close to the promise of creating a new you via a web browser and E-commerce. Transformational ads are more common in the gaming and entertainment markets, though they are almost always delivered with humor and a tongue-in-cheek attitude.

Transferal

The transferal ad promises to provide a desired attribute or property to the buyer in return for an actual purchase. The most common promise is money, or "value." Other promises may include "knowledge" and "power." Of course, the promise of transformation or protection is always implicit in a transferal ad, but it is at least once removed from the initial purchase. For instance, that new presentation package may allow you to create better presentations and that may lead to a promotion, which may lead you to being transformed into the president of the company. Transferal ads are the most popular type in most industries, with the notable exceptions of healthcare and insurance.

Protective

Protective ads provide a shield against a perceived danger or threat. They generate a type of fear often referred to as "friendly fear." The threat is real, and is personified through imagery and description, but the ad always offers a safe solution. (There's not much point to scaring your audience if you're not prepared to help them out.) Classic examples of these ads are found in the medical and insurance industries. They're also popular in the computer industry, where protection against power failure, viruses, being stuck with yesterday's product, lagging behind the technology curve, etc., speak to the fears of buyers everywhere.

Assuagement

An assuagement ad seeks to "make it up" to a consumer who is perceived to be abused by a product, company, or fate. The ads from Exxon Corporation after the Valdez disaster are classic examples of assuagement advertising. Pure assuagement ads are rare in most industries. However, attack ads, a variation of the assuagement ad, were popular in the late 1970s and early 1980s. A typical attack ad assigns the role of victimizer to another party, then selflessly offers your product as the remedy for the beleaguered customer's ills. Attack ads are rarely used in software marketing, though Microsoft has been known to deploy them.

Advantages and Disadvantages

Each ad type has its advantages and drawbacks. While transformational advertising is powerful, it also strains credibility. God or an ab smasher may be able to change who you are, but can software?

Transferal ads are safer, but because they are so common, they get lost in the clutter. Everyone promises value—performance—ease of use. It's boring and repetitive, and advertisers rarely offer creditable proof of their claims.

Protective ads rely on people's fears—particularly their feelings of personal inadequacy. Yes, we will die, and we should take steps to protect our loved ones. Your hard drive will crash, and therefore you really should back-up to the Internet. But these are depressing thoughts, and people tend not to spend their money when they're depressed.

Assuagement ads are often associated with goofs, foul-ups, and disasters. Who wants to deal with these? And attack ads have always suffered credibility problems, and leave the attacker vulnerable to a counterstrike.

Few ads are pure examples of any one type; most combine elements of each. For example, many religious ads advertise salvation at a relatively inexpensive price (transform your life **and** save money). An ad for a power supply may also promote the bundled software utility or game (protection and transferal).

Ad Components

All ads are built from the same basic components:

- Design elements.
- Information items.
- Emotional resonators.
- Corporate or brand identifier.

Design elements are either tactile (in the broader sense of conveying the illusion of tangibility) or visual.

Tactile elements include:

- Smell (e.g., scratch n' sniff).

- Touch (e.g., fur and cloth samples).
- Sound (e.g., bundled music chips).
- Sight (e.g., LEDs, glow strips).

Visual Elements include:

- Color.
- Type.
- Drawing.
- Photography (Images).
- Animation.
- Video/Film.

Information Items

Information items inform the buyer of key facts about the product and its positioning. Ads aimed at selling a product focus on:

- Product price.
- Where it can be purchased.
- Key positioning information.
- Key statistics or facts about the product.

While ads aimed at selling a company highlight:

- Company size and location(s).
- Products sold by the company.
- Key industry markets.
- Endorsements from other companies.

Emotional Resonators

Emotional resonators result from combining design elements and information to produce the ad's emotional tone. The most popular emotional resonators are:

- Empathy/Sympathy.
- Fear.
- Value (or, if you're cynical, greed).

- Humor.
- Sexual Attraction.
- Shock.

The most common emotional resonator used in software advertising, indeed, in all advertising, is value. Value is most often defined by money, though sometimes time and productivity are substituted for cash. While value claims are always of interest to a prospective buyer, they are also overused and lack impact.

The next most common emotional resonator is humor; it is considered safe, and people like to buy things when they're amused and feeling good. However, humor is hard to do well. If you doubt this, take a look at the ad copy in any PC publication and count the number of times you even smile when reading through ostensibly funny copy.

Power is also popular in high-tech advertising, where the larger your microprocessor, the larger your other attributes. Like value, power claims are overused, but they can be subjected to objective analysis in the software industry. There are people who must have the latest and greatest, and if you demonstrate you have it, they will pay for it.

Fear must be handled carefully. It is always easy to go overboard and exceed the boundaries of good taste and acceptability. If you're going to invoke friendly fear, you had better be ready to offer a completely creditable solution or you're simply going to scare people away.

Sex is an eternally powerful emotional resonator and is widely used in many industries. Not, however, in U.S. software publishing, which is a full of political correctness. It should be noted, however, that ads with sexually attractive people featured in them tend to do well everywhere.

Shock is used from time to time, but of all emotional resonators, this is the most dangerous. Famous shock ads include the Hayes "exploding modem" piece where Hayes claimed that other modems could abruptly drop off line, "blowing up" your data. It outraged many. Another even more egregious example was the "Feels Good," Feels Better" campaign run by a company whose name we won't mention out of pity. One ad in this series pictured a baby urinating. It outraged **and** disgusted many.

Most ads mix different emotional different resonators. Which one predominates depends on the product, the concept, and the goal.

CORPORATE OR BRAND IDENTIFIER

The corporate or brand identifier in an ad tells the customer who created the ad and transmits its brand equity to the product. Most ads include this component, usually nothing more than the company name and logo, because buyers want to know who made what they're buying.

A strong brand identifier in your advertising can be a two-edged sword. If your brand equity turns negative, either through misfortune or by a competitive attack, your product advertising can be heavily affected. For example, when Borland's positive brand equity turned negative due to its ongoing and well-publicized financial woes, developers began abandoning its programming tools—not because these products received poor reviews or couldn't create professional applications—but because the developers did not want to rely on products that might soon be market orphans.

In some cases, your ad may also be required to incorporate a partner's brand component. For the vendors who participate in the "Intel Inside" branding campaign, the advantage is very tangible–they're paid to use the Intel logo and jingle in their ads. The intangible benefits include, in theory, increased credibility, increased interest in the product, and a more powerful ad.

TRADITIONAL ADVERTISING MODEL

Now that we've examined the basics of ad types and their components, we need to understand the psychological interaction between advertising and potential buyers. An objective look at both the process and culture of advertising in America reveals a strange dichotomy: there is tremendous distaste for advertising. Agencies are often portrayed as swamps of intrigue and venality. The models and actors are empty-headed airheads. The artists are flacks. Everyone is embarrassed to work in advertising, and hopes one day to do something truly worthwhile with their lives.

Yet, most of us like advertising. (Even while noisily proclaiming how much we hate it.) We watch ads all the time. We respond to their inducements. We remember and discuss them. We use their music, design, and "stories" to mark the passage of time and memorable events in our lives and society.

The key to this dichotomy lies in the traditional advertising model. Fundamentally intrusive, it regards the mind of the buyer as an obstacle to be overcome. This metaphor is reflected in the jargon: an ad is designed to "get into" a person's head, "break through", or "grab" the buyer by the throat. The objectives of the traditional advertising model can be described as stalk, immobilize, penetrate, and conquer.

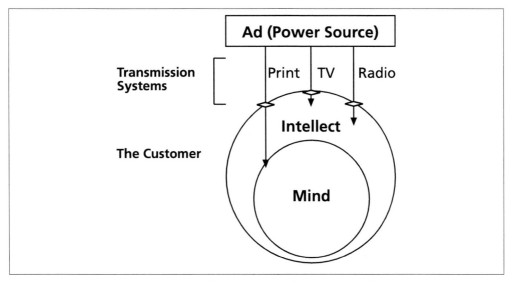

Figure 5-1. The Traditional Advertising Model

This approach runs directly afoul of some of our most primeval fears. We all possess a strong aversion to aggressive intrusions into our mind or body. Most people who saw "Alien" will never forget the famous "chest burster" scene, where the creature springs out of the body of its hapless victim. "The Manchurian Candidate," wherein a Medal of Honor winner is revealed to be a brainwashed assassin, exemplifies our fear of the ability of modern science to "get into" our heads and make us act against our will. In the mythology of "Max Headroom," the world's first virtual celebrity (and now a virtual has-been) was a by-product of an evil corporation's creation of "blip verts," subliminal ads that made your head explode. (Insert your own joke here.)

The Ad Space Environment

But despite the imaginings of advertising mavens everywhere, no ad has the power to "get into" our head. We do not perceive ads "in" our mind, but rather "outside" of it, in a virtual showroom we call the "ad space" environment. Here, the buyer is always in control—interacting with the product, projecting the consequences of their purchase, and deciding whether or not to do it. Effective marketers understand the reality of this environment, and design ads to take advantage of its unique properties. They understand that ad space is fundamentally a collaboration between the imagination of the ad's creator and the buyers who interact with it.

THE AD SPACE MODEL

The ad space model depicts a highly dynamic environment with three components: the **siren**, the **portal**, and the **ad space proper**.

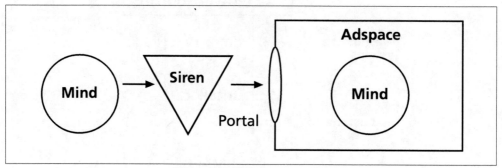

Figure 5-2. The ad space model

The Siren

The first thing an ad must do is attract the viewer into the virtual showroom. This is achieved by combining information items, design elements, and emotional resonators into an image or message that halts the eye and entices the viewer into the ad space environment. We call this component of the ad space model the "siren," and like the Greek creature of myth, an effective siren is one that is irresistible.

Creating the Siren

More time and attention are paid to creating the siren than to any other component of model. This emphasis makes a lot of sense; if buyers don't enter your virtual showroom, they can't make a buying decision. Which visual and tactile elements are used to create an effective siren depends on the type of product, audience target, competitive issues, and current fashion. For example, in the cosmetics industry, the use of tactile elements is fairly common, despite their relatively high expense. Experience has shown that if you're selling a new perfume, it is very effective to allow potential buyers to smell it before they buy it.

The use of tactile elements is very rare in software advertising, though a recent game in Seirra's **Gabriel Knight** series used a blinking LED on the packaging to attract attention. While most of us don't care about sweet smelling software or fuzzy office suites, the Internet places sophisticated animation, video, film, and complex music elements, heretofore only available to companies large enough to afford TV and radio advertising, within reach of many software publishers. Combined with virtual reality modeling language (VRML) settings and techniques, Internet advertising has the potential to reach levels of "tangibility" never before experienced. A few years from now, when conventional modems are no longer the standard for connecting to the Web, some of this potential may be realized.

In the meantime, the software industry relies heavily on visual elements and information items to create sirens. Most common is the combination of type and image, although you can find some sirens that are constructed from pure design elements. Network Associates' ad for their active firewall product, in Figure 5-3, is an excellent example of combining information, typography, and imagery to create a compelling siren. The ad is a protective type, and employs a striking image that creates an emotional resonator of friendly fear.

Figure 5-3. An effective siren

The Portal

Once the siren has captured the attention of your potential customer, he or she has to be convinced to enter the ad space. This is the job of the "portal," the key information items and emotional resonators that provide the rationale to enter and "shop" further. In a conventional print ad, a portal is often represented by a subheading combined with a product picture, drawing, or similar visual element.

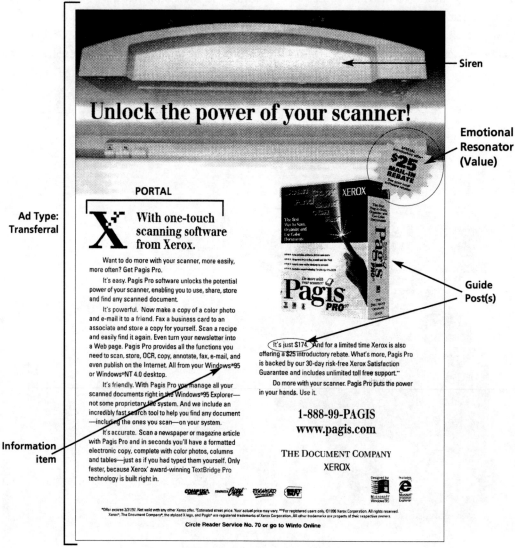

Figure 5-5. Xerox Pagis Pro Ad

For example, let's examine an ad for Xerox's Pagis Pro (see Figure 5-5), an OCR and document management product. The product's siren is a combination of visual image and text proclaiming "Unlock the power of your scanner." This siren makes strong use of color, a loud chartreuse that contrasts sharply with black text. The portal is built from the sub-heading "With one-touch scanning software from Xerox." This is a basic information item with a low emotional resonator.

The portal is also where the buyer interacts with the ad's type. In the Xerox ad, no claim is made that the buyer's life will significantly change as a result of using their scanner software. They aren't offering protection. And Xerox isn't apologizing for anything. By default, the ad is a transferal one; the product promises to transfer the power of easy scanning to the customer.

Of course, a shift in the situation could change the nature of this ad. For instance, you could design a protective ad that showed a burnt house, burnt documents, a scanner, and an optical disk in a vault. The portal's message would then point out how much easier it is to settle insurance claims when a homeowner's valuable documents are scanned and stored someplace safe. (We don't claim this is a good idea for an ad; it's just an example of how you might use similar elements in an ad of a different type.)

Establishing Emotional Resonance

The portal is also where the ad's emotional resonance is established. The Xerox ad has almost no emotional resonance. (It's difficult to become overly passionate about scanning software, though the product's nature might lend itself to an injection of humor.) In this piece, a gentle appeal to power is the prevalent resonator. The ad does establish that its informational content will be fairly high, as one would expect when discussing this category of product.

The Dynamics of Ad Space

Once buyers cross the portal's threshold and enter the ad space proper, they begin to incorporate the ad's components into their buying decision. The ultimate goal once they are in ad space is to persuade them that their purchase will match the happiness and satisfaction they experience in ad space. Interestingly enough, even when reality does not match the pleasures of the imagination, the memory of an effective ad can still persuade the buyer that the purchase was ultimately justified.

As buyers move through ad space, their imagination interacts with your ad's components, giving rise to highly individual and subjective experiences. Even though no two viewers will have the same experience, most ad space sojourners look for certain guideposts to help them in their buying decision.

The first guide post is information about the product category or price. Next may come a hunt for the box, or other appropriate physical representation of the product (or service). This search for the physical is important for psychological reasons, especially in the case of a new company or new product as it provides reassurance that the product is real.

Unfortunately, many ads are often marred by huge, overblown shots of the product's box. The customer is not that interested in your packaging and the space can be put to better use providing more "room" for the customer to move around in the ad space. In most cases, a simple proportional picture is enough.

There are, of course, exceptions. For instance, in the September 1997 issue of *Windows Publication*, an ad for Safeguard Interactive's Backup featured an over-sized picture of the box, which was deliberately designed to look massive and safe; it even had a bank door on the front. The ad was a protective type, offering to save the customer from data loss, and the design enhanced the ad's message.

After stopping at the guideposts, buyers next create a series of internal dialogues and buying simulations where they interact directly with your product. To a large extent, ad type determines the nature and direction of these simulations. For example, a transformational ad encourages buyers to directly "see" how they will feel and look after they purchase the product. Some cosmetics ads have even combined product samples with little mirrors built directly into the piece so the buyers can directly experience their newly youthful appearance or improved skin tone. Less dramatic elements and resonators may include pictures of people who appear to be changed or transfigured by their purchase.

The internal journey through a transferal ad is more concrete, as you would expect. These ads often help the buyer visualize a task completed, an item created, or money saved. A wide variety of visual elements are appropriate for this type of internal dynamic: bulleted points, pictures, and quotes from users or reviewers.

Like transformational ads, protective ads also encourage the buyer to visualize reality in a personal way. Visual elements that include images of children or that appeal to health, safety, and security are often integrated into these ads. The Safeguard ad is a good example of this; a bank vault is a quintessential image of safety. The virtual reality the ad hopes to create in the customer's mind is the safety and satisfaction experienced from knowing something important is locked away in an impenetrable safe. In the Network Associates ad, most buyers would transform the image of the vulnerable guard into an invulnerable one who can protect an Internet server from any attack.

Assuagement ads are tricky to develop, and tend to be devoid of almost all visual elements (except in the case of the attack piece). For instance, Exxon's ads after the oil spill were all text, with minimal design elements. What, after all, was Exxon going to show? Happy petroleum-coated birds? The pretty rainbows you can see in an oil slick? In many cases, the objective of an assuagement ad is limiting the customer's internal mental journey, and **not** encouraging additional scenarios (like lawsuits).

FOCUS STORY: "THE WORST SOFTWARE AD OF ALL TIME"
Company
Intuit

Product
QuickBooks

Company Background

Intuit's Quicken changed the way millions of PC users manage their personal finances. Capitalizing on this success, they introduced QuickBooks into the small business accounting market in 1992. But this market was more competitive than the personal finance niche Intuit dominated, and Intuit decided to develop an ad campaign to make QuickBooks stand out. Intuit employed the traditional advertising model of reaching out and grabbing their audience by their throats. To distinguish their product from the competition, and inject some excitement into what is not normally a market associated with high-energy advertising, Intuit created what their own CEO, Scott Cook described publicly as "the worst software ad ever created."

The ad can best be described as a celebration of "extreme accounting." It combined loud colors, jazzy type, and a radical-looking bald fellow, the type you might see with tattoos and body piercing gyrating in a cyber punk band's mosh pit.

The ad generated exactly one response and was quickly pulled—no one was interested in extreme accounting. Their new print ads were more conventional, and a short-form infomercial for QuickBooks featured mild-looking yuppies with full heads of hair and no tattoos or body piercings. As of this writing, QuickBooks is the leading product in the small business accounting category.

LESSONS

The problem with Intuit's initial approach should be apparent. People who buy accounting software are not interested in radical anything when it comes to their money and they don't want anyone grabbing their throats. Think about the possible scenarios the ad was creating in the minds of potential buyers. Imagine their virtual meeting with the extreme accountant; it must have been an unsettling experience. The accountants we meet in the real world tend to be conservative in dress and demeanor, reassuring us that they are managing our money in safe and conservative ways. An ad whose siren and ad space dynamic are so at odds with an audience's expectations and desires is bound to fail.

WHERE TO ADVERTISE

Over the last several years the computer publication market has undergone extensive segmentation. In addition to the major general-purpose publications, such as *PC World* and *PC Magazine,* new publications have emerged to serve:

- Database developers and users
- Direct purchasers
- Entertainment
- Enterprise management
- Home office
- The Internet
- Linux
- Multimedia
- Networking
- Notebook users
- PC novices
- Software development
- Web management and development
- Windows
- Windows NT
- Wireless and handheld communications

CHANNEL ADVERTISING

In addition to end-user publications, ads are also placed in channel publications such, as *Smart Reseller* or *VAR Business* in support of a channel MDF program. It is important to understand that these ads are not intended to generate end-user sales or inquiries—they help "push" products through the channel to the end user.

Selecting the Right Vehicle

The dilemma facing marketing managers is deciding how best to reach their target audiences. Placing an ad in a major publication like *PC Magazine* is an obvious tactic, but the expense and noise levels are high (about $40K for a one-page, one-time, four-color ad). Using more highly focused books may be a better way to target your market. Consider the following when choosing your placements:

- What is the publication's circulation?
- What is the publication's target audience? This is especially important when comparing general-purpose publications. For example, are there basic differences between the readers of *PC Magazine* and *PC World?*
- What are the readership demographics, including:
    - Age ranges
    - Gender
    - Income levels
    - Education
    - Job descriptions and responsibilities
    - Buying habits
    - Price sensitivity
    - Geographic location

There are no hard and fast rules; experience and common sense must be used in making placement decisions.

AD COSTS

Ad costs are affected by many factors, including:

- Color vs. black-and-white. A black-and-white ad costs between 25% and 50% less than a comparably sized color ad. Of course, color has more impact on a reader's eye and is more likely to be noticed.

- The size and circulation of the publication. Prices for full-page ads in niche-market publications range between $5K and $40K per page. The larger the circulation, the more expensive the ad.

- Ad size. The most common sizes are 1/4-page, 1/2-page, and full-page.

- Integrating supporting collateral into the ad, such as bingo cards or demo disks.

- Discounts for multiple placements. This is always a tricky subject with publishers. Depending on the ad's size, position (inside the front and back covers and in the middle are the most coveted spots), frequency, and placement in other publications owned by the publisher, discounts can range as high as 50%. Often, publications offer value-added marketing services in lieu of discounts. These can include basic research, surveys, focus groups, marketing consulting, etc. The number of ads placed and their frequency determine the type and availability of such extras.

- Co-op placement. When it is mutually beneficial, larger companies may assist smaller publishers in placing ads.

- Barter arrangements. While most publications are reluctant to publicize these programs, opportunities do exist to trade product for ad space. In some cases, fulfillment is done directly by the publishing side of the publication; in others, a third party handles it. In most barter deals, the publication receives all revenue from product sales until the ad placement is paid for. Revenue from additional product sale is then paid to the publisher or split between the publisher and the publication. Barter arrangements are usually offered only to new companies that the publication believes may "grow up" to be regular advertisers.

Before placing an ad, always request the publication's media kit, which should outline the publication's rates, readership, demographics, and value-added services. In addition, media directories can also help you with the ad-placement evaluation process.

Advertising Frequency

Once you decide to launch a major ad campaign, the ability to advertise consistently over a period of time is vital for the campaign's success. If you have to choose, it is better to run a 1/4-page ad every month for a year rather than a full-page ad three times a year. On average, readers must see an ad three times before it begins to sink into their consciousness.

Working With an Ad Agency

There are two reasons to use an ad agency for an advertising program. The first is ad quality. Many smaller publishers attempt to create their own ads, and it usually shows. Creating an attractive, appealing ad looks deceptively simple but is actually quite difficult. Ads by amateurs often use unappealing or out-of-date typefaces, contain typos, are clumsily laid out, and lack key information items, such as prices, addresses, and phone numbers.

The second reason is managing the negotiation and placement process. A good ad agency will have established working relationships with the different publications and alternate ad vehicles. They will have a good feel for the different market segments they address and their demographics. Agencies know the discount structure, how to negotiate favorable rates, and which value added-services may be worth considering.

MANAGING THE AGENCY

When you hire an ad agency, you have taken on a strategic partner, who needs to learn about your company and your products. They need to understand their positioning, target audience, features and benefits, strengths and weaknesses with respect to the competition, future release plans, and so forth. For this relationship to be successful, an agency must be managed almost as if it were an integral part of your company.

It is foolish and dangerous to think that an ad agency provides turnkey services. You must expect to supervise and/or participate in every aspect of your advertising—from design, to copy, to printing. Pay particular attention to proofing copy. Every year a major publisher or vendor places an ad that contains inappropriate or incorrect copy. The only way to prevent this is to proof, then proof again, and then final proof any and all copy with your company's name on it.

Agencies have even been known to design ads that don't ask for the sale or allow the buyer to purchase your product. Your phone number or web site address should appear in readable type in a prominent place in the ad—making it easy for the buyer to call or contact you and make the purchase. It is a mistake to simply refer the buyer to a local reseller. Even if your product is sold exclusively through a channel, you should always allow the buyer to contact you to begin the purchase process. Some buyers will be ready to buy immediately after seeing the ad. Always be ready to clear the way for the sale.

Because of the critical nature of the publisher/agency relationship, we have included a special questionnaire, in addition to the checklists, to help improve your marketing focus and assess an agency's overall performance.

Use the Review Summary to provide a quick overview of the agency's performance. If you feel you need a more detailed look, the optional in-depth survey will help you pinpoint the agency's strengths and weaknesses. You may also find it useful to fill out the overall summary and supplement it with those portions of the in-depth survey that deal with specific issues or problem areas.

ADVERTISING OBJECTIVES/EVALUATION CHECKLIST

OBJECTIVES	EVALUATION

Marketing Goals

1. Increase product sales from baseline

    # sales _____ _____ _____

    # leads generated _____ _____ _____

    # leads converted to sales _____ _____ _____

    # product inquiries _____ _____ _____

    # bounce-back inquiries _____ _____ _____

2. Generate favorable company image

    # positive articles,
    mentions, etc., in press _____ _____ _____

    # press interviews with
    key personnel _____ _____ _____

3. Increase pull through channel from baseline

    % increased SKUs shipped
    to channel _____ _____ _____

Audience

1. Reach target audience

    # responses to coded ads _____ _____ _____

Budget

1. Reduce ad costs

    % discount received _____ _____ _____

    # value-added services
    received _____ _____ _____

ADVERTISING SUCCESS CHECKLIST

1. **Develop advertising strategy, including objectives, budget, and schedule** _____

2. **Obtain approvals**
   - ☐ Product Marketing _____
   - ☐ Finance _____
   - ☐ Senior Management_____

3. **Assign advertising coordinator**
   - ☐ Ad specialist _____
   - ☐ Product Marketing _____

4. **Choose either in-house or outside ad services**_____

5. **Select advertising agency**

   A. **Use the following criteria:**
   - ☐ Experience with microcomputer software industry_____
   - ☐ Creative abilities _____
   - ☐ Industry relationships _____
   - ☐ Cost control _____
   - ☐ Research abilities (statistical, etc.)_____
   - ☐ Responsiveness _____
   - ☐ Ability to conduct focus groups and surveys _____

   B. **Brief agency on product, audience, objectives, etc.** _____

   C. **Set production schedule from development through ad placement**_____

   D. **Define tasks, deliverables, responsibilities, etc.** _____

   E. **Generate "get started" purchase order** _____

6. **Information required for ad development**

   A. **Product**
   - ☐ Customer problems solved _____
   - ☐ Description _____
   - ☐ Hardware requirements_____
   - ☐ Hardware requirements_____
   - ☐ Key differentiators _____
   - ☐ Key exclusives _____

☐ Key features/benefits _____

☐ Key product messages _____

☐ Name _____

☐ Platform(s) supported _____

☐ Position _____

☐ Price _____

☐ Software requirements _____

☐ Web site address _____

☐ Which platforms are supported _____

B. Target audience

☐ Demographics (age, title, sources, etc.) _____

☐ What is their perception about the product? _____

☐ What do they know about the product? _____

☐ What excites them? _____

C. Competitive information

☐ Who, market share, strengths, weaknesses? _____

☐ Intelligence from their product launches, promotions, mailings, etc. _____

D. Current product's perception in market _____

7. Select media vehicles

☐ General audience _____

☐ Specialty _____

☐ Product-specific (e.g., Linux users, notebook users) _____

☐ Industry-specific (e.g., legal, accounting) _____

☐ Channel publications _____

8. Obtain editorial calendars from media vehicles

☐ From publishers _____

☐ From media services _____

9. Ad development process

A. What are you selling?

☐ Company _____

☐ Product _____

B. Determine ad type

☐ Transformational _____

☐ Transferal_____

☐ Protective_____

☐ Assuagement _____

C. Pick ad components

☐ Tactile elements _____

   ▨ Touch _____

   ▨ Sound _____

   ▨ Smell_____

   ▨ Sight _____

☐ Visual Elements_____

   ▨ Color_____

   ▨ Type _____

   ▨ Drawing _____

   ▨ Photography (Images) _____

   ▨ Animation _____

   ▨ Video/film _____

☐ Pick Information Items _____

   ▨ Product price _____

   ▨ Place it can be purchased _____

   ▨ Key positioning information _____

   ▨ Key statisics and facts _____

   ▨ Company size _____

   ▨ Location _____

   ▨ Key markets _____

   ▨ Endorsements from other companies _____

☐ Pick emotional resonators _____

   ▨ Empathy/sympathy_____

   ▨ Fear _____

   ▨ Value (or, if you're cynical, greed) _____

   ▨ Humor _____

   ▨ Sexual attraction _____

            ▓ Shock_____

☐ Decide on corporate/brand identifier

            ▓ Yours_____

            ▓ Partners_____

D. Design ad space environment

☐ Siren   _____

☐ Portal   _____

☐ Ad space guide posts_____

            ▓ Price_____

            ▓ Picture of product _____

E. Test against sample target audience _____

F. Choose best concept based on test results_____

G. Product Marketing provides:

☐ Packaging for photo shoot _____

☐ Screen shots _____

☐ Output samples _____

H. Agency submits production and placement cost estimate

☐ Color vs. B&W_____

☐ Ad size _____

☐ Frequency _____

☐ Placement _____

☐ Discounts_____

☐ Use of bounce-back device _____

I. Budget approved (allow for overruns) _____

J. Produce ad _____

K. Ad proofing cycle (at least 3 edits)

☐ Product Marketing _____

☐ Development (for technical accuracy only) _____

L. Place ad _____

10. Track and evaluate results_____

AGENCY PERFORMANCE CHECKLIST
(VENDOR/SUPPLIER)

Use the following questionnaire to assess overall agency performance and designate areas for improvement for both the client and the agency.

For a quick overview, we have provided a one-page general assessment for your use.

For a more detailed look, we have included an optional in-depth survey to help you pinpoint specific strengths and weaknesses. You may find it convenient to fill out the overall assessment and supplement it with those portions of the in-depth survey that pertain to specific issues or problem areas.

We encourage you to review and discuss your assessment with the agency; this will help ensure that both parties are fulfilling their roles in maintaining the relationship and maximizing marketing effectiveness.

AGENCY (VENDOR/SUPPLIER) PERFORMANCE REVIEW SUMMARY

1. WHAT ARE THE AGENCY'S MAJOR STRENGTHS?

    _____
    _____
    _____

2. WHAT ARE THE AGENCY'S MAJOR WEAKNESSES?

    _____
    _____
    _____

3. DURING THE LAST PROJECT, WHAT WERE THE MAJOR PROBLEMS IN THE AGENCY/CLIENT RELATIONSHIP?

    _____
    _____
    _____

4. WHAT CLIENT FACTORS MAY HAVE CONTRIBUTED TO AGENCY PROBLEMS?

    _____
    _____
    _____

5. WHAT WERE THE AGENCY'S MAJOR ACCOMPLISHMENTS DURING THE LAST PROJECT?

    _____
    _____
    _____

6. PRODUCT TEAM/DEPARTMENT OVERALL EVALUATION OF AGENCY'S PERFORMANCE

    Excellent   Good   Average   Fair   Poor

7. WHAT HAS CLIENT/AGENCY AGREED TO DO TO IMPROVE PERFORMANCE?

    _____
    _____
    _____

CLIENT ASSESSMENT OF AGENCY PERFORMANCE
(5 = Excellent)

PLANNING

Background knowledge of markets and products

    Rating: 5   4   3   2   1

    Reason:_____

Initiative in developing facts and ideas

    Rating: 5   4   3   2   1

    Reason:_____

_____

Evaluation and recommendation of media

    Rating: 5   4   3   2   1

    Reason:_____

_____

Understanding of advertising fundamentals

    Rating: 5   4   3   2   1

    Reason:_____

_____

EXECUTION

Overall administration

    Rating: 5   4   3   2   1

    Reason:_____

Responsiveness to requests

    Rating: 5   4   3   2   1

    Reason:_____

Cost-consciousness

    Rating: 5   4   3   2   1

    Reason:_____

Quality of "art" (including adherence to guidelines)

    Rating: 5   4   3   2   1

    Reason:_____

Quality of copy (including adherence to guidelines)

    Rating: 5   4   3   2   1

    Reason:_____

Quality and efficiency of ad production (including adherence to guidelines)

    Rating: 5   4   3   2   1

    Reason:_____

Ability to make effective presentations

    Rating: 5   4   3   2   1

    Reason:_____

FOLLOW-THROUGH

Maintenance of schedules and processing of paper work

    Rating: 5   4   3   2   1

    Reason:_____

Budget control

    Rating: 5   4   3   2   1

    Reason:_____

Attention to detail

    Rating: 5   4   3   2   1

    Reason:_____

Use of advertising research

    Rating: 5   4   3   2   1

    Reason:_____

Communications with client

    Rating: 5   4   3   2   1

    Reason:_____

ACCOUNT REPRESENTATION AND SERVICE

| ALWAYS | OFTEN | OCCASIONALLY | SELDOM | NEVER |

1.   Account reps act with *personal initiative.*_____

2.   Account reps *anticipate needs* in advance of direction by client._____

3.   Account group *takes direction* well. _____

4.   Agency readily *adapts to changes* in client's organization or needs. _____

5.   Agency makes reasonable *recommendations* on budget allocations._____

6.   Account reps function as *marketing advisors* as well as creative advisors. _____
     _____

7.   Account reps *contribute effectively* developing new programs. _____

8.   Account reps respond to *client requests* in a timely fashion. _____

9.   Agency recommendations are *founded on sound reasoning* and supported factually._____
     _____

10. Account reps submit *alternative plans,* vs. a single plan/campaign/ad for client review. __
     _____

11. Account reps have a *firm point of view* and "sell" their recommendation._____
     _____

12. Other areas not mentioned:
     _____
     _____
     _____

OVERALL EVALUATION OF ACCOUNT REPRESENTATION AND SERVICE

| EXCELLENT | GOOD | AVERAGE | FAIR | POOR |

GENERAL COMMENTS ON ACCOUNT REPRESENTATION AND SERVICE

_____
_____
_____
_____

CREATIVE SERVICES

| ALWAYS | OFTEN | OCCASIONALLY | SELDOM | NEVER |

1. Agency produces *fresh ideas* and original approaches._____

2. Agency *accurately interprets* facts, strategies, and objectives into usable ads and plans. _
   _____

3. Creative group is *knowledgeable* about company's products, markets, and strategies. ___
   _____

4. Creative group is concerned with *good advertising communications* and develops
   campaigns/ads that exhibit this concern. _____

5. Creative group *produces on time.*_____

6. Creative group *performs well* under pressure. _____

7. Creative group operates in a businesslike manner to *control production costs* and other
   creative charges. _____

8. Agency presentations are well organized with sufficient *examples of proposed
   executions.*_____

9. Creative group *participates* in major campaign *presentations.*_____

10. Agency presents *ideas and executions* not requested but believed to be good
    opportunities. _____

11. Agency *willingly accepts ideas* generated by other locations/agency offices vs. being over-
    protective of its own creative product. _____

12. Other areas not mentioned: _____
    _____
    _____
    _____

OVERALL EVALUATION OF CREATIVE SERVICES

| EXCELLENT | GOOD | AVERAGE | FAIR | POOR |

GENERAL COMMENTS ON CREATIVE SERVICES

_____
_____
_____

MEDIA SERVICES

| ALWAYS | OFTEN | OCCASIONALLY | SELDOM | NEVER |

1. Media group actively *explores new uses* of the various media available. _____
    _____

2. Agency media recommendations reflect *sufficient knowledge* of company's markets, audiences, products, and objectives. _____

3. Agency keeps client up to date on *trends and developments* in the field of media. _____
    _____

4. Agency exhibits a *broad capability* in media as opposed to specializing in one particular medium. _____
    _____

5. Agency subscribes to and makes use of available and applicable *syndicated media services*. _____
    _____

6. Agency engages in *original research* relating to the selection and use of media. _____
    _____

7. Agency provides client with a regular review and analysis of *competition's media usage*.
    _____

8. Agency *media administrative practices* are adequate, including coordination of media schedules, contracts, and ad/media verification._____
    _____

9. Agency is effective in media negotiations for *best possible position* for company advertising. _____
    _____

10. Agency has proven to be an *efficient bargainer* in cases where negotiated media purchases are possible._____

11. Other areas not mentioned: _____
    _____
    _____
    _____

OVERALL EVALUATION OF MEDIA SERVICES

EXCELLENT   GOOD   AVERAGE   FAIR   POOR

GENERAL COMMENTS ON MEDIA SERVICES

_____

_____

_____

_____

_____

_____

_____

_____

RESEARCH SERVICES

ALWAYS   OFTEN   OCCASIONALLY   SELDOM   NEVER

1. The agency's *research responsibilities* and relationship to the client are clearly defined and implemented. _____

2. Agency research programs are *reviewed by client,* including research objectives, methodology, interpretation, and conclusions._____

3. Agency uses research in the *development of campaigns* and basic strategies. _____

4. Agency provides *adequate pre-testing* in developing advertising campaigns. _____

5. Agency utilizes research to measure *advertising effectiveness* (attitude surveys, etc.). ___

6. Agency *provides client with evaluations* of syndicated research._____

7. Other areas not mentioned:_____

OVERALL EVALUATION OF RESEARCH SERVICES

EXCELLENT   GOOD   AVERAGE   FAIR   POOR

GENERAL COMMENTS ON RESEARCH SERVICES

FINANCIAL AND ADMINISTRATIVE SERVICES

ALWAYS	OFTEN	OCCASIONALLY	SELDOM	NEVER

1. Agency *billing procedures* reflect a well-run internal accounting operation. _____

2. Agency *production billings* usually come close to agency cost estimates. _____

3. Agency maintains appropriate and adequate files and documentation for *audit requirements*. _____

4. Whenever possible, agency obtains three bids on work performed by *outside vendors*.

5. Other areas not mentioned: _____

OVERALL EVALUATION OF FINANCIAL AND ADMINISTRATIVE SERVICES

EXCELLENT	GOOD	AVERAGE	FAIR	POOR

GENERAL COMMENTS ON FINANCIAL AND ADMINISTRATIVE SERVICES

6

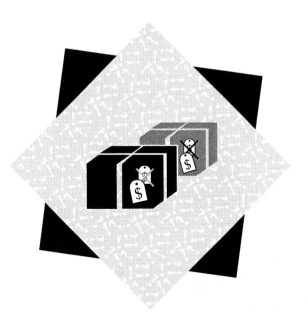

Sales Promotions

There is a lot of confusion about what constitutes a sales promotion. As a result, it is often difficult for publishers to plan why, how, where, and when to effectively employ a sales promotion as part of their overall marketing strategy.

Definitively, a sales promotion is a special offer or program designed to generate increased or incremental sales over your baseline sales and marketing efforts. If your promotion is not designed to do that, then it is not a promotion but another form of advertising or perhaps a price reduction. It is important to remember that while promotions can support your strategic advertising and marketing programs, they are inherently tactical in nature and it is a mistake to substitute them for a coherent product positioning strategy. If a promotion achieves a dramatic and unexpected long-term upsurge in your product's sales or audience, your product's positioning is flawed. Your marketing effort has not identified a key customer base and its needs, and should be redefined to address these customers at a strategic level.

Our focus in this section is on programs that clearly aim to sell more products to current and potential customers. Therefore, we have omitted any discussion of channel MDF programs, as many of these programs have little to do with promoting product, but function more as tolls publishers pay to access the distribution system.

Sales promotions are targeted to a particular type of customer, such as:

- A customer who has never heard of your product.
- A customer unsure about buying your product.
- A customer deciding which among several different products to buy.
- A customer who already owns your product and is considering upgrading.

In all cases, the goal of a sales promotion is to overcome the interested customer's normal purchasing inertia (a wallet at rest tends to stay at rest…), assuage lingering objections, and convince the potential buyer that a failure to take action and purchase **now** means missing an important opportunity to save money, increase productivity and/or personal satisfaction, or all of the above.

REASONS FOR SALES PROMOTIONS

There are four reasons why you would initiate a sales promotion strategy:

- You are launching a new product.
- You see an opportunity on the horizon.
- Your product's sales are declining due to its maturity.
- You are upgrading your product.

TYPES OF SALES PROMOTION

There are four types of sales promotions:

- Introductory.
- Situational.
- Defensive.
- Upgrade/Continuity.

Each type of sales promotion has its own advantages and disadvantages; therefore, which one you use should be an appropriate response to specific circumstances, with your goals and objectives clearly understood.

Introductory Promotions

A launch is a unique period in a product's life, a time when the market's attention and interest in your product and its success (or failure) is highest. Your marketing and sales effort should function as a strategic spearhead into the market, timed to take advantage of this unique opportunity. After the launch, there will be an inevitable drop-off in the attention and resources given to your product. An introductory promotion is the right tactical tool to support your marketing and help your product make the maximum gains possible during its launch period.

GOALS

If intended for channel release, your introductory promotion is a success if you reach the following goals via your resellers and distributors:

- Your product supplants the competition for the duration of the launch. This means achieving at least 50% market share during the launch.
- Your product achieves dominant "mind share." This means that anyone who asks for your product is steered toward it before any other product. You've achieved dominant mind share when:
  - 70%+ or more of your distribution system recommends your product ahead of the competition.
  - Every major and secondary publication mentions your product during the promotional period.
  - Every piece of software allocated for sales through the promotional period is moved out of inventory. Not a piece should remain on a reseller's shelves or in your inventory.

If designed for release through a direct sales force, your specific sales objectives can differ based on your product and market segment. Nonetheless, your primary goals are still to achieve 50% market share, dominant mind share among influencers and recommenders in your market, increased press coverage, and increased sales over your normal projected baseline numbers throughout the life of the promotion.

Situational Promotion

A situational promotion seeks to take advantage of a holiday period, a shift in technology, a perceived weakness in a competitor, a strategic partnership, etc. One of the most common situational promotions of the last several years has been the "competitive upgrade." Pioneered by Borland, a competitive upgrade has become a raid on another company's installed base. It is most effective when used against a company whose user base is growing restless waiting for an upgrade to their current product.

Seasonal opportunity promotions are also becoming more popular. As the small office/home office (SOHO) market continues to grow, software is becoming a popular holiday gift. Games, personal and small business productivity applications, and home design and management software are all good candidates for seasonal promotions.

GOALS

Goals for these promotions are the same as for a launch promotion, with the added proviso that if you are not the leader in your category, your promotion should supplant the leader in product sell-in to the channel and sell-through to buyers for the duration of the promotion. If the major player in your market is simply too big and entrenched for that to be realistic, then switch your sights to the number two player.

Defensive Promotion

A defensive promotion is called for when a product is aging, technologically ailing, or very late to market. For retail products, the most common symptom is channel warehouses stuffed with your slow-selling product. For direct-sales or VAR-class products, warning signs include:

- Requests from your customers for conferences with senior management on your strategic directions.

- Quotes from your current or potential customers in the press about their interest in new technology and product alternatives.

- Cancellations of planned purchases based on "strategic" considerations.

The need for a defensive promotion is most commonly sparked by a publisher's failure to upgrade its product on a timely basis. In the major and secondary markets, a product must be updated within 12 to 14 months after a major release. Failure to do this makes you a prime target for a competitive upgrade promotion.

GOALS

Your goal is simple: **halt erosion in market share and product sales at all costs**. A defensive promotion is usually the most difficult and costly to execute. If you need to run promotions like this often, you have a serious marketing or managerial problem that needs to be fixed.

Upgrade/Continuity Promotion

For a publisher with a significant installed base, upgrade programs are the most important promotions of all. Companies such as Oracle and Microsoft have installed bases in the millions, and upgrades represent a predictable, forecastable, annualized revenue stream for them. A dedicated installed base can sustain a company for years. Long after MicroPro lost its hold on the word processing market, loyal upgraders to WordStar kept the company alive, even when sales of the program to new buyers had stopped.

A continuity program is a close relative of the upgrade promotion, but violates the usual rule that a promotion must provide reasons and incentives to persuade a potential customer to buy now. The continuity promotion is necessitated by the fact that a certain percentage of your customers will never upgrade to a new version of your product no matter what incentives are offered. Therefore, always allow users to upgrade to a new version. You can set limits about time period, version, and cost, but if you shut down the upgrade path, you are sending the user elsewhere.

GOALS

- At least 50% of your installed base should upgrade from the current version of your product to its next release.
- At least 70% should upgrade with the second major release.
- And you should reach 90% with the third major release.

SALES PROMOTION OFFERS

There are only three types of sales promotion offers: one cuts price, the second adds value, and the third tries to combine the two. The industry is currently awash with price-cutting, though the type of destructive price wars launched by Borland in the early 1990s have become rare.

Less popular are value-added offers. Two logical candidates for the software industry are offering increased support or offering application design assistance. Many publishers are investigating value-added programs as an alternative to price slashing, but as of now, few such programs have been implemented.

ELEMENTS OF A SUCCESSFUL OFFER

All successful promotions must incorporate the following elements:

- **A compelling hook comprised either of price, value, or a combination of the two**. For example, offering a competitive upgrade price of $249 when a competing company's competitive upgrade price is $149 is not going to work, especially if you're not the market leader.

- **A clear and simple "call to action."** The benefits of the promotion must be clear, and easy for the customer to achieve.

- **A realistic understanding of your product's sales process**. For instance, if selling your application requires a multi-step process, whereby you first gather leads, then close sales via a direct sales force or VAR channel, your promotion planning should incorporate the right mix of contact, bounce-back, and closing programs and collaterals.

- **Consistent follow through**. This does not mean you cannot alter details of the promotion to respond to the market. It does means that once you commit to a promotion you should allocate enough resources to carry it through. Avoid front loading a promotion—spending all the money on events at the beginning—and you will have enough money to make any needed adjustments.

- **A firm end date**. This provides an incentive to act on the offer. A promotion without an end date is not a true promotion, but a permanent change in the price or configuration of the product. Consumers and the channel are not stupid. If your promotional pricing does not end, it is the "new" price and all discounts, margins, profits, will be based on this new price. If the promotion involves a continuing bundle, then the product's users and the reviewing press will inevitably wonder why the extra features offered by the bundled software aren't incorporated into the main product. The rule of thumb for a promotion's duration is that at least six weeks are needed for buyers and the channel to learn about the promotion, and that it should end after 12 weeks.

- **Channel notification**. Always notify the channel of your end-user promotions. Even when a promotion is not channel oriented, the increased interest and demand will usually increase retail activity and interest in your product. In addition, from the channel's perspective, promotions are an indication of your company's commitment to its products.

- **Flawless execution**. For instance, if you're running a reseller seminar, make sure to have any goodies you've promised to give away available the day of the seminar. If you don't, you're sure to disappoint and anger your audience, who will remember nothing about the seminar except that they never received their promised freebie. Microsoft has committed this mistake several times in the past, resulting in nasty letters to channel publications and angry discussions on online forums and discussion groups.

IMPLEMENTATION TACTICS

Once you have decided on the basic sales promotion type and offer, you must choose how to implement it. For example, you decided to cut price. How will you do that? We could write a book that described all the possible tactics you might employ. In the interests of brevity however, we have chosen to describe here the more common ones used with each type of sales promotion. Our schema is informed by common sense, but we should note that ingenious marketers can usually figure out how to fit any tactic to any type of promotion.

Competitive Upgrade (Introductory, Situational)

This tactic offers a user of a competing product to upgrade to your product at a reduced price. For a competitive upgrade promotion, an erosion of 10% or more of a competitor's installed base is considered a success.

Come Back Home (Upgrade/Continuity)

This is the promotion that violates the end-date rule. The come-back-home tactic is aimed at users who have failed to upgrade but still (presumably) use your product. It is designed to keep them in the family, and encourage them not to consider other solutions and products.

Coupons (Situational, Introductory)

Coupon programs are a quick and inexpensive way to add value to a product. A popular variant of this tactic involves including a book or catalog of coupons in the product box. This allows the publisher to advertise "Package contains X amount of savings" and grab the customer's attention.

Free Offer (Introductory)

The goal of a free offer is to build an installed base quickly and make money on upgrades. It is an expensive tactic, but some companies think it is worth it. Computer Associates (CA) executed one of the most aggressive programs seen to date with their Simply Money and Simply Tax programs. For the $14.95 price of shipping and handling, customers received fully functional copies of both programs. CA ended up shipping over 100K copies of Simply Money, calculating that approximately 30% of this new user base would be willing to upgrade to the next release. However, Simply Money received only mediocre reviews, and less than 10% of the installed base ever bothered to upgrade. Today, CA has exited this market. Needless to say, a company must have deep pockets to carry out this type of promotion, and you cannot rely on the fact that the product is free to carry your product to success.

Net-to-Zero (Introductory, Situational)

This is a recent promotional development heavily employed by large and medium-size software companies through resellers such as Staples and CompUSA. This tactic offers products for sale with an accompanying rebate that reduces the product's price to…nothing. (The customer receives no rebate on local sales taxes.) The objective is make a dramatic introductory splash, quickly build market share, and hope that enough people do not return the rebates and thereby lessen the publisher's financial burden. Retail resellers are enthusiastic about these programs as they tend to build store traffic and increase impulse purchases.

But Net-to-Zero promotions present several dangers to publishers, including:

- **Miscalculating rebate redemption rates**. Software vendors offering rebates of $25, $30, and $50 have been caught by surprise at redemption rates of 70%, 80% and 90%.

- **Failing to provide rebates on a timely basis**. This is guaranteed to generate tremendous amounts of bad will. Several Internet SIGs and forums are currently lit up by angry debates and accusations aimed at publishers who have been tardy in sending out checks.

- **Potential legal liability**. Slow redemption rates, and failures to send rebates have generated a tremendous amount of interest in states attorney general offices across the nation. You can anticipate legal action against certain vendors in the future.

Price Cuts (Introductory, Situational, Defensive)

A tactic that is usually effective over the short run, always expensive, and sometimes self-defeating in the long run.

Rebates/Refunds (Introductory, Situational)

This tactic is a popular and often effective way to move product out of inventory. The nice thing about rebates is that the customer doesn't receive the money until after the sale. The bad thing about rebates is that they require a great deal of after-sale administration to fulfill them. Recently, several software publishers have bundled free or reduced-price web access with their products via rebates.

Seminars (Introductory, Situational)

Typically a half-day (sometimes a full day) spent presenting a publisher's products and technology, and are best suited for direct- or VAR-class applications; they are rarely used to introduce retail-oriented products. The seminar is either hosted by the publisher or in cooperation with a local reseller. The ideal seminar audience is either potential VARs who address your market or potential customers with significant purchasing and influencing power. It is usually a big mistake to invite both to the same seminar; in fact, you should actively discourage local VARs from slipping into end-user seminars that they are not sponsoring.

Seminars can be a highly effective prospecting tool as the upcoming focus story illustrates, but they are time consuming and expensive to plan and execute. If you are planning a seminar series, success depends on following these steps:

- If your seminar series is national in scope, you will need to use both DM and EDM to announce the seminar schedule and dates. Your piece should arrive in conventional and electronic mailboxes at least four to six weeks before the date of the first seminar. Follow up regularly via E-mail.

- Your presentation team will need to check the facilities and set-up a day in advance of the seminar. Their travel and accommodation plans should reflect this. Very rarely do things go right the first time. To be safe, think of a seminar as a mini-trade show, and plan accordingly.

- You will need to schedule hotel and executive office space at least three months in advance. If your seminar is taking place near a major holiday period, plan to book space at least six months in advance.

- To increase attendance, in many cases you will need to place advertising in local newspapers, business magazines, web sites, and radio stations. (In rare cases, publishers have also placed local television ads.)

- In many cases, local sales offices will need to coordinate with your corporate marketing group for facilities arrangements, placing local advertising, and inviting key customers to attend.

- Consider charging a nominal sum for attendance. This may raise seminar attendance and lower your no-show rate. To reward attendees, you can rebate the cost of the seminar back to them via a giveaway whose retail value clearly exceeds the cost of attendance.

  Anticipate at least a 50% no-show rate among booked attendees if the seminar is free. Assume a 10% to 25% rate among paid attendees. Plan your seating accordingly.

- Plan in advance how you will capture attendees' names.

Room rental	$250 to $600 per day
Coffee refreshments	$8 to $15 per person
Lunch	$15 to $35 per person
Equipment	
White board	$0 to $30
Overhead projector	$50 to $100
VCR rental	$120 to $200

Figure 6-1. Cost breakdown for typical full-day seminar at a hotel, seating for 30, classroom configuration

FOCUS STORY: BENTLEY SYSTEMS—HAVE A HAPPY J DAY!
Company

Bentley Systems, Incorporated

Product

MicroStation/J

Market Situation

Bentley Systems is the rapidly growing number-two player in the microcomputer-based computer aided design (CAD) and engineering market. Founded in 1984, they have grown from revenues of $30M in 1990 to over $150M in 1998 and now serve more than 250K professionals in building/plant engineering, geoengineering, and manufacturing engineering. Their flagship products MicroStation and ModelServer are in use at more than 70% of the largest U.S. engineering firms. Versions of MicroStation are available for Windows NT, Sun, OS/2, Silicon Graphics, Unix and Linux platforms. And Bentley Systems was listed as the largest privately held company on the 1998 Softletter 100 and named to the 1998 Upside Hot 100.

In 1998, Bentley released a new version of MicroStation called MicroStation/J. The new release incorporated several major new features, including solid modeling from Parasolid, an extended Java Virtual Machine designed to support CAD development; a new version of Bentley's development language for MicroStation; and bundled applications for building, civil, geo, plant, and manufacturing engineering. The product's single-user retail SRP was $4795 US, and was sold through Bentley's one-tier reseller channel of over 100 MicroStation VARs.

Bentley released MicroStation/J at the same time they were also implementing a new positioning strategy for their products. Historically, the chasm between an enterprise's engineering data and its business systems created islands of automation that prevented firms from integrating and sharing their information stores. Incorporating a new technology, called ProjectBank, that replaced the current file-based paradigm for storing CAD designs with one that operates at the component level, MicroStation/J enabled users to create more comprehensive engineering models and share information within their enterprises in ways not previously possible. ProjectBank automatically links CAD files with related information, tracks file revisions, logs files in and out of a project, enables multiple users to access and work on a file simultaneously, and supports both MicroStation and market-leader AutoCAD files.

Bentley believed that integrating advanced modeling technology, industry-specific engineering capabilities, and component management justified repositioning some of their products under a new product category: engineering enterprise modeling, or EEM. Their category claim has received support from market research giant Dataquest, which reported on the new category in a recent white paper.

As discussed in the *Positioning* chapter of the **Handbook**, declaring a new category, or attempting a recategorization strategy requires an extensive market education effort. To support MicroStation/J, the new EEM positioning, and its market education effort, Bentley implemented an extensive U.S. seminar promotion named "J Days." These free seminars ran from October 1998 through January 1999 and consisted of a half-day MicroStation/J presentation and discussions of how EEM would impact the CAD market. Attendees were notified about the seminars through a combination of direct mail and telemarketing from Bentley, postings on the Bentley web site, E-mail, and local reseller marketing. By the promotion's end, over 225 J Days had been conducted.

The J Day promotions were conducted in partnership with Bentley's reseller channel, and local VARs were responsible for booking facilities or hosting the seminars at their offices, inviting potential and existing customers, and conducting the seminars. In some areas, Bentley sales and marketing representatives provided assistance, but all sessions were co-sponsored and conducted by the resellers. To capture customer names, resellers required each attendee to fill out an identification card either before or after the seminar. These names were kept by the local resellers for follow-up sales activity and sent to Bentley for corporate marketing purposes.

To support the J Days, Bentley's Marcom group created and shipped a comprehensive launch kit to each seminar location, containing the following:

- Brochures.
- Datasheets.
- Demo disks.
- Demo templates.
- Electronic presentations (in PowerPoint format).
- Posters (to put on the walls of the seminar room).
- Press reprints.
- Presentation scripts, providing a suggested agenda, outline, and timing for each segment.
- A product availability and order matrix.
- A video.
- White papers.

Most of the printed materials were provided in a three-ring binder for easy organization. In addition, each reseller co-sponsoring a J Day received extra collaterals to support follow-up sales activities.

Bentley also offered a series of promotional incentives to both resellers and J Day attendees. VARs who reached attendance goals received free "for sale" software and business consulting. For customers, Bentley ran a series of upgrade, support, competitive upgrade and site promotions keyed to J Day attendance. In addition, anyone who responded to a J Day mailing was entered in a drawing for a free trip, and all J-Day attendees were entered in a drawing for a free Silicon Graphics workstation (a unit much prized by engineers).

Results

At the end of the seminar series, over 4000 people had attended Bentley's J Day promotions, creating a highly qualified base for both upgrade and new product sales. In addition, VARs used the collaterals and seminar sessions to educate their customers and themselves about EEM. The J Day promotions also helped support and generate interest in a series of follow-up technology showcases.

LESSONS

One difficulty facing Bentley was producing collaterals on a timely basis. Bentley had sponsored a user conference just prior to the promotion and planning and managing that event drained time and resources from the promotion program. As a result, planned seminar materials were in short supply at some of the initial seminars. Bentley quickly rectified the problem, but decided that in the future all supporting collaterals would be available two to three weeks before the first seminar.

Bentley's J Day promotion exemplifies the activities a publisher can expect to take to support a seminar series. Publishers should take particular note of Bentley's use of follow-up promotions. Many publishers make the mistake of launching this type of promotion without plans for a strong follow through. Bentley's program was designed to capitalize on the immediate post-seminar sales momentum. Bentley's offer of free business consulting to its high-performing VARs was also very innovative. Increasing the business acumen of its sales channel benefited Bentley as well. Few publishers give much thought to training their resellers on how to be a more effective sales force, assuming they understand their own business. This is often not the case, and an investment in helping resellers improve their business planning and execution can often pay handsome dividends for the publisher.

Software/Hardware Bundles (Introductory, Situational, Defensive)

Bundles have always been popular with software publishers and they are often integrated via direct mail programs. This tactic can be very effective when used to:

- Add value to a product during a launch.
- Provide the publisher with the opportunity to generate incremental dollars on the sale of the bundled product. (This depends on whether or not you buy the bundled product at the right price.)

- Help a publisher address a product's competitive weakness until the next release.

Hardware bundles are far rarer, and should be approached carefully. Inevitably, a hardware bundle increases product support, invites bundle breaking in your channel, and requires more complex assembly and shipping.

SPIFs (Introductory, Situational, Defensive)

SPIFs, short for special performance incentive funds, function like a gratuity paid to sales representatives in return for recommending your product. They are paid either on a per-unit basis or when the total volume of sales exceeds a set level. SPIFs are only effective during the life of a promotion, and do not build long-term sales loyalty. In fact, sales often slump after the SPIF ends. This is particularly true of channel SPIFs, where they are an ongoing fact of life. SPIFs have always had a faintly unsavory air about them, but they do focus a sales channel's attention on your product like no other promotion does.

If you are going to use SPIFs, consider these points:

- SPIFs are expensive. They typically range between $10 and $100 per unit.
- SPIFs are not recommended for publishers with a one-tier VAR channel. This class of reseller is more interested in product margins and receiving high-quality support from publishers.
- The SPIF needs to be delivered directly to the sales representative. It is usually a mistake to assign SPIF money to a "general" or "manager's" fund and expect to see any results.

Trial Offers (Introductory, Situational)

An old standby, the trial offer allows customers to try the product for a preset time period. A popular tactic is to ship the product, then bill the credit card automatically if the product isn't shipped back when the free-trial period ends. This program is often integrated with a telemarketing effort.

Trips and Prizes (Situational, Introductory)

Although a channel staple, trips and prizes tend to have little appeal to potential software purchasers.

Technology Showcase (Situational, Introductory)

A technology showcase is a vendor show or series of presentations held at a customer's site. In some cases, several vendors will participate in a technology showcase, though most publishers dislike the prospect of participating in the same venue with their competition. Showcases are most effective when they are scheduled by the publisher and focus only on their products. Most customers reserve showcases for publishers who have a strategic impact on the market or whose technology has a major impact on the the their business. However, any publisher should consider participating or scheduling a showcase if the opportunity arises. There are few better opportunities to display your product and company in its best possible light.

User Conferences (Situational, Introductory)

User conferences are company-specific trade shows, and consist of seminars, exhibits, press releases, keynote speeches, reseller meetings, and product announcements all focused on one publisher and their products. These conferences also sometimes allow third-party publishers who have built ancillary and add-on products around the primary publisher's products to show off their wares and make sales. User conferences can be a very effective marketing tactic. A company large and influential enough to hold them is regarded as a major force in its market segment, and can count on the conference generating a great deal of press and user attention. However, conferences are very expensive and time consuming to plan and manage, and only a larger publisher should consider hosting one.

PROMOTIONAL AIDS

Promotional aids are particularly valuable in one-to-one direct sales efforts or as a relationship builder with key channel personnel. As discussed in the *Collaterals* section of the **Handbook**, they comprise a wide range of items, including key chains, coffee mugs, watches, etc. and typically function as ice breakers. However, promotional aids work best when they directly support the sales process and function as a continuing advocate for your product and company.

To make your use of a promotional aid as effective as possible, follow these guidelines:

- Avoid giving away something too expensive (at least at the beginning of the sales call), or the client may be too distracted to pay attention to your presentation.

- Tie the promotional item directly into the sales process. For instance, if you're using a pen as a giveaway, offer it to the customer to jot down notes about the products under discussion.

- Use your promotional items to gain a strategic position in the client's workspace, such as a desktop, wall, or display area.

- If possible, tie your promotional items into the personal interests of the client. For instance, if the client is a golfer, a golf shirt or golf balls emblazoned with your company or product logo can be effective.

- Integrate promotional aids into your sales follow-up. Consider, for instance, sending a memo pad to the client before calling to remind them of actions items scheduled for completion during the previous call.

PROMOTIONS AND THE CHANNEL

Unless your products are sold directly, your promotion strategy will also encompass the channel. Ideally, channel promotions focus on the monetary benefits to the channel of selling your product. Remember—distributors and resellers are not the users of your product. Their function is to make your product widely available and easy to purchase. They are middlemen, and their primary interest is their return on investment when selling your product.

For firms publishing VAR-class software, managing channel promotions is a far easier task than that facing publishers offering retail products. In a one-tier system, the publisher is in a far better position to plan, execute, and measure the results of a channel promotion. In a two-tier system, matters are far more difficult to manage, as a publisher must negotiate carefully around the MDF minefield described in the *Channel Distribution* chapter of the **Handbook**.

QUALIFYING CHANNEL PROMOTIONAL PROGRAMS

When planning a channel promotion, you must be prepared to ask your distributors or reseller to help you quantify the incremental ROI that you, the publisher, will receive on your investment. For example, if you commit to $20K in end-cap expenditures for a three-month period, or decide to offer extended support, how many extra copies of your product can you expect to sell? Will the extra copies sold cover the cost of the promotion? Significantly boost your market share? Will the extra copies sold via the promotion cover the cost of the promotion **and** provide a ROI on your investment? How much will the ROI be? Ten percent? Thirty? Fifty?

In a retail environment, if the answer is "depends on the product," then you should ask how many extra products did the publisher with a title similar to yours sell? The distributor or reseller may be reluctant to answer, but always ask for proof of prior performance. Remember that it is up to you to press for information, qualify programs, negotiate the terms of your participation, and decide which types of promotions best fit your marketing and sales goals.

GENERAL VS. LIGHTHOUSE PROMOTIONAL STRATEGIES

Before launching your channel promotion, you must decide whether or not to pursue a general or "lighthouse" promotional strategy. A general strategy invites all of your (appropriate) channel partners to participate in the promotion simultaneously. The advantage of this approach is that if the promotion is compelling and properly structured, your promotion will achieve maximum impact and scope within the channel. The disadvantages are that you have less room for error and testing, and the expense of launching, maintaining, and fulfilling your promotion may break your budget and exceed your operational capabilities.

For smaller publishers, the alternative lighthouse strategy may be more advantageous: you can test the promotion, tailor it more specifically to the needs of a specific channel entity, and more closely manage your budget and company resources.

For a successful lighthouse strategy, we recommend you follow these guidelines.

- Identify the channel partners most likely to succeed with your promotion.
- Focus your promotional efforts on helping them succeed with the promotion.
- Refine and improve the promotion.
- Offer the promotional opportunity to other channel partners.
- Use your success (the lighthouse) to attract the channel to your promotion and improve your bargaining position *vis a vis* the promotion specifics.

CONTRACT FIELD SERVICES

Contract Field Services (CFS) groups are "sales force for hire" organizations who can put product and computer-literate personnel into the channel on a nationwide basis. Their responsibilities range from simple detailing to promotion execution and management with costs ranging from $25 to $45 per visit per store. Publishers unable to manage a nationwide promotional program with a reseller can turn to these organizations to provide the needed resources, but they must be managed while under contract as if they were employees. A publisher must be able and willing to provide sales support, training, and ongoing supervision; otherwise, the CFS group will become unmotivated and ineffective.

MEASURING CHANNEL PROMOTIONS

The easiest way to measure channel promotional performance is to ask for reports. Distributors can tell you which resellers are ordering your product and which stores are selling your product. Resellers, both retail oriented and VAR-class, can tell you how much of your products they've sold during a promotional program, both on an enterprise and on a store-by-store basis. In some cases, the channel will ask you to pay for this information. (Strenuously resist making such payments.) This information can help you judge which channel MDF and promotion programs are working. But this information will not be provided to you unless you ask for it. You then need to be prepared to integrate the data into your internal marketing and sales-tracking system.

PROMOTIONS AND THE RETAIL SELLING TERRAIN

If your product is retail-oriented, then the selling terrain must be carefully inspected. If your product is meant to "live" on CompUSA's shelves, your goal is to make it the most visible in its class within the particular sales environment; that is, you want to achieve the maximum "eyeshare" for your product during the promotion. To do this, plan on contacting the targeted resellers at least three months in advance and spending money to control key reseller space, including shelves, walls, cashier areas, window fronts, etc. If you can't seize control of these areas legitimately, consider "guerrilla marketing." Build highly survivable tent cards, shelf talkers, brochures, anything you think you can manage and place them where you can. This tactic is often a second-best strategy, but it may be the best you can do.

INTEGRATING PROMOTIONS

The most effective channel promotions are always integrated, with each element supporting the other. For instance, if you are running a retail in-store promotion, your giveaway item should be attached to a card that includes a picture of your latest ad, along with the rules of your ongoing sales contest, which sends the winner on a free trip to Bermuda and posts the lucky winner's name on your web site—when they sell enough units of your product, of course.

TESTING PROMOTIONS

In many cases, it is a good idea to test a promotional idea or concept. Most promotional fiascoes do not occur because of subtle or hard-to-discover problems. And testing does not have to be an expensive or time-consuming process. For example, local stores are excellent test beds for retail-oriented promotions. If your promotion involves a change in product packaging or the use of in-store merchandising, the marketing manager should always go in person to local stores to scout out the selling environment. Talk to store managers and show them your new packaging or promotional pieces. Put it on the shelf and see if it fits. Talk to the store representatives. Take the time to see what other companies are doing. Watch the customers. Ask them questions. You will learn a great deal in a short time.

Publishers working with a one-tier reseller system are also in an excellent position to test and evaluate different promotional ideas. If you've established a reseller council, they can provide good advice on which types of promotions best fit their market. Also, some of your resellers may be happy to let you test different promotions in their areas, and thus develop a profile over time on what works best in your market.

Another effective way to test promotions is by actively cultivating intelligence about other companies' promotions. Reading through channel and industry publications and newsletters is a useful way to find out what types of promotions are in favor. In addition, distributor and reseller marketing managers can be useful sources of promotional information, especially if you've taken the time to develop good personal relationships with them. Finally, make it a point to collect promotional material distributed and mailed by other companies. This material will be an invaluable aid when you design, plan, and evaluate your own promotional programs.

Conventional and electronic direct-mail promotions are also fairly easy to test, as it makes it easy to test different price points, offers, and combinations of the two. List segments and sub-segments can be broken out, mailed to, and the results carefully tracked.

Formal testing, especially for larger companies, is always an option. This can include using focus groups; telephone, in-person, and online surveys; brand and name studies; etc. If your small company's budget can't stand the strain of outside formal testing, then use employees, friends, or even family to conduct informal studies. While these won't offer the "clean room" environment of professional marketing services, you can still get useful feedback and uncover all but the subtlest problems.

What Should You Test?

Depending upon the type of promotion, the most common items to test include:

- **The price point**. A surprisingly common mistake many publishers make is pricing a promotion too low. At a certain point, depending on the product's positioning and target audience, consumers are willing to pay a particular price for your product. Going below that price simply "leaves money at the table."

- **The target audience**. Is your promotional offer appropriate to the audience? For instance, an elaborate bundle may be the wrong type of offer to match to your upgrade base.

- **Promotional packaging and merchandising**. Will a specially created product bundled with another company's product fit on your resellers' shelves? How easy will it be for your resellers to tear the bundle apart and sell the components separately?

- **Promotional bundles**. Certain products will fit one product's positioning and features better than another.

- **Administration issues**. Many publishers make administering and tracking their promotions too complex—both for themselves and for their buyers. Too much paperwork will immediately short-circuit a promotion's success.

- **Fulfillment capabilities**. If your promotion is successful, can you ship enough product to meet demand? If you are using a web or FTP site to download product instead of shipping boxes, have you tested your server's capacity to respond to high download traffic? Can the user resume an interrupted download? Is the file compressed for downloads? Have you tested how it unpacks itself on the user's system? What happens if customers don't have enough disk space to unpack the file?

EXECUTING PROMOTIONS

The final point to remember about promotions is that the most common reason for failure is the inability to execute a promotion. It does you no good to have the phone ringing off the hook for product information if you have no collaterals to send or product to ship. It will hurt your image if your web site tells potential buyers to come back later because the site is too busy. To help you avoid these problems, keep these key points in mind:

- Promotions should be as simple as possible to administer. All forms, both real and virtual, and promotion procedures should be simple enough for an older child to complete.

- You must be able to fulfill your promotion. If you are not sure you can, hire a professional to do it for you.

- Promotions must be managed from beginning to end. At no point will you be able to relax on auto pilot. If you cannot dedicate someone to manage your promotion, then either hire someone to do it for you or don't do it at all.

SALES PROMOTIONS OBJECTIVES/EVALUATION CHECKLIST

OBJECTIVES   **EVALUATION**

Marketing Goals

1. **Increase direct product sales from baseline**

   # SKUs sold direct   _____ _____ _____

   # leads generated   _____ _____ _____

   # leads converted to sales _____ _____ _____

   # product inquiries   _____ _____ _____

2. **Increase channel sales via customer pull**

   % increase SKUs shipped
   to channel   _____ _____ _____

3. **Increase participating resellers' sales**

   % increase in direct
   run rate   _____ _____ _____

   % increase sales through
   distributors   _____ _____ _____

4. **Increase upgrade sales**

   % increase in direct
   run rate   _____ _____ _____

   % increase sales to
   channel   _____ _____ _____

5. **Decrease channel inventory levels**

   # units shipped from
   warehouse   _____ _____ _____

6. **Increase market share**

   % increase buying
   product   _____ _____ _____

OBJECTIVES	EVALUATION		

Audience

1. Increase buyer mindshare from baseline

*% increase asking for
product*   _____   _____   _____

*% increase calls to
company*   _____   _____   _____

*% increase product
inquiries*   _____   _____   _____

2. Reach new buyers

 # new user registration   _____   _____   _____

 # coded offerings   _____   _____   _____

SALES PROMOTIONS SUCCESS CHECKLIST

1. **Select reason for promotion**

   A. **Product launch** _____

   B. **Opportunity** _____

   C. **Declining sales** _____

   D. **Upgrading** _____

2. **Promotion type**

   A. **Introductory** _____

   B. **Situational** _____

   - [ ] Seasonal _____
   - [ ] Competitive upgrade _____
   - [ ] Other _____

   C. **Defensive** _____

   - [ ] Channel inventory too high _____
   - [ ] Product sales have slowed _____

   D. **Upgrade/Continuity** _____

   - [ ] Need to keep users on board _____
   - [ ] Never heard of your product _____
   - [ ] Undecided about buying your product _____
   - [ ] Deciding which product to buy in your product category ___
   - [ ] Considering upgrading your product _____
   - [ ] SELECT type(s) _____
     - Contest & sweepstakes _____
     - Coupon _____
     - Free offer _____
     - Net-to-zero _____
     - Price cut _____
     - Rebate/Refund _____
     - Seminars _____
     - SPIFs _____
     - Technology showcase _____

    ▓ Trial offer _____

    ▓ Trip & prize _____

    ▓ User conference _____

    ▓ Other _____

4. Develop plan, including objectives, budget, test plan, and schedule

A. Select who will do promotion

☐ In-house staff _____

☐ Outside vendor _____

☐ Contract vendor(s) _____

☐ Select via competitive bid _____

☐ Use a single-source vendor (handles subcontractors, printing, etc.) _____

B. Decide if co-sponsor

☐ Distributor _____

☐ Reseller _____

☐ Other vendor/publisher _____

☐ Other _____

C. Select who will do fulfillment

☐ In-house staff _____

☐ Outside vendor _____

☐ Distributor _____

☐ Reseller _____

☐ Other publisher _____

D. Identify internal key contacts for the following activities

☐ Collaterals needed _____

☐ Fulfillment _____

    ▓ Take orders _____

    ▓ Pick and ship orders _____

☐ Manufacture product _____

    ▓ Inventory levels _____

    ▓ Different product versions _____

☐ Produce sales promotion materials _____

    ▓ Who writes/designs promotion piece? _____

    ▓ Who prints/E-mails promotion piece? _____

▨ Who purchases promotion bonus? _____

☐ Plan seminar _____

  ▨ Book space _____

  ▨ Capture attendee information _____

  ▨ Provide food _____

  ▨ Provide scripts_____

☐ Support _____

  ▨ Pre-sale _____

  ▨ Channel_____

  ▨ Technical _____

  ▨ Customer _____

☐ Sales

  ▨ In-house sales personnel _____

  ▨ Contract sales force_____

  ▨ Problem resolution_____

  ▨ Technical _____

  ▨ Product support _____

  ▨ Follow-up _____

  ▨ Bounce-back for complementary product(s)_____

  ▨ Direct mail piece(s)_____

  ▨ Electronic direct mail piece(s) _____

  ▨ Qualify leads _____

  ▨ Questionnaire _____

☐ Appropriate to respondent _____

☐ Captures useful data _____

☐ Easy to fill out and capture data _____

☐ Specific plan for analyzing data _____

☐ Web based _____

☐ Sales call _____

☐ Telemarketing _____

E. Select promotion development coordinator _____

F. Decide scope of promotion

☐ General _____

☐ Lighthouse_____

G. Set promotion(s) start and end dates _____

5. Specify the OFFER

A. Determine for each audience

☐ Frequency of promotion _____

☐ Characterize each audience _____

☐ Associate each offer to each audience_____

☐ Code each offer _____

B. Determine what to include

☐ Letter _____

☐ Sticker or special sleeve _____

☐ Use bullets to highlight _____

☐ Emphasis on benefits not features _____

☐ Should answer:

   ▒ Why buy or upgrade _____

   ▒ Why buy now _____

   ▒ How to buy or upgrade_____

C. Specify offer requirements _____

D. Identify time or quantity limits/restrictions_____

E. Link to a direct-mail piece _____

F. Link to a electronic direct mail piece _____

G. Link to another promotion _____

H. Estimate quantities _____

6. Specify the CALL TO ACTION

A. Select response mechanism

☐ Business reply card _____

☐ Coupon _____

☐ In-store bundle _____

☐ Seminar attendance _____

☐ Telephone _____

☐ 800# _____

☐ Regular _____

☐ Web site registration _____

B. Display prominently _____

C. Coordinate with fulfillment organization

☐ Establish codes _____

☐ Implement procedure for capturing codes _____

☐ Implement schedule for reporting results _____

7. Cost by element

☐ Bonus purchase _____

☐ Contest/sweepstakes _____

☐ Contract sales force _____

☐ Design _____

☐ Promotional materials _____

☐ Special packaging _____

☐ Direct mailing _____

☐ Electronic mailing _____

☐ Facility rental _____

☐ Fulfillment _____

☐ Printing _____

☐ Telemarketing _____

☐ Trip/prize _____

☐ Web site design _____

☐ Travel _____

TOTAL PROJECT COST ESTIMATE _____

8. Test the promotion before final production of materials

A. Test

☐ Administration requirements _____

☐ Bundle types _____

☐ Fulfillment capabilities _____

☐ Packaging _____

☐ Durability _____

▨ Size _____

▨ Other _____

- [ ] Forms and procedures _____
- [ ] Price points _____
- [ ] Target audiences _____
- [ ] Web site registration _____
- [ ] Web site download _____
- [ ] Server capacity _____
- [ ] Compression handling _____
- [ ] Other _____

B. How to test

- [ ] Industry intelligence _____
- [ ] Publications and newsletters _____
- [ ] Channel contacts _____
- [ ] Other companies' mailings and offers _____
- [ ] Informal market research _____
- [ ] Focus groups _____
- [ ] Small surveys _____
- [ ] Web site surveys _____
- [ ] In-store research _____
- [ ] Interview store personnel and customers _____
- [ ] Test packaging and merchandising material _____
- [ ] Professional market research _____
- [ ] Focus groups _____
- [ ] Internet surveys _____
- [ ] Surveys _____
- [ ] Telemarketing and interviews _____

9. Produce all materials _____

10. Launch promotion(s) _____

11. Manage contract sales force (if using) _____

12. Follow-up activities

A. Lead generation

- [ ] Qualify _____
- [ ] Distribute _____

B. Sales generation

☐ Order entry _____

☐ Sales reports _____

C. Evaluation

☐ E/R for direct sales _____

☐ Channel sales _____

▓   Request for promotion to continue _____

▓   Promotion copied by others _____

▓   Promotion receives press coverage _____

☐ Cost-per-lead for lead generation _____

☐ Coded offers _____

☐ Price points _____

☐ Target audience _____

☐ Packaging and promotion materials _____

D. List management

☐ Merge/purge operations _____

☐ Update in-house list(s) _____

E. Feedback

☐ Product Marketing team _____

☐ Marketing Communications _____

☐ Senior Management _____

☐ Distributor _____

☐ Reseller _____

☐ Outside vendor/publisher _____

☐ Other _____

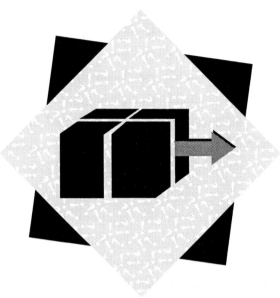

7

Direct Marketing

The idea that direct marketing (DM) once had a bad reputation in the microcomputer software business now seems quite silly, given that DM is a key component of practically every software marketing program, and accounts for about 20% of retail microcomputer software sales. Direct and VAR-class publishers also make extensive use of DM for both lead generation and to close sales.

While DM is often thought of as a synonym for direct mail, this is too limited a view. Direct marketing also includes:

- **Card decks**. These are useful for lead generation and can generate incremental sales for certain products.

- **Catalog sales**. Typically, software companies have used catalogs to sell add-on and complementary products to support sales of flagship products. This is still effective and a source of incremental dollars. But as publishers recognized the value of their mailing lists, some began to experiment with selling other products as an additional source of revenue. The one restriction is that most companies, for good reasons, will not sell competing products to their user base.

- **Direct fax campaigns**. These have faded a bit in general popularity, but they are still a useful way to reach a highly targeted niche.

- **The Internet**. The growth of electronic direct marketing is growing steadily, and will soon be regarded as both an adjunct to and replacement for conventional DM. It is the one area where the web has met expectations. This topic is covered in greater detail in the *Electronic Marketing* chapter of the **Handbook**.

- **Infomercials**. While not for everyone, infomercials can be a powerful marketing tool if your product fits the right profile.

- **Trade shows**. Many companies now regard trade show appearances not simply as marketing events, but as selling opportunities. This is covered in greater detail in the *Trade Show* chapter of the **Handbook**.

- **Telemarketing**. Telemarketing can be used independently or in support of other direct vehicles. Many publishers now use telemarketing as a follow-up to upgrade mailings, to support sales of home and small office/home office (SOHO) products, to follow up on leads generated by a high-end mailing, and to support infomercials. Close rates in these circumstances can be as high as 50%, though the typical range is between 15% and 30%.

WHO BUYS DIRECT?

As the industry matured, many buyers began purchasing desktop and SOHO products based strictly on features and price. In addition, purchasers of high-end products became far more receptive to DM. Network management tools, marketing management, and enterprise budgeting products are just a few of the categories whose products are successfully sold via DM programs. While conventional direct marketing revenues are projected to remain fairly flat for the near future, it will continue to be a major factor in the software sales mix.

WHAT DIRECT MARKETING CAN ACCOMPLISH

Direct marketing can accomplish several things, including:

- Generating additional incremental sales of your product. Remember, many buyers prefer to buy product this way, particularly retail-class products. Regardless of how your distribution channel may feel about it, your first obligation is to satisfy buyer demands.

- Generating awareness and sales leads for your products. This is the primary focus of direct marketing for high-end products. DM can reach customers for products of any class and cost. The idea that DM is strictly for low-end commodity products is obsolete.

- Increasing sales of your product through other channels. Despite channel skepticism about this, there are still many more people who prefer to lay down their money and walk out with a package or buy from a live body. For these buyers, direct marketing spurs their interest, informs them, and encourages them to walk into a store, pick up a phone, or visit a sales office and find out more.

- Putting you in direct contact with your customer. You can learn a great deal from a failure to sell. Direct marketing can uncover flaws in your assumptions about who your customers are and what they are looking for in a product. It can also educate you about the proper offer type and techniques you need to employ to reach your target audience.

- Allowing you to closely tie sales to marketing expenditures. Unlike advertising, where quantifying results based on sales is always difficult and sometimes impossible, you have far more control over your direct marketing. You know who you're calling or mailing, how often, and how many times they've purchased a product.

- Increasing upgrade sales. A publisher must direct market its upgrade product(s). You cannot allow the channel to control your upgrade programs or sales. While some publishers include the channel in upgrade programs, it is a mistake to rely on the channel for more than incremental contributions to any upgrade effort.

HIGH-END DIRECT MARKETING

DM programs for high-end software, defined here as a product with an SRP of $995 or above, require that you consider alternatives to conventional DM strategies. This need is driven by practical considerations. In many cases, high-end offers are targeted at upper management, people with purchasing authority and approval such as CEOs, CFOs, CIO, controllers, etc. This audience is usually surrounded by a coterie of gatekeepers—secretaries, administrative assistants, mailroom employees—who are often instructed to screen out anything that smacks of a commercial or DM offer. Some large companies have even instituted policies that automatically consign all third-class mail to the recycling bin.

Less Is More and Dimensional Mailings

There are two ways to get around the gatekeepers. One is the "less is more" school of direct marketing, which eschews bright envelopes, snappy teaser copy, and promises of fabulous premiums on the outside of the piece. Instead, it has a first-class stamp, the address is printed on a high-quality printer, and sometimes even uses a typeface that simulates handwriting or that classic "Selectric Script" look to persuade the addressee to open the piece. Another tactic, highly effective, but expensive and slow, is hand-addressing envelopes. They **will** be opened. For small scale, highly focused mailings, it may be worthwhile. Less is more is usually reserved for lead generation pieces, though in some cases a call to buy may be appropriate.

The other is the dimensional mailing. This consists of "bulking up" the piece or packaging it in such a way that it escapes the mail room and ends up on the recipient's desk. Some publishers have used mailing tubes, boxes, or express delivery services like Federal Express or Airborne to ensure delivery. Another alternative, highly effective but less costly, is using Priority Mail. It also tends to "get through," and at $3.00 per package, is considerably cheaper than a FedEx delivery.

Another sometimes effective tactic is to offer an incentive or "gift" as a way to intrigue and encourage prospective buyers to consider the offer more carefully. The gift should tie in directly to some aspect of the customer's job or business environment. White papers can also be effective, and some publishers have mailed copies of an article discussing trends in the customer's industry. In the case of Sterling Software, a vendor of VM-based data center management tools, the publisher sent prospective clients an information kit that included a "VM Expert" pin. In a VM environment, advocates don't mind making their OS preferences visibly apparent.

MAILING AND LEAD LISTS

Mailing and lead lists are at the heart of any DM effort. Therefore, the first rule of direct marketing is to purchase or build high-quality lists. Your product, pricing, and promotions can all be on target, but if you're mailing to the wrong people, none of that will matter.

There are several types of lists. Ranked in order of importance, they are:

- **The house file (or internal list)**. This is your most important list. It should contain the names of every individual who purchased your product or inquired about it. Estimated hit rate (EHR) on a good house file is 15% to 50%, depending on the offer, the product, and the promotion. There are several primary sources for a house file:

- *Registration cards from your product.* If you are not capturing your user base via conventional and/or electronic registration, you are failing a marketing fundamental. There is no excuse for not capturing registration information.

- *Registration cards from other products from your company* (if there are any). Many marketers make the mistake of not talking to other marketers in their company about complementary lists, promotions, and direct promotions.

- *Names from internal promotions, mailings, reader response cards, etc.* In a large company, different marketing groups may be running different promotions. Often the lists created represent a gold mine for an alert product manager. However, if these lists have been allowed to sit in a corner and molder for over a year, don't bother. A mailing list decays steadily and irrevocably from the moment it is created. After a year of non-use, most lists are useless. On average, decay rates range between 20% and 50% per year.

- **Complementary External House Files**. These are lists held by other publishers who sell products that complement, not compete with, your own. Publishers often trade use of these lists in return for joint marketing opportunities, or as part of bundling or joint promotions. EHR is 2% to 4%; however, it is possible to do much better, depending on the products involved and the type of promotion.

- **Buyers Lists**. These are lists of people who buy products through the mail. EHR is 1% to 2%; average price per thousand (APPT) is $70 to $100.

- **Subscription lists**. These are lists of individuals who subscribe to magazines and services that relate to your product. EHR is .75% to 1%; APPT is $70 to $100.

- **Demographically compiled lists**. These are lists of people who meet a specific profile—women over 40 who subscribe to PC Magazine, for example. Frequently, you may only obtain a job title and address—not a name and a title (e.g., Jane Doe, Purchasing Agent). EHR is .5%; APPT is $25 to $30.

Many new publishers make the mistake of depending on purchased lists to achieve lofty sales goals. This is a mistake. The point of using purchased lists is to feed your house file; significant profits are made by using your own high-quality house file(s).

LIST BROKERS AND WAREHOUSES

Buyers, subscription, and compiled lists are usually purchased from list brokers or warehouses who create, manage, and sell lists. When evaluating list brokers, keep in mind the following:

- Any broker can purchase any list. The key to a successful business relationship is picking a broker who will work hard for your company and your product.

- The list broker you work with should have experience in working with national lists. Very few publishers, with the exception of some who sell VAR-class software into certain niches, sell software on a regional basis.

When purchasing a list from a broker you should obtain a "rate card," that is, a description of the list's characteristics. These characteristics should include:

- **The "RFM" of the list**. RFM stands for recency, frequency, and monetary value. These rate how long ago, how often, and how much someone paid for items they purchased via a direct campaign.

- **The exact number of "hot-line buyers."** These are individuals who have purchased a product in your category within the last three to six months.

- **The list source**. Lists can be built from different sources, including public records, other lists, market research, etc. Knowing how the list was assembled will help you to qualify it.

- **Basic demographic information**. This can include age, sex, education, income, location, etc.

- **The average size of orders placed within that list**. You don't want a list of $19.95 buyers for a $149.95 product.

- **The list's form factor**. Do not buy lists from sellers who will not make the list available on computer tape (the DM industry has been using mainframes for over twenty years) or on disk in a standard database format. To avoid mistakes and duplicate mailings, most lists need to have duplicate/wrong names filtered out (often called a merge/purge operation); this requires that the list be available on disk or tape.

CARD DECKS

Card decks are an inexpensive way to generate leads and test different offers and approaches to your market. Cards normally come in 3.5" x. 5.5" and 5.5" x 7" sizes.

Deck mailing lists are usually derived from magazine subscriber lists, though some may be compiled from multiple sources. They are normally mailed once a quarter according to a preset yearly schedule. The size of the mailing range from 10K to 250K, with an average cost per impression between 2 and 5 cents, depending on frequency of placement, use of color, and the mailing list. Response rates average between 1/4% and 1/2%.

When placing your card, always negotiate your appearance. Areas for negotiation include:

- **The cost of appearing**. Most publishers will offer a first time advertiser a discount, usually about 10%. If you are willing to commit to multiple placements, you can negotiate further.

- **Where in the deck you will appear**. The front and back are the best locations. "Bracketing the deck," having a card at the front and back, is also highly desirable.

- **How many times you will appear in the deck**. You can often negotiate a two- or even three-card placement in the same deck for the same or marginally higher cost. This allows you to test different offers and designs simultaneously.

- **A larger card**. Again, depending on the deck and the list, you may be able to get a 5.5" x 7" slot for the same or slightly higher price as a 3.5" x 5.5" placement.

Card Deck Design

A good card deck design is an exercise in the art of marketing wrought small. Your card design must be extremely clean and to the point. You have very little real estate to work with, and every square inch counts. To help you maximize your miniature, keep these points in mind:

- **Use your web site or an 800 number to capture responses**. Try to avoid a design that requires the recipient to fill in information and mail the card back. This doubles the amount of real estate you have to work with. If you require respondents to write on the cards, as many as 20% of the cards sent back will have incomplete or illegible entries, and using the web site to handle response saves you money.

- **Use color**. The amount of money saved with black-and-white design does not justify the loss of visual impact.

- **If you're stretched for resources, most card deck publishers will design your card for you**. We suggest you do the work yourself, but this option can save your time and resources. Allow at least a month lead time for the publisher to create an acceptable card and be sure to review it before placement.

- **Decks are more effective as lead generators than close pieces**. To begin the process of converting a prospect to a sale, plan on what type of offer or bounce-back device will generate the best response to your card; for example, a free web download, free trial offer, white paper, seminar, etc.

DIRECT FAX

Direct fax campaigns were extremely popular in the early 1990s, but their use decreased sharply after the passage of federal legislation requiring companies to obtain permission from potential customers before faxing them and allowed recipients to collect civil penalties from firms that sent unsolicited faxes. Fax broadcasting to compiled or subscription lists does not perform particularly well; a response rate of 1% is considered high. Internet mail programs are now seen as the logical alternative to direct fax.

Direct fax also suffers from the inherent quality of fax technology. There is no such thing as an attractive fax. The most hopeful specimens can best be described as "not ugly." Documents designed for fax should therefore be designed with the goal of transmitting information, not making a visual statement. It is best to avoid graphics as they slow transmission and can tie up the receiver's fax for a considerable period. If you have to use graphics, keep them simple and small. Costs for fax broadcasts range between 10 and 30 cents per minute, depending on the amount of time purchased. In most cases, assume one minute for every 8.5" x 11" page broadcast.

Up to 4,999	$0.16
5,000 to 9,999	$0.13
10,000 to 19,999	$0.12
20,000 to 49,999	$0.11
50,000+	$0.10

Figure 7-1. Typical fax broadcast rates

Despite the drawbacks and legal issues, direct fax programs are still a useful adjunct to a direct marketing program, when:

- You are mailing to an installed base. These recipients will be more interested in receiving information about your product and will be less concerned about high-quality graphics.

- You are mailing to a highly qualified list. As with an installed base, these groups tend to be less concerned with graphics and high-quality collaterals.

- Your fax campaign is integrated with other programs, such as mailing or telemarketing. In this case, the fax serves as a "tickler" and can help support the other components of an integrated program.

To ensure you adhere to legal strictures, follow these rules when mailing to a fax list:

- Use opt-in lists (lists of individuals who have agreed to receive faxes from you).

- Consider Internet faxing. This is a bit cheaper than conventional fax broadcasting, though the same legal rules apply.

- Incorporate fax permission into your registration cards and other bounce-back collaterals received from customers or people interested in your products.

- Immediately remove from the fax list anyone who requests it.

HOME SHOPPING CLUBS

As of this writing, little software, with the exception of closeout merchandise purchased by liquidators, has been sold by home shopping clubs such as QVC. There have been some experiments selling entertainment and home titles in the holiday periods, with fairly good results. However, the current image of home shopping clubs does not wear well with a high-tech audience, and concerns about reputation and credibility have led most publishers to abandon this approach. This may change in the near future, as the expansion and segmentation of cable may lead to increased opportunities with shopping channels dedicated to highly specific audience segments.

Another problem is that home shopping clubs typically purchase products for resale at heavy discounts. Requests for 60 to 80 points off SRP are not atypical. This type of discount structure does mesh with most publishers' pricing structures, and is another reason to avoid this marketing venue.

INFOMERCIALS

Despite images of Chia pets and "no money down" real estate deals, infomercials have been used successfully by Apple, Phillips, Microsoft, Intuit, Jump Software, and several other high-tech firms and software publishers. This marketing approach may or may not be appropriate to your product, but the well-rounded marketing strategist needs to understand the dynamics of this form of TV advertising and how it works.

Background Information

Infomercials began appearing in 1984, after the Reagan administration lifted the ban on no more than 16-minutes of commercials per hour. This freedom, combined with the growth of cable and the 800 number system, sparked explosive growth in infomercial use. The modern infomercial follows in the "glorious" wake of earlier direct-response campaigns, including the never-to-be-forgotten Popeil Pocket Fisherman; the Ginsu knife; Peter Lemongello (an album featuring songs sung by, uh, Peter Lemongello); and of course, K-Tel records (who figured out that recycling old hits was a profitable business long before Sierra and Activision). Infomercials are just another element in what insiders call direct-response TV (DRTV). Other elements include home shopping networks, direct response ads on TV, airplane in-flight ads, and so forth.

Infomercial Basics

There are two infomercials formats, the long form and short form. The long form is a 30-minute piece, while the short form can be 30, 60, 90, or 120 seconds long. A few intermediate 15-minute forms have been produced, but they're difficult to place since most cable and broadcast stations won't book them. As cable networks have grown, they're less inclined to run two-minute spots so costs for these time slots have risen.

There are definite economic benefits associated with the long form since the rate cost is not 30 times that of a one-minute spot. In fact, the cost per minute of a 30-minute infomercial ranges between15% and 50% less than for a short form. Also, 30-minute infomercials are not run whenever the station feels like slotting it in; the specific half hour is bought in advance, hopefully in the most productive time slot for your product. Knowing the exact time makes it possible to schedule 800 number response staffing exactly when you need it.

Infomercials have, in theory, an incredible reach. A $2 million investment in media placement over one year has the potential of being seen by over 150 million+ potential buyers. Compare your cost per impression for print, or even the Internet, and the possibilities become intriguing. When infomercials, initially appeared, they were primarily creatures of cable, but these networks only reach about 50% of the total 89 million television viewers. Infomercials have now made the jump to broadcast networks, with about 60% of their revenue coming from airtime sales. It is rare, however, to see an infomercial running in a prime time slot. Experience has shown that various "off periods," such as Saturday morning, or after certain sports events, are usually far more profitable.

The Show Infomercial vs. The Storymercial

Infomercials are divided into two types—the traditional show format and the storymercial. The show format usually consists of a moderator, celebrity guest, testimonials, and an appropriately enthusiastic audience. In most cases, a careful illusion of a show is maintained, with the product functioning as the star.

The storymercial often incorporates the same elements, but it also includes a story revolving around the use of the product to solve a problem or fulfill a desire. All things being equal, a storymercial is more expensive to produce, given the need to develop the script, hire actors, and shoot a convincing story. Which type you employ depends on the type and price of your product. To date, most high-tech and software firms have used the storymercial format.

Regardless of the format, the internals of the infomercial will be similar. In a 30-minute one, the program should be divided into three segments. This is mandated by the fact that most people will not watch the complete infomercial; on average, they will watch about 10 minutes of the program before reaching their buy/no buy decision. That is why a call to action is displayed after each segment, along with an 800 or 888 number (absolutely necessary), listing of all credit cards accepted, (you must accept Visa, MasterCard, and Discover), 30 day no-questions-asked guarantee (also required), price, shipping and handling costs, and often an extra bonus for ordering now.

A point about the call to action. Not every infomercial asks for the money now, though most do. Microsoft, to support the rollout of Windows 95, aired a 30-minute program with Bill Gates and ER star Anthony Edwards to support the rollout of Windows 95. Interestingly enough, Microsoft sold ad space to appear in the ad.

Once produced, an infomercial is copied to tape and sent to various TV and cable station across the country. Station size can vary from small rural cable markets to prime time locations in major metropolitan markets. Approximately 500 new infomercials are shown every year, and the industry has achieved billion-dollar-a-year status. Approximately 25% of the viewing audience has made a direct purchase, based on seeing a TV ad, with the other 75% needing the security of a retail environment. (A very similar proportion to what exists in direct mail.) A common misconception is that women make up the bulk of infomercial buyers: the infomercial's audience is split evenly between the sexes.

A sobering fact is that most infomercials fail. Current industry estimates are that only one of every 20 infomercials aired makes money. The high-tech track record, however, though small, has been surprisingly good. Infomercials by Intuit, Jump, Phillips, Apple, and Microsoft have all been solid successes.

If you believe your product may benefit from an infomercial, consider the following points before going ahead:

- **Your product should have broad general appeal** (an audience of at least 5 million potential buyers) and a price point ideally between $99.95 and $249.95. The lower your price point, the broader your market needs to be.

- **You may need a celebrity endorsement**, though this is not always the case. However, most high-tech infomercials have used them.

- **A hardware/software bundle is a more powerful offering**, as infomercial buyers are used to purchasing something more tangible than a floppy disk or CD.

- **Your product's COG should be no less than 1:4 of SRP** (a $30 dollar product should sell for at least $120), and ideally 1:6. If you can't achieve this, an infomercial is a dangerous prospect, as the cost of media placement can chew through your marketing budget at frightening speed.

Infomercial Goals

In most cases, the primary goal of an infomercial is to create a self-amortizing advertising campaign that drives retail purchasing. A 1:4 ratio of direct sales to retail sales is considered ideal. There are exceptions to this rule. Some products perform so well that their introduction into a retail channel is deferred until direct sales begin to sag. But, these are comparatively rare, and your planning should not include the assumption that you will perform at these levels.

Your secondary goal is to generate incremental revenue from your DRTV program. This, in most cases, is icing on the cake. If your infomercial achieves break even, consider it a success.

Equity Companies

For companies unwilling or unable to bear the expense of producing their own infomercial, there is an alternative—an equity company. These firms "take over" the marketing of your product and provide you with a royalty for every product sold. On average, only one of every 100 products submitted to an equity company is accepted for production. In addition, most of these companies expect, on average, to make their money by reselling the product at five times COG; your profit comes after this formula has been applied. If your product fits into an already proven niche, or seems to have special appeal, you may be able to strike a better deal. No two equity contracts are ever the same.

Most equity companies claim to be full service, offering production, media test and placement, and fulfillment. However, at this point, we question whether any of these companies is well prepared to deal with the challenges of selling software.

Testing Your Infomercial

Once you've produced your infomercial, you need to test it by purchasing airtime in selected markets (called day parts, in industry parlance.) Costs range from $20K to $50K, depending on the product and the potential audience. It is important to understand that you never stop testing your infomercial in an attempt to maximize your return on investment.

Initially, most tests target regions on different channels and networks and compare results. Many of the regions are close to major metropolitan or sectional centers, but in secondary markets, so as to hold down costs. A typical test might include placement in Boston (Northeast): Greenbay, WI (Midwest): Orlando (the South, but upscale income): Phoenix (the West): Dallas (Southwest), and so forth. Some of the most popular cable networks include CNBC, The Discovery Channel, ESPN, CNN, Lifetime, the Family Channel, and Mind Extension University. Popular air times include Saturday and Sunday mornings, weekday afternoons, and late nights.

The Infomercial Financial Model

We've included a simple spreadsheet below that illustrates the basic financial mechanics involved in infomercial planning. Measuring ROI is different than with other types of DM, where you work with a defined universe of pre-qualified customers. For instance, when mailing to a 100K list of prospective customers, you know that a 2K response will break even, and you can calculate your costs and expected revenue in advance of the mailing.

Best Infomercial Cost and Media Model

Ratio	Units	Gross Sales	Media Cost Per Order	Profit	Profit After Media Placement
1:1	10,000	$2,200,000	$200	$1,000,000	-$1,000,000.00
1.5:1	15,000	$3,300,000	$133	$1,500,000	-$1,5000,000.00
2:1	20,000	$4,400,000	$100	$2,000,000	$0.00
3:1	25,000	$5,500,000	$80	$2,500,000	$500,000.00
3.5:1	30,000	$6,600,000	$67	$3,000,000	$1,000,000.00
4:1	35,000	$7,700,000	$57	$3,500,000	-$1,500,000.00

PRODUCT COSTS		REVENUE	
Unit Costs:	$100	Sales Price:	$200
Fulfillment Costs:	$20	Shipping & Handling	$20
Total Costs:	$120	Total Revenue:	$220
Available for media placement:	$100	**Media Placement Assumptions**:	$2,000,000

Figure 7-2. Infomercial financial model

Infomercial ROI is calculated differently. Since the main goal of the infomercial is to create a self-amortizing advertising campaign, the crucial figure in this model is the ratio of sales to media purchased, with your break-even point usually hovering around 2:1. As you move forward with your campaign, you will look for markets where you can meet and exceed this figure.

Placing the Infomercial

After testing the infomercial, you have to place it, and you can expect to spend between $1 and $4 million per year on placement. Who does the purchasing, how it is done, and the quality of the time purchased are all crucial to your success. The infomercial producer may not be the person who should place it for you.

Your goal in buying time is to generate at least two dollars in revenue for every dollar spent on media placement to achieve your break-even point. You're good at 2.5 to 1, excellent at 3 to 1, and smoking at 3.5+ to 1. The key question, of course, is how much time do you need to purchase to succeed? In our model, we've assumed $2 million, a good starting point. For smaller companies, $2 million seems to be the sweet spot, but it is possible to purchase around $1 million, and still be successful. On the high end, $4 million most likely places you close to saturation and the point of diminishing returns.

Response and Fulfillment

Responses to your infomercial usually break down as follows: a purchase rate between 20% and 30%, requests for more information from another 50%, and 30% chafe (wrong number, kids calling, no credit card, etc.). In conjunction with outbound telemarketing, you can expect to close between 20% and 30% of your leads.

Finally, there is fulfillment. This has been a danger point for high-tech products. Software and hardware products have far higher support costs associated with them, and the infomercial industry is not staffed and prepared to deal with these problems, although techniques are under development. Be prepared to spend extra time and effort in providing assistance to telemarketers via assistance screens, detailed scripts, and more advanced training. Some companies are investigating direct relations with support companies to help separate the support problem from the sales cycle.

FOCUS STORY: CHER SELLS SOFTWARE! INFOMERCIALS COME TO SOFTWARE
Companies

> Intuit
>
> Jump! Software

Market Overview

Intuit and Jump! Software are pioneers in the effective use of infomercials to support their software marketing. A look at their programs reveals the differences between the various forms and approaches and the results they can generate.

Intuit and the Short Form

Intuit has focused on the use of the short form to support QuickBooks, its market-leading small business accounting program. The company decided to use a short infomercial after considering the ROI of print advertising for their product. Product awareness was comparatively low, and the PC-based publications Intuit was most familiar with reached only a small sub-segment of their potential market.

Intuit's first ad was a basic, low-cost affair. It was a one-minute infomercial, shot on videotape, with an avuncular pitchman explaining the benefits of accounting with QuickBooks. All the action took place on a single set, with plain vanilla production values. Development and production together cost about $75K. (This is very inexpensive.) Another $60K was allocated for media testing (somewhat higher than usual). Intuit's goals were straightforward: build retail sales, generate direct orders, and increase awareness of the product.

Their second ad was far more polished. Using an upgraded set, running for two minutes, and employing two attractive actors, the infomercial portrayed a man and woman discussing the problems facing their companies. One person was portrayed as already owning QuickBooks, and extolled the virtues of the product to the other (a testimonial ad).

To test the infomercials, Intuit used a multi-media development tool that created stills of the ad overlaid with narration. This allowed them to test different concepts before spending thousands in production. The ads can then be shown to focus groups, or prospective buyers for evaluation and refinement. Costs range between $6K and $10K for testing three to six potential ads, depending on the type. Quicken tested six concepts for their first infomercial and four for the second. After development, the infomercial was placed in a mix of regional and cable networks. Testing determined that cable placement was most effective, and the eventual 3,500 placements focused on these media outlets.

In both cases, neither ad asked for an order for the full product up front. Instead, prospective buyers were offered the chance to call in and order a trial version: $8 dollars initially, then for free. The product was designed to shut down after a certain number of uses, but could be reactivated after the user called to pay the full SRP price of $89.95.

Jump! Software and the Storymercial

Jump! Software represents an even more dramatic example of success using an infomercial. Their principal product, Piano Discovery System, is an application that teaches people to play the piano. Music instruction is a new and emerging niche in the home market, with companies like Microsoft and Midisoft competing for leadership. To break out of the pack, Jump! decided it needed to do something dramatic to create product and company awareness. So, they created a hardware/ software bundle of a midi-keyboard and their Piano Discovery System software and marketed it via a 30-minute infomercial starring jazz great Herbie Hancock.

Jump!'s target audience was middle- to upper-middle class families with children in elementary and middle-school grades. The entire market size was estimated at 30 million households, with parents interested in purchasing a piano for their children as the primary decision makers. Computer-system requirements of Win 3.X or 95, Sound-Blaster compatible card, and a midi-port met the criteria for mass market appeal and infomercial suitability. The product was priced at $249, with an additional upsell to $299 for additional software and accessories.

Jump!'s primary marketing appeal was positioned to assuage parents' fear of the emotional and financial drain of teaching their children to play an instrument. The learning software was multimedia based, colorful, highly accessible to children, and did not require a great deal of parental involvement—and the midi keyboard cost only a faction of what even a small piano would cost. Parents could get their children involved in music without spending a small fortune.

From the beginning, Jump! decided to create a high-quality infomercial. The ad, "Discover the Music Inside," was shot primarily in 16mm (intermixed with some videotape) with Herbie Hancock as host and pitchman. Mr. Hancock discussed music and demonstrated the product in an elaborate set constructed for the infomercial. In addition, numerous off-set locations were filmed, adding to the cost. And, Mr. Hancock received substantial remuneration for his involvement. All told, the infomercial cost close to $500K to produce, about the top end of what you should pay in today's market. Media test costs were $60K, twice what was originally budgeted.

Jump! used the "storymercial" format for their ad, believing this approach to be more appropriate to their audience. In the introduction, Mr. Hancock briefly demoed the system and set the basic theme for the infomercial: music liberates and enhances your life. The ad then transitioned to the story of a young girl whose mother has purchased the Piano Discovery System for her. We follow her first encounter with the system, watch her progress in capability and confidence, and watch the climax of the story, a home "recital" attended by beaming friends and relatives who watch our newly minted impresario perform Beethoven's "Ode to Joy." The story is interrupted by testimonials from other users, including a music teacher, and more supporting narration by Mr. Hancock. Typical of 30-minute infomercials, it was interrupted three times by a call to action.

The infomercial was ready for airing in mid-1996, and was shown over 2000 times until the end of the 1996/97 holiday season. The potential number of viewers was over 100 million, with 11 million people confirmed to have seen at least part of the ad.

It should be noted that Jump! took a risk in terms of the optimal 1:4/6 cost of goods to price ratio. Despite this, they went ahead, believing the lack of competition and product quality would win out. However, you should keep this ratio firmly in mind when planning your own infomercial.

Results
INTUIT

Intuit achieved their sales goals. Conversion rate for the trial product was approximately 30%. Where Intuit was able to measure retail impact, sell through was approximately 1:4/5; for every one package sold direct, four to five were sold at retail. Today, QuickBooks is the number one product in the small business accounting market. Intuit credits their infomercials with playing a key part in QuickBooks' success.

Intuit also learned some interesting lessons with respect to which techniques worked best. Despite expectations, the "pitchman ad" worked better than the "testimonial." Also surprising was the discovery that the second, two-minute ad performed no better than the first, one-minute ad. Not surprising was the fact that the free trial offer had more audience appeal, with higher inquiry to sales conversion rates.

JUMP!

The results were dramatic. For the six months preceding the 1996/97 holiday season, the ad ran over 2000 times in different regional and cable networks. Direct sales exceeded initial projections by 15%, with 30% of the purchasers choosing the $299 upsell offer. In sharp contrast with Intuit, Jump! discovered that regional and spot placement in local markets was more effective than cable network placement, and their media mix reflected this.

Caller response was as follows: 30% purchased immediately, 40% requested further information, and 30% were non-productive. The purchase rate of callers contacted via an outbound sales effort ranged from 15% to over 40% (the higher rates were reached by in-house Jump! efforts).

The impact on retail sales was also substantial. The expected 1 to 4 direct-to-retail-sale ratio was sustained, though Jump! occasionally had trouble in stocking local outlets in tandem with the infomercial's appearance. Jump! achieved particular success with the bundle in such consumer chains as Lechmere's and in buying clubs such as Costco. Infomercials are expected to work particularly well in the club environment, where demo tapes and unattended demo stations are proven sales generators. For consumer retailers and discounters, the ability of the infomercial to contain a drop-in (a quick mention of a local reseller) helped push sales into a particular market or region. In addition, Jump! approached music specialty stores such as Guitar Center and Sam Ash, and was successful in selling product through these alternate channels.

Interestingly enough, the bundle was not successful in CompUSA, although the software-only product was and is highly successful. This is puzzling, but conversations with other publishers suggest that this reseller is not easily able to adjust its retailing model to meet different marketing situations.

TELEMARKETING VS. TELESALES
Telemarketing vs. Telesales

Some confusion exists about the difference between telesales and telemarketing programs, especially since the two terms are sometimes used interchangeably. A telesales program is designed to close business immediately after contacting a customer. A telemarketing program is primarily focused on generating leads. The telemarketing group may work in conjunction with your channel or a direct sales force to assist the sales process, but unless they take the order directly, it is telemarketing and not telesales. The group that staffs and executes either type of program is referred to as a "call center," and is charged with managing calls, fax and web responses, interactive video, and mail. For brevity's sake, we use the term "telemarketing" to refer to situations and technology applicable to both telesales and telemarketing programs.

Outbound vs. Inbound Call Centers

When planning your call center, you need to decide what percentage of its operations will be dedicated to outbound calls and inbound calls. By its nature, an outbound center is more proactive and involved in either closing sales or generating leads. An inbound center is more focused on taking orders, answering questions about product availability and shipping dates, and resolving fulfillment problems. An inbound center can develop personal relationships with customers by creating a profile of their purchasing habits and preferences, building a history of their calls, resolving any problems quickly, and contacting them with appropriate offers and opportunities as they are introduced.

In-House Call Centers vs. Outsourcing

Once the decision has been made to implement telemarketing, the next decision is whether to outsource the function or create an in-house call center. There are advantages and disadvantages to each approach.

Advantages to an in-house center include:

- It is easier to train and maintain in-house center personnel. Development of scripts, answering technical questions, and solving support issues can also be executed more quickly.

- An in-house group can react to changing market circumstances more quickly. Programs not performing up to expectations can be quickly fine-tuned and improved by employees close to the situation.

- All things being equal, an in-house group will outperform an outsource call center. Employees, or even an internal group of subcontractors, will develop a closer bond with the company, product, and personnel involved with the product, which usually translates into greater *esprit de corps* and better sales.

Advantages of outsourcing include:

- Outsourcing is useful for testing the viability of different telemarketing campaigns and tactics for your products.

- It takes time, money, and management resources to manage an in-house call center. Some companies believe they can hire part-time workers, students, or college interns and achieve the type of results produced by experienced telesales personnel. They are almost always disappointed.

- Outsourcing is useful for seasonal or situational programs where a full-time call center is neither appropriate nor needed.

In-House Call Center Technology

If you are going to establish an in-house call center, new advances in computer telephony integration (CTI) have made it possible for even a small publisher to provide levels of customer service and response that only a few years ago could only be offered by outsourcing centers. At the heart of an inbound-call center is an automatic call distributor (ACD) system. Available on both proprietary and PC-based platforms, these systems allow a call center to provide:

- Automatic call routing to an operator, voice mail system, or interactive voice response (IVR) menu. (Be careful of systems that automatically route a customer into a voice mail system even when a live operator is available.)

- Call queuing, with messages about estimated wait times, the customer's position in the cue, entertainment recordings, or even messages about other products.

- Queue jumping (moving a customer out of the queue and connecting them to an operator).

- Hang up tracking.

- Phone traffic analysis and reports.

On the outbound side, predictive dialers can automate dialing customers and displaying customer information. They work by downloading call lists from a host system or outside list source, then dialing out. The software can screen out busy numbers, no-answers, answering machines, and disconnected numbers.

More advanced systems track call length and try to predict when an operator will be available. They can synchronize caller ID with customer information via a "screen pop" with customer information from a database, and can distribute the customer database across multiple locations.

While predictive dialers can increase telemarketing productivity, there are drawbacks. Most systems have a lag between the answer and the operator pickup; astute listeners can identify this lag, and have learned to hang up before the operator can say "hello." Also, for high-end telemarketing where the call list may target upper management, a manual call method may still be best. Another drawback is burnout; these systems tend to push your personnel hard and can increase feelings of rejection and failure. Over time this will manifest itself in slumping morale and sales.

CTI and the Web

Call center technology is beginning to blend with the web with "callback" and "callback tag" features being added to ACD systems. With this capability, web surfers can click on a callback button on the web site and a form pops up asking for their name and phone number. When they submit the form, the web server sends the information to the firm's phone system, where it is placed in an outbound queue for the next available operator. A callback tag allows the outbound agent to receive a screen pop of the web page the customer is viewing and prepare to answer questions the customer may have about the product or service. A more sophisticated variant on this technology allows a message to be sent to the call center automatically scheduling a call between the two parties. Finally, a "click and connect" capability allows a customer to directly ring the operator's phone and talk directly to the call center.

Call Blending

Call blending manages the relationship between inbound and outbound call center activity. They monitor inbound and outbound activity, and notify managers when an operator or call center agent needs to be reassigned to either inbound or outbound duties. Most call centers implement call blending when inbound agents become idle waiting for calls, and it makes sense to reassign them to an outbound campaign. Ideally, using call blending, a center can staff for peak volumes and still remain productive during slow periods.

Script Development

The core of all successful telemarketing operations is a good script. Script development is done on a custom basis, and incorporates the following elements:

- A greeting that makes the customer feel good and develops quick rapport.
- A friendly presentation that proactively allows customers to act on the offer while leaving them in charge of the decision.
- A trial close.
- Answers to the most common objections.
- A friendly goodbye even if the customer does not purchase anything. This is particularly important if you're going to be working with an installed base list. While the customer may not buy now, they may be interested in a future product or upgrade. Always leave the door open for further contact.

Appropriate Audiences for Telemarketing

A popular perception surrounding telemarketing is that it is only appropriate for low-end, retail-class products. This is not true. Telemarketing can be very effective for both direct- and VAR-class products, and can be successfully targeted to members of upper management, such as CEOs, CFOs, and CIOs. For telemarketing to succeed with this audience however, call center operators need extensive training on speaking with upper management, as well as scripts that address upper-management's business issues. High-level telemarketing usually, though not always, is most successful when it focuses on lead generation as part of an overall sales effort.

OUTSOURCE COSTS	
Inbound operator costs	$1.50 to $2.50 per call (depends on script length and number of fulfillment actions, i.e., offer an upsell, take credit card number, provide product information, the agent must undertake) or a percentage of the selling price (dependent on negotiations).
Inbound script and setup	$500 to $750
Outbound operator	$30 to $40 per operator. Prices will depend on the number of fulfillment actions the agent must undertake.
Outbound script and setup	$1K to $2K
Initial tests	$500 to $1.5K
IN-HOUSE COSTS	
In-house Call Center Technology (include ACD, predictive dialing, and basic hardware	$20K to $250K (price dependent on number of operators, software, hardware, and maintenance charges.
Personnel	$50K to $65K for managers, $20K to $35K for full time personnel, $7 to $11 per hour part time (geography, call center objectives, and skill level needed will effect these costs).
Commissions	2% to 15%, depending on whether the activities focus around telesales or telemarketing.

Figure 7-3. Typical telemarketing costs

THE OFFER

Direct marketing offers can come in a wide variety of types, price points, and special offers. Regardless of the specifics, all successful offers incorporate the following elements:

- An immediate and compelling offer. Direct-mail pieces frequently print an attention grabbing "teaser" right on the envelope. A telemarketer may begin a conversation with a description of the savings buyers will realize if they act on the promotion right now.

- An incentive to purchase within a set time frame. Without a deadline, purchases are far more likely to be deferred.

- If not intended to sell but to generate a response, then an incentive to respond within a set time frame.

- Crisp copy that clearly explains the offer, highlights the advantages of buying the product or responding to the offer, and asks for the order or response.

- Coding. This allows your company to analyze list performance and determine who responded and who didn't.

- Your 800 number—everywhere. Make it very easy for a buyer to give in to the impulse to call right now and order or respond. If your web site supports e-commerce, your URL should be equally prominent.

COMMON MISTAKES

Common mistakes in direct marketing include:

- Failing to code the offering. You need to not only code by offer, but also by list. This allows you to find out which lists and which buyers are not receptive to your offering. This is doubly important if your company is generating several different offers. If the offer is not coded, a telemarketer may have to ask the buyer to describe the particular offer so they can book it; this is a tremendous waste of time and money. And even if only one offer is currently in the mail, you can anticipate calls months later from previous offers.

- Failing to track pricing. This is very important in bundles and catalog sales. While you will usually have control over your own product's pricing, this is not true when you are dealing with another company's products. Try to negotiate price protection into your bundling and catalog offers so that should a publisher drop their product price, the value of your bundle or the effectiveness of your catalog or telemarketing offer is not damaged.

- Attempting to use advertising pieces as direct-mail pieces. This is especially true if your ads encourage the buyer to ask questions about a product rather than close the sale right then and there. A direct-mail piece is most effective when it closes, and it should be designed from the start to result in a sale, not an inquiry. If integration among various parts of your marketing campaign is needed, creative use of graphics and text is essential.

- Mixing inappropriate products and pricing. This is particularly critical in the catalog business. A $1995 item will not sell well in a catalog of products ranging between $49.95 and $149.95; the pricing mix must be rational. Also be careful when picking premiums. One time a publisher of accounting products picked an adventure game without knowing that the game began with a crooked CPA stealing a company's funds. Fortunately, the premium was changed before the mailing went out!

- Directing customers to a web site for a free download when the objective of your DM campaign is to sell **now**. When you direct users to a web site for a trial copy, you must put into place a mechanism to contact the customer and convert them from a prospect to a customer. This converts a close campaign into a lead-generation program. If this is not your objective, forget the free download.

- Forgetting to offer a money-back guarantee. This is required in DM. When offering a money- back guarantee, use positive language. For instance, "Try it for 30 days without risk or obligation" sounds better than "Your Money Back if not Satisfied." And longer guarantees, 45-, 60-, or 90-days usually generate better responses than 15- or 30-days. (Life-of-the-product can be effective as well, but the nature of software makes this a bit dangerous.) The longer guarantee period gives your customer more time to use your product, integrate it into their working environment, and increase their desire to hold onto it.

- Misusing the word "free." Under FTC regulations, you cannot state that something is "free" if the customer has to send payment to obtain it, or without some clear statement of the specifics in close proximity to the word "free." For example, "Yours FREE with offer inside" implies that the prospect has to agree to something else in order to get the "free" gift. Thus a "Free Trial" must include a "bill me" option with no up-front payment. A "Risk-Free" Trial, however, can require payment with a refund option clearly stated.

- Trying to sell two things at once. Usually, this occurs in the context of offering a secondary product at a discounted price, often as an inducement to purchase the primary product. This dilutes your marketing message since the customer must now make two buying decisions. Worse, necessity will demand the secondary product be given comparatively faint praise within the offer. However, offering a premium pack as a reward for purchasing can be a very effective tactic.

- Scaring people. After the Unabomber, it is a mistake to send DM pieces in a brown Kraft #10 envelope stating: "Open by Addressee Only," and "Confidential." Your piece is likely to end up in a tub of water.

- Using mailing labels. If at all possible, directly print an address on the piece. Labels have a mass market, "cheap" look, detract from your message, and discourage recipients from opening your offer.

- Deciding it is too inconvenient to send out a promised premium. Incredible as it seems, some publishers actually try to get away with this. This is called "mail fraud." Don't do it.

DIRECT MAIL COSTS

Direct mail costs are calculated by multiplying the number of pieces mailed or distributed by the total cost of the piece including design, postage, printing, preparation, mailing, and fulfillment. Your largest costs per piece will normally be mailing and fulfillment costs. Price per piece will typically range between $1.25 and $2.75 per piece. This will change if you are executing a dimensional mailing or sending out an expensive premium.

If you are mailing via the Post Office, your options on saving money are limited. The Post Office is a legal monopoly, and you have no place else to go if you want to move conventional mail. However, there are a few things to keep in mind that will save your campaign money and boost your image:

- Consider sorting even first class mailings. This will save you a couple of cents per piece.

- It is usually not necessary to go the expense of buying your own bulk mail stamp (indicia) if you're using a fulfillment house; you can use theirs.

- Consider using bulk mail stamps if you decide bulk mailing is appropriate for your offer. These give your piece a "first class look" and will boost response.

- If you're going to use bulk mail, use the nine-digit system. A good fulfillment house can massage your list with a "Zip+4" program to make sure you realize the extra savings.

- For a dimensional mailing, look into companies who produce FedEx or Priority mail look-a-like packaging. (The Post Office hates these companies.) These can be sent for about half the price of a priority mail piece, but are very likely to be opened. Remember that despite their appearance, they are treated like first class mail (and perhaps a bit worse!)

Envelope	$.03 to $.05 (regular bond, two color)
Design	$2,500 to $25,000
Four-color brochure	$.12 to $.20
Cover letter	$.015 to $.04
Mailing	$.20 to $.33
Fulfillment	$4 to $9.95
Reply card	$.03 to $.05
Total Cost per Piece	$1.25 to $2.50

Figure 7-4. Typical direct marketing piece costs (assumes a 25K mailing)

PRODUCTION PLANNING

Production issues are the perennial bane of direct marketers. Last minute changes in paper stock can mean adhesive fasteners now don't fasten. Failure to supervise the production of personalized letters can lead to thousands of inappropriate letters being mailed. Failing to check the competency of a translation group creating an instruction manual can lead to a scatological term being substituted for the word "screw." (These examples have all happened!) Almost all production problems can, in theory, be avoided, through careful, exhaustive testing. The key words are exhaustive testing. Most beginners cannot resist the urge to cut corners and expenses. This is always a mistake.

Mailing List Ordered (assumes use of list broker)	7 to 10 days
Merge/Purge, Postal Sorts, Taple/Label/Disk/Output	10 to 14 days
Output conversion to mailing house format	2 to 3 days
Laser proofs to client for approval	2 to 3 days
Client approval of laser proofs	1 to 2 days
Laser forms	4 to 5 days
Burst and fold personalized forms	1 to 2 days
Insert, seal, meter, sort and bag mailing pieces	5 to 10 days

Figure 7-5. Typical direct mail preparation schedule (assumes a 100K mailing with four inserts)

FULFILLMENT

While many companies spend a lot of time worrying about offers and price, too few worry about fulfillment. This can be fatal. American buyers are picky. They will not wait long on the phone to place orders. And once they have ordered a product, they want it to arrive immediately, if not sooner. Publishers need to bulletproof their fulfillment capabilities and track performance. The average time per call (ATPC) should be about five minutes, with a 2% to 3% abandonment rate; 5% is not acceptable. Overnight and/or two-day shipping options are critical.

Because it is difficult to build a professional fulfillment capability internally for a major campaign, most publishers are best served by third-party fulfillment houses that specialize in shipping and providing product. A good fulfillment house can provide:

- The ability to ship product in a variety of ways, including overnight, two-day, bulk, COD, etc.
- The ability to build special bundles for the publisher. This can include taking delivery of product, assembling it, and shrink-wrapping it as needed.
- Accurate reports on run rates on a daily, weekly, monthly, and yearly basis by a variety of criteria. In addition, the fulfillment house can build custom reports to a publisher's specifications.
- Telemarketing and telesales capabilities. This can include order taking, cross- and up-sells, surveys, etc.
- Insurance in the event a fire destroys inventory stored in their warehouse.

Common fulfillment mistakes include:

- Failing to test a new electronic online order entry system if you are fulfilling internally. These will always crash when first brought up; therefore, your testing should be extensive and exhaustive—for at least three to six months. If not, then plan on using a manual system or an outside fulfillment firm.
- Failing to plan cross-sells and up-sells in advance. This is especially crucial in telemarketing activities. There is no better opportunity to sell something else than when a customer is on line already making a purchase. For example, if someone is buying a network drawing tool, why not offer them an upgrade to the network device database? Or perhaps a discovery or monitoring tool? These are cross-sells. Or offer them the opportunity to purchase a network management framework? This is an up-sell. The key to success is planning. The telemarketer can't waste time rummaging through a price list and trying to sell anything they think of. Extra offers should be thought out, built into the script, and make sense. If the customer doesn't bite, the sales representative should say "thank you" and move on to the next call.

- Failing to have products available. While this may not be a concern if you're selling your own products, it's a crucial issue when you are selling someone else's. A mailing offer full of unavailable products is very unappealing to a potential buyer.

- Failing to factor in the cost of fulfillment when calculating the cost of the campaign. This can be a serious mistake for a campaign dedicated to selling a product in the $29.95 to $149 range. Be sure to build your fulfillment overhead into your offer or shipping and handling charges.

TESTING

Unlike other marketing efforts, such as advertising, direct selling can be carefully tested. In fact, all direct campaigns should include testing as an integral, ongoing part of your DM activities. The minimum mailing size that provides a valid statistical return is about 5,000. You should be testing the following things:

- The price of an offer. Both high and low price points need to be tested. The goal is to find the price point that returns the maximum revenue.

- Applicability of a special offer. For instance, is one product bundle more appealing to your buyers than another? Why?

- Audience focus. Are you direct selling to the right audience? Are there potential audiences you're not mailing to that you should be?

Remember, no direct campaign should ever begin without plans for testing different lists and offers when the mailing is sent.

FOCUS STORY: DOING IT RIGHT
Company

Borland (Inprise)

Market Overview

Borland, now Inprise, has always had an affinity for direct marketing. Its introduction of Turbo Pascal in the early 1980s at a direct price of $79.95 sparked a revolution in the pricing of computer languages. Its success laid the foundation for the company's growth into one of the top microcomputer software publishers, and the microcomputer DBMS leader. During the dark day's following Borland's withdrawal from the desktop applications market, their expertise at DM and generating revenue from its installed base were key factors in the company's continued survival. Borland can still direct market with the best of them, and they closely follow the formula they developed in their upgrade program for Borland C++ 4.0. This was one of Borland's most successful efforts and can be used as a model for any publisher planning a DM campaign.

The Borland promotion was aggressively priced ($149.95, down from an SRP of $499) and effectively executed. This classic direct mail piece incorporated the following elements:

- A clear statement on the outside of the offer envelope stating its contents— "Announcing Borland C++ 4.0." Underneath was a strong teaser statement— "Our Meatiest Upgrade Ever." Underneath the teaser was a simple graphic of a shishkabob (get it?). The outside was also stamped "Second Notice," adding further urgency to the message. (This was the second upgrade mailing to this list.)

The inside of the envelope contained the following key elements:

- A postage-paid return envelope. This is an absolute necessity. Most buyers resent being asked to spend their money for the privilege of spending their money.
- A premium offer for an arcade-style "shoot-em-up" game printed on a 3" x 6" gaudy, three-colored slip, stating that the offer is only good while "supplies last." This added further urgency to the offer. The 800 order number was also printed on the slip.
- A four-color, fold-out brochure describing the product's key features and benefits. The design of the brochure allowed buyers to open it to the key features they were most interested in. The 800 order number appeared on one side of the brochure.
- A cover letter that immediately stated the offer and the price. Cover letters are popular and effective in direct marketing, as the buyer expects to find a letter in an envelope. Key points in the letter were underlined, and it contained a subset of the key points listed in the brochure. It was not overwritten, and made good use of white space. The 800 order number was on the back of the letter.

An order form for people who prefer to buy by mail. It had the following characteristics:

- Simple to fill out.
- A check-off box where buyers could request that they not be placed on any additional mailing lists.
- A check-off box where buyers could notify Borland if they were receiving duplicate mailings. This helped Borland clean and refine its list.
- An offer to buy a CD-ROM version of the product and receive a free product valued at $49.95. A smart offer, since the CD version has a lower COG.
- An offer to buy a complementary product for $99.95 (the cross-sell).
- A premium, listed as FREE, as a line item on the order form. The buyer has to make the effort to decline this free premium. This is a visual incentive to buy, since free is the strongest word in the marketing language.
- The 800 order number appears on both sides of the form.
- A money-back guarantee.
- An end date.
- An offer code on the order form. If you called Borland to purchase this product, the telemarketer requested this code.

LESSONS

Borland's piece exemplifies good direct marketing. The order number appeared at least six times throughout the piece. An attractive premium was offered and the buyer didn't have to do anything to get it. A cross-sell offer was made, as well as an additional offer to buy a more profitable version of the product. The options to not have the buyer's name brokered and to find out about duplicate mailings were both courteous and smart. The copy was clean and readable. The offer was made several times, and the buyer encouraged to act now. The only changes necessary to bring this piece up-to-date are the inclusion of a web site address, and perhaps not offering an incentive to buy the CD version of the product.

DIRECT MARKETING OBJECTIVES/EVALUATION CHECKLIST

OBJECTIVES	EVALUATION

Marketing Goals

1. Establish market visibility

*% increased calls
to company* _____ _____ _____

*% increased product
inquiries* _____ _____ _____

*% increased SKUs shipped
to channel* _____ _____ _____

% increased direct sales _____ _____ _____

*% increased mentions,
articles, reviews, etc.,
in press* _____ _____ _____

2. Move product to market quickly

Monthly run rate _____ _____ _____

3. Build a strategic position in the market

*% increased reseller
recommendation rate* _____ _____ _____

*% increased reseller
mindshare* _____ _____ _____

*% increased buyer
mindshare* _____ _____ _____

*# orders from channel for
other product(s)* _____ _____ _____

*# orders from channel for
new product(s)* _____ _____ _____

*# product reviews, first-
looks, and articles
in press* _____ _____ _____

OBJECTIVES	EVALUATION		

4. Establish a direct business for the product

% increased direct sales _____ _____ _____

5. Increase channel sales via customer pull

% increased SKUs shipped
to channel _____ _____ _____

6. Increase market share v.a.v. competition

% increased buying your
product _____ _____ _____

7. Leverage off an installed base

% increased cross-sells _____ _____ _____

% increased up-sells _____ _____ _____

8. Develop a self-amortizing

Ad campaign

amount product sold in ratio

to media placement _____ _____ _____

Audience

1. Offer(s) reached target audience(s)

 # responses to coded
list offers _____ _____ _____

DIRECT MARKETING SUCCESS CHECKLIST

1. **Select type of Direct Marketing**
   - [ ] Card decks _____
   - [ ] Catalog _____
   - [ ] Direct fax _____
   - [ ] Direct mail _____
   - [ ] Regular piece _____
   - [ ] Dimensional piece _____
   - [ ] Electronic marketing _____
   - [ ] Home shopping clubs _____
   - [ ] Infomercials_____
   - [ ] Telemarketing_____

2. **Determine target audience(s)**
   - [ ] Characterize each audience _____
   - [ ] Identify sources for names for each audience _____
   - [ ] Set priorities among audiences _____

3. **Determine number and types of offers**

   A. **Number of offers**_____

   B. **Types of offers**
   - [ ] Bundling offers _____
   - [ ] Different price points _____
   - [ ] Value-added offers_____
   - [ ] Other _____

   C. **Associate offer(s) to target audience(s)** _____

4. **Develop direct marketing plan, including objectives, production, fulfillment, measurement, budget, schedule, and follow-up activities**

   A. **Determine who will coordinate offer development and execution**
   - [ ] Agency _____
   - [ ] Consulting firm_____
   - [ ] In-house personnel_____

   B. **Determine who will do fulfillment**
   - [ ] In-house staff _____
   - [ ] Outside vendor _____

    C.   **Determine who will do list processing** _____

    D.   **Identify internal key contacts for the following activities:**

- ☐ Manufacturing _____
- ☐ Deliverables, inventory, and availability _____
- ☐ Problem determination _____
- ☐ Marketing person named in offer letter _____
- ☐ Technical expert _____
- ☐ Support _____
- ☐ Pre-sale _____
- ☐ Channel _____
- ☐ Technical _____
- ☐ Customer _____
- ☐ Follow-up _____
- ☐ Qualify leads _____
- ☐ Telemarketing vs. follow-up mailing _____
- ☐ Bounce-back for complementary products _____

5.   **Select type(s) of list(s)**

    A.   **Internal list**

- ☐ Registration cards from your product(s) _____
- ☐ Names from other internal promotions, mailing, offers, inquiries, etc. _____

    B.   **External list (purchased or swapped)**

- ☐ Buyers list _____
- ☐ Compiled list—matches a demographic profile (usually least effective) _____
- ☐ Opt-in (for direct fax/EDM _____
- ☐ Subscription list _____

    C.   **Decide whether or not to use a list broker** _____

    D.   **If you purchase or swap for a list, note the following:**

- ☐ Average # orders placed _____
- ☐ Basic demographics _____
- ☐ List form factor _____
- ☐ List source _____
- ☐ Number of "hot line buyers" _____

6. **Develop the direct marketing piece**

MAILING

   A. **Letter—at least 2 pages ending with a P.S. that repeats the offer**
   - [ ] Emphasis on benefits, not features _____
   - [ ] Should answer:
       - Why buy, upgrade, or act now_____
       - How to buy, upgrade, or act _____
   - [ ] Prominent display of web site/800-number_____

   B. **Brochure**
   - [ ] Describe new features and old _____
   - [ ] Focus on features/benefits_____
   - [ ] Should answer:
       - What product does _____
       - What is new in product_____
       - How it differs from prior versions_____
       - How it differs from competition_____

   B. **Envelope**
   - [ ] Address correction request _____
   - [ ] Appropriate return address _____
   - [ ] First class vs. third-class bulk _____
   - [ ] Include teaser message _____
   - [ ] Use word "REMINDER" on follow-up mailings to same person _____

   C. **Postage-paid return envelope** _____

CARD DECK
   - [ ] Decide size _____
   - [ ] Design _____
   - [ ] Card deck publisher _____
   - [ ] In-house_____
   - [ ] Design uses both sides of deck _____
   - [ ] Design uses color _____
   - [ ] Negotiate card _____
   - [ ] Price _____
   - [ ] Placement _____

    ▓ Bracket _____

    ▓ Front/back of deck _____

    ▓ Size _____

DIRECT FAX

☐ Avoid graphics _____

☐ High information content _____

☐ Integrated with other campaign _____

☐ Internet fax _____

INFOMERCIAL

A. Decide criteria

☐ Celebrity endorsement_____

☐ Hardware/software bundle _____

☐ Product COG 1:4 _____

B. Equity Company vs. self-produced _____

C. Long form vs. short form _____

D. Traditional vs. storymercial _____

E. Purchasing and media placement

☐ Different regions_____

☐ Different cable networks _____

☐ Different regional networks _____

☐ Other _____

TELEMARKETING

A. Telemarketing _____

B. Telesales _____

C. Target audience

☐ Retail-class customers _____

☐ Upgraders _____

☐ Upper management _____

☐ Other _____

D. Outbound _____

E. Inbound _____

F. In-house call center

- [ ] ACD _____
  - ▦ Call queuing _____
  - ▦ Queue jumping _____
  - ▦ Hang up tracking _____
  - ▦ Phone traffic analysis and reports _____
  - ▦ Screen pops _____
  - ▦ Web-based callback tags _____
  - ▦ Web-based click and connect _____
- [ ] Predictive dialing _____
- [ ] Call blending _____

G. Outsource call center _____

H. Script development

- [ ] Effective greeting _____
- [ ] Friendly presentation _____
- [ ] Trial close _____
- [ ] Answers to common objections _____
- [ ] Friendly goodbye _____

7. OFFER Elements

- [ ] Added value _____
- [ ] Any restrictions/limitations _____
- [ ] Attractive price _____
- [ ] Clear description _____
- [ ] Combination _____
- [ ] Cross- or up-sell offer _____
- [ ] Link to promotion _____
- [ ] Money-back guarantee _____
- [ ] Next-day or 2-day shipping (standard or option) _____
- [ ] Option for buyer's name not to be brokered _____
- [ ] Option for buyers to indicate they are receiving duplicate mailings _____
- [ ] Powerful teaser _____
- [ ] Premium _____
- [ ] Software _____

☐ White paper _____

☐ Other _____

8. The CALL to ACTION

☐ Response mechanism _____

☐ Business reply mailer (card) _____

☐ Coupon _____

☐ Fax number _____

☐ Modem automatic order _____

☐ Web site _____

☐ Telephone via 800 number _____

9. Involvement device

☐ Questionnaire _____

    ▨ Appropriate to respondent _____

    ▨ Captures useful data _____

    ▨ Easy to fill out and capture data_____

    ▨ Specific plan implemented for analyzing data _____

☐ Paste-on sticker(s)_____

10. Order form or business reply mailer

A. Coded to identify mailing/product/audience: _____

☐ Source of activity _____

☐ Audience response _____

☐ Mail-drop effectiveness _____

☐ Complies with postal regulations _____

☐ Easy for order entry to process _____

☐ Easy to fill out _____

☐ Instructions are clear and obvious _____

☐ Lots of space to write in _____

☐ Prominent display of 800 number to order _____

☐ Prominent display of web site URL to order _____

☐ Unique to specific audience _____

11. Select vendor(s)

☐ Assembly & mailing _____

☐ Fulfillment _____

☐ List broker _____

☐ List management _____

☐ Printing _____

☐ Production _____

12. Cost by element

☐ Mailer preparation _____

☐ Mailing (include postal permits and P.O. Box)_____

☐ Measurement _____

☐ Merge-purge service _____

☐ Production _____

☐ Purchased list _____

13. Obtain all necessary approvals

☐ Finance _____

☐ Product Marketing _____

☐ Senior Management_____

14. List/mail activities

A. Code all mailers by list sources

☐ Merge decoy names to: _____

▓ Examine vendor quality of delivered mail _____

▓ Time postal/internet delivery process_____

▓ Check for name theft _____

B. Merge/purge to eliminate duplicates _____

C. Postal presort for postage savings _____

D. P.O. Box and postal permits in place _____

15. Fulfillment activities

☐ All deliverables available before mail drops _____

☐ All internal systems ready to accept activity_____

☐ "Live test" system prior to volume mailing _____

☐ Web site e-commerce system ready _____

☐ Measurement system ready at mail drop with sample reports ___

☐ Order-entry scripts tested and in place _____

16. Measurement activities

☐ Evaluate cost per lead _____

☐ Exact sales measurement _____

☐ Identify and qualify sales leads _____

☐ Measure coded activity _____

☐ Measure conversion of leads to sales _____

☐ Measure ratio of sales to media purchase _____

☐ Measure response to piece _____

☐ Measure sale vs. no-sale activity _____

☐ Measure Webster response _____

17. Marketing follow-up activities

☐ Lead-conversion program _____

☐ Evaluate mailer contact per audience response _____

☐ Update mailing list(s) _____

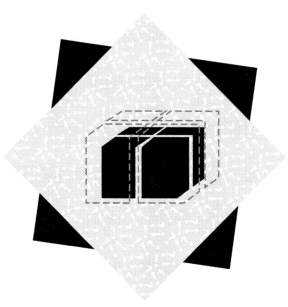

8

Bundling

Bundling, that is, using software as a value-added inducement to purchase products, has been a part of the software industry since its inception. Osborne Computers, one of the early microcomputer pioneers, rode to fame on the "incredible" amount of software it offered with its 33-pound "portable," the Osborne 1. Their bundle included Basic, WordStar, and SuperCalc. Today, the spirit of Osborne lives on in the new software suites that have proved so popular with buyers.

TYPES OF BUNDLES

There are three bundle types in the software industry.

- **Hardware or original equipment manufacturer (OEM) bundle**. This consists of bundling software product(s) with hardware. While the most common type combines software with a computer, such bundles can also be designed around other popular types of hardware, such as printers, scanners, mice, cameras, etc.

- **Software bundle**. This consists of packaging two or more software packages together.

- **Book bundle**. This consists of packaging a software product with a book.

Hardware Bundles

Of necessity, a bundling arrangement is an attempt to reconcile differing objectives and viewpoints; this is particularly true with hardware bundles. From the software publisher's perspective, the most important reason to bundle is to build an upgrade market and generate incremental dollars. However, since hardware manufacturers are always looking for aggressive discounts off retail SRPs (discounts of 90% and even more are not uncommon), the dollar volumes associated with such bundles can be quite low. In some cases, first-tier hardware vendors, such as Compaq, are asking publishers to **pay them** for the privilege of bundling their software with Compaq hardware. Publishers need to carefully plan their bundling price strategy in advance of taking their product to the market.

While a low cost of goods (COGs) and quick cash can be enticing, the low dollar volumes make it difficult to build a large cash flow. If, for example, the hardware manufacturer builds the product, the publisher is basically just "selling labels," and can expect to make, **at most**, 3% to 10% of the product's SRP. While very profitable from a percentage standpoint, the dollar volume going to the publisher is low. In some cases, the dollar volume will be non-existent.

WHY DO HARDWARE MANUFACTURERS BUNDLE?

Hardware manufacturers bundle software with their products primarily to enhance its value and differentiate it from the competition. They will be looking for the following from their software partners:

- Assurance that the applications they're bundling will clearly add value to their hardware in the minds of the purchasers. To convince a hardware manufacturer of this, software publishers should be ready to discuss the following in detail:
  - Size of the market for their product.
  - Growth of the market for their product.
  - Type of user likely to buy their product.
  - Readiness of users to buy their product.
- The ability to enhance and customize the software to differentiate the manufacturer's hardware product. This can include:
  - Simple customization to produce brand identity. This may mean creating a "splash" screen with the manufacturer's name on it, creating special "wall paper" or screen effects, adding support for other devices made by the manufacturer in the software's installation program, and so forth.

– The ability to support a proprietary or branded device and/or capability built into their hardware. This could include multimedia or sound card support, for example.

– The ability to provide special versions of the product. This might include a "lite" version, or one with reduced hardware or memory requirements.

• Competitive pricing with a variety of packaging options. This can include:

– Full product built by the hardware manufacturer.

– Full product provided by the software publisher.

– Special versions of the product with partial documentation (the reference guide might be an extra purchase for the user, for example).

– Pre-loaded "locked" versions of the product, which require the buyer to call the manufacturer or publisher to unlock the product for use. Currently, most locked product is loaded onto the system's hard disk drive, but interest in CD-ROM for OEM distribution and fulfillment is growing. In this case, the buyer must call either the hardware vendor or more typically the software publisher for an unlocking code. One advantage to locked product is that it allows the software publisher to capture information for all its product users.

– Partially locked versions of the product. Game companies often use this approach. ID software used this technique to gain widespread acceptance of their blockbuster hit, Doom. The product was distributed via the Internet and retail channels with the beginning levels unlocked. Once the customer was hooked, they had to call ID directly for the privilege of wiping out hordes of gruesome demons with a variety of firearms currently outlawed by the Geneva Conventions.

- A coupon program for obtaining the software either at a special price or even for free. While considered a "second-best" strategy because it delays gratification and buyers don't usually like that, it does offer an inexpensive way for a vendor to add value to a product.

- Internet availability. Using this technique, buyers receive a code that enables them to log onto a web site and download the bundled product.

• Ease of use. Hardware manufacturers tend to steer clear of overly complex products. Even if the publisher agrees to provide full support, a high percentage of buyers will call the hardware manufacturer for support when they encounter problems with the software.

KEY NEGOTIATING POINTS

The following key points should be negotiated for a hardware bundle:

- How will registered users' names be captured? This is a crucial point for software publishers, since a key objective of bundling is to build a target audience for upgrade offers. If the hardware manufacturer primarily sells direct the logistics are fairly straightforward. If the manufacturer sells through the channel, capturing names is much more difficult.

- Who will support the product? Generally, the software publisher supports entertainment and business applications. However, the reverse is often true for operating systems, with the hardware manufacturer bearing the support burden.

- Who will manufacture the software? In some cases, the manufacturer takes delivery of a master disk and copies the product to a hard disk. In other, the software is copied onto a CD with other bundled products. In these cases, the publisher is basically "selling labels" and the pricing negotiations will reflect this. In rarer cases, the publisher provides product and documentation, usually a limited OEM version sans fancy graphics and color covers. In some limited cases, the hardware manufacturer produces the documentation from masters provided by the publisher.

KEY ADVANTAGES TO HARDWARE BUNDLES

From a publisher's standpoint, there are several advantages to hardware bundling.

- The publisher doesn't have to "chase" hardware sales. Since the buyer receives the product with the hardware, the publisher can focus on persuading the buyer to register the product and, eventually, purchase an upgrade. However, if the product is not locked, discovering who the buyers are can be difficult.*

- The COG should be lower on a bundled product. Elaborate, four-color, O-ring binders and fancy cardboard boxes are usually not included with bundled products. In addition, if the product is pre-installed on a hard disk or on a CD-ROM, the publisher can eliminate floppy disks from the packaging—an important COG consideration in an era of larger and larger software programs.

- A publisher can quickly create an installed base and a target market for upgrades. In many cases, this is how a publisher generates significant profits for its products. For this to occur however, the publisher must capture the buyers' names.

*If your bundled product is not locked, there are a number of things you can do to capture buyers' names. Ask the manufacturer to share its customer list with you. Offer an incentive to register by tying technical support or a premium offer to product registration.

KEY DISADVANTAGES OF HARDWARE BUNDLES

Hardware bundles do have some potential disadvantages.

- They can create "channel conflict." Some resellers are concerned that bundled software robs them of retail software sales. One approach used to mollify resellers is to bundle limited or "lite" versions of a flagship product. Sometimes, buyers perceive these offers as "poor relations" and don't buy them. Another approach is to offer a secondary or "lite" product with an easy upgrade path to a major product. Many of the low-end integrated products—Microsoft Works, the various home office products, etc.—are used for this purpose.

- Track product sales to determine if the sales of bundled product are creating an incremental opportunity, or simply cannibalizing retail sales. This can be difficult to determine if the hardware manufacturer distributes products through a broad variety of distribution vehicles.

- They can anger major reseller and distributor partners, who have a knee-jerk dislike of bundling arrangements because they perceive bundles as cutting the distribution system out of the sales cycle. A publisher can help soothe these wounded feelings by focusing on other sales opportunities in the marketing mix.

- They can cause retail cannibalization. Every buyer who receives your product free is a buyer who does not have to purchase it from you. Remember to factor in the sales you are not going to make while your bundling offer is underway before you decide that the bundle deal is compatible with longer term goals.

Software Bundles

Software bundling has grown dramatically over the last few years. It is now one of the most popular methods publishers use to add value to their products and to differentiate themselves from the competition.

There are four basic software bundle types.

- **Suite bundles**. A good example of a suite bundle is Symantec's current bundle of its market leading Norton-brand utilities. Sold as Norton SystemWorks, this two-layer bundle was created in response to pressure from rivals such as McAfee and Computer Associates. The first layer consists of full versions of venerable mainstays such as Norton Utilities, and the second of "lite" versions of several other Symantec products, including pcANYWHERE, WinFax, and so forth. The goal of the second layer is to generate incremental revenue from buyers of SystemWorks who sample the "lite" versions and decide to upgrade to the full products.

- **Promotional Bundles**. These bundles are now a staple of direct marketing offers; usually they consist of several products offered as an accompaniment to the central or flagship offering. Many publishers offer these bundles in a variety of configurations, including base product without the bundle, the base product with the bundle at a higher price point, and the base product with an option to buy it singly or in combination with the bundled products.

- **Enhancement Bundles**. These are bundles designed to highlight the particular capabilities of a product or compensate for a technical weakness in a product.

- **Premium Bundles**. Publishers offer premium bundles to provide an extra incentive to purchase a product or as a "thank you" to the buyer. They are frequently packed into the box with the main product and usually consist of either a small utility or entertainment product. Borland was particularly successful with this tactic, offering a golf game and an arcade-style game with past releases of their product. Currently an underused tactic in software marketing, a premium bundle can play different roles in your software marketing strategy, as the focus story illustrates. The company supplying the premium will frequently supply it at marginal cost in hopes of generating an upgrade base.

KEY NEGOTIATING POINTS

The following key points should be negotiated with a software bundle:

- How will the names of registered users be captured? This is crucial, since the pricing arrangement may make building an installed base the only reason for the software bundle.

- Who will support the product? In most cases, each publisher will support its respective product(s), unless the bundled product is "built into" the primary product. However, many buyers will call the publisher of the primary product first for help if they have problems.

- Who will manufacture the product? Some publishers prefer to build the bundled products from supplied master disks and documentation, while others prefer to simply ship full product supplied by the other publisher. Both models are frequently used. If the primary software publisher does manufacture both products, the secondary publisher is again basically "selling labels" and the pricing negotiations will reflect this.

KEY ADVANTAGES TO SOFTWARE BUNDLES

Software bundles offer several advantages.

- Promotional bundling offers the opportunity for a publisher to make incremental dollars on the sale of the bundled product. This is more likely if the bundled products can be bought at discounts of 80% off SRP or better. With direct mail offers, it is a good idea to test different combinations of price and value to arrive at the optimum offer.

- Bundling can be a quick and inexpensive way to add significant perceived value to a publisher's product.

- Bundled products can be very effective point-of-purchase (POP) merchandising in reseller stores. The degree of effectiveness is very dependent on the packaging design, which should clearly and forcefully call out the bundled product(s) and explain the added value to the customer.

- From the standpoint of the publisher whose product is being bundled, the chance to penetrate another publisher's installed base, build an upgrade base, and begin to develop up-to-date mailing lists are all significant opportunities.

KEY DISADVANTAGES TO SOFTWARE BUNDLING

The major disadvantages of software bundling concern pricing and potential for bundled products to cannibalize sales of retail product.

To minimize these, publishers can do several things:

- Develop or offer a "lite" or out-of-date product for bundling.

- Offer a complementary product to a desirable flagship product. A variant of the first technique, it avoids the stigma some associate with old or "lite" versions.

- Offer bundled product in some channels but not in others. For example, some publishers sell bundled product through large mail-order merchandisers who have developed loyal followings. The people who buy through these merchandisers often comprise a different buying audience than the typical microcomputer software and hardware buyer.

- Use scaled-down packaging and documentation to differentiate bundled product from retail. In addition, publishers can strip premiums from bundled product or offer reduced support to differentiate product.

Book Bundles

Bundling books with hardware, and more commonly software, is an inexpensive way to provide educational information about the primary product, supplement or replace standard documentation, and differentiate or add value to products. The negotiating points, advantages, and disadvantages closely resemble those of a software bundle.

FOCUS STORY

Companies

Planet Corporation

Enteractive Corporation

Product(s)

Business Maestro

Picture Perfect Golf

Market Overview

Planet Corporation is a small software publisher focused on the enterprise budgeting market. Their target audience consists of chief financial officers (CFOs) and controllers, an ideal audience in many respects, since these senior managers combine purchasing influence with purchasing authority. These individuals spend much of their day crunching numbers and reconciling the budgets coming to them from different locations and departments. To make sense of it all, many have turned to the ubiquitous spreadsheet. Unfortunately, these programs are ill suited to the task, as spreadsheet technology makes it difficult for a template to be distributed across the enterprise and then consolidated. One change in a row or column position, or to a key macro, and the model becomes useless or dangerously misleading. And CFOs have little interest in developing compiled spreadsheets and commissioning programmers to create uniform interfaces for their templates.

To meet the need for budgeting uniformity and consolidation, Planet focused on developing an object-oriented alternative to the spreadsheet. Their flagship product, Business Maestro, priced at $995 for the desktop and $2495 for the enterprise, incorporates this concept. Budgets and plans are regarded as a business object that a CFO can distribute across the enterprise. Line managers can alter it, use it to run projections, report on financial performance, and then submit the results back to the CFO for fast and uniform consolidation. This approach to budgeting fits many companies' needs, and Planet has created a niche for itself among medium-sized broadcasting, manufacturing, and high-tech firms. Most copies of Business Maestro are sold via direct marketing and a limited one-tier reseller channel.

Unfortunately, companies using Business Maestro have to learn a new approach to budgeting and give up the bad habits they learned working with spreadsheets. This fact, combined with weaknesses in the product's documentation and the lack of certain features, led to a return rate of approximately 30%.

Planet was aware of these weaknesses, and its next release of Business Maestro addressed many key user requests, including much improved documentation. In the meantime, Planet turned to a bundling promotion to lower returns. Planet bundled a free complementary program for cost-center budgeting and a free copy of **Picture Perfect Golf** from Enteractive Incorporated. They picked the golf game because of its appeal to the upscale demographics associated with CFOs and controllers and its low cost of under $1.50 (retail value of $29.95). They offered the game with the promise that Business Maestro would save the CFO enough time to enjoy a few rounds of virtual golf. The goal of the promotion was to add enough value (and a bit of sly fun) to persuade users to keep the product and wait for the next release.

The bundling strategy was a success and the return rate was cut in half. As a test, some customers were only offered the golf game as a "thank you" for their purchase. In those cases, returns dropped about 10%, a fine ROI when you contrast the cost of the golf game with that of Business Maestro.

LESSONS

Bundling can be used in a wide variety of tactical purposes and publishers need to be flexible and inventive when considering bundling options. And remember that bundling doesn't have to be limited to retail-oriented products.

Bundle Breaking and the Channel

Bundles are a popular promotional item with the channel and probably the most effective method of in-store merchandising. Unfortunately, retail resellers are notorious for ripping bundled product apart, selling the separate components, then trying to return components they've damaged for full credit. They are also prone to accepting broken bundles back from end users, then attempting to return the product back to you (for full credit, of course). This is an ongoing problem, and can be addressed in several ways.

- Build break-proof packaging. Use adhesive tape, special wrapping, special marking, or a combination of all three. You can also build special boxes for the bundled applications rather than packaging them independently and shrink wrapping them together. Of course, this drives up the product's COG.

- Use plain or unappealing packaging, such as plain white cardboard stock or stock that doesn't stand up well by itself, to hold the bundle.

- Omit the bar-coding label on the individual products in the bundle, which will make them unsellable at most large resellers.

- Refuse to take back bundled product from either the reseller or distributor. This is one of the most effective methods to curtail bundle breaking, but many publishers are afraid to do it. To administer this effectively, you will have to serialize all your packages so you can track what went where and to whom.

- Consider Internet-only availability. This method lowers product COGs to almost nothing for both parties, and allows you to achieve 100% user registration. The downside to this approach is that many people still lack Internet access, and as many as 30% of those who do have access will never bother to go to the site and obtain the bundled product.

Resourceful resellers have found a way to bypass all methods used to discourage them from bundle breaking. The key is to make it difficult and costly for them. If a publisher is vigilant about this problem and makes things difficult enough for the reseller, bundle breaking can be reduced to nuisance status.

BUNDLING OBJECTIVES/EVALUATION CHECKLIST

OBJECTIVES	EVALUATION

Marketing Goals

1. **Generate incremental sales**
   # sales generated _____ _____ _____
   Over what period? _____ _____ _____

2. **Establish upgrade paths**
   # names added
   to mailing list _____ _____ _____
   # names added to
   installed base _____ _____ _____

3. **Reach buyers w/o tracking hardware sales**
   # buyers reached _____ _____ _____

4. **Sell into another company's installed base**
   # added to mailing list _____ _____ _____

5. **Improve internal (in-house) mailing list**
   # qualified names added
   to mailing list _____ _____ _____

6. **Minimize channel conflict**
   # complaints received _____ _____ _____
   # resolved (comment how) _____ _____ _____

7. **Minimize bundle breaking**
   # returned/broken units _____ _____ _____
   # requests to return
   broken bundles _____ _____ _____

8. **Limit retail sales erosion**
   # sales lost _____ _____ _____

BUNDLING SUCCESS CHECKLIST

1. **Select bundle options**

   A. **Hardware bundle**

   ☐ Full product manufactured by software publisher _____

   ☐ Full product manufactured by OEM vendor from masters _____

   ☐ Special version with partial documentation _____

   ☐ Pre-loaded, locked version _____

   ☐ Pre-loaded, partially locked version _____

   ☐ Coupon for separate purchase of product at reduced or no cost _____

   ☐ Internet available _____

   B. **Software bundle**

   ☐ Suite _____

   ☐ Promotional _____

   ☐ Enhancement _____

   ☐ Premium _____

2. **Identify hardware and/or software vendor(s) with input from:**

   ☐ Product Marketing _____

   ☐ Hardware and/or software sales personnel _____

3. **Establish key contacts with hardware and/or software vendor personnel**

   ☐ Sales

   ☐ Manufacturing _____

   ☐ Legal (contracts) _____

4. **Establish pricing for common bundle options with input from:**

   ☐ Hardware and/or software vendor sales personnel _____

   ☐ Channel Sales personnel _____

   ☐ Product Marketing _____

5. **Conduct market research and establish bundling strategies prior to vendor negotiations**

   A. **Describe your product's marketing opportunities with respect to:**

   ☐ Market share _____

   ☐ Growth _____

   ▒ Installed base _____

   ▒ Upgrades to installed base _____

      ▨ Anticipated incremental sales _____

☐ Product awareness _____

      ▨ Volume and frequency of advertising _____

      ▨ Number and quality of product reviews _____

      ▨ Product visibility and acceptance _____

☐ Target audience _____

      ▨ Audience readiness to buy product _____

B. Define customization and enhancement capabilities

☐ Screen customization _____

☐ Proprietary/special device support _____

☐ Special product versions _____

☐ Other   _____

C. Develop volume purchase discount schedule for each bundle option

☐ Full product manufactured by software publisher _____

☐ Full product manufactured by OEM vendor from masters_____

☐ Special version with partial documentation_____

☐ Pre-loaded version _____

      ▨ Hard disk_____

      ▨ CD-ROM _____

☐ Coupon for separate purchase of product at reduced or no cost_____

☐ Internet key for download _____

6. Conduct vendor negotiations—get answers to questions

☐ How will buyers' names be captured? _____

☐ How often and in what format will these names be provided? _____

☐ Who will provide product support? _____

☐ Who will manufacture the product? _____

☐ How will returns be handled? _____

☐ Who pays for broken bundles?_____

☐ What is royalty payment schedule? _____

☐ License restrictions? _____

7. Present plan and obtain approvals, where required

☐ Senior Management_____

☐ Finance _____

☐ Legal _____

8. **Sign contract with vendor** _____

9. **Develop different product versions (reduced price or special function), if necessary, with input from:**

    ☐ Manufacturing _____

    ▨ Disks _____

    ☐ Marketing _____

    ▨ Packaging _____

    ☐ Documentation _____

    ☐ Development _____

    ▨ Locking code _____

    ▨ Special "lite" version _____

    ▨ Special key code for web site _____

10. **Develop bundle packaging strategy**

    ☐ Break-proof packaging _____

    ☐ Special packaging _____

    ☐ Omit bar code, if necessary _____

    ☐ Serialize packages _____

11. **Develop joint marketing program**

    ☐ Announce to press _____

    ☐ In-store marketing/merchandising _____

    ☐ Direct marketing _____

12. **Deliver product** _____

13. **Track and evaluate results** _____

9

Electronic Marketing

Electronic marketing includes both demonstration and distribution vehicles. Traditional electronic systems include commercial and hobbyist bulletin board systems, kiosks, and CD-ROM distribution. The Internet is now supplanting all of these.

WHY USE ELECTRONIC MARKETING?

Interest in electronic marketing and distribution is exploding for a number of reasons. Chief among them are:

- The difficulty and expense of penetrating the U.S. channel. Many publishers hope electronic marketing will allow them to create alternate distribution channels and methods so they can reach buyers more quickly. Retail-class publishers, in turn, hope this will persuade the distribution system to accept their products with more alacrity.

- The opportunity to carefully measure response and learn more about a market. In theory, electronic and Internet purchasing should allow higher end-user capture rates and the ability to precisely track who is buying a product and why.

- The ability to reach large numbers of buyers quickly. For example, an electronic direct marketing program reaches its target audience within minutes of distribution at a fraction of the cost of conventional direct marketing. And once a product has been posted for sale on a web site it is immediately available to millions of potential customers. Current estimates are that between 42 and 65 million Americans have regular access to the Internet (The Gartner Group).

- The ability to build relationships with your customers, or as it is popularly called, "relationship marketing." For example, USENET naturally segments the market by common interests, and it is safe to assume that most people will consistently visit web sites that appeal to their specific interests and hobbies. Home pages can even be designed to react interactively with requests, theoretically allowing a company to create a buying environment specifically tailored to an individual's shopping preferences, though the current phone system makes much of this impractical. But the Internet also allows shopping to become a purely price-driven exercise. Technologies are in use that allow users to use agents and "bots"(canned search and retrieve routines) to shop the Internet for items on a best-price basis. In such an environment, purchasing becomes a purely commodity-driven exercise, with no real customer interaction.

The purest expression of this in high tech can be found at web auction pioneer Onsale, Inc.'s new atCost program. Onsale has recently made a deal with international distributor Tech Data to buy hardware and software at wholesale and sell it with no markup at their site; however, the customer does pay credit card, shipping, and inventory processing fees. Onsale developed the program in response to the growing shortage of obsolete and excess inventory to fuel its online auctions. The goal of the program is to increase Onsale's web traffic and ad revenues, with the software and hardware acting simply as an inducement to shop the site.

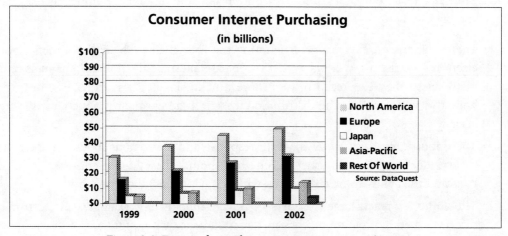

Figure 9-1. Estimated growth in consumer Internet purchasing

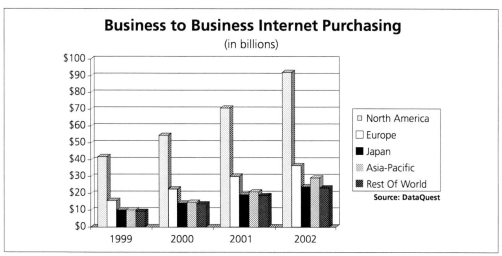

Figure 9-2. Estimated growth in business to business Internet purchasing

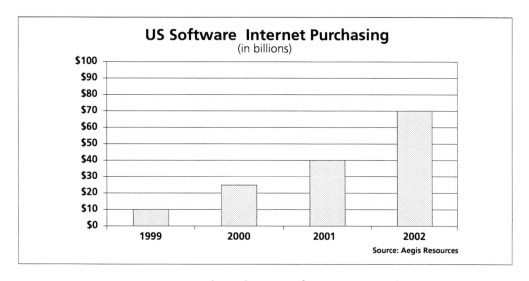

Figure 9-3. Estimated growth in U.S. software Internet purchasing

CD-ROM DISTRIBUTION

In the early 1990s a glorious future was predicted for CD-ROM distribution as an alternative to conventional bricks-and-mortar distribution. The Internet quickly brought an end to these predictions, and CD-ROM is used primarily as a pillar of shareware and TBYB distribution. One of the most noted users of CD-ROM distribution is America Online, which used repeated mailings of floppies and CDs to encourage 12 million people to join their service. A few publishers and resellers still use CDs to sell products into niche markets, but we are unaware of any publisher who has realized significant revenue from these programs.

KIOSK SYSTEMS

A kiosk system is an electronic marketing display designed to be installed in a retail location. These units can display text and graphics about products and services, and the user interface is a menu system that allows the shopper to view different screens describing the following:

- Product features.
- Special offers.
- Reviews and endorsements.
- Demo screens.

Kiosk systems have the potential to complement retail sales efforts in various ways.

- They can act as a surrogate sales representative for customer education and demonstrations.
- Sales personnel can use the system to keep abreast of product features and new release information.
- They can, in theory, help persuade retail personnel to push particular products.
- They can be designed to allow special ordering of non-stocked inventory items.

Previous kiosk systems never achieved much penetration in the computer industry, and current systems under development use the Internet as their underlying technology. While not an important marketing factor in the industry at this time, kiosk systems may become more important if resellers begin to implement electronic distribution at their locations.

BULLETIN BOARD SYSTEMS (BBS)

Bulletin board systems are single-site electronic messaging, file transfer, chat, and forum systems that can run on a wide variety of equipment, from micros to mainframes. Prior to the Internet, there were thousands of hobbyist and non-profit bulletin boards in use throughout the country, with dozens appearing and disappearing each month. There are only a handful of these systems now in use, with most of the survivors transferred to the Internet. Bulletin board systems are useful in special situations where the lack of connectivity is an advantage. Some publishers still use them for support and limited file transfer operations, but their use is rapidly being supplanted by the Internet.

THE INTERNET

Well, what is there to say? Driven by the introduction of the World Wide Web in 1989 at CERN, a European research facility dedicated to particle physics research, interest in the Internet exploded in 1994 and 1995. The attention dedicated to this "new" phenomenon (in point of fact, the Internet has existed since the late 1960s, and was first incarnated as ARPANET, a Department of Defense program designed to explore the feasibility of an interconnected system of computer systems that could survive an attack by the late Soviet Union) has reached a fever pitch of err... "nuclear" proportions. Thousands of companies have rushed in to exploit this wondrous new Mecca where REAL money lies waiting to be picked up off cyber sidewalks of gold. Each day brings new stories of millionaires being created on the Internet! And they are! Not, please note, from the **profits** that have been made from **selling** products on the Internet. Rather, newly minted Internet moguls are being churned out by the stock markets on the **promise** of the profits that will **someday** be made from selling products on the Internet. Take Amazon.com, for example, the Internet's most famous success story to date. It was founded on the concept that users could browse through its virtual shelves and order books of any type, at any time, at attractive discounts. Amazon succeeded in establishing itself as a major web site, and after its public offering saw its stock price shoot to dizzying heights and its market capitalization reach $**19.7 billion** dollars on approximate sales of $600 million worth of books, videos, and music in 1998, while losing about $80 million. Contrast this with bricks-and-mortar bookseller Barnes & Noble's capitalization of $2 billion on sales of $**3 billion** and profits of $53 million. Despite its sales growth, Amazon is not projected to be profitable for the next several years.

Now, skepticism aside, many companies are making money on the Internet from product sales. Early success stories included flower and swimming pool sales companies. In high tech, estimated 1998 online sales of $3 billion for Dell Computer, accounting for 20% of the hardware giant's total revenue, and the $6 billion network heavyweight Cisco took in at its site testify to the power of the Internet as a direct marketing tool. Total retail sales on the Internet were $43 billion in 1998 and are projected to reach $1.3 *trillion* by 2003. This is a healthy figure, but contrast this number with the $2.3 *trillion* in-store shopping dollars targeted by Sears and Wal-Mart.

Publishers should also keep in mind that the wild claims for the future of the Internet often ignore basic reality and common sense. One writer for *NewMedia* magazine recently made the breathless prediction that the Internet would soon replace the country's malls and retail stores. In their place would be a vast sprawl of distribution centers and warehouses serviced by fleets of vans designed to ensure product delivery to your door within four to six hours.

This is fairly silly stuff. If one learns anything from history, it is that new methods of distribution and payment rarely supplant existing systems; either they are integrated into the existing system or become an additional enhancement. If you doubt this, take a coin out of your pocket and inspect this product of Bronze Age technology carefully. Coins are heavy, hard to store, and difficult to transport. Are they obsolete? Ask a vending machine operator or a Las Vegas casino. Scattering vast new warehouse complexes around the country sounds nice to some, but where are they to be located? There are areas of the country where building a new gas station or restaurant is reason for environmental angst. And direct marketing with overnight delivery is nothing new in this world. People who enjoy direct shopping via the mail of course enjoy direct marketing on the web, and there are few complaints about the current efficiency of the delivery system for goods. Rather than replace the retail system, we can expect to see the Internet integrated into the system. The exact nature of this integration and the new capabilities and inducements it will offer shoppers remains to be seen.

INTERNET COMPONENTS

Despite the public's single-minded focus on the World Wide Web, the Internet consists of several elements and technologies, including Telnet, file transfer protocol (FTP) sites, USENET, and Internet relay chat (IRC). Telnet sites can be thought of as electronic libraries where information can be accessed. FTP sites contain programs and files available for downloading. USENET is the portion of the net dedicated to forums and special interest groups. Topics and subjects covered include everything from collecting old Barbie dolls to careers in taxidermy. There are over 13,000 USENET sites nationwide, and the number is constantly growing. IRC allows Internet users to chat in real time with like-minded people about a vast array of topics.

Before we go any further, it is vital to understand that no one owns the Internet. There is no central authority, no agency to appeal to if you don't like how things are going, and no board of trade to set the rules. Nor is there a publicly maintained central index to services or web sites on the Internet. The companies and entities that DO maintain such indices are under no obligation to do so, and they answer only to the market for the quality and utility of their indices. Most users rely on experimentation, research, and various Internet browsers and utilities to build idiosyncratic lists of their favorite sites. This means the customers are in control of their viewing experience; nothing locks them into any site, any portal, or any service.

THE INTERNET AND THE WORLD WIDE WEB

What is the Internet?

The Internet is an interconnected series of computer networks; any computer network can be a part of it. Mediating communications among these disparate networks is the transport control protocol/internet protocol (TCP/IP). Most computers are physically linked to each other via the phone system, though an increasing number are linked via alternate cabling such as fiber optic. Most users currently connect to the Internet by means of the lowly but ubiquitous modem, which communicates with an Internet service provider (ISP). Most ISPs, in turn, connect to the Internet via such high-speed alternatives as T1 and T3 lines, digital systems cable of transmitting data at millions of bits per second over their lines as contrasted with the current phone line maximum of 53K (and few people actually ever connect at such rates). New technologies such as cable modems, which use your TV cable lines to pump Internet bits at high speed to your computer; DSL and ADSL technologies, which speed up transmission on your phone lines; and ISDN all offer the hope of universal high-speed access in the near future. Many corporations already enjoy fast Internet browsing, but most of the home market remains stuck at 28.8K bandwidth. Your Internet marketing and development plans must always keep this in mind.

Web Sites

Technically, a web site is am Internet site designed to display or "serve" documents formatted in HTML (**h**ypertext **m**arkup **l**anguage). These are posted on the site and read by visitors using a web browser, a viewer optimized to decode and display HTML-formatted documents. That's too abstract for marketing purposes. By applying the lessons of conceptualization from Chapter One, a web site can be presented as a store or a mall, information kiosk, magazine, card catalog, auction house and even perhaps as a neighborhood hangout. Which description best fits a site depends on its content and underlying technology.

Auction Sites

Auction sites were the web's first major commercial success (if one ignores the pornography sites), and gave an early indication of the web's power as a direct marketing tool. Auction sites originally focused on selling obsolete and excess inventory, but their reach and functionality are changing rapidly. New sites are being developed to allow business-to-business auctions, bidding for government contracts, even bids for information and technology consulting (we'll give you a great deal!). Auction site fans are currently among the Internet's most loyal, and these sites develop consistent and stable audiences.

Basic Web Sites

A basic web site can be conceptualized as an online brochure. The vast majority of the millions of web sites fit this model, whose purpose is to provide information about products and companies quickly and easily.

Channels (Push Technology)

Web channels, often referred to as "push technology," were pioneered by PointCast Systems, and represent an attempt to transform your PC desktop into a type of TV set. Hailed in 1996, hyped in 1997, and hung out to dry in 1998, web channels allow you to subscribe to different web sites that broadcast a constant stream of information to your web browser. This sounds like a great idea, and if you are a stock trader, the ability to set up a real time ticker tape on your monitor, one of the principal uses for channels, is very useful.

Unfortunately for the technology, after the initial novelty wore off, most people found push systems annoying, intrusive, and slow. Most web surfers prefer to visit sites when they want to and not have sites reach out to them. The excitement surrounding web channels quickly subsided and the technology no longer receives the same breathless attention it once commanded.

Despite these discouraging words, push has started to make a place for itself in sales automation environments and as the online analog of automated call centers. Financial services companies, the traditional stronghold of push, are discovering that channels are good for notifying users that their bank balances have dropped below predetermined points, informing them that deposits or wire transfers have been received or executed, and notifying customers of market changes.

Portals

Technically, a portal is simply a web site composed of an aggregation of links to other sites, and can be conceived of as an information kiosk. Many of the major portals began life as search sites that, over time, added other links and content in order to draw even larger numbers of surfers. Today however, portals are perceived as key strategic jumping-off points for Internet eyeballs. The ultimate goal of portal marketing is to grab the favored home page "slot" in a user's browser and attract millions of eyeballs that will in turn attract millions of advertising dollars.

Search Sites

Technically, a search site is an Internet "card catalog" designed to help users find information on the Internet. Over time, these sites have evolved from useful indexing tools into strategic jump-off points, playing a dual role in Internet marketing. On the one hand, since large numbers of users go to these sites to begin their quest for Internet-based information, products, or services, some software publishers have found them useful areas in which to place web advertising. On the other hand, the keywords and phrases these sites accept to power their web queries can dictate how and in what order web sites that meet the queries' parameters will be displayed. This, in turn, can have a profound effect on how many visits a web site receives and how much exposure a product will receive.

TARGETED KEYWORDS AND TRADEMARKS

A recent controversy has broken out about the practice of search sites selling "targeted" keywords. These sites often charge a premium for "desirable" key words and have included such terms as "playboy" and company names as part of their inventory. Prices range between $10 to $60 per thousand impressions for desirable keywords, depending on the site's size and demographics. When the user submits these targeted words to a search engine, the search site displays a keyword purchaser's advertising. Companies such as *Playboy Magazine* have objected vociferously to the practice of porn sites purchasing the "playboy" keyword in order to advertise their fleshy wares. *Playboy Magazine* feels strongly that the "playboy" should be reserved to allow the company to sell **their** fleshy wares, instead. Law suits have been launched by various companies who feel their trademarks are being impinged on. No resolution on this issue has been reached in the courts, but if you are in the least concerned about the impact of a lawsuit on your company' financial health, it may be best to steer clear of controversial targeted keywords.

MINI-PORTALS

While general purpose portals such as Yahoo! are regarded as the current model for this type of site, portals can be built to different scales and more precisely target particular audiences. A good example of a "mini-" portal is Matt Drudge's site, **The Drudge Report**. It began as a collection of links to different news and political columnist sites, along with a small column written by Drudge. The site is now one of the Internet's most widely bookmarked, even though to this day it is a plain-vanilla effort that eschews fancy graphics and visual pizzazz.

While Drudge had no background or training in journalism or writing, his web site's association with some of America's most noted political pundits transferred a certain patina of legitimacy and credibility to his work. Over time, interest in his site grew, more people bookmarked it, and political operatives began to use Drudge's inside reports and tips, some of which proved to be true. Drudge began the transformation from nobody to Internet journalist and when he succeeded in scooping *Newsweek Magazine* by printing details of its Monica Lewinsky investigation before they did, his fortune was made. Today Drudge has a TV show, appears on some of the major network news shows, and his site is an Internet mainstay.

The same tactics can be used for software publisher web sites. Astute publishers have discovered that creating a mini-portal can establish their sites as "must visit" locations, and transfer credibility to their company and products through association with other related products or companies with established market credibility. For example, if you're trying to sell network design software, a mini-portal with links to all the major networking sites will attract people interested in buying, evaluating, and learning about networks. Over time, as they come to rely on your site, you can shape the portal to ensure that a large percentage of "its" visitors eventually decide to visit "your" site as well. Of course, a publisher can use marketing to invite and publicize a primary site, but many users will refuse to respond to any direct commercial offer.

A mini-portal uses a two-step process to attract and build site traffic. The first step is to attract viewers to the mini-portal via DM collaterals, web links, EDM, and word of mouth. Step two is to subtly attract viewers by your strategic position on the portal and offers of interesting content. Publishers in the networking, Internet development, and accounting markets have effectively used this tactic.

An effective mini-portal contains the following elements:

- A very plain appearance. This helps build credibility, makes navigation quick and easy, and assures the user the portal is all about information, not marketing.

- A wide variety of links, including links to competing products. For a mini-portal to have credibility, it must comprehensively cover a targeted market.

- Fresh content. While the ostensible purpose of the mini-portal is to provide links and information, its marketing function is to provide credibility. Articles, news, updated links and discussions about your market and related topics will draw a fresh stream of new visitors to your mini-portal and then on to your site.

- No overt marketing. If your portal starts to sprout commercial messages for great savings on your software, it will soon be seen as a direct extension of your site, and lose credibility.

CONTENT PORTALS

Another version of the mini-portal is the "content portal." During the web's initial growth, "content" was seen as the main engine of web growth. Magazines, books, and newspapers were going to become obsolete as everyone flocked to the Internet to read.

This has not happened. The Internet is not a comfortable reading environment, and most people have not abandoned the convenience and flexibility of printed materials for the web. Nonetheless some software publishers have discovered, as the following focus story illustrates, that the web is an appropriate medium in which to offer content that was difficult to distribute using conventional marketing tactics.

FOCUS STORY: FROM BOX TO CONTENT
Company

Lyriq Software, At-the-Crossroads

Product

Lyriq Crosswords, At-the-Crossroads, Inc.

Market Overview

Founded in 1991, Lyriq software entered the gaming and education market as the early fascination with CD-ROM multimedia titles was growing. The company introduced several educational and edutainment titles in this period, but made its mark with Lyriq Crosswords. Crosswords are a daily pleasure for about five million Americans and the product's clean interface and high-quality puzzles propelled it to leadership in this niche category. As a result, Lyriq Crosswords achieved high retail penetration and built significant brand awareness over the next several years.

The only problem was that despite high unit sales, the cost of marketing Lyriq Crosswords precluded high financial growth. At a retail price of $29.95, channel, advertising, and COG costs made it difficult to generate a significant revenue stream from even a market-leading title.

Lyriq was not unaware when it developed the title what the impact of channel and marketing costs would be. A crossword product fits the classic "give away the razor and sell the blades" marketing model perfectly. Lyriq anticipated that users would soon work through all the puzzles in the retail product and want more. The original marketing plan assumed that the company would develop a strong after market of add-on puzzle sales to Lyriq Crosswords owners.

Unfortunately, after market sales never reached the expected levels, for a number of reasons:

- To build a large installed base, Lyriq needed to achieve high user registration levels for Crosswords. Unfortunately, the technology of the early 1990s made electronic registration expensive and difficult to implement, and registration card returns never exceeded 20%.

- Delivering new puzzles was a highly labor intensive and expensive exercise for a small company. The only practical way to provide new puzzles to many users was to mail floppy disks. Lyriq did offer a crosswords service on AOL, which at the time was a closed and proprietary service offering no Internet ISP capabilities.

- Publicizing and providing information about new puzzles was also difficult. Crossword puzzle players like to play puzzles about different subjects and of different complexity. Conventional puzzle packs made it hard for players to pick out just the puzzles they find interesting, and put Lyriq at risk of building hard-to-sell inventory.

Lyriq never did succeed in solving the after-sales marketing problem, and when the company merged with Enteractive in 1996, the crosswords product was allowed to languish.

In 1997 Gary Skiba, one of Lyriq's founders, decided to resurrect Lyriq Crosswords via a new web site service, At-the-Crossroads. After some analysis of the current Internet gaming and entertainment situation, he decided to create an online service that he conceptualized as the game page of your local newspaper. In addition to crosswords, the site offered a code cracking program, cryptograms, various card games including cribbage and several variants of poker, and a kids section, which included chess and checkers. Most games were posted under a "duplicate gaming model;" that is, each visitor to the site played the same daily word or card game, and could compare how they did with every other site visitor. The site posted a daily leader board, and visitors could also set up gaming leagues and enjoy online competition with their favorite games. The games were free, but visitors were required to fill out a membership form before they could play.

At the Crossroads went online in late 1997, and initially depended on word-of-mouth marketing, strategic links with other sites, and a co-labeling arrangement with *The New York Post*. Visitors to the newspaper's site were also able to visit "NY Post At the Crossroads," which consisted of the ***Post's*** banner wrapped around At the Crossroads. The site grew slowly but steadily, and by the end of 1998 had developed a base of over 10K members with daily visits by gamers averaging about 1.2K. At the Crossroads was designated on several occasions as "Cool Site of the Day," a rolling Internet award that can build both traffic and brand awareness for the lucky site. Equivalent "worst site of the day" awards also exist, but At the Crossroad managed to avoid them!

The type of audience attracted to At the Crossroads tends to be well read, upper income, and demographically very desirable. The site began to attract advertisers, and At the Crossroads was solicited by web advertising firm Flycast to join its network. All ads run on At the Crossroads are sold on a CPM basis, though the site is evaluating whether to offer click through opportunities. Growth at the site has been rigorously controlled to ensure reliability and uninterrupted gaming, vital components in retaining the membership's interest and loyalty.

Results

As of this writing, At the Crossroads is now operating on a break-even basis, quite an accomplishment for such a young enterprise. The site will soon go into the black, and is growing at a steady clip while building a desirable, stable, and highly measurable user base. At the Crossroad's highly targeted marketing efforts provide an interesting contrast to the current "throw everything at the wall and see what sticks" tactic used by many web sites and portals. The site also provides a look at how software publishers who were not able to make content part of the software sales equation in the past may be able to solve this problem in the future.

BOTS

A bot (ro**bot**) is an automated software agent or routine that searches the Internet based on a series of user-supplied parameters. The most popular bot is the shopping bot or shopbot, which scans the Internet looking for items based on price and availability. Infobots look for information. Cancelbots look for messages posted by other people and erase them. (More on cancelbots later in the legal section of this chapter.)

Shopbots are the bane of many web sites, and some sites have implemented technology to block their use. Which, of course, leads the bot developers to develop even more sophisticated bots designed to bypass these systems. Which leads the web sites to deploy even more…well, you get the idea.

The reason for the distaste for shopbots is that they erase site identity, brand equity, and any chance of relationship marketing. Shopbots have the potential to turn the web into a hyper efficient market, driven by price and price alone. For marketers, bots could be the ultimate nightmare! The best way to combat bots, other than blocking their use, is to provide information and content that build site loyalty.

Roguebots and adbots present marketers with a different series of headaches. Adbots can generate inflated web ad impressions by visiting a site repeatedly and scanning for graphics. The bot searches the site map and tricks the web server into offering up its banner ads, thus inflating the sites impression count between 5% to 15% on average.

Roguebots inflate the traffic count on CGI-generated, in-line GIF advertising images. These graphics are usually displayed and counted when a web page determines a site visitor is legitimate by receiving information from the client's http referer field. A rogue bot pretends to be a "visitor" by sending the site a fake http reference and IP address. Roguebots are less common than adbots, but their use is growing.

Spiders and crawlers, another class of bot, are software programs that visit virtually every page on the Web to create indices for search engines. These programs are usually benign, but poorly written code can cause them to continually request the same text page, leading to performance issues and potentially making it difficult to accurately measure advertising impressions.

Forums and Chat

Forums, special interest groups (SIGs), and online chat also predate the web, and they are still imperfectly integrated into the fabric of most sites. This is a bit surprising, since a well-run forum is capable of building site loyalty and repeat visits unlike any other service or feature offered on the Internet today.

Chat is the ability for a user to send and receive real time messages while on line. It is a mainstay of AOL, and can be fairly easily implemented on web sites via various programs. It is more popular with younger audiences since it provides a means for people to gossip and "talk" to people from all over the world at low cost. Adults and professionals make far less use of chat, since response times tends to be slow and time constraints often make it impractical.

Far more important in software marketing is providing a forum capability, where visitors can read messages, reply to ones that interest them, then return at a later date to read responses and post further replies, if they so desire. A record of previous postings is maintained in a "thread," allowing visitors to peruse through the discussion and join if they wish.

Both AOL and CompuServe have built and maintained their user base on the quality and quantity of their forums and chat capabilities. The CompuServe forum system remains the best example of how a forum should operate, and no web equivalent yet matches it in power and flexibility. Forums can be formed to provide technical support, discuss product use and deployment, and provide a social outlet for people with common interests and outlooks.

Services

Web services such as America Online, CompuServe, and Prodigy predate the web, and have now been subsumed by it. A service can be thought of as a super portal that charges a membership fee that it justifies as ISP charges. AOL currently reaches a nightly "audience" of over 12 million people, while CompuServe (now owned by AOL) and Prodigy have memberships of about 2 million, respectively.

Because of its size, AOL is considered the Internet's behemoth, and its recent purchase of Netscape, owner of one of the Internet's busiest portals, hammers the point home. In recent years, AOL has tended to position itself more as a TV network than an Internet service, claiming its "mass audience" equals a TV network's reach. The analogy is somewhat misleading; AOL, like any online entity, must deal with the interactive nature of the web. No one is dialing into AOL to "watch" chat rooms or send E-mail. However, one thing services can provide is more precise demographics about the type of audience that uses them since they always request some basic information about their subscribers during the sign-up process.

Web Malls

A web mall is a collection of web stores. Early in the web's development pundits predicted a glorious future for the mall concept, but to date the performance of web malls has been disappointing, and the concept has been eclipsed by portals. Several reasons have been offered to explain the failure of web malls, but the most probable one is that the early sites attempted to reproduce the conventional mall environment Americans are accustomed to and to charge publishers outrageous fees for an unproven concept. In fact, some early web mall development efforts made heavy use of virtual reality modeling language (VRML) to create 3-D sites that slavishly resembled actual stores. Unfortunately, as users waited for these sites to slowly load into their browsers, the web developers inadvertently managed also to reproduce the real world experience of walking into a store and waiting endlessly for some service. All of these approaches ignored the fact that Internet is a highly interactive environment that allows individuals to create their own "personalized" malls. Little value was added to the shopping experience by these malls.

Web Stores

A web store is a "commerce enabled site," i.e., you can buy product(s) and submit your credit card to the site to pay for your purchase. The early Internet audience showed little interest in the initial efforts to extract dollars from web surfers. These early failures occurred because of doubts about the safety of web commerce; ill-conceived ideas about charging for "content," i.e., web-based magazines, newsletters, and newspapers; and "nickel and dime" micro-payment schemes intended to nick users for micro downloads.

This is changing rapidly. New tools make developing basic stores easy, and the public has woken up to the fact that the web is probably a more secure place to hand over a credit card number than a restaurant or store, where they obtain a sample of your handwriting in addition to your card number. Credit card companies and local banks are quite willing to work with even the smallest publishers, and making money a buck at a time is much more fun than doing it dime by dime. A well tested, easy-to-navigate and use web store can be an excellent adjunct to a publisher's marketing and sales efforts. Smaller publishers in particular have found them a good way to start to build an installed base and revenue stream.

WEB SITE DEVELOPMENT ISSUES

The web is in a constant state of change and development. The choices you make in respect to your site's development can have a profound impact on your development cycle and site costs. As you consider which marketing and sales goals you want your site to achieve, keep these points in mind.

- Despite talk of the wonders of XML (eXtensible Markup Language), do not expect it to render HTML obsolete. HTML will remain the simplest way to publish data quickly on the Web, and is the best choice for sites designed to act primarily as collateral sites and information kiosks.

- Carefully evaluate any development choices in the context of their portability to other platforms, and decide if this is an issue of concern to you. For instance, Microsoft's popular active server page technology, which processes interactive pages at the server and not at the client or "browser" level, runs only on Microsoft operating systems.

- Consider carefully whether your site requires a **static** or **dynamic** design. A static site can be thought of as an electronic piece of paper or form. Changes made to your sites are done off line, and re-posted back to the web when they are completed. All users see the site the same way, and interact with it in the same fashion. A dynamic site is a magnitude of order more expensive to develop and complex; it interacts with the user on a one-to-one basis, and programmatically alters the services and features it offers based on user input. When you hear about sites that deliver customized catalogs to online shoppers or create personalized newsletters, you are talking about the world of dynamic sites. In today's market, basic static sites can be planned and implemented in a matter of a few weeks, and for a few thousand dollars. A dynamic site can take months of design and testing before its ready to go online, and costs often start at $100K and go up from there.

- Decide if your site requires implementing electronic commerce (E-commerce), a fancy way of saying "accept credit card numbers over the web." E-commerce is all the rage, but it makes your site's development more complex and lengthy. Implementing a secure commercial site that protects credit card numbers is not a trivial exercise. Practical experience has shown that posting an 800 number is still an effective way to generate sales from a web site, though it must be noted that even the slight delay dialing a phone number engenders will lose some sales. And if your site's revenue stream depends on a monthly subscription model, E-commerce is a requirement.

- Go easy on the Java. Java may be a wonderful language, but over the phone system, the principal means by which people connect with the Internet, it can slow things down. Use it sparingly and for quick impact. Plan on coding to the 1.1 standard, as 1.2, now called Java 2, is not projected to become the web standard until sometime in 2001.

- Obtain your domain name now from the Web Site Internet Network Information Center (Internic). The cost is $70 dollars for a new registration, and $35 for a yearly renewal. Some publishers prefer to use registration services that automate the submission process. These services charge on average between $19 and $230 dollars per registration (in addition to Internic fees.) We suggest you avoid higher priced services. We also suggest you register your company's name immediately, if you have not done so already, even if you are not currently using a web site This lessens the chance that your name will appropriated by another company. In some cases, company's who have found their domain name in use by another firm have had to pay substantial fees to gain rights to a particularly valuable web address. However, if you find your name already taken, and the other company does want to sell or release it, don't panic. An underscore or hyphen is enough to distinguish one domain name from another, and consistent marketing efforts will usually suffice to insure your domain name is added to the bookmark files of your market's web browsers.

WEB SITE DESIGN, NAVIGATION, AND WRITING

As we pointed out earlier in the *Collaterals* chapter, the **Handbook** is not a graphics design guide. Nonetheless, we've spent enough time looking at and suffering through a wide variety of web sites to have arrived at some basic conclusions. Please remember that circumstances and brilliant design execution can nullify some of our good advice, but violate the following precepts with care.

Design

When designing your site, remember the following:

- Plan on uploading fresh material and offerings at least once a month. This is acceptable for smaller publishers, but as your company grows, weekly, then daily updates will become necessary.

- Be on the constant lookout for new cross-link opportunities. If you're offering cross-links to other sites, you need to review those sites as well for their quality and "freshness" on a monthly basis.

- Check your spelling! Misspellings stand out even more glaringly on a web site than in a printed piece.

- Ensure all pages download in less than 15 seconds over a 28.8K modem.

- Check that every page contains phone number, mailing information, and E-mail contacts.

- Place a copyright notice on every page.
- Use HTML fonts for maximum speed.
- Make your text blocks short and to the point. And make liberal use of bullet points where appropriate.
- Keep a single page size between 20K to 30K, and set a maximum of 50K.
- Do not use dark backgrounds with light letters as they're almost impossible to read, and difficult to print.
- Avoid the use of colored table cells in forms.
- Keep multimedia presentation graphics on a separate page and warn users what lies ahead before they click on the link.
- Remember to test your designs on every major browser. This includes all versions of Netscape Navigator and Communicator, Microsoft Internet Explorer beginning with version 3.0, and Opera.
- Use BACKGROUND and BGCOLOR parameters in the BODY tag so the site visitor doesn't have to see gray while the background image is loading.
- Stick with the GIF format for your inline images (integral parts of your page, as opposed to offline images, which are loaded as links). While support for JPEG on line has grown, you are far better off sticking with the GIF format.
- Never place a survey in front of a purchase procedure. There is no faster way to kill an online sale.
- Extensively test your shopping cart procedures. This has been a sore point on many commercial sites, and only recently has the technology stabilized and become more idiot proof.

Navigation

To improve navigation on your site, you should:

- Provide alternate ways to navigate a site: buttons, site maps, search engines, drop down menus, etc.
- Design navigation pages to load in less than eight seconds.
- A data sheet page should load in less than 30 seconds.
- Provide multiple paths to key site information.
- When linking to another site, launch a new browser window, keeping your own window open.
- Regularly test for broken links, faulty E-mail addresses, and broken graphics.

Writing

People tend not to read the web pages, preferring instead to scan through them looking for keywords and phrases. If they find them, they'll read on and will be more likely to act on what they learn. As a result, marketers need to use a writing technique that lends itself to quick scanning and a "pick and chose" reading style. This technique employs:

- A sharply reduced word count. On average, use 50% less words than what would appear in printed collaterals.

- Bulleted lists. They are easy to read, and lend themselves particularly well to a web site.

- Highlighted keywords that link to more information. This allows the user to progressively discover more about a topic if they choose to do so.

- Short paragraphs (ideally, no more than three sentences) that express a single idea.

- An "inverted pyramid" disclosure of information. Conventional English exposition teaches us that the conclusion follows the disclosure of supporting facts. In web writing, this paradigm is turned on its head. Get to the point immediately, and allow the reader to decide if they want to know more.

- Good grammar and spelling. This seems obvious, but it is surprising how many sites display fractured English and obvious misspellings. These are far more noticeable in a web environment than in conventional collaterals.

- Clear call to action. If your piece asks the user to do something, that request should lead the piece.

- Overall composition that avoids the need to scroll. Studies have shown only 10% of web surfers scroll past the information displayed when the page is first shown.

WEB SEARCH ENGINES

Part of the process of advertising your web site and developing traffic is to register your site with popular search engines. The intent is to direct web surfers searching for specific information to your site. Some of the most popular search engines are HotBot, AltaVista, Yahoo, Webcrawler, and Lycos, with new search sites being constantly introduced and old ones fading away.

There are four basic ways to register a site:

- You can manually register your site yourself by visiting each of the large engines and submitting your web site's address, keywords and description. This is time consuming, but fairly easy to do.

- You can use "submit-it" type services where you enter your information once into a form and then click on each of the search engines to submit to that site. One example of this service is www.submit-it.com.

- You can pay a registration service to input key words and a description and register your URL to the various search engines. If you haven't got the time or the ability to create the meta tags discussed below, this may be the option for you.

- You can purchase different software packages that automate the process of registering your site (there are also some freeware tools available for this job).

Meta Tags

Meta tags are hidden HTML tags that provide site owners with some degree of control over how their web pages are indexed by "spider" or "robot" search engines. They are used by most, though not all search sites, Excite being a notable exception (Excite does read **Description** meta tags). Properly formatted and composed meta tags can increase the "relevancy" of a web page in relationship to a search query and raise your site's position in the list of likely pages. This can be crucial in building site traffic; the first five sites listed from a search will capture over 90% of the potential visitor base. Search engines that index meta tags include AltaVista, HotBot, Infoseek and Webcrawler; new search sites are constantly being introduced.

There are two meta tags that relate to search engine indexing and relevancy:

<META NAME="Description" Content="Your web page description">

<META NAME="Keywords" Content="Your web page keywords">

The meta **Description** tag should contain a concise description of your page and the services or information it features. Ideally, the contents of your description meta tag will be displayed with your URL if it comes up in search engine results. We recommend that you keep your description to 15 words or under. If it's too long, it will simply be truncated.

The meta **Keywords** tag is intended to contain keywords or key phrases that you think people interested in your site might be searching for. A comma followed by a single space should separate each word or phrase. Some word repetition is permissible but be careful of overdoing it—many search sites now check for excessive keyword repetition, formally known as "spamming. Excessive spamming can result in your pages getting lower relevancy to searches, or being banned from the search engine.

In addition to spamming, there are other techniques a web site can use to raise its site's relevancy index. These include:

- **Metajacking**. Copying the meta tag of another site that receives high search engine ranking to use in another site's code.

- **Spamdexing**. Adding the same keyword over and over to a page by including it in comment tags.

- **Fontmatching**. Adding keywords with the text set to the exact color of your background. This renders the type invisible but indexable.

- **Keyword Gateways**. Using a meta refresh tag so fast that it can't be seen to direct a viewer away from an indexed dummy page to another page.

As with spamming, search sites are on the lookout for such techniques and are constantly implementing new programs designed to discourage these tactics. For example, Infoseek has recently implemented a new feature in their search engine called clustering, which groups all pages submitted from the same domain and indexes them together. This help prevent companies from pushing the competition's pages down to the next page of search returns by indexing a large number of pages from the same site with the same keywords.

WEB SITE LEGAL ISSUES

Developing and maintaining a successful site also involves taking steps to avoid running afoul of the law. Key points to consider when developing and running your site are:

- Do not post untrue or defamatory comments about other people on your site and do not allow others to do so. Nothing about a web site provides you with any protection against slander and libel laws.

- Do not use the likeness of famous people without their permission or paying licensing fees. If you stick a picture of Michael Jordan up on your site to draw traffic, you can expect to hear from Mike's attorney very soon. Also remember that dead people leave estates, and these estates can own rights to the deceased's likeness. If you have any doubts about whether it is legal to use a likeness, call your attorney to check it out.

- Charge sales tax on out-of-state purchases if you have an office in that state or your company owns property in that state. This area of the law is in constant flux, so check with your lawyer if you have any doubts.

- Obtain copyright licenses for any material that is not original content. And remember that while it is technically easy, you can't simply appropriate another site's graphics, music, text, HTML code, ActiveX controls, Java scripts, and code without permission.

- Do not violate another company's trademark. And remember that while you may have established a local trademark in your town, state, or region, you may still violate another company's national trademark. To protect yourself, go to www.micropatent.com or www. thomson-thomson.com and run a national trademark search. If your search comes up clean, file a federal trademark application. If it is approved, place a (®) next to any goods or service you sell on your site. Place a (™) or sm next to any goods or services for which you are seeking a national trademark.

- Securely guard any customer credit card information you receive. If you are careless with credit card numbers, you can lose your merchant status and possibly be sued by your customers.

- Avoid the use of "cancelbots." They are often used to counter spammers, but filters and firewalls are a better solution. Cancelbots raise potentially "tortuous" (someone can sue you) issues since they pretend to be someone else as they do their work and their use can be construed as an illegal restraint of trade and freedom of speech.

WEB SITE ADVERTISING
Image vs. Product Advertising

As with conventional advertising, there are two basic classes of ads a publisher can create for the web: image or brand ads and product ads. As with conventional ads, most publishers should focus on product advertising and building brand equity through product superiority. This said, larger publishers are finding the web an intriguing venue in which to place brand advertising. Banner advertising, with its quicksilver nature and almost subliminal impact, lends itself uniquely well to building name recognition and purchasing comfort over time, the chief intangibles offered by strong brands.

Banner Advertising

Most web advertising is done via banners, those colorful blocks of text and graphics adorning millions of web sites. The banner is the web's most popular form of advertising for several reasons, including:

- Banners are part of the HTML specification, load quickly, and are easy to implement.
- Banners can incorporate graphics, animation, and color, making them effective eye candy.
- Banners can also incorporate navigation elements such as drop down boxes, dials, and buttons, making their use even more appealing to users.
- Banners are relatively non-obtrusive. In today's web browsing environment, few people wish to wait while their browsers load full-page ads.
- Banners can be automatically rotated after a specified period of time. This allows a web site to consistently refresh the advertising environment, and avoid tiring the viewer's eye with "the same old thing." It also allows a site to show more ads.

Unfortunately, banners suffer one major drawback: they are easy to block. Since banners are an integral part of HTML, their use on a site is easy to detect. Industry watchers currently estimate that 6% of web surfers operate their browsers with graphics off, though in this mode the banner's text stays visible. Recently, however, new browser add-ons and plug-ins have appeared that allow users to turn off banners completely, block links that make outgoing view requests, and stop automatic cookie transmission.

Banner Design

When developing your banner ads, the following design tips may prove helpful:

- Always place your ads above "the fold" (the scroll point), if possible. As with text, few readers bother to scroll down in their browsers.
- Consider using some animation in your banner.
- Always use color. Black-and-white no longer works well on the web.
- Bright color schemes tend to grab greater eye share.
- If appropriate, use pull down menus, pick lists, and other devices that encourage the user to interact with the ad.
- Integrate an offer with your ad if at all possible.
- Develop compelling text to accompany the banner.

Banner Incentives

The interactive nature of web advertising makes it easy to add buying incentives directly to banner ads. There are three basic approaches presently in use:

- Instant wins.
- Points earned.
- Cash back.

An instant win strategy awards a user some sort of bonus simply for clicking on the ad. Prizes can include T-shirts, caps, consumer goods, pre-paid phone cards, and similar merchandise. Some programs reward every click through, but most give the surfer a "one in X" chance of winning the bonus. Effective instant win programs can increase click through rates an average of 5% to 20%, depending on the bonus and associated offer.

Points programs assign points to a user for a click through and for subsequent purchases. Popular awards include gift certificates to such stores as Target or Best Buy, frequent flyer miles, and software discounts. Points programs have highly varied success. They are more difficult to administer since a user's visits must be monitored and their points accumulated. Click through rates typically rise between 3% to 8%, based upon the program's award structure.

Cash back awards usually revolve around offering buyers purchasing discounts or entrance into a sweepstake in which the user can win cash. Some programs offer a small cash award directly to the user for their click through, usually under a dollar. As with points programs, click through rates typically rise between 3% to 8%, based upon the program's award structure. Some experimental programs have been implemented that offer larger amounts, typically between $5 and $10 dollars. This is extremely expensive, but click through rates can easily exceed 50%.

Ad Networks

Web-based ad networks aggregate sites for potential advertisers, making it easier for them to place ad blocks at targeted sites. When a site joins a network, it agrees to accept advertising and splits on a 60 (site) to 40 (network) basis, though this is often negotiable. If your site is part of an ad network, you can control how much of your site's ad "inventory" (the maximum amount of ad space your site can offer over a given period of time) is available to the network and refuse to accept advertising from a particular advertiser. Ad networks are a blend of both high activity and niche sites, depending on the type of audience the network is targeting. Some publishers have found that participation in networks can help a site approach break even, though to become profitable a combination of network and direct advertising sales is usually required.

Measuring Web Advertising

There are two primary methodologies used to sell Web advertising: the "cost per thousand impressions," or CPM system previously discussed in the *Advertising* chapter of the **Handbook,** and "click through. In a web environment, an impression, sometimes called an "exposure" or "page view," occurs when a visitor to a web site is served up a web page containing an ad. The web server counts the number of impressions, but as with print advertising, you have no way of knowing whether the user paid any attention to the ad. The ad's placement on the web page has no effect on the impression measurement.

Impression Costs

Costs for impression-based web advertising range between $.03 and $.20 per impression, though some "premier" sites will attempt to charge amounts comparable to those commanded by conventional direct marketing list brokers, $75 to $150, on average. We do not believe that any web-based list or site is worth these prices. Web advertising rates have recently undergone something of a collapse, and some networks have sold ad inventory at prices as low as $.002 per impression.

Please remember that impressions do **not** necessarily translate into individuals. Most sites have repeat visitors, and most view more than a single page of information, so your 100,000 CPM may translate into 10,000 to 40,000 unique visitors who may have been exposed to your ad more than once. As with conventional advertising, it will take at least three exposures before you can be assured that a majority of the viewing audience has "seen" your ad.

Surveys, subscription counts, and even telemarketing are used to supplement site traffic estimates. Depending on the site and negotiations, some impression counts may be guaranteed, though usually only an estimate is offered. Also, some sites will charge a flat rate for estimated impressions, and if the actual count is higher, will let you keep the "over-deliveries" at no extra cost. As with conventional advertising, many popular sites offer ad agency and volume or frequency discounts. The ad agency rate, known as the **net** rate, is typically a 15% markdown from the **gross** rate, the amount charged a company that buys their advertising directly from the agency.

Hits and Page Hits

When purchasing advertising, some sites may tout their "hits" and "page hits," but experienced advertising purchasers usually discount these measurements. A site registers a hit any time text or a graphics file is served, and a page hit occurs when a complete HTML page, including text and graphic files, is served. A site can typically generate hit ratios of 10 to 1, or two to four page hits per impression.

The Click Through Model

The major alternative to the CPM system is the ""Click Through" or "Cost Per Click" model. This model directly measures ad response and performance, and combines advertising and direct response techniques. A click through occurs when the visitor sees or reads an ad and clicks on it, going directly to the advertiser's web site. Click through rates can reach as high as 25% though 2% to 3.5% represents the normal range. As with all your marketing efforts, success will be determined by the site's audience, the quality of your ad, and quality of your other marketing efforts. Cost to the advertiser range between $.30 and $.60 per click.

Many web sites try to avoid selling ad space under the click through model since their revenue stream depends on the advertiser's ad, product, and offer. Of course, from a publisher's standpoint, the click through model is ideal, since you pay only when the advertiser delivers a "virtual" live body to your site. Some sites offer hybrid programs that combine reduced impression rates with higher click through costs.

Finally, as befits the sprawling nature of the web, numerous deals and barter programs are constantly being experimented with and implemented. Some involve reciprocal trades of unsold inventory across sites, others involve selling ad space based on a percentage sales, while some involve paying bounties on software downloads, etc.

Measuring Advertising

Advertising is measured primarily by tracking software and monitoring server-activity logs. Unfortunately, many aspects of Internet technology can contribute to server undercounting. Most problems center around the use of web caches, site mirroring, and firewalls. With caching and site mirroring, the ad page is delivered to a local cache server, where the page is available for fast local viewing. This prevents the server site from accurately counting impressions. The recent development of "cache buster" programs from MatchLogic and Imgis can help ameliorate this problem, as these programs view inside the cache and count impressions.

Corporate firewalls using proxy servers create similar problems. These systems can identify 10 or 10,000 employees with the same visitor address, leading to server impression undercounts. A more subtle problem occurs when a site assigns the same IP address to a new user as the previous user logs off. This technique, used by some ISPs during peak activity periods, also leads to undercounting.

Evaluating a Web Site

When evaluating whether to place ads on a web site, portal, service, ad network, or any other web entity, an astute publisher asks the same questions they'd ask any vendor looking to relieve your marketing budget of its dollars.

- What is the size of the site's base?
- How often do they visit the site?
- What are the site subscriber base demographics? Average age? Income? Gender? Profession?

If you are dealing with a computer reseller, you will also need to know:

- What is the average size of the software purchase?
- What is the average frequency of purchase (e.g., three purchases over the last 12 months, two, etc.)?
- What percentage of buyers purchase software?
- What type of software do they most often purchase (e.g., entertainment, utility, business, etc.)?
- What are the total annual sales of software purchased through this site?

Web Cookies

One solution to these problems is the use of "cookies," small data files your browser exchanges with the web site when you first visit. Your "site identity" is stored in the cookie file, and on subsequent visits the cookie "helps" identify the visitor in conjunction with the IP address. However, cookies can be turned off within a browser, new utilities automate the process, and sites can easily be sent a "false" cookie file.

ELECTRONIC DIRECT MARKETING (EDM)

The age of electronic direct marketing may be said to have officially begun on April 12, 1994, when a pair of lawyers by the name of Canter and Siegel "spammed"

USENET. To do this, they commissioned the creation of a program that automatically sent a direct response piece to approximately 6000 USENET newsgroups advertising that their firm would help resident aliens obtain green cards. Their campaign generated about 1000 responses, floods of hate mail, cancelbots, and tons of notoriety, which they then parlayed into a book deal.

Since this exciting beginning, Internet-based EDM has grown steadily, though without the feverish attention paid to the web. EDM is thought by many people to be synonymous with the hated and maligned spam that shows up regularly in electronic mailboxes and, as a result, many publishers have shied away from learning about EDM. This is a mistake; EDM has a bright future, and no software marketer can afford to be ignorant of this increasingly important marketing tool.

EDM is currently divided into three different types: spam, USENET, and opt-in. A basic description of each type, as well as its marketing advantages and disadvantages, can be found below.

EDM TYPES
Spam

Spam or spamming consists of bulk mailings to unqualified or untargeted lists. Spam has been much vilified, though some of the hysteria seems rather out of bounds. Most Americans receive healthy doses of junk mail daily, and we seem to survive the experience. Indeed, DM creates a great deal of wealth, provide millions of jobs, and is an integral part of the American economy. And while spam does tend to contain a great deal of offers to buy useless health products, visit porno sites, and outright fraud, no one who has ever received a piece of junk mail containing an offer to buy swampland in Florida should be that shocked.

More to the point, spam is a waste of marketing resources. There is simply no point in wasting time sending out mass mailings to unqualified and uninterested audiences. There are several reasons why you don't want to do this, including:

- Large amounts of your mail will never be delivered. There is an ongoing battle against bulk mail being waged by different groups and individuals. Much of your spam will be knocked out of cyberspace via spam filters and blocking sites.

- Spam does not allow you to test different lists and audiences. This alone makes it useless for marketing purposes.

- Spam can generate bad will, and even attacks on your web site.

- Response rates are minimal, and usually do not justify the expense of the lists and the cost of the software.

USENET Marketing

USENET marketing is analogous to joining a club and talking up your business to the members. USENET groups are, in theory, a marketer's dream. The very nature of the environment, a collection of people who have segmented themselves into self-contained, easily targeted market segments, makes sales and direct response specialists salivate. Unfortunately, most USENET groups still frown upon receiving unsolicited mail and a broad-based USENET advertising campaign is guaranteed to generate flame mail, letter bombs, and ill-will.

One way past this problem is to is to target specific USENET groups and become a participant. You will need to spend time with the specific groups, gain trust and credibility, and eventually receive an official or a *de facto* invitation to post a low-level pitch for your product(s). This was precisely the strategy used by the New Zealand-based publisher of Ghost, the popular disk imaging utility recently purchased by Symantec. The word-of-mouth advertising this publisher developed by participating in forums dedicated to storage and backup helped build interest and awareness for Ghost and bolstered the company's sales efforts.

A variant of this tactic is to offer a service or product that integrates your advertising with your product. For example, some publishers of software development tools post newsletters on USENET groups discussing coding and product development. These newsletters typically offer tips and techniques and information on where the reader can obtain products and services. Executed carefully, this technique can be effective.

Also used on USENET groups are "clackers," individuals who are paid or incented to talk up a product on a forum. Clacking is viewed by some as ethically dubious, and you should think carefully about whether you wish to use this tactic. On the other hand, there is nothing wrong with contacting someone who has voluntarily decided to praise your product and thanking them for their efforts, nor with providing them with useful information about your products if they wish to receive it. If in doubt about the ethics of a particular situation, full disclosure about any marketing relationship is the best way to allow people to make up their own minds about what they wish to believe.

Online marketing is often criticized as "viral marketing," described by one pundit as "the rapid spreading, by word of mouth, of a product or service." Unfortunately, the pundit believes this is a bad thing since, "…it's likely to have grown from a marketing budget petri dish." This, of course, is silly, and any marketer who does not seek to create widespread favorable word of mouth for their product by any means possible, including the Internet, should be assigned to an important post in a country such as North Korea, where, presumably, this is not a major issue.

Opt-In EDM

Opt-in mailing is the Internet's most powerful direct marketing tool, and its use and reach are steadily growing, driven by the explosive growth of the use of E-mail; nearly 135 million people will communicate regularly via email by 2001. Fifteen percent of the U.S. population (approximately 30 million adults age 16 and over) use E-mail now. More than 3 billion "permitted" commercial email messages were sent in 1997 and this number will grow to 250 billion by 2002, creating a market that will soar from less than $8 million in 1997 to more than $950 million in 2002 (Forrester Research).

In an opt-in system, a publisher accesses or contracts with an Internet-based list broker to E-mail product or service announcements to lists of people who have expressed an interest in a particular service or product and have given their permission to receive E-mail about these items. Current costs range between $.10 and $.50 per name; contrast this with costs of $1.25 to $2.50 typical of conventional direct marketing. Most EDM mailings measure results by web site responses, though a handful direct the call-to-action to an 800 number. In some cases, companies use an "autoresponder," a temporary E-mail site set up to accept responses and relay them to your site. However, we do not recommend their use unless you have a particular reason to convert responses into a two-step process. Publishers who want to conduct some quiet market research sometimes make use of autoresponders.

Most opt-in systems work by allowing you to access an EDM site, pick names from a series of lists, generate a mailing piece, and then mail the piece via the site's ISP services. In some cases, the service will review the piece before mailing and make suggestions, or even write the piece for you. These services generally do not allow you to download the names to your system.

EDM lists do not yet match the quality and selectability of conventional DM, though this is changing rapidly. Current systems do allow subscriber selection by region; country; when they were last mailed; and in a limited fashion, by job title. You can usually choose to mail to the entire list or a subset of it. Few systems use SIC coding or similar systems, though most promise to add this capability soon. EDM list data cards typically provide the list source, approximate size, price per name, price per list (assuming you mail to the entire list), and a general description of the list's composition.

Despite its limitations, many publishers still find EDM mailings to be a valuable source of leads and, in some cases, sales. Assuming the existing lists target your product's audience, EDM response rates typically generate a 2% to 5% response rate within a 48-hour period. The nature of EDM mailings makes it possible to easily test different audiences, offers, and price points, particularly if the piece points the recipient back to your web site. Sales-to-response conversion rates range between 1/2 of 1% and 1.5% for retail class products—though this can be heavily influenced by your offer and other marketing factors. For direct- and VAR-class products, conversion rates are dependent upon your ability to follow up on your leads.

List Servers

As an adjunct to your EDM efforts, consider adding a list-server capability to your web site, which allows your visitors to subscribe to a "mail to" list administered by the server. The usual process is to direct visitors to a submission section on your web page where they fill out a simple form. Some programs allow the site to manage multiple lists; visitors can pick out which lists they wish to join. Once the form is submitted, the server sends out a "welcome" note and adds the information to an EDM list.

List-server technology is robust and predates the web. Over time, you can use a list server to build a highly qualified list of individuals and companies amenable to receiving E-mail about your products and services. A good list server can automatically broadcast E-mail or electronic newsletters to an entire list, purge bad electronic addresses, report on how many pieces of E-mail were sent and to whom, and allow recipients to easily unsubscribe themselves from the list. Many publishers decide not to implement their own list servers, but rent this capability from companies offering this service. If you decide to use a third party for your list-server needs, avoid companies that charge a very low monthly or yearly fee and charge for the number of times you use the list server or on a per name basis. Instead, look for firms that charge flat yearly fees and state clearly their extra costs. Yearly rental costs should range between $500 and $1500, depending on the company and the services offered.

Writing and Creating Effective EDM Pieces

An effective opt-in EDM piece consists of:

- Crisp, highly focused copy. Even in an opt-in environment, individuals are far more prone to send commercial mailings into the bit bucket. Your EDM piece should lead with a to-the-point header; make strong use of bulleted points; reference, if possible, any favorable reviews or mentions of your product from the press, users, or a research firm; contain a compelling call-to- action; and be short.

- Integrated follow-up for direct- and VAR-class software. The most effective EDM programs often use DM, telemarketing, or telesales to further qualify leads and close sales.

- Effective web-fulfillment capabilities. If your offer encourages a potential buyer to download a TBYB or demo version of your product, make sure your site or host has enough bandwidth to handle the increased traffic.

As with conventional DM, test components. Use every mailing as an opportunity to experiment with different offers and prices.

ELECTRONIC SOFTWARE DELIVERY

As noted in the **Channel Distribution** chapter of the *Handbook*, electronic software delivery (ESD) has the potential to completely change the current software distribution model. In 1997, worldwide sales of software via ESD systems were estimated at $200 million and projected to reach $5.9 billion by 2001. Even more significant is the projected growth in electronic license distribution (ELD), with market penetration projected to reach 100% by 2008.

What is ESD?
ESD TRANSACTIONS

An ESD transaction is the electronic purchase and delivery of software with no transfer of physical inventory. Internet transactions that involve shipping shrink-wrapped software are not true ESD transactions, nor do we consider current CD-ROM distribution schemes and shareware marketing to be electronic distribution, though these programs share some characteristics with ESD.

An ESD transaction is defined as follows:

- The software publisher creates and locks a software master for ESD distribution.
- The publisher or its fulfillment partner prepares the master for electronic distribution. The protected master is posted on the publisher's web site, or, optionally, also released to the appropriate channel partners.

- Customers go online and buy the product.
- The publisher or online reseller fulfills the product electronically.
- The publisher or reseller notifies the ESD fulfillment vendor (for payment of royalty).
- Returns, re-installs, and post-purchase cross- or up-sells complete the ESD transaction.

The issue of returns is a particularly thorny one for ESD distribution. Current ESD systems rely on the honor system when customers "return" software. No current feasible system now exists to "prove" that a piece of downloaded software has been removed from a buyer's system after they have received their money back. All discussions about how to implement such a system require the introduction of new copy-protection and system-snooping schemes, technology that is currently anathema to users everywhere.

Why Use ESD?

From the customer's viewpoint, ESD offers several potential benefits, including:

- Shopping convenience, though this is somewhat overstated. People like to shop, and the Internet will not change this.
- Immediate delivery, unless the Internet crashes, and it can and will.
- Product availability on a 24 x 7 basis.
- Global access to products. Start-up publishers are finding that ESD is an excellent way to establish a preliminary international channel.
- Easier and faster access to upgrades and new products.
- Improved asset management within corporate customers.

From the publisher's viewpoint, there are also many potential benefits to ESD.

- Potentially lower COGs, though this may be overstated. While packaging costs will go away in some instances, the need for high-quality help systems and electronic manuals will partially offset these savings.
- Increased market access for niche market, component-class (middleware, code libraries, graphics routines, etc.), and lower-volume products.
- The potential to achieve 100 per cent customer registration.
- Increased upgrade sales via larger captured installed bases.
- Fastest time to market for new products or replacing existing products.

- More flexible pricing models, including time-limited licensing, software rentals, subscriptions, and web-hosted applications.
- Faster and more accurate market feedback.

The role of the current distribution system in an ESD environment is not clear. Internet-only resellers and distributors would like to operate under the same margin structure as conventional distributors, whose business model is predicated upon their control of retail shelving and vast warehouse and inventory management systems capable of tracking and shipping physical inventory.

But 40-point margins and fat MDF expenditures are hard to justify in an ESD world. What value-added services does the channel offer in such an environment? Warehousing and shipping services are irrelevant in an ESD environment. Inventory management would also appear to be irrelevant; most products would, presumably, be shipped directly to the customer upon purchase from the publisher's web site.

Of course, a retail shopping environment will continue to exist for years to come, so perhaps the channel will offer value to a limited subset of software publishers. But as Internet bandwidth increases, it is easy to conceive of no-inventory retail environments, where software is downloaded and packaged on an as-purchased basis. In such a world, marketing clout will be worth something, but precisely what? The answer is not clear.

For products that are not designed for retail distribution, the issue becomes even murkier. For publishers who rely on a one-tier reseller channel, the impact of ESD will be more profound in the areas of licensing, support, and upgrade sales. But the role of distributors in such an environment, where they are already a secondary factor, becomes even more marginal.

Channel advocates predict that the current distribution system will transform itself from simply a shipping service into a true marketing resource for software publishers. This could happen at several levels. Resellers may build powerful and compelling portals that attract publishers' ad dollars. The channel may begin to offer different outsourcing services, including marketing, customer service, and true technical support, and offer them as an outsource to new publishers unwilling or unready to shoulder such burdens. But for these changes to occur, the channel will have to abandon its "toll keeper" revenue model and adopt one that generates dollars by providing sales and services tied to performance. Needless to say, the current channel system is totally unprepared for this eventuality, and does not regard it with much enthusiasm.

Another proposed alternative is that the industry will undergo a greater integration of distribution, services, and software than has been seen to date. Under the current model, distribution avoids directly competing with resellers, and no distributor has ever made a significant attempt to sell software. This could change. Some observers think AOL has made the first step toward building this new model. With its acquisition of Netscape, the online giant is in a position to advertise and distribute software, as well as sell competitive Internet development, server, and browser tools.

ESD Resellers

The ESD reseller model is currently in flux. For standard shrink-wrapped software, the existing margin structure used by bricks-and-mortar distribution is also applied to online resellers. For software developed with ESD distribution in mind, it is a mistake for publishers to pay out similar margins. The reseller has no inventory, shipping, shelving, or physical returns costs. Discounts should reflect this, and we suggest publishers negotiate with ESD resellers to use a model that ties discounts to advertising and sales performance. MDF programs should also be tied to measurable incremental sales performance.

But while we're waiting for the future to arrive, innovative publishers are already learning how to succeed with ESD. Despite all the Buck Rogers rhetoric, the current state of technology offers real online opportunities for aggressive publishers, as the following focus story illustrates.

FOCUS STORY: ESD, PLAIN AND SIMPLE
Company

Brooks Internet Software

Product

Remote Print Manager (RPM)

Market Overview

Brooks Software publishes **Remote Print Manager (RPM)**, a print utility that integrates printing capabilities in a mixed environment of PCs, mid-range systems, and mainframes linked by WAN or a TCP/IP protocol. A Windows-based program, the application remotely sends a print job from a mainframe to a remote printer and maintaining document formatting while automatically sizing the document to fit the printer's paper and using its fonts. A key market for this product is college campuses, where students registering for classes can have their schedules prepared and printed out immediately at a registration terminal in lieu of waiting for a mainframe to prepare a batch job and print it out in the MIS building somewhere on campus. RPM is priced at $99.95, with a site license of $39 per additional seat.

When Brooks began preparing to launch RPM in 1995, it originally planned a conventional rollout, but the cost of packaging, conventional direct marketing, and limited channel opportunities encouraged the company to give ESD a try. An additional incentive was the ability to offer web-based updates and patches to their customer base, lowering support costs.

Brooks' ESD model was simple. Potential customers could download a limited copy of the software and try it out (the product would only allow X number of uses). Customers wanting to buy the product would call an 800 number or E-mail Brooks to receive an unlock code. (Many companies also offer fax service.)

The first hurdle Brooks faced was finding a reliable vendor to implement their TBYB lock; they decided not to try to create their own system, though some publishers do. Two basic TBYB lock approaches were available: time-stamping the application, and shutting it down after a set period via a usage counter. Time stamping was the favored approach, but usage counters were proving more popular for higher-end applications, as experience showed that encouraging users to work with products, as opposed to putting them under a date gun, generated more sales. In addition to an unlocking capability and 24 x 7 service, Brooks also needed its TBYB technology to generate and track software licenses, both for end users and resellers (a point often overlooked by many publishers).

Finding a firm to implement a reliable TBYB capability for RPM proved to be more difficult than initially expected. Many companies had jumped into the field, and support and responsiveness varied widely. RPM initially chose a product from Mr. Phelps Software, but had to change directions when the company went under. Brooks also considered Portland Software, which offered E-commerce fulfillment capabilities in addition to TBYB. They settled on Timelock from Preview Software, in spite of experiencing some difficulties with service and support.

Brooks negotiated a royalty charge per unlock, somewhere between 2% and 8% per transaction. Such charges depend on the price of the product, number of units unlocked, and the type of fulfillment services, if any, contracted for with the ESD vendor. Some ESD companies also provide the option to purchase a one-time license, which can make sense for a high-volume publisher.

Brook's Internet marketing program was a fairly bare bones effort. The company purchased keywords from some of the largest search engines and that was it. No web advertising, no banners. They also purchased space in a couple of card decks.

Outcome

Brook's ESD system went on line in mid-1995. The product was first posted on a web-service hosted by an ISP, then later moved to an internal Brooks server. Sales results were excellent. In the first month, product sales quadrupled, then quadrupled again through the next month. Growth remained strong over the next 18 months. Company revenue grew from zero to close to a million dollars, almost exclusively through ESD.

Brooks also used its ESD system to build a one-tier distribution system. Over time, the company recruited 20 resellers, many of them outside the U.S. Brooks set up a system whereby a reseller could purchase the product electronically at 40 to 50 points off RPM's SRP. The reseller also purchased the ability to transfer a software license to the end user. Initially, all resellers were recruited strictly by "electronic" word of mouth, though Brooks later became more proactive in seeking them out.

PAYMENT OPTIONS

Despite all the excitement about web-based transactions, Brooks has found conventional payment options to be more than adequate for most prospective purchasers who can purchase RPM via an 800 number, credit card, fax, or corporate PO. In the first 18 months of operations, exactly two customers requested a web-based transaction capability. Requests have slowly risen, but the majority of customers still find conventional payment options suitable in most cases.

LESSONS

Publishers should note that despite its success, Brooks did not regard its ESD system as a replacement for conventional marketing. As the company has grown, it has placed ads in appropriate books, executed a more aggressive PR campaign, and used conventional direct marketing.

Another lesson Brooks learned from its ESD implementation is the need to include full electronic documentation with an ESD "retail-class" product. Initially, Brooks hoped the extensive help system built into RPM would suffice. This did not prove to be true, and the company developed an electronic manual for the product that accompanied each download.

ELECTRONIC MARKETING OBJECTIVES/EVALUATION CHECKLIST

OBJECTIVES   **EVALUATION**

1. **Establish alternate distribution method**

   # direct sales through
   ESD _____

   # channel sales
   through ESD _____

   % total sales through ESD _____

2. **Develop EDM capability**

   # SPAM mailed
   (not recommended) _____

   # of USENET groups
   participate in _____

   # of opt-in pieces
   mailed _____

3. **Leverage product into the channel**

   % increased calls from
   channel _____

   % increased orders from
   channel _____

4. **Leverage web site**

   # visits to web site _____

   # demo downloads _____

   # requests for
   more info _____

5. **Quickly showcase a product to many users**

   # web impressions _____

   # web click throughs _____

   # Kiosk requests _____

OBJECTIVES	EVALUATION

6. Learn more about the market for your product

Demographics on
ESD buyers _____

*Web-based surveys*_____

Internet/Usenet/Service
Forums/SIGS threads _____

ELECTRONIC MARKETING SUCCESS CHECKLIST

1. **Select type of electronic marketing you will use**

   ☐ CD-ROM distribution _____

   ☐ Electronic kiosk _____

   ☐ BBS _____

   ☐ Internet web site _____

   ☐ Auction site _____

   ☐ Channels (push) _____

   ☐ Search sites _____

   ☐ Portals _____

   ▓ Major _____

   ▓ Mini _____

   ▓ Content _____

   ▓ Web stores _____

   ▓ Web malls _____

   ▓ Services (AOL, CompuServe) _____

   ▓ Forums/chat _____

   ☐ EDM _____

   ▓ Spam _____

   ▓ Usenet _____

   ▓ Opt-in _____

   ☐ ESD _____

   ☐ Direct from site _____

   ☐ ESD reseller _____

2. **Develop web site**

   ☐ Development _____

   ▓ Decide core technology (HTML, XML, etc) _____

   ▓ Consider portability issues _____

   ▓ Choose between static vs. dynamic design _____

   ▓ Decide whether to implement E-commerce _____

   ▓ Decide which Java SDK to use _____

   ▓ Design _____

   ▓ Plan on regular updates _____

   ▓ Check cross-links _____

▨ Check spelling _____

▨ Ensure pages download quickly _____

▨ Every page contains contact info _____

▨ Copyright on each page _____

▨ Use HTML fonts _____

▨ Text short and to the point _____

▨ Multimedia graphics on separate link _____

▨ Test designs on major browsers _____

▨ Careful use of surveys _____

▨ Test of shopping cart procedures_____

☐ Navigation

▨ Alternate ways to navigate site _____

▨ Navigation pages load in less than eight seconds _____

▨ Data sheets load in less than 30 seconds _____

▨ Launch new browser window on links _____

▨ Regular test for broken links_____

☐ Writing

▨ Sharply reduced word count_____

▨ Bulleted lists _____

▨ Highlighted keywords _____

▨ Short paragraphs _____

▨ Inverted pyramids_____

▨ Good grammar_____

▨ Clear call to action _____

▨ Avoid scrolling _____

3. Check WEB SITE legal issues

☐ Credit card information protected _____

☐ No bots _____

☐ No unauthorized likenesses_____

☐ No defamatory comments, posts, or links _____

☐ Sales tax where applicable_____

☐ Obtain copyrights _____

☐ Trademarks acknowledged _____

4. Develop WEB Advertising

A. Design banner

☐ Placed above fold _____

☐ Incorporate graphics _____

☐ Incorporate navigation elements _____

☐ Incorporate animation _____

☐ Integrated offer _____

☐ Compelling text _____

B. Develop banner incentives

☐ Instant win _____

☐ Points off _____

☐ Cash back _____

C. Participate in ad network _____

D. Measure ad response

☐ Impressions _____

▓ Click throughs _____

▓ Hits/page hits _____

▓ Purchases _____

▓ Other _____

5. If purchasing web advertising

A. Do basic research

☐ Site demographics _____

▓ Size of subscriber/visitor base _____

▓ Percentage of subscribers visiting service _____

▓ Number of times they visit service _____

☐ Buyer demographics _____

▓ Age _____

▓ Sex _____

▓ Education _____

▓ Income _____

▓ Profession _____

☐ Purchasing Demographics _____

▓ Type of product they buy _____

▓ Average amount of sale _____

▓ Amount of products sold _____

▓ Frequency of purchase _____

▓ Amount of purchase _____

B. Determine costs

☐ CPM Cost _____

☐ Click through cost _____

☐ Percentage paid on each sale _____

☐ Other _____

C. Negotiate participation

☐ Tie advertising to performance (set measurable objectives)_____

☐ Ask for test participation _____

☐ Check references _____

6. Search Engine Submission

A. Submit Web Site to Search Engines

☐ Manual _____

☐ Submit sites _____

☐ Registration service _____

☐ Software submission products _____

7. Develop EDM program

A. Pick EDM type

☐ Spam (not recommended)_____

☐ Usenet _____

☐ Opt-in _____

B. Develop piece

☐ Focused copy _____

☐ Integrated follow up _____

☐ Effective web fulfillment _____

☐ Test components _____

8. If using ESD distribution:

A. Determine costs to:

☐ Lock software _____

☐ Lock demos _____

- ☐ Lock books, documentation, etc. _____
- ☐ Interface _____
  - ▓ DOS _____
  - ▓ Macintosh _____
  - ▓ OS/2 _____
  - ▓ Windows _____
  - ▓ Linux _____
  - ▓ Others _____
- ☐ Lock/unlock mechanism_____
- ☐ Fulfillment _____

B. Determine pricing

- ☐ SRP discount structure _____

C. Determine fulfillment

- ☐ Internal _____
- ☐ External_____

D. Determine ESD vendor notification _____

E. Determine returns program _____

9. If using ESD reseller

- ☐ Tie discounts to advertising and sales performance _____
- ☐ Tie promotional programs to incremental sales performance _____

10. Determine type(s) of electronic promotions/programs you will offer

A. Number of offers_____

B. Types of offers

- ☐ Price cuts _____
- ☐ Promotional pricing _____
- ☐ TBYB version _____
- ☐ Other _____
- ☐ Bundle(s) _____
- ☐ Note: Any type of promotion used elsewhere would also work here

C. Associate offer(s) to target audience_____

11. Develop electronic marketing plan, including objectives, production, fulfillment, measurement, budget, schedule, and follow-up activities

A.   Determine what will be in the electronic offer

☐ Product (full, lite, limited) _____

☐ Documentation _____

☐ Web-based collaterals _____

☐ Graphics _____

☐ Electronic registration card _____

☐ Electronic catalog _____

B.   Determine who will develop the electronic offer

☐ In-house staff _____

☐ Outside vendor _____

C.   Determine who will do fulfillment

☐ In-house staff _____

☐ Outside vendor _____

D.   Determine internal key contacts for the following activities:

☐ Manufacturing _____

▓ Deliverables, inventory, and availability _____

☐ Problem determination _____

☐ Support _____

▓ Pre-sale _____

▓ Technical _____

▓ Customer _____

☐ Follow-up _____

☐ Bounce-back device for complementary product(s) _____

12.   Track and evaluate results _____

10

Trade Shows

Trade shows are a specialized form of both marketing and direct selling. As such, they can be an important part of a company's marketing equation. Software publishers, hardware vendors, and the channel all use trade shows to take the industry's pulse, develop new marketing strategies, sell product, and obtain intelligence about competitors. The key to successful trade show participation is deciding why you are going to a show, picking the show or shows that best fit your strategy, carefully planning your participation, executing the plan, and following up after the show.

TYPES OF TRADE SHOWS

Trade shows fall into several categories, including:

- **Conferences and expositions**. These shows are a mix of lectures and exhibits, and usually focus on a particular class or type of product. They offer a wide variety of classes and forums by experts knowledgeable about their market segment as well as different publishers' exhibits. One example is Internet World, held by Mecklermedia in New York City's Javits Center.

- **Industry shows**. These shows are where companies display their marketing prowess, announce new activities to the press, meet business and channel partners, and gather competitive intelligence. Depending on the show's policies, obtaining sales leads and selling product can also be key activities.

- **Reseller shows**. These shows are put on by different channel elements and designed to allow publishers and distributors or resellers to meet and plan channel promotions, negotiate publisher MDF participation, and stay up-to-date on channel trends. Resellers are the main attendees at distributor-run shows, while corporate buyers, franchisees, sales personnel, and store managers attend reseller-hosted shows.

- **VAR shows**. Here, publishers gather leads for future sales activities. Attendees include a mix of publishers and resellers who service a particular industry (legal, accounting, construction, etc.).

- **"White box" shows**. Here, participants sell product to the attendees. As some mainline trade shows do not allow publishers to sell or take orders for product on their exhibition floor, a series of local "white box" shows, held in hotels, schools, and similar venues across the nation, has emerged. These shows are dominated by local resellers who offer a wide variety of separate components, OEM merchandise, pre-configured generic systems, used equipment, and software. While larger publishers are rarely ever seen at these shows, smaller publishers with limited marketing budgets have found them to be a useful adjunct to their marketing as well as an opportunity to sell product.

WHY GO TO TRADE SHOWS?

Publishers go to trade shows for a variety of reasons, including:

- **The opportunity to gather sales leads**. Ideally, a good trade show contains an audience that is pre-qualified and interested in your company and/or products.

- **The chance to sell products**. This is especially true of selling shows. While they won't replace the channel, they can offer the opportunity to generate some nice incremental dollars.

- **Generate favorable publicity**. The press and buying public tend to take more notice of a company that exhibits at shows—it is regarded as an indicator that a company "has arrived."

- **Recruit sales personnel**. Resumes are always flying about at major trade shows. It is a good opportunity for job recruiters and job hunters to meet.

- **Meet the press and gather intelligence about other companies**. Major shows like COMDEX are hotbeds of gossip, rumor, and sometimes rock solid information about what's going on. If you're not there, you'll miss it.

- **Meet resellers and distributors**. Like publishers, the channel uses trade shows as a chance to see what's new and interesting. In addition, many major shows hold special resellers and distributor events designed to bring publishers together with the channel.

- **Close major sales directly**. This tends to be a fairly rare occurrence, but it does happen.

- **Because everyone else is doing it**. Despite constant grumbling about show costs and time, no one wants to be the only company not exhibiting at an important show. Failure to exhibit/participate can lead to speculation and gossip about why you weren't there.

OTHER TRADE SHOW ACTIVITIES

In addition to exhibiting at a show, there are a number of other show activities you can participate in or use as part of your marketing efforts.

- **Keynote addresses**. At major shows, the CEO of a major company will give a keynote address. At smaller shows, middle managers may sometimes give keynotes. These events can be useful in generating favorable publicity for your company. Remember that a keynote address is not supposed to be a blatant ad for your company and its products. Your advocacy will have to be subtly packaged.

- **Seminars**. Seminars can be useful opportunities to learn about industry trends, gather intelligence, and, if you are participating on a seminar panel, raise your company's market "mindshare." Participating in seminars is an underutilized trade show technique.

- **Advertising**. Major shows often print daily "newspapers" or publish elaborate directories in which publishers can buy ad space. It can be an effective, but expensive, way to cut through the marketing clutter. This type of advertising should be used sparingly.

Other programs offered by trade show promoters include:

- **Direct mailing and card pack mailing to trade show attendees**. In most cases, publishers will be better off using more targeted decks to reach customers.

- **Links from the show's web site to yours**. Publishers who have participated in these programs report they are of limited use in creating booth traffic.

- **EDM notification to show attendees**. While more effective than web links, a publisher can probably carry out these activities more cost efficiently by generating the mailing directly.

Publishers can stage their own show events, including:

- **Promotions**. This covers a wide variety of programs and ideas. In the past, they have included placing go-go dancers in booths; renting Disney World for a night; providing breakfast in bed for show attendees; product giveaways; hiring jugglers, clowns, magicians, mimes (be careful, everyone is tired of mimes), celebrity impersonators; etc. Use common sense when planning promotions. Your goal is almost always to encourage attendees to come to your booth and see your product. Handing out freebies or collateral that does not accomplish this is a waste of money. Of course, your appearance at a trade show should be posted on your web site. An EDM campaign is also an effective way to notify attendees that you will be at a particular show.

- **Hospitality suites**. This involves renting a hotel room and using it as an entertainment center for show attendees. Usually a supply of liquor and light food is kept on hand for guests. In some cases, a computer(s) may be set up for demo purposes. A suite offers its users a quiet respite from the hurly burly of the show floor and a chance to talk privately with customers, potential employees, and channel partners. To save money, many smaller companies rent a suite in lieu of exhibiting on the floor, allowing them to establish a show presence without incurring substantial exhibitor's costs.

- **Parties**. While they tend to be expensive, parties can be highly productive from both a competitive intelligence and good will perspective. Publishers have used parties as a substitute for show attendance, or to tweak the nose of a competitor by throwing a bash nearby a conference or show to which they've not been invited or wish to disrupt (Sun and Microsoft have both indulged in these sorts of hi jinks). If you're going to throw a party, keep these points in mind:

  - *Over invite*. There is nothing worse than attending a party inhabited by a few lonely souls. But don't overdo it, either. A rule of thumb is to invite 150% of the number of attendees you've planned for.

  - *Spring for the open bar*. It's far easier to chat up a member of the press or potential business partner holding a glass of Chardonnay than a glass of coke.

- *Make sure you have enough food.* Your party will die quickly if stomachs begin to rumble.

- *Have a greeter at the door, someone friendly and personable.* Also, if feasible, hand out an appropriate giveaway or "chatchka" (Yiddish for knickknack) to make your party more memorable.

- *Check the event schedule to avoid conflicts.* For instance, it's probably a big mistake to schedule your COMDEX party opposite Micrografix's famous "Chili Cookoff" party.

- *Have a contingent of company employees available to handle unexpected events, such as a crush of people deciding to mob your party.*

TRADE SHOW EXPENSES

It is very expensive to attend a trade show. And it is difficult to do them "on the cheap." Prices for attending COMDEX in Las Vegas can range between $30K and $350K. Union rules will often lock you into fixed booth setup and installation expenses. You have to purchase or build a booth. You may have to purchase or lease computer equipment on which to demo your product. And all materials have to be shipped there and back. Also, premium shows such as COMDEX and PC Expo do not need to be flexible in negotiating booth space. If they are, you can be assured you're going into an undesirable location or a new, untested exhibit area.

In addition to actual exhibit costs, you will also have to plan on paying for travel, lodging, food, entertainment, transport, last minute shipments of the power cords you forgot to pack, etc., etc. There will be at least one last-minute emergency. If you do not have the time or money to plan or pay for this, think about attending trade shows next year.

BOOTH PERSONNEL

Your booth personnel are your company's representatives to the public. As such, standards of dress and behavior must be high. In matters of dress, the trend at several U.S. shows over the last few years has moved away from formal business attire to sport casual, while European and South American shows still rely on traditional business dress. In fact, at some shows the traditional suit and tie can make you seem a bit out of touch or overly formal. The answer is to do a bit of research beforehand.

If there is any doubt as to the image you wish to project, business attire is always a sensible choice (and you can always take off the jacket). For men, in all cases, leave the ponytails, T-shirts, and funky jackets at home. For women, revealing or provocative outfits should also be left in the closet. Shoes should be sensible and very comfortable as you'll be standing on your feet for many hours. Also, no chewing gum, smoking, or eating in the booth; company personnel on break should leave the booth and walk around. This gives them the chance to decompress, eat, and look at what the competition is doing. If company personnel stay near the booth, attendees will inevitably ask them for information and become annoyed if told "we're on a break."

Depending on the size of your company, it is also a good idea to have a mix of personnel at the show to handle different situations. For example, channel sales managers and representatives should be present to deal with retail inquiries and leads. Technical personnel should be present to deal with people who come to the booth with questions or problems about the product (a common occurrence). Be sure that your technical personnel have been trained on proper booth strategy. Programmers and support people tend to be forthright; overheard at a recent trade show," You won't believe some of the bugs we fixed in this release and there are **still** a couple of winners in there." Remind everyone that a trade show is an opportunity to put the company's best foot forward.

Also be careful how you deploy personnel hired only for the show. Many companies hire professional models and greeters to put a more attractive face on their exhibit and free employees for more substantial work. If you decide to use temporary employees for show duty, it is probably a mistake to allow them to demonstrate product or answer any questions about the company or its products. They will not be knowledgeable about either, and it will show. This is not the type of image you wish to portray.

In all cases, booth personnel need to be responsive and polite. And, they must also be able to qualify potential customers. A certain percentage of attendees who stop by the booth are not interested in your product and are just "kicking tires." Train your booth personnel to ask questions that cut deftly and quickly to the possible sale: What business are you in? Are you interested in buying this product? What is your time frame for purchase?

It is also a good idea to plan on staffing for alternating shifts. Trade shows are exhausting. The floors are hard, backs will ache, and voices will become hoarse. Even the most motivated personnel will wilt by the end of a big show like COMDEX or PC Expo if not relieved on a regular basis.

A last note about booth manners. At a well-attended show, booth personnel may need to manage several attendees at once. In such cases, it is a mistake to focus on one customer without acknowledging the other. The usual result of being ignored for several minutes is that the attendee will walk off in disgust with ill will toward your company. A superior technique is to ask one attendee if you can ask someone waiting to talk to you what they need, then make a decision to, A) ask them to wait and give them an estimate of how long that will be, B) refer them to someone else in the booth, or C) answer a simple question quickly and return your attention to the first attendee.

LEAD GENERATION AT TRADE SHOWS

Gathering sales leads is always a prime objective of any trade show, but few companies are effective at using these leads. Most of the time, publishers gather leads only to deposit them in a corner and ignore them until they are useless. To prevent this, plan your lead strategy in advance, and make these important decisions.

- **How you will code trade show leads**. There are many different ways to do this. Some trade shows use electronic reading devices that scan an attendee's badge or business card and capture their name and address. This is a good technique for building mailing lists, but offers little ability to qualify the person. For booth attendees who show special interest in a product, a ready-made form that allows booth personnel to quickly write down basic information and qualifying data can be very useful. If you do use a form, make sure you use a form with a qualifying "check-off" mechanism that can't be read by the attendee. It is not good PR for visitors to see themselves rated as having low sales potential or as a possible "5 out of 5" when a "1" is what you're looking for. Using abstract symbols on these forms or on a business card is a better approach.

- **How you will entice attendees to stop by your booth and give you information**. Collecting business cards in a fishbowl in return for being entered in a drawing for a free product is a popular technique, but you'll end up with a lot of useless cards from people only interested in show freebies. A better technique is to offer attendees the chance to enter the drawing if they'll step into the booth and allow you to qualify them or sit through a presentation. All freebie programs should use a similar qualifying tactic.

- **How you will respond to inquiries**. Someone who has stopped by your booth and requested information about a product should receive that information within two weeks of the show. Leads that have been categorized as "hot" should be contacted within three days of a show. This can only happen if you have a clear plan of execution to follow once the show is over.

INTELLIGENCE GATHERING AT TRADE SHOWS

Trade shows offer an excellent opportunity to network and gather competitive intelligence. Major trade shows such as COMDEX, PC Expo, or N+I offer publishers the unique opportunity to inspect an industry and gather valuable information on the current competition, newcomers to the market, new trends, as well as meet key movers and shakers in your market. To maximize your efforts, preplanning and setting goals are necessary. Your pre-show activities should include:

- **Obtain show demographics**.
- **Develop a brief outline of the key facts and trends you wish to investigate at the show, and assign personnel to find the necessary data**.
- **Obtain a profile or demographic breakdown of the show's attendee list**. This information may include attendee titles, company size, company type, and related information. This data will help you shape your show's marketing message and focus. You should also find out if the show will provide you with a complete attendee list after the show.
- **Check the party and special event schedule for the show, decide which you want to attend, and obtain an invitation**. (You won't always be able to party crash). Keep in mind that the largest parties are not always the best. Smaller parties attended by people who are key influencers or who write about your market segment may be a better bet.
- **Check the conference and seminar sessions for the show, and sign up for the ones you want to attend**. Also remember that it can be very useful to speak to a presenter during the informal pick-up sessions that often follow each session.
- **Hold a pre-show meeting with show staff; hand out show maps with key booths highlighted and checklists of items and information you want them to gather**.

YOUR LOCATION AT A TRADE SHOW

As in real estate, the value of your trade show booth is determined by location,

location, location. If you are tucked away in the back of the hall near the janitorial closet, no one will come to see you no matter how compelling your presentations or how well trained your booth personnel. To ensure that you obtain a favorable location:

- **Register early**. Especially at new shows, early registrants will receive the pick of the better locations.

- **Examine the floor plan of the show prior to signing up**. The more desirable locations include booths near the main entrance, near a major food concession, and near major companies such as Lotus or Microsoft (if they'll be attending the show). If the show is organized by product category, a booth on the aisle leading to that section is desirable.

- **Keep track of late cancellations**. If an exhibitor pulls out at the last minute, it may be possible for you to obtain their more desirable floor location at little or no extra cost.

TRADE SHOW INSTALLATION

Since most major shows are held in large civic exposition halls under union control, your company personnel may be barred from setting up or installing the booth. Union rules may require that a union member plug in the power cords, lay the carpet, and put the computers on the pedestals. You will pay a handsome fee for this to happen, and it will not happen very quickly or be done very well in most cases. There is nothing you can do about it, so be prepared to budget for the expense.

Booth personnel should be ready and able to fix any problems that arise just after the installation and during the show. Items to bring with you include:

- Numerous rolls of packing tape.
- Marking pens.
- Extension cords, power strips, and adapters.
- Collapsible luggage carts for toting boxes around.
- Extra light bulbs for booth lighting.
- Basic tools (a Swiss Army Knife can overcome a world of omissions).
- Shipping labels for shipping boxes back after the show.
- Extra power cords.
- Duct tape.

THE PRESS AND TRADE SHOWS

You can expect to see the press at major trade shows, and should plan in advance to generate as much favorable press notice and stories as possible. If you're using a PR firm, they should handle much of the details. Your plans should include:

- **Check the trade show listings for which publications will be sending representatives** (these listings are usually only prepared by major shows).

- **Schedule as many meetings with interested press members as realistic**. If you have a PR firm, they should take the lead on this activity. Also take this opportunity to set up after-show meetings and demonstrations.

- **Prepare in advance any press releases and announcements you want to release at the show**.

- **Investigate any opportunities to participate in any "Best of Show," "Best of Category," "Best New Product," etc., contests**. If you win, be prepared to immediately send out a PR release and announcement trumpeting your victory.

All booth personnel should be briefed on what a press badge looks like, and warned to be on their best behavior when being quizzed by members of the press. If a member of the press begins to ask questions about the financial health of the company, or begins to ask questions about company gossip or future plans, booth personnel should be instructed to bring the press member over to a public relations specialist or someone who has been designated to handle these types of questions.

Trade shows are often a good opportunity for marketing managers to make contact with key editors or reviewers. To facilitate this, many publishers will have private showings of new or unannounced products for the press. In many cases, these showings will take place in a hotel suite or room off the main exhibit floor. Most showings should be scheduled in advance and take place in a relaxed atmosphere. For a crucial or particularly influential reviewer, the product manager, a PR specialist, and perhaps a senior manager should all be present to answer questions and handle objections. Do not invite reviewers from competing magazines to attend private showings at the same time. The atmosphere will be anything but relaxed.

RESELLER SHOWS

Reseller shows are a special breed of trade show, and need to be approached somewhat differently. Publishers participate in these shows hoping to convince the distribution system to purchase their product. To meet this objective, your show strategy should include, but not be limited, to the following:

- **If this is a show aimed at the retail channel, a high-quality booth**. From a reseller or distributor's viewpoint, your exhibit is an indication of your company's financial health and ability to commit to marketing programs. While less important at shows targeted for VARs or vertically oriented-distributors, your booth should still be of good quality and well maintained.

- **A place in the booth to meet privately for private demos and business discussions**. In many cases, the reseller or distributor will have a busy schedule, and not have time to meet elsewhere on the show floor or in a suite.

- **A well thought out channel marketing strategy that focuses on key marketing programs**. For example, if you believe an end cap program is important for your product's in-store success, be prepared to discuss these programs at the show and lock in your participation. However, it is usually a mistake to commit to secondary MDF or co-op programs at this time.

- **Set up a series of follow-up meetings with key channel figures you meet at the show**. These meetings are good indicators your product is being seriously considered for distribution.

SHOW SPECIALS

Attending trade shows is an expensive form of marketing, no matter what the objectives. To offset costs, many companies offer "show specials," a one-shot, deep-discount offer on a product or service offered only at the show. In addition to offsetting costs, show specials can:

- Increase attendance at your booth.

- Increase excitement about your presence at the show.

- Help raise employee morale and excitement. Most employees find it exhilarating to make sales anytime, anyplace.

- Help generate interest in your product among corporate evaluators.

- Help deflect requests for free product from show attendees who claim to be "evaluators."

Some shows, such as COMDEX, prohibit product exchanges taking place on the show floor. In these cases, publishers can fulfill sales and specials directly through a telesales system. The product is then mailed directly to the purchaser's home or office.

SHOW SELLING

In addition to show specials, more and more companies are also using trade shows as selling opportunities, where they offer products at attractive discounts, but not at the same levels as the show specials. Show selling is most effective if your company:

- Can offer a broad variety of products to sell, including software, books, accessories, etc.

- Has the personnel to staff the booth and take orders, unpack inventory, and manage customer crowds.

- Has a telesales capability.

FOCUS STORY: HOW MUCH FOR THAT KEY CHAIN IN THE WINDOW?
Market Overview

IBM founded its Independent Vendor League (IVL) in 1992 to support the development of OS/2-related products and services such as consulting, books, training videos, and courseware. Led by an aggressive marketing staff, the IVL saw an opportunity to use trade shows to increase support for OS/2 and generate incremental sales into the rapidly growing OS/2 installed base. The initial design and intent of its trade show participation was to highlight the growing support of OS/2 by third parties. The IVL set up its own booth at major trade shows and invited various vendors supporting OS/2 to share the booth in order to showcase their products and services.

With the dual objectives of increasing traffic and capturing names, the IVL turned to a series of outbound tactics. Personnel were stationed at key show entrances and strolling through the show handing out promotional items designed to both encourage show attendees to go to the booth and to equalize traffic within the booth. One tactic involved handing out a mock passport. If show attendees visited every vendor in the IVL booth and had their passports "stamped," they received a prize when they turned it in, at which point their vital information was captured.

Then in 1993, the IVL shifted its focus to catalog sales of third-party OS/2 books, videos, courseware, etc., and paraphernalia such as key chains, shirts, mugs, and other items. To drive traffic into the booth, the IVL again used aggressive outbound tactics. Catalogs containing discounts and premiums designed to entice attendees to come to the booth were handed out on the show floor and at every entrance. Once at the booth, visitors could inspect the various items for sale, purchase them via a telesales system, and either walk away with their purchase or have it shipped to a specified location. While show sales never completely covered the costs of attendance, they helped to substantially offset costs and provided an excellent audience for the IVL catalog, which became profitable.

The IVL also offset show overhead by hiring flight attendants to help work the various shows. They were able to build a core of attendants who, because of their flexible schedules, could arrange to be in the different show cities. The IVL did not have to pay for airfare or accommodations, only for hours worked in the booth and on the show floor. And, flight attendants proved very adept at dealing with people in a polite and professional manner, even under stress. The IVL's use of flight attendants proved to be a cost-effective way to increase attendance and provide aggressive floor coverage.

Finally, the IVL used the captured attendee information to both pursue hot leads in a timely fashion and to enhance its internal mailing lists.

LESSONS

The IVL used promotions and show selling most effectively. Their plan included the following tactics:

- Aggressive in-show marketing.
- The use of incentives to encourage people to visit the booth and allow important information to be captured for future marketing efforts.
- The use of capable and cost-effective temporary personnel to offset show costs.
- An effective way to capture important attendee information.
- Effective use of the captured attendee information.

Too often companies go to shows with vague ideas about "marketing exposure" and "leads" but with no concrete plans. In that case, trade show participation becomes an expensive, all-expenses-paid vacation for all concerned. If your company has the budget for that kind of thing, fine. If not, make sure you plan your participation and carry out critical pre- and post-show activities.

TRADE SHOWS OBJECTIVES/EVALUATION CHECKLIST

OBJECTIVES   **EVALUATION**

1. Sell product

   # show product sold   _____ _____ _____

2. Obtain sales leads

   # sales leads   _____ _____ _____

   % qualified sales leads   _____ _____ _____

3. Generate favorable publicity

   # mentions, articles, etc.

   in press   _____ _____ _____

   % increased product

   reviews, first looks, etc.   _____ _____ _____

4. Meet the press and gather intelligence

   # editors/reviewers added

   to database   _____ _____ _____

   competitive research   _____ _____ _____

   market research   _____ _____ _____

5. Meet key channel partners

   # key channel contacts   _____ _____ _____

   # product inquiries   _____ _____ _____

   % increase channel orders   _____ _____ _____

6. Recruit personnel

   # resumes gathered   _____ _____ _____

   # interviews conducted   _____ _____ _____

 # new hires   _____ _____ _____

7. Close major sales directly

   # sales closed   _____ _____ _____

TRADE SHOWS SUCCESS CHECKLIST

1. Determine type of trade show(s) you will attend

- ☐ Selling show _____
- ☐ Industry show _____
- ☐ VAR show _____
- ☐ Conference and/or exposition _____
- ☐ Reseller _____
- ☐ White box _____

2. Develop trade show plan, including objectives, strategy, lead handling and disbursement, intelligence, budget, schedule, staffing, equipment, promotions, etc.

A. Determine who will coordinate show activities

- ☐ In-house person _____
- ☐ Business show coordinator (consultant) _____

B. Determine which show-related activities you will participate in Advertising _____

- ☐ Event conflicts _____
- ☐ Official greeter _____
- ☐ Hospitality suites _____
- ☐ Party _____
- ☐ Emergency contingent _____
  - ▒ Keynote address(es) _____
  - ▒ Promotions _____
  - ▒ Seminars _____
- ☐ Over invite (150% rule of thumb) _____
  - ▒ Open bar _____
  - ▒ Sufficient food _____
  - ▒ Other _____

C. Determine type of booth

- ☐ Use booth provided by show _____
- ☐ Build/purchase own booth _____

D. Determine floor space requirements

- ☐ Location _____
- ☐ Size _____

E. Determine staffing requirements

☐ Establish booth coverage (work schedule)_____

☐ Arrange relief shifts _____

☐ Coordinate travel/hotel arrangements _____

☐ Brief staff on booth behavior, dress, etc._____

F. Press activities

☐ Check trade show listings _____

☐ Enter different show contests _____

☐ Prepare press releases _____

☐ Schedule meetings _____

G. Attendees _____

☐ Review show manual and show rules with staff _____

H. Determine equipment requirements

☐ Bring own _____

☐ Arrange packing & shipping _____

☐ Rent _____

I. Determine how you will promote your participation in show

☐ Advertising (trades, show manual, exhibitor book, etc.) _____

☐ EDM _____

☐ Discount/free tickets_____

☐ Free drawings _____

☐ Literature/lead card _____

☐ Premium giveaway (mug, key chain, etc.) _____

☐ Print/broadcast media (local radio, cable TV, etc.) _____

☐ Web site _____

☐ Product giveaway _____

☐ Other _____

J. Determine costs

☐ Payment terms _____

☐ Refund policy _____

☐ Discount opportunities_____

☐ Additional cost considerations _____

☐ Amperage _____

☐ Audio-visual _____

☐ Carpeting _____

☐ Electrical outlets _____

☐ Lighting _____

☐ Sound _____

☐ Telephone/data lines _____

☐ Travel/hotel/car rental for staff _____

☐ Plastic bags with company and/or product name/logo _____

☐ Other giveaways _____

K.   Develop lead capture program

☐ Card/badge reader _____

☐ Drawing _____

☐ Fill-in card _____

☐ Promotional program _____

☐ Other _____

L.   Develop intelligence gathering program

☐ Check conference and seminar sessions _____

☐ Check party and event schedule _____

☐ Outline of goals and trends _____

☐ Pre-show meeting with staff _____

3.   Make "go–no go" decision _____

4.   Obtain necessary approvals

☐ Product Marketing _____

☐ Finance _____

☐ Senior Management _____

5.   Pre-show activities

A.   Inspect show site and floor space assignment _____

B.   Inspect rental booth _____

C.   Purchase/design own booth _____

D.   Review show manual and show rules _____

E.   Obtain show demographics _____

F. Staff meeting _____

☐ Assign staff responsibilities _____

☐ Emergency contacts/procedures _____

☐ Establish expected conduct, dress, etc. _____

☐ Review written schedule _____

G. Buy insurance _____

H. Arrange booth security _____

I. Arrange storage for equipment, boxes, product, collaterals, etc. _____

J. Reserve equipment passes _____

K. Reserve badges for booth staff and others attending show _____

L. Hire cleaning service _____

M. Reserve/rent equipment _____

N. Rent/buy plants, decorations, etc. _____

O. Arrange shipping (to show and back) _____

P. Arrange labor for booth set up and tear down _____

Q. Mail free/discount tickets to potential customers _____

R. Prepare presentations, demonstrations, etc. _____

S. Produce/order collaterals _____

6. Show activities

A. Set up booth _____

B. Install equipment _____

C. Unpack all collaterals, literature/lead cards, etc. _____

D. Check all presentations, demonstrations, etc. _____

7. **Post-show activities**

   A. **Pack/ship equipment, literature, etc.** _____

   B. **Obtain show attendee list** _____

   C. **Lead capture** _____

   ☐ Identify hot leads _____

   ☐ Verify that all leads were handled _____

   ☐ Implement follow-up _____

   ☐ Direct mail _____

   ☐ Direct sales call _____

   ☐ Telesales _____

   D. **Track and evaluate results** _____

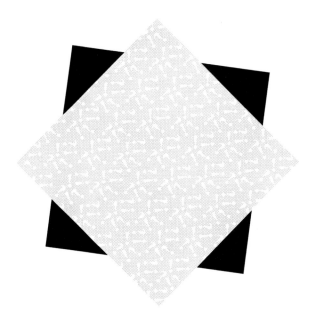

Basic Product Marketing Concepts and Organization

Marketing gurus like to categorize software companies—it makes it easier and more interesting to talk about a company if we can compare its mission and/or marketing focus with another and contrast the differences. Some of the more common classifications include:

THE TECHNOLOGY-DRIVEN COMPANY

The technology-driven company is controlled by the desires and direction of its development staff. MicroPro International, publisher of one-time market leader WordStar, was a classic example of this type. The most common problem with the technology-driven company is that it builds products that satisfy its development staff, rather than providing the features and benefits the market wants. Early in WordStar's evolution, for example, many users requested the ability to format text in side-by-side columns, useful for many types of writing, particularly resumes and newsletters. The development group refused to add it and, noted that over time, user requests for side-by-side columns diminished. This was absolutely true! Users wanting this feature purchased WordPerfect or Microsoft Word.

THE SALES-DRIVEN COMPANY

Ashton-Tate was a classic example of a sales-driven company, myopically focused on fulfilling quarterly sales quotas. When demand for certain products weakened, they would offer product at special prices, bundle slow sellers with quick movers, offer special returns, stock swap—anything in an effort to meet unrealistic quotas. At one point, the distribution system had backlogs of over 24 months for certain products, but Ashton-Tate had satisfied its quotas, for the time being. Of course, much of this product eventually came back, and the revenue piper had to be paid, with much wailing and gnashing of teeth and layoffs.

THE MARKET-DRIVEN COMPANY

This company is motivated by the needs and desires of its customer base. This is often the most successful because all functional groups sublimate their egos to their customers' needs. While this is an easy philosophy to preach, it is a hard one to put into practice. A current example of a company that listens to its customers is IBM. Once famed for this ability, IBM became increasingly deaf to the market in the late 1980s and paid a severe price in 1992, when the company was forced to report a staggering $5 billion loss.

Under Lou Gerstner, IBM has turned around and the company's resurgence can be directly traced to their regained ability to shut up and listen. For example, after years of commitment to OS/2, in 1995 IBM finally faced reality and began to incorporate such products as Windows, particularly Windows NT, into its sales offerings, helping them regain lost ground in key corporate markets.

But market-driven companies have their own problems. Often, they lose the will to lead. Or they can become too reactive and fearful of change, waiting for the safe road to appear while missing opportunities stemming from an aggressive but intelligent proactive strategy.

THE FINANCE-DRIVEN COMPANY

During the 1980s, auto industry observers noted that General Motors was a finance-driven company. The road to upper management usually led through GM's accounting department. Over time, GM implemented many cost-saving programs that made it more economical to create cars that nobody wanted to drive.

Few companies are perfect examples of any one type. Most are a mix, but it is important to understand which type(s) best describes your company. This understanding will provide you with insight into the potential "cultural" issues that await you.

Software Publisher Titles and Responsibilities

When organizing a successful company and marketing team, one must learn to work with a fairly wide spectrum of product, development, and sales specialists. The industry's use of different names for people doing the same job can make things confusing.

To assist you, we've included a list of typical job titles and responsibilities. Use this as a guideline only and remember that responsibilities will vary widely. In some cases, a project manager may be doing a product manager's job, and a collateral specialist handling feature sets (usually not very well, in both cases). Nonetheless, necessity demands that a publisher's basic business functions be divided along the lines described. Be aware that it may take research and detective work to find the basic structure underneath conflicting titles.

Marketing Titles

Product Manager. The person responsible for the coordination of all the functional groups responsible for the creation of a product, including development, marketing, quality assurance, support, documentation, sales, and marketing. The best product managers are marketing oriented and also possess strong technical skills. In some companies, the product manager is given bottom-line responsibility for his or her product's performance, as well as control over the product's budget. Some companies divide the product manager's functions into one or more specialized roles. The most common are:

- **Product Marketing Manager.** The person responsible for coordinating advertising placement, collateral development, and PR for a product. This individual may also focus on post-launch activities.

- **Product Manager.** The person responsible for pre-release product development issues, customer wish-list management, and pre-release review management.

Marketing Communications (Marcom) Manager. The person responsible for coordinating collateral and PR activities. Marcom positions are usually divided into a number of specialized positions including:.

- **Public Relations (PR) Manager.** The person responsible for building and maintaining good relations with the press and computer-industry publications.

- **Channel Marketing Manager.** The person responsible for long-term sales and marketing development for channel programs, including merchandising, advertising, and MDF and co-op funds allocation.

- **Channel Account Manager**. The person responsible for implementing programs and maintaining relationships throughout a channel account, including contacts in the channel partner's sales, marketing, promotions, and purchasing departments. They also handle distributor or reseller requests for publisher participation in new or existing programs and promotions.

- **Collaterals Manager**. The person responsible for creating and printing product collaterals, including brochures, demo disks, specification sheets, in-store merchandising items, and so forth.

- **Ad Placement Manager**. The person responsible for placing advertisements in publications, after determining which offers your product the best audience for the best price. They also coordinate the extra services publications may offer in return for a sizable ad placement.

- **Trade Show Manager**. The person responsible for booking and coordinating trade show attendance and activities.

Sales Titles

Sales Manager. The person responsible for selling product to end users and the channel. Depending on the size of the organization, sales positions can be divided into a number of different special functions. The most common are:

- **Corporate Sales Representative**. The person responsible for sales to major corporations and national accounts.

- **Channel Sales Representatives**. The person responsible for sales to important or major distributors and resellers. Larger publishers often assign a dedicated representative to major distributors and resellers.

- **OEM Sales Manager**. The person responsible for selling product for OEM integration to other publishers or to hardware manufacturers.

- **Promotions Sales Manager**. The person responsible for selling product for bundling and promotional programs.

Development Titles

Project Manager. The person responsible for coordinating product development and implementing product specifications. The project manager coordinates all aspects of a product's development and evolution and usually represents the viewpoint of development to the marketing and sales departments.

- **Product Architect**. The high-level designer responsible for a product's overall design and philosophy.
- **Integration Specialist**. The specialist responsible for integrating third-party modules and OEM code into the core product.
- **Engine Specialist**. The programmer responsible for developing the core product code.
- **Driver Specialist**. The person responsible for developing product-device drivers.
- **Support Specialist**. The person responsible for providing technical to end users and the channel. In some cases, especially in larger publishers, support will be part of a separate customer service organization.
- **Quality Assurance Specialist**. The person responsible for product testing and reliability.

Customer Service Titles

Depending on the publisher, customer service is either part of the sales or marketing group, or a separate functional group.

- **Customer Services Manager**. The person responsible for managing customer inquiries about product pricing, availability, and ordering.
- **Customer Product Specialist**. The person responsible for providing specific information about a specific product or product line's pricing and availability.
- **Customer Inquiry Specialist**. The person responsible for handling customer inquiries about shipping status of products, complaints, and problem resolution.

The Product Team

Please understand that when we discuss product teams, we are not talking theory. The team always exists. Building a product, whether it is a car, a bar of soap, or a successful software package, is always a collective effort. Different groups within a company must contribute their skill and expertise to the product. What often distinguishes one company's success from another's failure is the degree to which they acknowledge the team's existence, and the amount of time spent coordinating and communicating the team's activities.

The most successful software companies are generally those that formalize the team's existence and provide the tools and incentives required to manage it. One way is to create a formal product team with members from each key functional group: development, sales and marketing, documentation, quality assurance, and support. In some cases, the "team" may be a virtual one, consisting of contractors and third parties.

Regardless of title or location, the team's objectives are to exchange information about each group's activities, coordinate each group's role in building and launching the product, and solve problems and conflicts. The team meets regularly to track progress and discuss relevant issues—in person, over the Internet, or at electronic conferencing facilities.

An important question is "who runs the team?" Many times, it is the product manager, whose responsibilities can vary widely from company to company. In some cases, the product manager has bottom-line responsibility for the product's financial success. In other cases, he or she functions more as a facilitator among the functional groups. In most cases, the best success is achieved when the product manager has at least some authority to ensure that the team adheres to its agreed-upon tasks and milestones.

Team Conflicts

A common problem in software companies is the natural tension that exists between functional groups. Each group has its own perception of the value it brings to a product and stereotypical perceptions about the other groups. For instance, the development group frequently regards the marketing group as a bunch of blow-dried "suits"—talking heads who lack understanding of product subtleties and key technical issues.

The documentation team often has an academic bent and believes that the other groups don't respect their efforts (the "nobody reads our documentation" whine). Worse, with competitive upgrades and price cutting, many retail products now skimp on documentation, and rely on third-party publishers to explain how their products work.

The support and customer service groups often feel that they are always cleaning up everyone else's mess. And the marketing group often feels that the development group is out of touch with the real world and should pay more attention to conventional grooming habits.

Subtle tensions can also arise between groups that would seem, on the face of it, to be natural allies. It is not uncommon for the sales and marketing groups to engage in unproductive sniping; sales argues that their direct contribution to bottom-line sales makes them the fair-haired boys. Marketing, on the other hand, will point out that with the wonderful company image created, crisp collaterals printed, and favorable press generated, a monkey could sell this stuff. And so it goes.

Perhaps the biggest problems arise when functional groups begin to take on roles for which they are inherently ill suited. For instance, product management should never be part of a development organization. A few software companies have attempted to do this with uniformly poor results. In all cases, the marketing function becomes weak and attenuated, failing to provide needed customer input before and during the development phase. In rare cases, technical support groups have been attached to sales forces or customer service to a direct sales force instead of marketing or technical support. Such management experiments are almost always short-lived and unproductive, as they violate internal business logic.

These tensions and issues are natural and cannot be reversed; however, they can be managed by recognizing that they exist, using humor and common sense to defuse areas of tension, and helping each group acknowledge the value and contribution of the other. The best marketing and product managers possess these abilities.

THE PRODUCT MARKETING PROCESS

As companies grow, they realize the need for process control—a structured methodology for managing projects and product releases, preventing surprises, and disseminating important information on a timely basis to employees and customers.

Product Release Bulletin (PRB) System

Many software companies implement a product release bulletin (PRB) system to manage product releases, changes in prices and availability, and product retirement. There are many different variants to this system, and we describe a generic approach here that can be easily adapted by any publisher.

Product Marketing Description

The foundation of the PRB system is the product marketing description (PMD), which functions as the product's marketing "bible," and reflects the product team's goals and expectations for the product. The PMD is usually developed by the product manager and circulated to contacts in the various functional groups for their review and response. The PMD is updated during the development cycle to as events dictate—most often to incorporate feature changes. A basic PMD describe the:

- Product's target audience.
- Basic features and benefits.
- Product's competitive strengths and weaknesses.
- Hardware platform(s) supported.
- Operating system(s) supported.
- Projected release date.
- Key marketing messages.
- Sales projections.

A high-level outline of the product marketing plan (at least). In some cases, a PMD will incorporate a complete product launch and marketing campaign. In others, this information will be covered in a separate document.

In some companies, the PRD is referred to as a marketing requirements document (MRD).

Preliminary PRB

As the product nears release, the product manager, with input from the product team, creates a preliminary PRB, which is then circulated as a "heads-up" to contacts in the functional groups involved in manufacturing, shipping, and supporting the product. A preliminary PRB should include:

- A basic product description.
- The product's stocking unit (SKU) number.
- The release date.
- Method of distribution.
- Medium for distribution, i.e., floppy disks, CD, tape, Internet, etc.
- Product superceded or replaced by previous release, if any.
- Known technical issues surrounding the release.

When development releases the product for production, a final PRB is created and the product becomes officially available for sale and distribution. A product without a PRB does not officially "exist" as far as the publisher's customers and business partners are concerned.

Product Termination Bulletin (PTB)

A product termination bulletin (PTB) is created whenever a new product supersedes an existing one or a product is being retired from general release. The PTB should include the following:

- Date of product termination.
- Product replacement.
- Date product support will be terminated.
- Suggested upgrade path for customers using the product.

Product Change Bulletin (PCB)

A useful adjunct to the system is a product change bulletin (PCB), which documents for internal use a significant change in a product's target market, pricing, or service and support.

Summary

The system described here is a generic one. To assist you in developing a process that suits your company's organization and internal structure, we've included sample PRB forms on the disk that accompanies the *Handbook*.

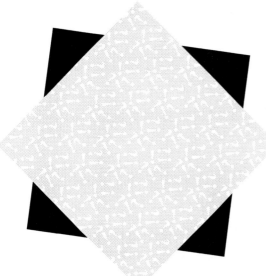

Product Marketing Cost Matrix

To assist you in creating marketing budgets, we have included this cost-matrix spreadsheet, which assigns costs, ranges, and percentages to the key marketing activities described in the ***Handbook***. You will find it useful when deciding which activities you should (or can afford to) participate in.

The numbers are based on current market conditions and charges. They can and do range widely. For example, when looking at channel costs, CompUSA MDF programs represent the high end of the spectrum, while Electronic Boutique's MDF programs are usually far less costly. The difference reflects each reseller's or distributor's target audience and influence in the channel.

Some costs, particularly printing and production costs, can be reduced by as much as 70%, depending on volume and design factors. On the other hand, postage costs are relatively fixed. And finally, in many cases, costs may vary depending on the savvy of your company, how big it is, and demand for your product. In other words, use these figures as signposts, not tablets written in stone, and remember that you can always negotiate.

POSITIONING, PRICING & NAMING	COSTS
Naming Studies	$3K-$50K
Legal Fees	
Basic Trademark Search	$150
Comprehensive National	$1K
Comprehensive International	$2K
Resolve Potential Conflict	$6K
Positioning Studies	
Focus Groups	$K-$10K per session
Market Research	$10K-$300K
Informal Research	$2K-$3K
Pricing Studies	
Focus Groups	$5K-$10K per session
Market Research	$10K-$75K
COLLATERALS	
End-User Collateral (Assumes 10M initial print run)	
Brochures (4-color)	$200 per thousand, assume a minimum set-up charge of $12 for any size run
Case studies	$1K-$2K for writing
Collateral CDs	$1.50-$3.00 per piece (includes production)
Comparison Sheets (2-color)	$150 per thousand
Corporate piece	$250 per thousand
Demo disk	$7.5K-$60K
Design	$750-$3K per piece
Electronic presentations	$1K-$5K per template
Folders	$450 per thousand
NFS SOFTWARE	
Full	$10-$35
Partial	$1.50-750
Reprints	$0.25-$1 per page, B&W
Spec Sheets (2-color)	$150 per thousand

SYSTEM OVERVIEW	
Design	$1.5-$3K
Writing	$1.5-$7K
Printing	$150 per thousand
VIDEOS	
Production	$60-$150 per hour
Tapes	$1.50-$2.50 per unit, depending on packaging
Talent	$100-$350 per hour
White Paper (Design and writing costs)	$5K-$10K
Channel Collateral	
Corporate Identity Manual	$200-$400
Comparison Sheets (2-color)	$150 per thousand
NFS	
Full	$10-$25
Partial	$1.50-$7.50
Order forms	$75 per thousand
Sell scripts (Design)	$3-$5K per thousand
Spec Sheets (1-color)	$75 per thousand
Merchandising Collateral (Assumes runs of 500 units)	
End-caps	$3-$4 per piece
Kiosks	$15-$20 per piece
Mobiles	$.25-$1.50 per piece
Monitor Wraps	$.75-$1.50 per piece
Shelf Talkers (Assumes run of 500)	$.10-$.15 per piece
Tent Cards	$.25-$1.50 per piece

Packaging	
Design	$3K-$5K
Printing (includes box and printing costs)	
Setup Box	$1.50 per box
Tuck Box	$1.10-$1.15 per box
Assembly	
Insert individual piece	$.10-$.25
Shrink Wrap	$0.15
Print Manuals (Assumes one piece with a 2-color cover)	
100+ pages	$1.10-1.50 per unit
200+ pages	$1.75-2.25 per unit
300+ pages	$2.50-3.00 per unit
Duplication (disks)	$.10-$.25 per floppy
Duplication (CDs)	$.50-$.85 per CD
Documentation Creation	
100+ pages	$7.5K-$12.5K
200+ pages	$15K-$25K
300+ pages	$30K+
CHANNEL MDF	
Distributor	
Ad Placements	$4K-$20K
Basic participation fees	$0-$10K
Buying Incentive	1%-2% of selling price
Catalogs	$1.5K-$2K
Co-op	50% matching funds
Detailing	$40-$60 per store
DM Programs	$2.50-$5.00 per piece
Product Management Services	$5K-10K per year
PR Programs	$1.5K-$5K per year

Publications	$1K-$10K per placement
Reseller Presentations	$1.5K-$7K per event
SPIFs	5%-20% of selling price
Technical Training	$0-$2K per hour
Telemarketer Presentations	$750-$2K
Telemarketer Programs	$0-$10K
Trade Show Appearances	$2K-$10K per show
Vendor Nights	$1.5K-$2.5K
Web Site Listings	$500-$10K per listing
Reseller	
Ad Placements	$4K-$20K
Bundling	80%-90% off SRP, may be 100% off SRP
Buying Incentive	1%-2% of selling price
Catalogs	$750-$10K
Co-op	50% matching funds
Demo Days	$35-$50 per store
Detailing	$40-$60 per store
DM Programs	$2.50-$5.00 per piece
In-store Kiosks	$3K per month
In-store Merchandising	$7K-$60K per month
Product Management Services	$5K-$10K per year
PR Programs	$1.5K-$5K per year
Publications	$1K-$10K per placement
SPIFs	5%-20% of selling price
Telemarketer Presentations	$750-$2K
Telemarketer Programs	$0-$10K
Trade Show Appearances	$2K-$10K per show
Web Site Listings	$500-$10K per listing

PR AND PRODUCT REVIEWS	COSTS
Review Management	
Review Guide	$5K-$15K
Pre-Release Editorial Tour (Assumes no use of agency, includes travel expenses)	$15K-$20K
Pre-release Editorial Tour Through Agency (10-city tour, does not include travel expenses)	$25K-$35K
PR Rep On Tour With Publisher	$1.2K-$1.5K per day
PR Management	
Launch Event	$5K-$20K
Press Kit	$2K-$3K (Design)
Press Mailings	$1K for 300 pieces
Business Wire Posts	$500
Electronic Posts	$100-$250
ADVERTISING	
Cost of development	$5K-$70K
Placement Fees	15% of ad cost
Cost by Magazine (Assumes 1-page, 4-color ad)	
First Rank (i.e. PC Magazine)	$40K
Second Rank (i.e., PC World)	$15-$35K
Niche (i.e. Publish Magazine)	$1K-$6K
Channel (i.e. CRW)	$1K-$15K
(Industry Specific (i.e. The American Law Journal)	$1K-$8K

SALES PROMOTIONS	COSTS
Bundling Promotions	
Product Costs	$0-$20
Design Development	$3K-$25K
Fulfillment	$5-$30
Price Promotions	20%-70%,depending on market and product
Free/Premium Offers	
Product	$0-$20
Books	$3-$5
Paraphernalia	$2-$15
DIRECT MARKETING	
Bingo Cards	$.02-$.05 per impression
Direct Fax	$.10-$.30 per minute
Direct Mail	
Per Piece (Standard)	$1.25-$2.50
Per Piece (Multi-dimensional)	$2.00-$6.00
Design (All pieces in mailing)	$10K
Copy (All pieces in mailing)	$4K
Cover letter	$24 per thousand
Brochure	$40 per thousand
Order form	$18 per thousand
Return Envelope	$16 per thousand
Cover Envelope	$20 per thousand

Postage	$.20-$3.20
Fulfillment (Assumes taking order, processing, and shipping)	$5-$12
Infomercials	$75K-$250K
Telemarketing & Telesales	
Inbound operator costs	$1.50-$2.50 per call
Inbound script and setup	$500 to $750
Outbound operator	$30 to $40 per operator
Outbound script and setup	$1K-$2K
Initial tests	$500 to $1.5K
BUNDLING	
Cost of bundled product	$0-$30
Cost of promotion	$10K-$70K
Cost of packaging (assumes box reengineering)	$1.5-$3
Cost of fulfillment	$1-$5 per piece
Cost of support (assumes extra costs of supporting third-party product, regardless of contractual terms)	$.25-$.80
ELECTRONIC MARKETING	
Kiosk	$1K-$2K (usually MDF expenditure)
Web Site Development	
Static Site	$2.5K-$20K
Dynamic Site	$20K-$150K
CD-ROM Distribution	$1K-$12K or an extra 5%-10% off SRP

Web Ad Development	
Banners	$1.5-$25K, highly dependent on scope of project
Web Search Engine Submissions	$30-$100 for software
Web Advertising	
CPM	$.01-$.05 per impression
Click Through	$.30-$.50 per click through
EDM	
Bulk mailings	$50-$500 per bulk list (Varies widely)
Opt-in	$.15$-$.50 per person
ESD	
Unlock royalties	2%-8% per unlock
Tradeshows	
Regional Shows(Northeast Computer Show)	$5K-$25K
Major Shows(i.e. PC Expo)	$15K-$150K
Theme Shows(Networld, OS/2 World)	$15K-$150K
COMDEX	$75K-$500K
Suite	$8K-$25K

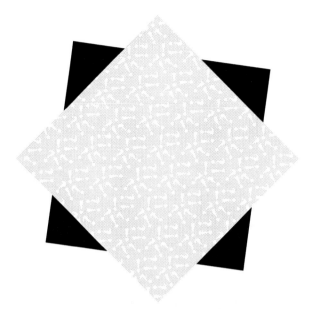

Marketing Resource Directory

Our original intention was to expand this section for the third edition of the *Handbook*. In the age of the Internet however, thick paper directories seem increasingly out of place. In this spirit, we have decided to include a small sampling of the names, companies, and resources found at www.SoftwareMarketSolution.com. This web site, sponsored by Aegis Resources, contains organized links to a wide array of companies and individuals who provide software publishers with different types of industry services and information.

Remember: If you need to contact companies for marketing consulting, distribution, collateral and design development, training, advertising, direct and electronic direct marketing, and related services and assistance:

http://www.SoftwareMarketSolution.com.

ADVERTISING

Moss Warner Communications, Inc.
56 Arbor Street
Hartford, CT 06106
Telephone: 860.233.5641
Fax: 860.232.5239
Contact: Daniel Weingrod
E-mail: weingrod@mosswarner.com

BAR (UPC) AND ISBN CODES

The ISBN Agency is the point of origin for International Standard Book Numbers. You will need an ISBN number for bookstores and libraries and to obtain a Books in Print listing.

The ISBN Agency
Telephone: 908.464.6800
Fax: 908.665.2895

The Uniform Code Council is the point of origin for the automated identification and capture (AIDC) industry. A publisher can begin the process of obtaining a bar code at their site.

Uniform Code Council, Inc.
Telephone: 937.428.3743
www.uc-council.org

For information on obtaining an international code, the EAN International site is a must visit.

EAN International
rue Royale 145
1000 Bruxelles - BELGIUM
Telephone: +32 2 227 10 20
Fax: +32 2 227 10 21
E-Mail: info@ean.be
www.ean.com

CHANNEL CONTACTS
Catalogers

MicroWarehouse
47 Water Street
South Norwalk, CT 06854
Telephone: 203.838.5484
Fax: 203.853.2267
www.microwarehouse.com

MicroWarehouse includes Mac, PC, Data Warehouse. They are the largest direct response
reseller of Mac products.

Multiple Zones International, Inc.
707 South Grady Way
Renton, WA 98055.3233
Telephone: 425.430.3000
www.zones.com

Target audience: SOHO, business, and entertainment. Publish catalogs for the PC, Mac, and
educational markets.

Programmer's Paradise
1157 Shrewsbury Avenue
Shrewsbury, NJ 07702.4321
Telephone: 908.389.8950
Fax: 908.389.9227
www.pparadise.com
Contact: Jeff Largiader, Vice President of Marketing

Target audience: Programmers, database developers, corporate developers. A principal reseller
targeting the software developers market.

PC Connection
528 Route 13 South
Milford, NH 03055.3442
Telephone: 603.423.2135
Fax: 603.423.5784

Famous for its raccoon mascots, PC Connection is considered the most influential of the
direct response resellers. As befits a star, the company has a reputation of being difficult to
approach. Their primary interest is in selling established products.

DISTRIBUTORS

Ingram Micro, Inc.
1600 East Saint Andrews Place
Santa Ana, CA 92705
Telephone: 714.566.1000
Fax: 714.566.7795

Types of software products stocked: Business, SOHO, education, entertainment, Unix, Linux and VAR/niche products. Ingram Micro is currently the largest international distributor of microcomputer software and hardware.

Merisel
200 Continental Boulevard
El Segundo, CA 90245
Telephone: 1.800.Merisel, 310.615.3080
www.merisel.com

Types of software products stocked: Business, SOHO, education, entertainment, Unix, and VAR/niche products. Merisel is the third largest international distributor of microcomputer software and hardware.

Tech Data Corp
5350 Tech Data Drive
Clearwater, FL 34620
Telephone: 813. 539.7429
Fax: 813.538.7429
Total 1997 annual sales: $7 billion

Types of software products stocked: Business, SOHO, education, entertainment, Unix, and VAR/niche products. Tech Data has overtaken Merisel to become the number two company in international high-tech distribution. They have traditionally been more adventuresome and more open to new opportunities.

Micro Central, Inc.
8998 Rte. 18 North
Old Bridge, NJ 08857.1009
Telephone: 732.360.0300
Fax: 732.360.1369
www.microcentral.ocm

Micro Central is a good starting point for a new software publisher interested in two-tier distribution.

Electronic Arts
209 Redwood Shores Parkway
Redwood City, CA 94065
Telephone: 650.628.1500
www.ea.com

Target audience: Entertainment. In addition to being a distributor, Electronic Arts is also an affiliate label publisher who markets and sells smaller publishers' products under its label, usually on an exclusive basis.

SOFTWARE-ONLY RESELLERS

Babbages
2250 William D. Tate Ave
Grapevine, TX 76051
Telephone: 817.424.2000
Fax: 817.424.2002
www.babbages-etc.com

Target Audience: Entertainment and SOHO. Most Babbages are located in indoor malls. Their primary market is entertainment, with a secondary emphasis on SOHO products.

STOREFRONT RESELLERS

Inacom
10810 Farnam Drive
Omaha, NE 68154
Telephone: 402.392.3900
Fax: 402.392.7214

Inacom subsidiaries include Valcom and Inacomp.

SUPERSTORES

CompUSA, Inc.
14951 North Dallas Parkway
Dallas, TX 75240
Telephone: 800.COMPUSA
Fax: 800.669.8329
www.compusa.com

Target Audience: Business, SOHO, and entertainment. The world's largest chain of computer super stores with over 200 locations.

DESIGN AND GRAPHICS

L'Artiste a la Carte
P.O. Box 506
Millbrae, CA 94030.0506
Telephone: 650.872.3411
Fax: 650.415.872.0737
E-mail: lartiste@lartiste.com
www.lartiste.com
Contact: Marc Richards

Specialize in illustrations, designs, and cartoons for the high-tech industry.

mle design
213 Cider Mill Road
Glastonbury, CT 06033
Telephone: 860.657.2156
Fax: 860.633.4688
E-mail: mle design@aol.com
Contact: Ray Campbell

High-quality and high-speed collaterals development. Multimedia video and slide shows. High resolution scans and Photoshop manipulation. Adobe Photoshop Certified. They also provide extensive print brokerage services.

Turner Duckworth
665 Third Street, Suite 509
San Francisco, CA 94107
Telephone: 415.495.8691
Fax: 415.495.8692
www.turnerduckworth.com
Contact: David Turner

Specialize in developing brand identity packaging and design, with an emphasis on creating a strong visual product identity. In business for six years, the company has both a U.S. and international clientele. They offer comprehensive personal services for smaller companies.

DIRECT MARKETING

Devol Services
20 Morgan Avenue
Greenwich, CT 06831.4940
Voice: 203.532.0969
Fax: 203. 532.9158
E-mail: Race73@aol.com
Contact: Bob Devol

Specialize in direct marketing for high-tech products. Portfolio includes successful mailings for IBM and Microsoft as well as business-to-business and consumer software product campaigns.

L.I.S.T. Incorporated
320 Northern Boulevard
Great Neck, NY 11021
Telephone: 516.482.2345
Fax: 516.487.7721
E-mail: info@l-i-s-t.com
www.l-i-s-t.com
Contact: Glenn Freedman, President

A good source of high-tech marketing lists and services.

21st Century Marketing, Inc.
2 Dubon Court
Farmingdale, NY 11735
Telephone: 516.293.8550
Fax: 516.293.8974
Contact: David Schwartz

In business since 1978, 21st Century Marketing is a leader in direct marketing for the high-tech industry. Services include list management, list brokerage, database creation, and data processing.

ELECTRONIC DIRECT MARKETING

NetCreations, Inc
378 W. Broadway
New York, NY 10012
Telephone: 212.625.1370
Fax: 212.625.1387
www.netcreations.com
Contact: Michael Mayor, Director of Sales

Operate the Postmaster Direct EDM service, one of the best places to start if you are interested in beginning an opt-in campaign.

INFOMERCIALS

KSL Media Direct, Inc
60 Madison Avenue
New York, NY 10010
Telephone: 212.481.0740
Fax: 212.481.4265
Contact: Michael Medico.

A leading developer of infomericals, with experience in selling high-tech products.

TELEMARKETING

Multitrack
125 Park Street, Number Six
Brookline, MA 02146
Telephone: 617.232.7780
Fax: 617.232.7854
Contact: Herb Fox

Specializes in helping companies evaluate and implement telemarketing services for high-tech products.

DOCUMENTATION SERVICES

DocuClear
79 Perry Street
New York, NY 10014
Voice: 212.691.4926
Fax: 212.255.1990
E-mail: info@docuclear.com
contact: Cheryl Morrison

Specializes in recruiting technical communications professionals for permanent jobs and contracting assignments in the information technology field. Placements include specialists in online and printed documentation and marketing materials. Also provide documentation and editorial consulting services for software developers and recruit other IT professionals.

Wiest Publications Management, Inc.
21 NE 5th Street
Minneapolis, MN 55413
Telephone: 612.379.0634
Fax: 612.379.0634
Contact: Lee Wiest, Director of Editorial Services

Specializes in training development and production, particularly as it relates to product knowledge and sales/marketing; foreign language translation and production of training materials, parts catalogs, maintenance manuals, and other technical materials; and publishing support for textbook publishers.

Write Type Associates, Inc.
78 Bartram Avenue
Bridgeport, CT 06605
Telephone: 203.384.9996
Fax: 203.368.6379
E-mail: fullgail@megahits.com
Contact: Gail Ostrow, President

A full-service writing, editing, and training consulting company, specializing in internal and end-user documentation, training materials, and collaterals.

DUPLICATION AND MANUFACTURING

Astraltech Americas
5400 Broken Sound Boulevard
Boca Raton, FL 33487
Telephone: 407.995.7000
Fax: 407.995.7001

Creator and duplicator of CD-ROM packages, video tapes, and disks. In addition, the company provides comprehensive product fulfillment services.

International Software Services
1560 Tilco Drive
Frederick, MD 21701
Telephone: 1.800.368.9900
www.softwareservices.com

Specializes in high-volume disk and CD-ROM duplication services, documentation printing, and software fulfillment. The author has used their services in the past, and continues to be impressed by their cost-effectiveness and responsiveness.

FULFILLMENT

Kea Technologies, Inc
17 Avenue D
Williston, VT 05495
Telephone: 802.658.3993
Fax: 802.658.3991
E-mail: sales@keatech.com

The best fulfillment service we know of.

UCA&L
699 Hertel Avenue, Suite 390
Buffalo, NY 14207
Telephone: 716.871.6444
Fax: 716.871.6459

Probably the industry's largest high-tech outsourcing company.

INDUSTRY ASSOCIATIONS

Software & Information Industry Association
1730 M St. NW, Suite 700
Washington, DC 20036.4510
Telephone: 202.452.1600
Fax: 202.223.8756
www.siia.net

The Software Publishers Association (SPA) and the Information Industry Association (IIA) merged on Jan.1, 1999 to form a new trade association representing the software and information industry.

MANUFACTURER'S REPRESENTATIVES

Lacom
55 South Broadway, 3rd Floor
Tarrytown, NY 10591
Telephone: 914.366.6200
Fax: 914.366.6220
E-mail: jimkanelg@aol.com

Lacom specializes in channel development for startup publishers.

Roman Marketing
3920 E. Coronado Street, Suite 206
Anaheim, CA 92807
Telephone: 714.632.7053
Fax: 714.632.7214
E-mail: duroj@earthlink.net
Contact: Jerry Duro

Roman Marketing specializes in working with startups and the distribution system. The company has extensive contacts within the major distributors.

MARKETING CONSULTING SERVICES

Aegis Resources, Inc.
35 Ridge Road
Stratford, CT 06497
Telephone: 203.380.8261
Fax: 203.380.8263
www.aegis-resources.com
Contact: Merrill R. Chapman, President

Publisher of *The Product Marketing Handbook for Software,* Third Edition and the sponsor of www.SoftwareMarketSolutions.com. Aegis Resources is also the creator of *The Aegis Product Marketing Forum*, a comprehensive three-day program designed to teach successful software marketing. Subjects covered include product positioning and pricing, channel distribution, public relations and product reviews, collaterals and packaging, sales promotions, advertising, direct marketing, bundling, and more. Contact them for information about when the forum will be conducted in your area or for pricing on custom sessions.

The Ambit Group (TAG)
665 Third Street, Suite 527
San Francisco, CA 94107
Telephone: 415.957.9434
Fax: 415.957.0504
Contact: Linda Kazares, President

Founded in 1988, TAG is a full-spectrum marketing and channel development company serving domestic and international high-technology clients. TAG develops strategic and tactical marketing plans for companies wishing to enter the U.S. market or expand their current presence.

Software Success
990 Washington St., PO Box 9105
Dedham, MA 02027
Telephone: 888.479.6663
Fax: 617.320.9466
E-mail: seminar@softwaresuccess.com
www.softwaresuccess.com
Contact: Rob Shapiro

A leading source of marketing information, seminars, publications and reports about the software industry.

MERCHANDISING AND DETAILING

Consumer Products Marketing Group (CPMG)

1601 East Plano Parkway, #100
Plano, TX 75074
Telephone: 800.251.0551
Fax: 972.881.29935
Contact: Ron Eisner, CEO; Chris Pelzl, President

Provide in-store training, detailing and merchandising, inventory tracking, software installation, market research, seminar presentations, trade show staffing, and customized publisher support programs.

Lees/Keystone

80 Business Park Drive
Armonk, NY 10504
Telephone: 914.273.7655
Fax: 914.273.9187
Contact: Michael Stoll

Provides a wide variety of promotional and merchandising items, including personalized (imprinted with your company or product logo) jackets, T-shirts, watches, pens, coffee mugs, etc.

Technology Advancement Corporation

298 24th Street, Suite 135
Ogden, UT 88401
Telephone: 801.393.1155
Fax: 801.393.4115

Operates several divisions, including Temp Reps and Blitz America and specialize in providing temporary field sales forces for product rollouts and promotions.

PUBLICATIONS

Software Developer and Publisher

Webcom Communications Corporation
10555 E. Dartmouth, Suite 330
Aurora, CO 80014.2633
Phone: 303.745.5711
Fax: 303.745.5712
www.webcom@pi.net

A must read for software publishers.

PUBLIC RELATIONS

Geibel Marketing Consulting
PO Box 611
Belmont, MA 02178.0005
Telephone: 617.484.8285
Fax: 617.489.3567
E-mail: 74752 3072@compuserve.com
Contact: Jeffrey P. Geibel

Specializes in placing articles and related editorial material in targeted periodicals. An excellent choice for software companies with a business-to-business orientation.

Media Map
215 First Street
Cambridge, MA 02142
Telephone: 374.9300
Fax: 617.374.9345
www.mediamap.com

Provides a leading directory service identifying editors, reviewers, and analysts from high-tech publications, as well as a series of print, CD, and software products designed to assist publishers in managing their public relations.

NetPR, Inc
146 Shady Lane
Freeport, FL 32439
Telephone: 850.835.2694
Fax: 850.835.6895
Contact: Kimberly Maxwell

An excellent public relations firm with reasonable prices. Kimberly Maxwell, NetPR's founder, has worked at Ziff-Davis and CMP.

Thomas Public Relations, Inc.
775 Park Avenue, Suite #222
Huntington, NY 11743
Phone: 516.549.7575
Fax: 516.549.1129
www.http://thomas-pr.com/
Contact: Karen Thomas

Specializes in PR parties and social events at high-tech conferences. They sponsor one of COMDEX's most noted social events.

RESEARCH

DataQuest
251 River Oaks Parkway
San Jose, CA 95134
Telephone: 408.468.8000
Fax: 408.468.8045
www.dataquest.com

DataQuest is one of the leading research and survey groups in the PC industry.

The Gartner Group
56 Top Gallant Road, Box 10212
Stamford, CT 06904
Telephone: 203.964.0096
Fax: 203.324.7901
www.gartner.com
info@gartner.com

The Gartner Group specializes in high end IT and MIS trends and forecasts.

PC DATA
11260 Roger Bacon Drive, Suite 204
Reston, VA 22090
Telephone: 703.435.1025
Fax: 703.478.0484
www.pcdata.com

PC DATA is the leading source of hard numbers on sales of retail products.

Simba Information
Box 7430
Wilton, CT 06897
Telephone: 203.834.0033
Fax: 203.834.1771
www.simbanet.com
Simba concentrates primarily on publishing and Internet-related media research.

SUPPORT

Stream Software
275 Dan Road
Canton, MA 02021
Telephone: 617.821.4500
Fax: 617.821.5688
www.stream.com

A leading provider of technical support outsourcing services.

TRADE SHOWS

Skyline Exhibits and Graphics, Inc
7 Johnson Avenue Suite B
Plainville, CT 06062
Telephone: 860.793.2814
Fax: 860.793.2817
www.skycorp.com

Well-respected booth graphics and design company.

WEB SERVICES

Write Type Associates, Inc.
78 Bartram Avenue
Bridgeport, CT 06605-3101
Telephone: 203.384.9996
Fax: 203.368.6379
E-mail: fullgail@megahits.com
Contact: Gail Ostrow, President

Provide web site needs analysis, review, design, and implementation services.

WEB SITES

SoftwareMarketSolution

Telephone: 203.380.8261
Fax: 203.380.8263
E-mail: aegis@aegis-resources.com
http://www.softwaremarketsolution.com
Contact: Aegis Resources, Inc

Sponsored by Aegis Resources, SoftwareMarketSolution.com is an excellent online source of links to different companies offering a wide variety of services and solutions for software publishers.

TechCalendar

Telephone: 415.447.6193
Fax: 415.447.6191
http://www.techweb.com/calendar
Contact: Rebecca Wetherby

Hosted by CMP Media in partnership with KnowledgeWeb, Inc., TechCalendar is an excellent online source of information about upcoming industry events and trade shows, and an opportunity for publishers to post information about their events.

The Spot for Web Site Builders

E-mail: kristi@on-the-net.com
http://thespot.i-depth.com
Contact: Kristi Stone

A first-class site for information on web development, advertising, public relations, E-commerce and marketing.

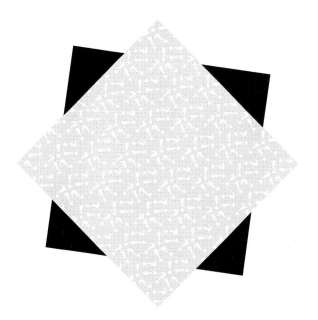

Software Marketing Pipeline

To illustrate when the various marketing tasks discussed in the **Handbook** occur, both individually and in relationship to each other, we have created the "software marketing pipeline." This is simply a metaphor, described both graphically and verbally, to give you an overall sense of when these important marketing tasks are planned, executed, and evaluated with respect to a product's launch. The pipeline is not intended to substitute for a project management tool; nor is it intended as a complete breakdown of all the myriad tasks that must be completed to support a product's release. Rather, the pipeline is designed to provide you with a simple, at-a-glance time frame for starting and completing the marketing tasks detailed in the checklists.

In most cases, the tasks outlined on the pipeline begin twelve months before a product launch or major upgrade and end twelve months later (please note where exceptions are indicated). For the sake of simplicity, we have divided the pipeline into three phases: a twelve-month preparation period, the launch period, and a twelve-month sustaining period. In today's competitive environment, 12 months of planning is all you can expect to have since your user base will usually expect an upgrade within a year of any major or new release.

Depending upon your company's size, resources, and bureaucracy, you may need more or less time to complete the tasks listed here. Adjust the dates accordingly. But be careful! Key tasks such as planning your product review strategy will not wait on your company's ability and willingness to execute them. Instead, you must be ready to meet market requirements. If not, expect to pay the price!

POSITIONING, PRICING, & NAMING

Because how you position your product drives just about everything else in your marketing plan, positioning is the very first marketing task you must complete. In fact, the entire preparation, launch, and sustaining process begins with this first step. Naming and pricing inevitably flow from this initial exercise.

Positioning, naming, and pricing tasks fit into the software marketing pipeline as follows:

Determine product category	12 months before launch
Determine product class	6 months before launch
Determine features and benefits launch*	6 months to 4 weeks before
Select name	6 to 3 months before launch
Develop pricing structure	3 months before launch

*Features can and will change right up to the last minute, which is guaranteed to drive your Marcom people crazy trying to keep their collaterals up to date! This can negatively affect your PR, advertising, and product review campaigns.

To ensure the least possible expense and aggravation, it is absolutely essential that you position your product as early in the preparation phase as possible. Naming your product early is also critical, as you may have to select an alternate name before the process is finished. And finally, having your pricing structure in place allows you to plan the distribution, promotions, bundling, direct marketing, and other strategies that are also required during the preparation phase.

CHANNEL DISTRIBUTION

How soon you begin your efforts to place your product in the channel depends primarily upon whether you are an established company with a new product or an "unknown" in the market. The hardship for a new company breaking into the channel is that it must sometimes initiate activities before the product even exists, a neat trick if you can pull it off. Suffice it to say that a new company with a new product must begin contacting the channel as early as 18 months prior to product launch.

For optimum success, channel distribution activities occur in the software marketing pipeline as follows:

New company/new product	18 months before launch

Contact distributors and resellers and obtain product evaluation forms. Fill them out and send them back to the appropriate channel personnel. You may have to repeat this cycle numerous times before anyone becomes interested in seeing the product.

Established company/new product	6 months before launch

Contact distributors about evaluation. Meet and discuss product. Submit evaluation forms.

All subsequent activities are the same for both new and established companies/products.

Plan channel promotions	3 months before launch
Plan telemarketing SPIF programs	1 month before launch
Plan maintenance promotion programs	3 months after launch
Plan second round of maintenance programs	6 months after launch

While it is certainly more difficult and more time consuming for a new company to break into the channel, no software publisher with channel plans is exempt from the need to plan and implement channel activities as part of its overall marketing plan.

COLLATERALS

After your product has been positioned, priced, and named, you can begin planning and developing your end-user and channel collaterals. Timing, as always, is critical. Your packaging may very well be used in your ad layouts, along with other collaterals such as brochures, spec sheets, etc.—all of which must be ready to go at launch time. Channel collaterals will also need to be shipped just prior to launch.

Typically, collateral planning and development fits into the software marketing pipeline as follows:

Plan collateral types and quantities	5 months before launch
Plan and design end-user collaterals	3 months before launch
Plan and design channel collaterals	2 months before launch
Design product packaging	2 months before launch
Plan all print runs	2 months before launch
Finalize package design	1.5 months before launch
Print all collaterals	1 month before launch
Distribute all collaterals	1.5 weeks before launch

Even the smallest publisher with the smallest budget can make the most of these valuable marketing tools if you plan early and carefully and insist on quality implementation.

PUBLIC RELATIONS & PRODUCT REVIEW PROGRAMS

It is almost never too early to begin planning and implementing your public relations and product review activities. However, logic dictates that you cannot begin these activities until you have positioned, priced, and named your product. Therefore, your formal PR program will probably begin about six months prior to your product launch.

Public relations and product review program activities fit into the software marketing pipeline as follows:

Public Relations Basics

Appoint PR coordinator	12-6 months before launch
Plan beta and non-disclosure previews	12-6 months before launch
Plan and implement controlled leaks	12-6 months before launch
Schedule and conduct press tour(s)	3-1 months before launch

Build press kits	1 month before launch
Write press releases and plan press mailings	2 weeks before launch
Mail press kits to weekly publications	1 week before launch
Courier deliver press kits	1 day before launch

Product Review Program Basics

Establish product review team	6 months before launch
Begin "review" beta	6 months before launch
Schedule user group appearances	6-3 months before launch
Update reviewer/analyst database	3 months before launch
Plan "first look" and feature articles	3 months before launch
Begin active review management process	3 months before launch
Develop product review guide	3-1 months before launch
Evaluate reviews and respond	1 month after launch
Evaluate review program	2-3 months after launch
Implement contingency plans, if necessary	2-3 months after launch

Public relations and product review programs are ongoing activities that must be carefully planned, implemented, and monitored. With proper management, such programs can add significantly to your product's success in the market.

ADVERTISING

Advertising plans have to be carefully thought out in the preparation phase prior to product launch because the publications in which you will want to advertise plan their editorial and advertising calendars up to 12 months in advance.

Advertising activities typically occur in the software marketing pipeline as follows:

Plan advertising budget/placement	6 months before launch
Review/select advertising agency	6 months before launch
Review budget, ads, placement strategy	3 months before launch
Place advertising	Coincide with launch
Review advertising/agency results	3 months after launch
Plan next advertising/budget placement	6 months after launch

Advertising is not an activity that is performed once and then forgotten. Your advertising budget and schedule should be reviewed during the sustaining phase and decisions based upon your marketing objectives and results. You will also be evaluating your client/agency relationship on an ongoing basis, as this is a strategic partnership that can significantly enhance your performance in the market, if managed effectively.

SALES PROMOTIONS

How far ahead you can plan your sales promotions depends entirely upon the type of sales promotion you will be implementing. Planning for either a launch or an upgrade promotion is relatively simple because launch and upgrade campaigns are planned events. Dealing with opportunity and defensive promotions is a little trickier as you don't always know ahead of time when you will have to react to something in the market. Keeping this in mind when you plan your sales promotion strategies during the preparation phase will make it that much easier for you to react quickly and effectively during the sustaining phase.

Sales Promotion activities occur during the software marketing pipeline as follows:

Launch Promotion

Plan promotion(s)	4 months before launch

Opportunity Promotion

Plan promotion	6-1 months, depending upon market events

Defensive Promotion

Plan promotion upon	2 months-3 weeks, depending
	market events

Upgrade Promotion

Plan promotion release	3 months before new version

Sales promotions can be both proactive and reactive. That is why careful planning, including "what-if" scenarios, is so important to the success of your overall marketing plan. Analyzing the possibilities before you need to act will always put you in a better position to either take advantage of a positive situation or take the sting out of a negative one.

DIRECT MARKETING

Direct Marketing is another one of those areas where some activities begin up to a year before your product is ready to be launched and may continue for as long as 8-12 months after the launch. Obviously, the more careful and detailed your planning is prior to launch, the more successful your direct marketing efforts will be during the sustaining phase.

Direct marketing activities occur in the software marketing pipeline as follows:

Card Decks

Pick appropriate card decks	6-3 months before launch
Design card deck piece	2-1 months before launch

Direct Fax

Identify fax services	2-1 months before launch
Broadcast faxes	7 days up to day of launch
Follow up faxes	Ongoing

Catalog Sales

Plan catalog	5 months before launch
Finalize product inclusions and catalog form factor	3 months before launch
Finalize printing and production	1 month before launch

Direct Mail

Begin internal list compilation	12 months before launch
Develop test offers	5 months before launch
Evaluate/hire list broker	4 months before launch
Mail test offers	2 weeks before launch
Mail direct offer (can be upgrade)	1 month after launch
Mail second offer	4 months after launch
Mail third or complementary offer	8 months after launch

Infomercials

Evaluate infomercial potential for product	8-6 months before launch
Produce Infomercial	4-3 months before launch
Test Infomercial	3-2 months before launch
Purchase air time for infomercial months before	3-2 months before launch
Run infomercial	Day of launch
Run infomercial in different markets	Ongoing, determined by sales results over the life of the product

Telesales

Decide if outbound vs. inbound	5-3 months before launch
Decide if in-house vs. outsource	3-2 months before launch
Test offers	1 month- 2 weeks before launch
Develop sales scripts and cross- and up-sells	3 months before launch

Fulfillment

If new system, test fully	3 months before launch
If existing system, test fully	6 weeks before launch

In reality, once you get past your first product release, direct marketing activities are constantly occurring as successive products are launched and the activity cycles of each launch overlap and continue.

BUNDLING

Selling product bundles typically occurs during the twelve-month sustaining phase. However, planning for bundling must begin at least six months prior to product launch if you want to implement bundling schemes that will benefit your bottom line when you need it. In addition, as you might not always be the initiator of a bundling proposal, prompt and effective responses to such requests from OEMs and other software publishers is essential.

In an ideal world, bundling fits into the software marketing pipeline as follows:

Hardware Bundles

Plan "lite" or alternate product for bundling	6 months before launch
Develop OEM pricing plan	3 months before launch
Preview product to targeted OEMs	1 month before launch
Begin sales calls to targeted OEMs	2 weeks after launch

Software Bundles

Identify potential bundling opportunities	3 months before launch
Contact potential vendors	2 months before launch
Begin bundle prospecting	immediately after launch

While it may not always be possible to follow such a "neat" calendar, it is important to factor bundle planning into your overall marketing plans. If this isn't done during the preparation phase, you will not be prepared to initiate or react to bundling opportunities during the sustaining phase. If bundling existing books, use a software bundling schedule. If bundling custom or new books, use a hardware bundling schedule.

ELECTRONIC MARKETING

Electronic marketing activities typically begin about three months prior to your product launch; however, you will have begun planning for them as early as possible to ensure that you are ready to act when the time comes. Planning early in the preparation phase will allow you to successfully execute these activities during the launch and sustaining phases.

Electronic marketing activities occur during the software marketing pipeline as follows:

Kiosk Systems

Plan kiosk appearances	2 months before launch

CD-ROM Distribution

Plan appearances	3 months before launch
Review CD distribution plans	1 month before launch
Review CD distribution activity	1 month after launch
Evaluate CD distribution activity	3 months after launch

Web Site Development

Build and "proof" basic static web site	3-1 months before launch
Build dynamic web site	12-6 months before launch
Follow up with search submissions	Every two weeks or monthly
Identify search engines for keyword placement.	1 month - 2 weeks before launch
Submit Information to search engines	1 month - 2 weeks before launch

Web Site Advertising

Plan advertising budget/placement	3 months before launch
Review/select advertising agency	3 months before launch
Review budget, ads, placement strategy	2-1 months before launch
Schedule placement	2-1 months before launch
Develop Web ads	1 month - 2 weeks before launch
Place web ads	Day of launch
Place follow-up ads on selected web sites	1 month after launch
Review advertising/agency results	Immediately after launch
Plan next advertising/budget	1 month after launch

As with conventional advertising, web advertising plans have to be carefully thought out in the preparation phase prior to product launch. However, unlike conventional advertising, you will have far more flexibility in how and when you purchase web-based advertising. The web has plenty of ad "space" available, and the development cycle for banners is far shorter than it is for print or TV pieces. Web ads typically have a far shorter life span than conventional advertising, and you should plan on at least monthly updates of your ad material. You will also be able to measure results quickly by metering web responses.

EDM

Again, unlike conventional direct marketing, EDM campaigns can be implemented and executed with lightning speed. However, their actual sales results will usually be much lower than conventional DM, since the abbreviated nature of EDM encourages inquiries, not sales.

Begin EDM internal E-mail list compilation	3 months before launch
Begin opt-in E-mail vendor evaluation	2 -1 months before launch
Develop test offers	1 month before launch
Mail test offers	1 month to day before launch
Mail direct offer (can be upgrade)	Day of launch
Mail second offer	1 week after launch
Mail third or complementary offer	2 weeks after launch
Follow-up mailings	Ongoing

TRADE SHOWS

Planning to participate in a major trade show like COMDEX must begin 12 to 18 months prior to show time. This may be difficult for a new company coming to market with a 6-month planning window at most. Therefore, it is imperative that you plan your trade show activities according to your time constraints. For the small and emerging company, a regional show may be the better option, saving a COMDEX appearance for the future.

Trade show activities occur in the software marketing pipeline as follows:

COMDEX

Plan participation	12 months before show
Plan staffing requirements	6 months before show
Plan and buy/build booth	6 months before show
Plan show promotions(s)	3 months before show
Plan lead follow-up activities	3 months before show
Plan travel/accommodations	3 months before show
Arrive, rehearse, set up	2 -1 days before show
Follow up all leads	3 days - 2 weeks after show
Evaluate results	2 weeks after show

National Show

Plan participation	12 - 8 months before show
Plan staffing requirements	6 - 3 months before show
Plan and buy/build booth	6 - 3 months before show
Plan show promotion(s)	3 months before show
Plan lead follow-up activities	3 months before show
Plan travel/accommodations	3 months before show
Arrive, rehearse, set up	2 - 1 days before show
Follow up all leads	3 days to 2 weeks after show
Evaluate results	2 weeks after show

Regional/Niche Show

Plan participation	6 months before show
Plan staffing requirements	3 - 2 months before show
Plan and buy/build booth	3 - 2 months before show
Plan travel/accommodations	3 - 2 months before show
Plan lead follow-up activities	3 - 2 months before show
Plan show promotion(s)	1 month before show
Arrive, rehearse, set up	2 - 1 days before show
Follow up all leads	3 days to 2 weeks after show
Evaluate results	2 weeks after show

The cost of trade show participation must be carefully weighed against the anticipated benefits. Planning as far in advance as possible will help you determine whether or not you should participate and assist you in setting realistic goals and expectations from your participation.

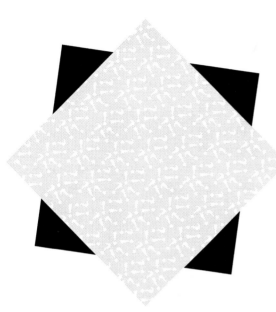

Glossary

ACD Automatic call distributor. A software/hardware system that manages inbound and outbound telemarketing campaigns.

ADSL Asymmetric digital subscriber line.

Ad space model A paradigm that describes the ad types, elements, and psychological space that combine to create a virtual buying environment for the customer.

ALD Affiliate label distribution. A re-marketing agreement between a small and a large (affiliate) publisher.

APPT Average price per thousand.

ATPC Average time per call.

Banner A type of web-based advertisement.

BBS Bulletin board system. A standalone software/hardware system for file transfer and messaging.

Beta

A publisher code base sent to end users for testing and evaluation.

BOM

Bill of materials

Books

Industry slang for the various trade and consumer publications.

Bounce back

A piece of collateral material sent to someone responding to a "Call to Action" in an ad, promotion, direct marketing piece, etc.

BRM

Bulk rate mail that is presorted according to US Post Office regulations, qualifying it for a lower rate.

Call to action

A marketing term for an offer that asks the potential buyer to act on an offer. It can be either a request to purchase, or an offer to provide more information, when the potential buyer returns a card, calls a number, or acts on the offer in some familiar fashion.

Card deck

A collection of advertising cards bundled together and mailed to a targeted audience.

CE model

Cost efficiency model. An advertising model that defines the relative balance of effectively meeting reach and frequency goals at the best price

Channel.

Industry term for the software distribution system. The term is used somewhat loosely and often refers to a channel segment, as in "the reseller channel."

Channel conflict

Undercutting the price structure of a channel segment, as when a publisher sells product to end users below the discounts offered to resellers.

Clacker

An individual hired or assigned to talk up a publisher's product on a SIG or forum.

Click through   An Internet ad model that measures response by the number of users who click on an ad that links to the advertiser's site.

Collateral   All material created to support a product, including brochures, posters, sample product, demonstration disks, mobiles, and T-shirts.

Compatible   Typically refers to a computer system that duplicates all aspects of the original's operation, including disk drive access, screen display methods, and memory schemes. A compatible must be able to run 99% of the software that runs on the original system to qualify as truly compatible.

Competitive upgrade   A software promotion designed to drain sales away from a competitor's installed base. Usually the product is sold at a price close to or below the upgrade price of a competing product.

COG   Cost of goods. The cost of publishing a product, including development, packaging, marketing, sales, and company overhead.

Cookies   Small data files your browser exchanges with a web site when you visit it.

CPM   Cost per thousand. Alternately, refers to a popular but now obsolete operating system for eight-bit microprocessors.

CPP   The cost per 1% for buying advertising space in a given periodical.

Cross-sell   An offer made to a purchaser to buy an add-on or complementary product upon purchase of a primary product.

CTI   Computer telephony integration.

DSL   Digital subscriber line. A new technology that allows high speed transmission over phone lines.

Duopoly	Refers to the near monopoly exercised over the PC industry by Micosoft and Intel ("The Wintel duopoly").
DVD	Digital video disc.
E-commerce	The process and technology that enables a web site to conduct electronic transactions.
EDM	Electronic direct marketing. Refers to sending E-mail via the web for commercial purposes.
EHR	Estimated hit (purchase) rate.
ELD	Electronic license distribution.
E/R	Estimated return.
ESD	Electronic software distribution.
ESP	Estimated street price. A product with no suggested retail price.
FTP	File transfer protocol. An Internet site designed for file uploads and downloads.
FSI	Free-standing insert.
GUI	Graphical User Interface. A software operating environment used by applications to present a desktop metaphor to the user. In the U.S. market, the dominant GUIs are Windows, Mac OS, OS/2, Motif, Open Desktop, KDE, and Gnome.
HTML	Hypertext markup language. A formatting language designed for viewing documents posted on the World Wide Web.
Infomercials	A form of television advertising.
Internet	A worldwide system of interconnected computer networks.

Internic	Internet Network Information Center. The agency that assigns Internet domain names.
IRC	Internet relay chat. A technology allowing real time chat on the Internet.
I/S	Information systems.
ISP	Internet service provider.
ISV	Independent software vendor. A developer or publisher of software products.
IVR	Interactive voice response.
Java	A programming language designed to compile and run under a virtual microprocessor or "machine."
LAN	Local area network. A group of PCs linked to run in a cooperative fashion.
MAP	Manufacturer's advertised price. A publisher program that provides a reseller marketing development funds in return for their agreement not to discount a product.
Marcom	Marketing Communications. The department in a publisher, distributor, or reseller responsible for creating and administering collateral development, PR, and advertising, along with the scheduling of trade show participation.
Margin	The difference, in percentage points, between a product's purchase and selling price. A product purchased for $200 and sold for $220 has a 10% margin.
MDF	Marketing development funds. Money given by a publisher to a distributor to fund channel marketing programs.

Merchandise   In industry parlance, arranging product in store locations to the best competitive advantage. This can include shelf placement, putting posters in reseller's storefront, leaving brochures near the cash register, etc.

MRD   Marketing requirements document.

Multimedia   A technology that allows an application to mix pictures, images, video, and sound from multiple sources such as hard disk, optical media, floppy disk, etc. within the application's framework.

NFS   Not for sale. Products specifically built for demo or complementary purposes. Can be limited-function software, software without the retail packaging, without documentation, etc.

NOS   Network operating system. An operating system designed to run a PC network.

OEM   Original equipment manufacturer. An alternate channel for developers building products designed to be incorporated into another product.

Opt-in   A type of EDM that sends mail to lists of pre-qualified individuals who have given their permission to receive commercial E-mail.

O-Ring   The removable cover found on many software products. Increasingly, publishers are choosing to print directly on the box.

OS   Operating system. A program that allows a computer system to operate its internal hardware, manage its memory, and communicate with application programs.

PC   Personal computer. A computer built around a microprocessor and intended for standalone or individual use.

PCB	Product change bulletin.
Platforms	Industry term that refers to different hardware and software environments; for example, a Sun workstation is considered a different development platform than an IBM PC.
PMD	Product marketing description.
Point release	An interim upgrade between major upgrades usually indicated by adding a point to the product's version number (i.e., 1.1 becomes 1.11). A point release usually fixes bugs found in the release; in some cases, minor features may be added.
Points	An industry abbreviation for percentage points. The amount of margin found in a product. A product with a 10% margin is said to have 10 points.
POP	Point of purchase. A location in a retail store. Desirable POPs include the storefront, cash register, and shelves.
Portal	A web site that aggregates links to other web sites.
POS	Point of sale. See POP.
Power user	A class of computer user comfortable with technology and interested in experimenting with new products. Within corporations, power users frequently influence the product purchase, as they are regarded as informal consultants and computer gurus.
PRB	Product release bulletin.
PTB	Product termination bulletin.
Pull	The process by which publishers persuade end users to request particular software products.
Push	The process by which the channel moves and markets software to end users.

RFM	Stands for recency, frequency, and monetary value; rates how long ago, how often, and how much someone paid for items they purchased via a direct marketing campaign.
RFP	Request for proposal.
ROI	Return on investment. The amount of money earned on investing in a particular program.
Royalty	A fee paid to a publisher on a per-product basis. In the software industry, royalties are usually paid on a quarterly basis and average between 10% and 12%.
RSP	Recommended street price.
Run rates	The rate at which a product sells in a given amount of time. If a product sells 120,000 copies yearly, it is said to have a monthly run rate of 10,000 units.
Search engine	A program designed to search through various web and search sites on the Internet.
Search site	A web site used for locating information or products on the Internet.
Sell-through	The amount of software sold out of distributor or reseller inventory, as opposed to the amount of product sold into it.
Server	The PC running the network operating system or a web server. Also referred to as a host system. A server can be dedicated—only network functions are performed, or non-dedicated—applications can be run in addition to the NOS.
SIC	Standard industrial classification. Categorizes industries and jobs within them.

SIG	Special interest group. A subdivision of a user group, dedicated to examining one particular application category or product. For example, a user group may have a word processing SIG, which might, in turn, be divided into smaller SIGs dedicated to specific word processing products.
Single-tier	A distribution model in which the publisher sells software directly to resellers, bypassing the distributor.
Site license	A license that typically allows a business to reproduce a program and its documentation for all the workers at a particular location.
SKU	Stock-keeping unit. The identification code assigned items in a warehouse.
SOHO	Small Office/Home Office. A class of products aimed at the home consumer and home worker. Includes titles such as "Build Your Deck," "Manage Your Investments," "Your New Baby," etc. This class of products is currently undergoing rapid market growth.
Spam	Unsolicited commercial E-mail.
Specialty reseller	A reseller concentrating on selling retail software and hardware for a specific market, such as desktop publishing or accounting.
SPIF	Special performance incentive fund. A cash payment made to a store or individual in return for their recommending a particular product to a customer.
SRP	Suggested retail price. The publisher's product price. SRP can vary widely from a product's street price, which reflects the discount offered by a particular reseller.

Stickering   A point-of-sale tactic where a publisher places stickers on their product advertising a joint promotion with another product. In some cases, publishers of add-on products place promotional stickers on titles already on display.

Stock balancing   A swap by a distributor or reseller of a slow-moving product for a better-selling one.

Storymercial   A form of infomercial that tells a story during the course of the advertisement.

Street price   The actual selling price of a product, as opposed to the SRP. Street prices can vary depending on publisher, channel discounts, and reseller competition.

Stuffing   A publisher tactic where product is sold into a distributor's or reseller's inventory despite a lack of end-user demand for the product. Channel stuffing can take many inventive forms, such as selling product to a distributor just before the end of a fiscal quarter, and then taking the product back immediately after the quarter ends.

Superstore   A very large retail location that sells a wide variety of discounted software and hardware.

TBYB   Try before you buy.

TCP/IP   Transfer control protocol/Internet protocol. The communications protocol used by Internet sites.

Turns   A shortened term for inventory turnover; refers to the amount of time it takes a given amount of product to be sold from inventory.

Two-tier   A distribution model in which the publisher sells software to distributors, relying on the latter to sell the product to resellers.

UPC	Universal Product Code in bar code terminology. All packages being shipped into the distribution system must be bar coded.
Up-sell	An offer made to a purchaser to buy a more expensive product when purchasing a primary product.
USENET	A collection of Internet-based forums.
User group	An organization of computer users who share common interests and who meet regularly to view new product presentations, exchange information, distribute public domain and shareware products, etc.
VAR	Value-added reseller. A reseller specializing in developing or installing application solutions, often for vertical markets, such as medical, legal, construction, and mapping.
VPA	Volume Purchase Agreement. A sales arrangement between a publisher and a buyer that allows the buyer to buy multiple copies of full product at a discount.
VRML	Virtual reality modeling language.
Web site	An Internet "location" that displays documents formatted in HTML.
White box	Refers to generic computer hardware purchased by resellers for local assembly and sale.
White paper	A formal document published by a company stating their beliefs and core sales and marketing strategies. A form of collateral, white papers are often long and technical as they are designed to be read by decision makers, consultants, and power users.

Wintel   Stands for Windows/Intel.

World Wide Web   An international network of sites displaying documents
                         formatted in HTML.

XML   Extensible markup language. A web-based formatting
                         language designed to allow more complex web formatting
                         and data transfer.

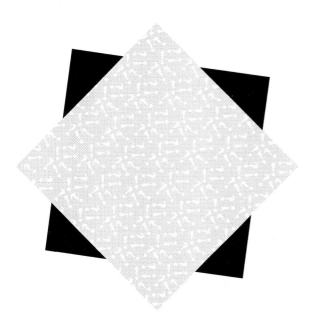

Index

B

Babbages, 373
banner, 401
banner advertising, 306
    incentives, 307
banner design, 306
bar-coding label, 278
Barnes & Noble, 287
BBS, 286, 401
Bentley J Day, 209
Bentley Systems, 206
beta, 390, 402
BOM, 402
book bundles, 269, 276
books, 402
bookstores, 47
booth personnel, 333
Borland, 24, 201, 255
    acquisition of Ashton-Tate, 24
    loss of markets, 24
    name change of, 24
    Quattro Pro pricing, 24
Borland C++ 4.0, 256
bots, 284, 295
bounce back, 402
brand identifier, 168
brand identity, 270
Branding
    integration and persistence, 19
    Intel and, 18
    need to defend, 18
    process of, 18
Brands
    attachment of, 19
    components of, 16
    definition of, 15
    equity of, 16
    investing in, 20
    limitations of, 19
    origin of, 17
break-proof packaging, 278
BRM, 402
broken links, 301
Bronze Age, 288
Brooks Software, 318
Bulletin Board Systems. *See* BBS
bundle breaking, 278
bundles
    reasons to, 270
    types of
        book, 269, 270
        hardware, 269
        software, 269

bundling, 69
business consulting, 209
Business Maestro, 277
buyers lists, 231
buying incentive programs, 64
buzzwords, 5

C

cable modems, 44, 289
cache buster, 309
CAD, 79, 206
Caldera, 42
call blending, 248
call center, 248
call queuing, 247
call to action, 202, 237, 402
callback tag, 247
cancelbots, 296, 305
cannibalization, 273
Canter and Siegel, 310
card deck, 402
card decks, 227
    design of, 233
    lead generation and, 234
    sources for, 233
catalog sales, 227
catalogers, 47, 48
    practices of, 47
CD-ROM, 272
CD-ROM distribution, 285
CE model, 402
CEOs, 229
CERN, 287
CFO, 277
CFOs, 229
CFS, 213
channel, 41, 402
    gaining access to, 60
    product demand and, 62
channel collateral, 102
    collateral CDs, 103
    comparison sheets, 103
    logos.
    ordering, 104
    sell scripts, 103
    specification sheets, 104
channel conflict, 273, 402
channel promotions, 212
    qualifying, 212
    VARs and, 212
channels, 290
chat, 296

The Aegis Product Positioning Workbook™

An Invaluable Companion to *The Product Marketing Handbook for Software, 3rd Edition* **for just 24.95**

The Aegis Product Positioning Workbook is a unique tool designed to help product marketers successfully execute this most critical of marketing tasks. Based on the the product methodology described in **The Product Marketing Handbook for Software, 3rd Edition,** the *Product Positioning Workbook* assists you in using the industry's most advanced product positioning methodology.

The goal of the *Workbook* is to help you create a product description that is self supporting, internally logical, and capable of being communicated to buyers with a minimum of confusion. To reach this goal, the Workbook steps you through the process of:

- Conceptualizing your product
- Visually identifying it
- Attaching favorable images and layering them
- Creating a compelling Marketing Vocabulary

Key Features and Benefits

- Unique visual format allows marketers to logically and quickly structure their product positioning.
- Prefaces and narrative detail the precise goals a marketer must achieve to clearly and successfully position a product and explain each positioning concept in relationship to the other.
- Expanded product positioning checklists break out each task and concept in complete detail, allowing marketers to control all aspects of their product positioning.
- Industry-specific examples, as well as examples from outside the software industry, allow marketers to compare their progress with other companies and products.
- Built-in notepads let you add details and guide you in dealing with special situations.
- Visual templates allow you to explore different aspects of your product's positioning, and build a unique 3-D view of your product positioning.
- Structure allows use as a powerful competitive analysis tool.

The Aegis Product Marketing Workbook™

An Invaluable Companion to *The Product Marketing Handbook for Software, 3rd Edition* **for just 24.95**

The Aegis Product Marketing Workbook is the only tool designed to help product marketers manage EVERY aspect of launching and sustaining a product in today's competitive software market. All **PMHB** checklists are easily accessible in a bound 8x1/2" by 11" workbook. Each section includes a preface covering key marketing points, notepad, and coordinator forms that let you add information about personnel who are working with you on your marketing projects. For companies that need to work on multiple products and projects, *The Aegis Product Marketing Workbook* is also available in economical **corporate** and **enterprise** packs.

The Aegis Product Marketing Workbook's checklists cover:

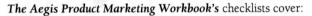

- Product Positioning
- Advertising
- Pricing
- Sales Promotions
- Naming
- Direct Marketing
- Channel Distribution
- Bundling
- Collateral Design and Production
- Electronic marketing (*including web marketing, advertising, electronic direct marketing and electronic software distribution*)
- Public Relations and Product Reviews
- Trade Shows

Key Features and Benefits

- Easy-to-read, easy-to-use format of PMHB checklists helps you manage all aspects of a successful product launch and sales campaign.
- Prefaces to each section covering key points helps you stay focused on critical tasks and goals.
- Coordinator forms allow you to track key contact information and responsibilities for all marketing team members.
- Built-in notepads let you keep track of added details and facts.

Aegis

The Aegis Product Marketing Forum™

The Aegis Product Marketing Forum is a program based on Collaborative Consulting™, an interactive mix of instruction, market simulations, case studies, and hands-on experience that enables software publishers to succeed in today's ultra-competitive environment. It is the only program of its type that focuses exclusively on software marketing. Not "high tech." Not hardware. Software. *The Forum* deals with the realities of this market, not theory. Participants will study every element of successful software marketing.

Forum Highlights

- Examine software marketing campaigns and learn what's working, what's not, and why.
- Work through a series of product launch simulations to get "hands-on" experience with the processes involved.
- Participate in mini-clinics where actual software packages, collateral and promotions are examined and critiqued for effectiveness. We'll even examine YOUR materials.
- Learn to use powerful marketing tools designed to help your company successfully execute the "heavy lifting" of managing and controlling effective marketing campaigns.

All forum sessions are led by software marketing veterans using real-life examples, case studies, class exercises, and mini-clinics. In the Direct Marketing session, for example, we look at actual direct mail pieces and offers, both good and bad. Forum participants will create their own direct mail piece. (It's not as easy as it looks!)

WHAT'S COVERED

- Positioning, pricing, and naming
- Distribution
- Advertising
- Bundling
- Sales promotions

- Collateral
- Public relations and product review programs
- Direct marketing
- Electronic marketing
- Trade shows

The Aegis Product Marketing Forum™

WHO SHOULD ATTEND

- Marketing and sales managers
- Brand managers and staff
- Public relations managers
- Senior managers of marketing and sales

- Product managers and staff
- Marcom managers and staff
- Entrepreneurs
- And anyone interested in effective software marketing!

To arrange for a custom session at your location, E-mail us at PMF@Aegis-Resources.com or www.SoftwareMarketSolution.com to find the schedule for the latest sessions in your area.

The Product Marketing Handbook for Software: Live!

*T*he Product Marketing Handbook for Software: Live! is the complete electronic version of *The Product Marketing Handbook for Software, 3rd Edition*, on CD. The *Handbook Live!* integrates text, video, and graphics of the ads, collaterals, packaging, and programs discussed in *The Product Marketing Handbook for Software, 3rd Edition* into a compelling learning and training tool.

When you purchase **The Product Marketing Handbook for Software Live!** you'll receive a four CD set containing:

- Video pops of the author discussing the **Handbook's** various topics. For instance, you may have READ about the worst piece of collateral ever created! Want to see it? How about the SECOND worst piece of collateral ever created! We've got that too! AND the worst direct marketing piece ever created as well!

- More invaluable content! There is plenty that didn't make it into **The Product Marketing Handbook for Software,** 3rd Edition because of space constraints! Additional stories about online marketing foolishness. More stories about successful and unsuccessful advertising campaigns and promotions. A discussion about the dangers of subtractive marketing. Information about the latest trends in electronic marketing. And much much more.

- Guest celebrities! We've invited executives from other software and marketing companies to discuss their most interesting flubs and successes.

- The Software Marketing Hall of Shame/Fame! Video pops and discussions of some of the best and worst programs, ads, promotions, collateral, and packages ever created.

- The complete text of **The Product Marketing Handbook for Software, 3rd Edition** in a convenient hyperlinked format. Jump quickly to just the sections you need to review, and print them out!

The Product Marketing Handbook for Software has been widely praised for being comprehensive, readable, and specific to our industry. **The Product Marketing Handbook for Software: Live!** is all that, **and** it's fun and interactive! It is the ideal tool to train your staff on successful marketing techniques, stay up-to-date on the latest trends and approaches, and help manage all your marketing processes and activities.

The Product Marketing Handbook for Software: Live! is only $149.95 and includes four CD's with the complete text of *The Product Marketing Handbook for Software, 3rd Edition* as well as integrated video and graphics. You can use the enclosed order form on disk or in the **Handbook** to order now and ensure you receive your copy early! Available for both PC and Macintosh systems.

For fastest ordering use our website at www.Aegis-Resources.com or call 1.877.BUY.PMHB (EST/EDT). U.S. and international fax orders: 1.802.846.8204. For bulk corporate and educational pricing please contact us at www.Aegis-Resources.com.

❑ Please send me _____ copies of *The Aegis Product Positioning Workbook* @ $24.95 each. _____

❑ Corporate Pack: Includes five (5) *The Aegis Product Positioning Workbooks*: $99.95 _____

❑ Enterprise Pack: Includes ten (10) *The Aegis Product Positioning Workbooks*: $189.95 _____

❑ Please send me _____ copies of *The Aegis Product Marketing Workbook* @ $24.95 each. _____

❑ Corporate Pack: Includes five (5) *The Aegis Product Marketing Workbooks*: $99.95 _____

❑ Enterprise Pack: Includes ten (10) *The Aegis Product Marketing Workbooks*: $189.95 _____

❑ *The Product Marketing Handbook for Software: Live!*: $149.95 _____

❑ MasterCard _____ ‡Shipping $8.95

❑ Visa Card #: _____ Subtotal_____

❑ AmEx _____ *Sales Tax_____

Exp. Date: _____ Total_____

Name _____Title _____

Company_____

Street Address _____

City _____ State _____ Country _____ Zip _____

Phone _____ FAX _____ E-Mail _____

*Conn. & Vermont residents are required to add 6% sales tax to entire order. ‡ **Multiple products & bulk orders please check our website for shipping prices.**

For fastest ordering use our website at www.Aegis-Resources.com or call 1.877.BUY.PMHB (EST/EDT). U.S. and international fax orders: 1.802.846.8204. For bulk corporate and educational pricing please contact us at www.Aegis-Resources.com.

❑ Please send me _____ copies of *The Aegis Product Positioning Workbook* @ $24.95 each. _____

❑ Corporate Pack: Includes five (5) *The Aegis Product Positioning Workbooks*: $99.95 _____

❑ Enterprise Pack: Includes ten (10) *The Aegis Product Positioning Workbooks*: $189.95 _____

❑ Please send me _____ copies of *The Aegis Product Marketing Workbook* @ $24.95 each. _____

❑ Corporate Pack: Includes five (5) *The Aegis Product Marketing Workbooks*: $99.95 _____

❑ Enterprise Pack: Includes ten (10) *The Aegis Product Marketing Workbooks*: $189.95 _____

❑ *The Product Marketing Handbook for Software: Live!*: $149.95 _____

❑ MasterCard _____ ‡Shipping $8.95

❑ Visa Card #: _____ Subtotal_____

❑ AmEx _____ *Sales Tax_____

Exp. Date: _____ Total_____

Name _____Title _____

Company_____

Street Address _____

City _____ State _____ Country _____ Zip _____

Phone _____ FAX _____ E-Mail _____

*Conn. & Vermont residents are required to add 6% sales tax to entire order. ‡ **Multiple products & bulk orders please check our website for shipping prices.**